Secrets of BETTER BASIC

Secrets of BETTER BASIC

Ernest E. Mau

HAYDEN BOOK COMPANY, INC.
Rochelle Park, New Jersey

To my father, who listens patiently to my complaints about my computers, and who acts as a sounding board for my ideas and procedures: you may not understand all of what I say, but you do listen. That in itself is a big help; without it, this book and most of the programs I use probably wouldn't exist.

Acquisitions Editor: M.C. VARLEY
Production Editor: RONNIE GROFF
Art Director: JIM BERNARD
Composition: McFARLAND GRAPHICS AND DESIGN, INC.
Printed and bound by: HAMILTON PRINTING COMPANY

Library of Congress Cataloging in Publication Data

Mau, Ernest E.
Secrets of better BASIC.

Includes index.
1. Basic (Computer program language) I. Title.
QA76.73.B3M38 1983 001.64'24 83-128
ISBN 0-8104-6254-0

Printed in the United States of America

1	2	3	4	5	6	7	8	9	PRINTING
83	84	85	86	87	88	89	90	91	YEAR

Preface

In 1971, I was working as a technical and marketing writer for one manufacturer of a minicomputer. I can still remember the stir caused when the company licensed its first high-level language. It was a major event, worthy of news releases to every trade publication in the electronics industry, and it was the recipient of major effort both in promotion and documentation. As crude as it was, that particular language was firing the imaginations of every minicomputer manufacturer, and its availability was cause for great celebration because it provided a way around many of the difficulties computer purchasers were encountering in programming their machines and making them perform useful functions. Today, we take that same programming language for granted and assume it will be provided automatically as part of our purchase. If you haven't already guessed, I'm talking about the language called BASIC.

In *Webster's New Collegiate Dictionary* (1980), BASIC is shown to be an acronym for *B*eginner's *A*ll-purpose *S*ymbolic *I*nstruction *C*ode and is defined as "a standardized language for programming and interacting with a computer." To clarify, a little historical perspective is in order. BASIC was developed in 1964 at Dartmouth College by Thomas E. Kurtz and John G. Kemeny and was conceived as an educational aid for students having their first contact with computers. As its name implied, it was a simple programming language closely resembling elementary English and algebra, so it could be learned quickly and easily by individuals with no previous computer experience. While it was useful for general problem-solving applications, it had limited capabilities and really wasn't intended to serve as the "standard" programming language it has since become.

However, BASIC really caught on! Because it was so easy to learn, its shortcomings were easily overlooked, and more and more computer manufacturers began to purchase the right to use it (BASIC was and may still be a registered trademark of the trustees of Dartmouth College). As they did so, they also began to expand its capabilities and to "enhance" the language so it could be applied easily to increasing numbers of computer applications.

The advent of the microprocessor was followed by the introduction during the mid-1970s of "personal computers" and "small-business computers," which suddenly made computer technology available to a great many individuals and businesses never before able to afford such a luxury. But those people were not skilled programmers, and the need for an easily learned language continued and even increased. Again, BASIC was a natural choice for the computer manufacturers. The core of the language already existed, and it had been proven useful over the years. Therefore, BASIC became a standard for microcomputers, and today it is available for and usually provided automatically with nearly every personal and small-business computer on the market.

However, BASIC is far from standardized. As I will show in this book, there are significant variations in the language as implemented from one computer to another, and considerable differences exist even between any two versions used on the same computer. Every supplier of BASIC, and that means virtually every computer manufacturer and every software house, has a different idea of what the language needs. Although certain "core" instructions remain relatively constant, "extensions" and "enhancements" differ widely so one version of BASIC may or may not function at all like another.

The version of BASIC that was implemented on the 1971 minicomputer I mentioned was very crude by today's standards. When compared to the Microsoft BASIC-80® widely used by modern micros, it seems especially limited. The 1971 version had only 18 program statements as compared with 46 statements in BASIC-80. Specifically, the 1971 version used only the program statements CALL, DATA, DIMension, END, FOR, GOSUB, GOTO, IF . . . THEN . . . , INPUT, LET, NEXT, PAGE, PRINT, READ, REMark, RESTORE, RETURN, and STOP. In Chapter 3 of this book, I'll be defining some elements of more modern BASICs, and you'll see how limited that early set was.

Furthermore, that 1971 version of BASIC contained no "intrinsic functions" for such operations as determining the sine of an angle or the logarithm of a number. BASIC-80 uses some 52 instrinsic functions, of which 16 are for arithmetic computations, 17 are for literal-string handling, and 19 serve special functions. In 1971, calculating the square root of a number took about 10 program instructions, usually in a subroutine. BASIC-80 now does the same thing by simply calling the

SQR () function. Obviously, BASIC has changed dramatically over the years, and it's still changing. It seems that every few months a new version of the language or a new release of an existing version appears.

Despite some of the difficulties and differences among BASICs, the language itself is probably the single most widely used programming language around—at least for the small computer systems found in homes and offices. There are many other languages available, such as FORTRAN, ALGOL, COBOL, Pascal, APL, LISP, and so on, plus the lower levels of machine and assembly languages, but the average user of a small computer usually starts with BASIC. Many programmers then stay with BASIC almost exclusively, venturing into the other languages only when it's no longer avoidable.

As I've said, BASIC is easy to learn. That was the intent behind its creation. That remains its real advantage even with the complications various suppliers try to build into it. The principles of BASIC can be learned in an afternoon, and a working program written within hours of first picking up the instruction manual. What isn't so easy is learning to use BASIC effectively. By that I mean using the language to write programs that run efficiently on a computer, with the least amount of the computer's operating time and memory wasted.

One thing you must understand—there's no such thing as a right or wrong way to write a BASIC program as long as that program works and yields the correct results. There is a running argument about whether programming should be called an art or a science, but that's really not important. If you take any 10 programmers and assign them the same problem, you'll probably find they come up with 10 different programs. Every one of those programs may be a perfectly valid solution to the problem. Yet important differences may be noted in how fast the programs arrive at the result and how much of the computer's available memory is required.

That brings me to the purpose of this book. There are many references around that will help you get started at using your computer and BASIC, most of which are devoted to defining the statements and functions available in the language and demonstrating one or two ways to set up some simple programs. But there are very few places to look for information on how to optimize a program. As long as you stick to short, simple programs you don't have a serious problem; you can be satisfied by just making the program work. However, once you begin to write long or complex programs, you have to start worrying about how long it takes to do individual operations and how much memory you are going to use for them. It's annoying to work for days or weeks on a program only to find out that it runs too slowly to be practical or that it takes more memory than your computer has available.

Over the past few years, I've spent most of my time writing very long, very large programs for word-handling tasks involved in the creation of word games and puzzles. In those applications, I've found both execution speed and memory utilization to be critical, and I've had to learn techniques of program optimization largely by trial and error. What I hope to do is save you some of the time and effort it took me to discover the advantages and disadvantages of different approaches. If you're a novice, you'll find the information valuable when you attempt your first large program. If you're an intermediate or advanced programmer, you should find some important hints on how to improve your work and achieve more effective use of your equipment.

Some of the hints and suggestions I'll be making may seem trivial or insignificant, especially when they save only a byte or two of memory or a small fraction of a second in execution time, but you have to remember that the effects are cumulative. Saving 0.1 second in a program loop may not seem like much at first. But what if that loop executes 1,000 times? The time saving then is 100 seconds or 1.6 minutes. If the loop executes 10,000 times, the time saving is 16.6 minutes. If, as is the case in some of my own programming, the loop executes 100,000 times, the saving is 2.8 hours. Furthermore, saving the same small fraction of a second in several different loops will simply increase the overall time savings.

This is where the art and the science of programming come together into one overall operation. The science is to construct a working solution to the problem at hand. The art is to make that solution both effective and efficient. I intend to address not the science but rather the art. You will not find a lot of information on problem solving and algorithms in this book, and you certainly can't use it as a "cookbook" of programming recipes. Instead, you'll find advice and suggestions on how to improve your program's performance once you have it written.

With a little practice and insight, you can minimize those long delays between starting a program run and obtaining the finished results.

Ernest E. Mau

Contents

1 AN INTRODUCTION *1*

The Computer System *3*
The Central Processing Unit *3*
The Memory *5*
The Input/Output Devices *10*
Mass-Storage Devices *18*

From Hardware to Software *22*

Programming Languages *26*
Binary Machine-Language Programming *26*
Hexadecimal Machine-Language Programming *28*
Assembly-Language Programming *29*
High-Level-Language Programming *30*

The Language Called "BASIC" *33*

2 GETTING DOWN TO "BASICS" *39*

"BASIC"—Some Pros and Cons *39*

Learning BASIC *42*

Computer Power and Computer Errors *46*
Handling Data *46*
Performing Repetitive Operations *47*
Altering Program Flow *49*
Computer Errors *50*
Using a Computer's Power *54*

Creating Your Programs *60*
Identifying and Evaluating the Problem *60*
Devising a Workable Solution *64*
Flowcharting a Program *67*
Coding a Program *72*
Testing and Debugging a Program *73*
Running the Program *75*

Program Readability versus Efficiency *76*

3 A "BASIC" UNDERSTANDING *85*

BASIC-Language Implementation *86*
BASICs Side by Side *91*
BASIC Commands, Statements, and Functions *95*

The "BASIC" Choice *128*

4 SOME "BASIC" TECHNIQUES *130*

Number-Handling Methods *131*
A Matter of Precision *131*
A Matter of Memory Consumption *137*
A Matter of Execution Speed *138*
Rounding versus Truncating *148*
A Practical Hint *150*

String-Handling Methods *151*
Storing Strings in Memory *152*
Allocating String Space *154*
Free-Space Determinations and String-Space Garbage Collects *157*
String Manipulations *164*

Defined Variable Types *179*

Handling Techniques Revisited *183*

5 MORE "BASIC" TECHNIQUES *185*

Random Numbers *185*
Random Numbers Returned *186*
Random-Number "Seeding" *188*

Defined User Functions *189*

Constructing and Using Loops *192*
Special FOR . . . NEXT Considerations *196*
Special IF . . . THEN . . . Considerations *207*
The "BASIC" Maneuvers *214*

6 SPECIAL "BASIC" TRICKS *215*

Manipulating the Variable Table *216*
Assigning Variable Names *216*
Forcing a Variable Name into the Table *218*
Using Array Variables in Loops *220*
Zeroing Array Variables *223*
Using Default Conditions *225*
Using Subroutines *230*
Subroutine versus Mainline Programming *231*
Positioning a Subroutine *233*
Recursive Subroutines *235*
Using Disk Files *236*
Random-Access Disk Files *236*
Sequential-Access Disk Files *241*
Closing Disk Files *243*
Choosing an Efficient Algorithm *244*
"Punch Up" BASIC *249*

APPENDIX A—ASCII Codes and Equivalents *251*

APPENDIX B—Numerical Systems and Conversions *255*

APPENDIX C—Some "BASIC" Functions *279*

APPENDIX D—Sample Disk and Memory Tests *288*

APPENDIX E—Some Useful Software *291*

INDEX *299*

An Introduction

Would you like to squeeze a little extra "mileage" out of your computer—to be able to put it through its paces a little faster, reduce some of those annoying delays in the middle of a program, and get your machine to do more things in less time? If your answer is "yes," I have good news for you: that's what this book is all about.

Throughout the several years that I have been programming and running my own microcomputers, the apparent lack of certain information has always bothered me. I do most of my programming in the language called BASIC, which may be the single most widely used computer language around. Even though I'd been involved with computers and programming for many years before acquiring my first system, I still had trouble getting my programs to run efficiently enough to be practical.

Although there's a great deal of information available in instruction manuals and tutorial-style books on how to write a BASIC program, most of it is limited to the fundamentals. What has been lacking is any single source of information on using BASIC effectively; I've found myself and other programmers being left pretty much to our own devices for discovering how to improve the programs we write so they can come up with the desired results in the least amount of time.

In this book, I intend to remedy that situation, at least partially. Some of what you'll be reading herein may be tucked away in some nearly forgotten part of your system's instruction manuals. Other things may be addressed at various times by individual magazine articles. Still others may not be discussed anywhere. In any event, the information often is difficult to acquire and usually is overlooked in the haste of getting a new program up and running.

One comment I've often heard from others who have done some programming is, "If my programs are running and giving me the right answers, why should I change them?" If the programs are small and don't require a lot of time, there's no reason to change them or to give much thought to improving their efficiency. However, if the programs are large, require a lot of computer memory, perform a great many operations, or work with very large amounts of data, efficient and effective programming becomes a major concern. There's little point in reducing a five-minute program to four and a half minutes, but there's a great deal to be gained by reducing a one-hour program to 30 or 45 minutes. In the simplest terms, using less time to run any one program increases the number of programs that can be run and thus the amount of work that can be done by the computer.

To illustrate, I use one computer primarily for producing word-game manuscripts, which I sell to a number of magazine publishers. This activity and the programs are described in *Create Word Puzzles with Your Microcomputer*, also available from Hayden Book Company, Inc. In that activity, the number of puzzles I can produce in a given amount of time is a direct measure of my income. When I first started to do one of my most salable types of puzzles by computer, I reached a stage where I had a very complex program that took about four hours to generate a single program—and that was after a lot of manipulating to get it down from 17 hours. With each puzzle paying me an average of $10, running the computer 24 hours a day gave me six puzzles or a potential income of $60 a day. But I had to keep the machine tied up on that one task continuously.

I could generate puzzles of the same type by hand in just over an hour each, so the computer program certainly wasn't keeping pace. By applying the techniques described later in this book, and without changing the overall program approach, I was able to reduce the execution time to an average of 30 minutes. This gave me the capability of generating 48 puzzles every day, essentially multiplying both my output and my potential income by a factor of eight. More important, it allowed me to divert a portion of the computer's time to other purposes such as designing new programs. I wound up using the computer for program development, word processing, and other tasks for eight or ten hours a day and then switching over to unattended puzzle production overnight or until I needed the machine again.

The process of optimizing that one program extended over a full year, mostly because I had to stumble over each improvement by accident. It amounted to a process of pure trial and error, with each subsequent approach tested against a stopwatch and either accepted for inclusion in the program or rejected as too costly in terms of time or memory consumption.

As you read through this book, you'll find a lot of comparisons between two or more ways of doing the same things. Whenever possible, I will supply simple examples with information on the length of time it takes to repeat the operations a given number of times, the memory consumption, or both.

Before going on, however, you must recognize that this is not the average book on BASIC for small computers. I'm going to make three assumptions: (a) you have a computer that runs some version of BASIC, (b) you have read and at least partially understood the instruction and programming manuals that came with your system, and (c) you are familiar with the fundamentals of using BASIC on your system and have spent some time writing your own programs. I do not intend to take a tutorial approach to either computers or BASIC, and you'll probably end up quite confused if you don't already know the basics of BASIC.

If you happen to be a novice and haven't used a computer before, I strongly recommend that you finish reading this chapter, set this book aside, and then work through your computer's instructional materials. After you've done that and have practiced a bit with writing some simple BASIC programs, you can come back to this book.

For those of you who are more advanced, the remainder of this chapter should serve as a review. You may be tempted to skip some or all of this background information on computers and programming, but I recommend that you at least scan the material. The following sections are included herein primarily for the purpose of defining terms that will be used later. Since there often is some degree of confusion about terminology and since people tend to use the same word to mean different things, it's important that you understand the words and their definitions as I will be applying them.

The Computer System

Figure 1-1 is a generalized and highly simplified block diagram typical of microcomputer systems. It shows that a system may be viewed as four separate and distinct components. In order to clarify some of the terminology, each of these components must be examined briefly.

The Central Processing Unit

The heart of any microcomputer system is its *microprocessor*. This is the device that manipulates data, performs various arithmetic and logical operations, and controls the movement of the data back and forth between other components of the system. In fact, the microprocessor *is* the computer—without it there could be no system. It's easily recognizable as an *integrated circuit* or *circuit chip* somewhat larger than most others around it, measuring two inches or less in length and

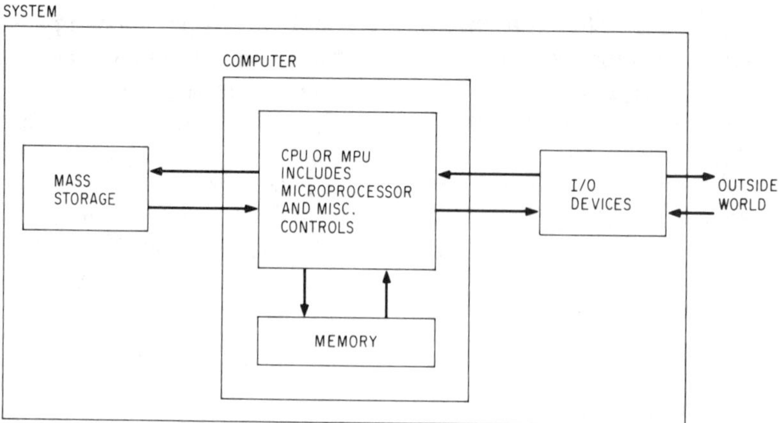

***Fig. 1-1.* Typical Microcomputer-System Block Diagram**

slightly less than an inch in width, and it's clearly marked with its identification number.

Microprocessors come in many types and have many names, including the 8080, 8085, Z-80™, 6502, and 6800, to name just five of the microprocessors commonly found in personal and small-business computers. There are, of course, many others. The exact type of microprocessor used in a system is of little concern to average home or business users, who don't do their programming in *machine language* or *assembly language.* For those who program exclusively in *high-level languages,* such as BASIC, there is little or no direct contact with the microprocessor, so an extensive discussion of the relative merits of each type would be inappropriate in this book. However, you should be aware that there are distinct differences among the various microprocessors that may be to your advantage or disadvantage if you ever attempt to use a lower level of programming language that accesses the microprocessor directly.

By itself, the microprocessor does absolutely nothing. It must be connected to other devices and electronic circuits before it can perform any useful operations. These are the miscellaneous controls that provide *clock* and *synchronization* signals, *status* indications, input and output *buffers,* and so on, all needed by the microprocessor so it can do its job properly. Again, the individual functions are of major concern only to those who choose to do their programming in machine or assembly language, and the individual circuits and controls are invisible to users of BASIC or other high-level languages.

Together, the microprocessor and the miscellaneous control circuits comprise the so-called *central processing unit* or *CPU.* Some hard-line traditionalists insist on referring to the *microprocessor unit* or *MPU* in talking about microcomputers in order to differentiate them from minicomputers and larger-scale machines. However, many manufacturers of personal and small-business computers based on microprocessors have elected to use the central-processing-unit or CPU terminology. Simply to keep in step with the majority of the manuals on my own systems, I'll be using the term "CPU" whenever I find it necessary to mention this group of components.

Generally, there are two approaches to constructing a CPU. One is to put the components, including the microprocessor and its miscellaneous control devices, on a *plug-in* circuit board, which is then installed into a connector providing contact with a *bus*. This is the approach used in both old and new *S-100 bus* computers and other *multiple-board* computers. A bus is nothing more than a group of electrical paths or lines that convey signals from one device to another. In the case of a plug-in CPU card, the card connector allows circuits of the CPU to contact the lines of the bus and thus transmit signals to and receive signals from other circuit boards also plugged into the bus. Advanced programmers working in machine language or assembly language often have to differentiate among such things as the *data bus*, the *status bus*, the *address bus*, and so on, but once again the individual communications lines and groupings of those lines into separate buses are rarely of any concern to someone programming in a high-level language.

The second approach involves the *single-board* computers, such as the Apple II.™ In such a machine, the microprocessor is installed on a *main board (motherboard)* that also contains the computer's memory, interface controllers, and other devices not properly a part of the CPU. The microprocessor itself may be identified easily and is right in front of the *peripheral connectors* on an Apple II, but the other components of the CPU may be somewhat more difficult to identify. In fact, the Apple II documentation tends to avoid the use of the terms "CPU" and "MPU," but the components are there nevertheless. In such cases, the miscellaneous control circuits of the CPU often are the integrated circuits immediately adjacent to the microprocessor chip.

The Memory

I've already mentioned that the microprocessor or "computer" performs certain operations such as basic arithmetic and that it controls the transfer of data to and from various other devices. To do this, the computer must have some means of storing the data, the instructions on what to do with the data, and the information about where to find a specific instruction or a particular data item. That storage is provided by the computer's *memory*.

Apple Computer, Inc., publishes a book called *The Applesoft Tutorial* in which the term "pigeonhole" is applied to the computer's memory. Actually, it's a pretty fair analogy, and it helps create a visual image of what computer memory is and what it does. At one time or another, you've undoubtedly seen a movie or television scene depicting a hotel lobby. Behind the front desk are two things of note: the desk clerk and a wall of boxes with one box for each room in the hotel. Those boxes are called pigeonholes. If you think of several thousand such boxes as being a computer's memory and the desk clerk as being the CPU, it's easy to demonstrate how the two interact.

Since each pigeonhole is assigned to a specific room, it has an *address* roughly comparable to that of a memory location. Each box is used to hold information pertinent to the room or the occupants thereof, and that information is comparable to the data held by a single location in a computer's memory. By inserting notes and information into the boxes and removing those items from the boxes, the desk clerk performs the same operations that a CPU performs with memory: inserting and removing data.

Now, assume that each box may contain only one piece of information at a time, specifically a number. That number may represent one of three things: (a) the number of days the room has been occupied, (b) the address of another box that contains some cost factor, or (c) a numerically coded instruction that tells the desk clerk what to do. For reasons of practicality, some boxes arranged in columns from top to bottom are reserved only for coded instructions, so those instructions can be found quickly and easily whenever necessary.

To follow a simple operation, let's say that the desk phone rings; the occupants of room 332 are checking out, and the clerk is to prepare their bill. To do so, the clerk goes to the first box reserved for instructions on what to do when a room is vacated. There he finds the instruction to get or "fetch" the number of occupancy days from the pigeonhole with room address 332. The next instruction box tells him to fetch the room price from some other designated box. The third instruction tells him to multiply the two numbers to get the room price. The fourth instruction tells him to put the calculated cost back into the pigeonhole for room 332 where it will be available when the occupants come to pay their bill.

The analogy can be extended to include fetching and adding sales taxes, dining-room charges, gratuities, and other such items before putting the final price back into the room's pigeonhole. There could even be cases where an instruction merely tells the clerk to look in one box to find the address of some other box that happens to contain a needed piece of information. The important point is that the desk clerk has manipulated data in and out of the pigeonholes very much as a CPU would manipulate data in and out of memory. In fact, by following coded instructions in a sequence of boxes, the clerk executes a simple form of a *program*.

In a computer, electronic pigeonholes are used to store data, addresses, and instructions, and the computer often is characterized by the type and size of its memory. The most common microcomputers are eight-bit machines—machines in which each memory address or pigeonhole will hold a single *byte* of information that consists of eight *binary digits* or *bits* (more information on bits, bytes, and their manipulations is provided in Appendix B). The number of bytes available in the machine's memory, then, is a measure of the amount of information it can handle at one time.

The usual representation of a computer's "size" is a number such as 16K, 32K, or 48K, in which the "K" indicates thousands of memory bytes. Those computers contain approximately 16,000, 32,000, and 48,000 eight-bit bytes respectively. I say "approximately" because, in computer jargon, 4K of memory isn't exactly 4,000 bytes; it's actually 4,096 bytes as a result of some of the design requirements encountered when the memory devices were first designed. Therefore, a 16K memory actually contains 16,384 bytes, 32K contains 32,768 bytes, 48K contains 49,152 bytes, and 64K contains 65,536 bytes. Occasionally, you may find a computer claiming 65K of memory, but it's the same size as another brand claiming 64K.

Regrettably, it is common practice to compare computers on the basis of their memory sizes. Since a larger memory allows more data, addresses, and instructions to be stored, it seems logical that larger memories always mean more computing power. Therefore, it's easy to assume that a 32K computer will be able to do more than a 16K machine, that a 48K computer will be able to do even more, and that a 64K machine will be able to do more than any of the others. That holds true as a good rule of thumb as long as you are comparing computers of the same type or brand name. A 48K Apple II will be able to work with larger programs and more data at one time than a 32K Apple II, and a 32K TRS-80™ will have more capabilities than a 16K TRS-80.

However, factors other than simple memory size have to be considered when computers of different types or different brands are compared. For example, it's not strictly true that a 64K S-100 bus computer such as an old Altair® 8800b or even a new Morrow Designs' Decision 1™ has a larger memory and greater storage capacity than a 48K Apple II. A great deal depends upon the memory design, the organization and utilization of different types of memory, the amount of memory used by essential system software such as the BASIC language interpreter, and the "efficiency" with which a particular language, such as BASIC, can be used on a particular machine. Since I operate a 64K Altair 8800b, a Morrow Designs' Decision 1, and a 48K Apple II Plus, I can use those systems as illustrations. But before I can compare them, I have to define two types of memory.

The two principal types of computer memory are known as *random-access memory* or RAM and *read-only memory* or ROM. There are other types as well, including *programmable read-only memory* (PROM) and *erasable programmable read-only memory* (EPROM). However, to keep matters as simple as possible, I'll limit present considerations to RAM and ROM.

RAM is the memory that can be used and manipulated by the computer, allowing information to be stored, retrieved, or changed. ROM allows only the retrieval of information preprogrammed into the chip, and a ROM device cannot be altered or modified by the computer in which it is installed. A further distinction is that RAM is *volatile* memory and ROM is *nonvolatile* memory. That is, any power interruption, whether deliberately turning the machine's switch off or suffering a loss of power from the utility lines, destroys the contents of RAM but has no effect on the contents of ROM.

In the hypothetical hotel situation, the pigeonhole boxes allow the desk clerk to remove and insert information at will—as does the RAM of a computer. But what if every time the lights go off someone stumbles into the array of boxes and tips them over? Their contents will be scattered, confused, or lost, and each box will have to be reloaded again once the lights come back on—as with a RAM device.

Now assume that such a loss of the instructions to the clerk is intolerable, so that instead of those instructions' being placed in regular pigeonholes, they are chiseled into an immovable marble block. Obviously, the clerk will be unable to alter those instructions unless he has his own hammer and chisel (and he then risks destroying the marble block itself), but he will be able to read the instructions any time he needs them. Now, when the lights go off and someone tips the pigeonholes over, the instructions chiseled into the block remain intact and accessible to the clerk, just as the contents of ROM remain accessible to a computer even when the contents of RAM are lost.

The way in which RAM and ROM devices are used in a particular computer directly affects the comparison of memory capacity. In a machine such as the Apple II Plus, the BASIC language known as Applesoft is stored or programmed into a nonvolatile ROM device and is available as soon as power is applied to the computer. Furthermore, Applesoft in ROM does not consume large portions of RAM, so the RAM locations remain free for use by individual programs. With my own 48K Apple II Plus, I have access to Applesoft from ROM while still having 47,100 bytes of available RAM memory. If, however, I load the Apple's disk-operating system, available RAM decreases to 36,348 bytes because that disk-operating system "resides" in RAM and makes that portion of memory unusable for other purposes.

I can go a step farther with the Apple and add a plug-in circuit board such as Microsoft's 16K RAMCard®, apply any one of several *memory-management-system* software packages available to move the disk-operating system into that RAMCard, and effectively have a 64K Apple

II Plus with about 46,800 bytes of usable RAM memory after Applesoft and the disk-operating system have been loaded.

In comparison, my 64K Altair, which does not provide BASIC in ROM, requires that all system software be loaded from an external disk device and stored in RAM. I have a number of different BASICs available for that machine, and each uses a different amount of memory. Depending upon which version I need for a particular application, my available memory after loading BASIC and its integral subsystems can vary from a low of 34,300 bytes to a high of 43,500 bytes. The Altair BASIC I use most often leaves me only 41,500 bytes of free RAM. As a result, I can have as much usable memory in a 48K Apple II as I have in a 64K Altair, depending upon the application, my need for disk storage, and so on.

There are a number of other factors that enter into any consideration of a computer's memory size and capability, including how much memory is needed to manage or control external devices. One such factor is whether or not the computer system uses *memory-mapped video,* in which every location of the display screen is controlled and continuously updated according to the current contents of a specific area of RAM. I'll be saying more about this in the section of this chapter on input/output devices, but it is necessary to mention here that memory mapping always reduces the amount of memory available for the programmer's use because reserved areas of RAM are utilized only to store the information to be displayed.

The effective use of memory by the programming language is another important consideration, and I'll be saying more about this subject throughout the book. One aspect that I'll discuss at length later is the difference between being able to predefine variable types and having to declare the type explicitly each time the variable name is used. The latter case requires adding an extra character as part of the variable name each time it appears in the program and can cost several thousand bytes of memory in the course of writing a large program.

Obviously, when considering the purchase of a computer system, it's important that you know how much "free" memory remains after the system is "loaded" and ready to be used. Since most computer documentation and many computer salesmen are quite slippery when it comes to this subject, it's advisable to request a check of free memory at various points throughout the demonstration of the system.

As a final amplification of the point that you cannot always judge the relative capabilities of two different kinds of computer systems simply by looking at the total size of the memory, I'll relate two experiences I've had in assessing popular computer models as possible replacements for or complements to my existing systems. I will not name the computer brands because my feelings toward them are rather negative, but you can quickly detect whether the problem exists in any machine you contemplate buying by performing a simple check of free memory space.

In the first case, I obtained a new computer on loan for a few days of trial and evaluation. According to the specifications, the unit was equipped with 128K of memory; on the surface, it appeared to have twice the memory capacity of my 64K S-100 machines. However, most of that memory was required for the various operating systems and *device drivers* needed to operate and communicate with the computer. The actual amount of memory available for programming use was only about 32K, with the remaining 96K all a part of the *system overhead.*

In the second case, I was contemplating the purchase of a personal computer that had some marvelous and unusual graphics capabilities. The unit was available with a 48K RAM memory and at first was very appealing. However, things changed abruptly as soon as I had the demonstration unit connected to a disk drive. On this particular unit, available RAM decreased to just over 22K with the drive connected and the operating system and the other elements comprising system overhead loaded into RAM.

Since I typically require a bare minimum of 35K to 38K for my own programming applications, neither of those two systems would do the job. Of course, I had the option of totally redesigning my programming approach, breaking individual programs into smaller sections, reducing the amount of data I handle in RAM at any one time, and applying numerous other techniques to get around the problem, but all that would cost me dearly in terms of overall execution speed, the possible complexity and quality of my final outputs, or both. Since I cannot tolerate either a loss of execution speed or a reduction in the amount of data I handle, I had no choice but to reject both of those machines as unusable, despite any other attractive capabilities they might have had.

I cannot emphasize too strongly the importance of determining the amount of *usable* memory in a computer system rather than the *total* memory listed in the machine's specifications. The actual memory you can utilize has a distinct effect on your later programming efforts. In the case of the second system, it took some pressing, but I eventually got the sales personnel to admit that they were aware of the excessive memory consumption when a disk drive was connected, that it had been the subject of numerous complaints about the system, and that the manufacturer was not particularly inclined to correct the situation.

The Input/Output Devices

So far, I've described two essential elements of a computer system, namely the CPU and the memory. Together, those elements often are thought of as the computer itself, and it's common practice to differentiate between the computer and the computer system. In strictest terms, the word "computer" applies only to the CPU, but it often is extended to include the memory and a few specialized devices, such as automatic start-up circuitry, that are interconnected directly. These usually are housed in a single box with a power supply that converts regular electrical current to usable voltages, fans that cool the electronic components, connectors that allow the use of other plug-in circuitry, and other miscellaneous supporting items. Taken together, that box and its contents often are called a *mainframe*, and the words "computer" and "mainframe" frequently are used interchangeably to mean the same thing.

However, such a computer still is of no practical use because it has no way to communicate with the outside world to receive its instructions or report the results of its operations. The process of building a computer system from a single computer is nothing more than the process of adding the necessary devices to effect that communication.

Connecting a device is known as *interfacing*. Interfacing consists of providing appropriate connections between the external device and the communications lines or input/output bus of the computer mainframe. I don't want to mislead you into thinking that interfacing always is a simple process. Designing an interface between an external device and a particular computer can be and usually is a complex task. However, the average computer user rarely becomes involved in the intricacies of designing an interface because prefabricated components are available for nearly every imaginable purpose. The user of such components need not be concerned with the actual design of the electronic circuits but only with the question of whether or not the particular component is compatible with the computer in question. At some later point, the user may have to design special programming to make use of the external component, but many manufacturers even provide that programming for the specific computers with which they intend their devices to be used.

In the simplest case, two external devices are required by any computer system. One of these allows you to "talk" to the computer, and the other allows the computer to talk to you. In other words, one is an *input device*, which allows instructions and data to be put into the computer by the user, and the other is an *output device*, which allows data and other information to be put out from the computer to the user. As a group, all such devices are known as *input/output devices* or *I/O devices* and are lumped together under the heading of *peripherals*.

Note, however, that I/O devices or peripherals include many different types of devices other than those you use directly to communicate with the computer. They include mass-storage units such as magnetic disk or tape drives, special devices that allow the computer to control electrical circuits that turn equipment on or off, devices that convert electrical voltages generated by a measuring instrument into numerical values that can be manipulated by a computer, and a great many other gadgets external to the computer mainframe.

In a book of this scope, it's impractical and unnecessary to attempt the description of all possible peripherals, so I'll limit my coverage to those few commonly found on most personal and small-business systems.

The Keyboard. Obviously, the first peripheral of concern is the one that allows you to input instructions and data to the computer. This is essentially a *keyboard* of one type or another, and it's used just like the keyboard of a conventional typewriter to enter letters, numbers, and some other special characters. All keyboards function in the same general manner: after you press a key, a numeric representation of the character is transmitted from the keyboard across the interface to the computer. That representation normally is an *ASCII* (*A*merican *N*ational *S*tandard *C*ode for *I*nformation *I*nterchange) code in which any alphabetic, numeric, or other character is represented by a particular numeric value.

Although computer keyboards all serve the same general function, there are some differences. The first difference is the physical location of the device. In computer systems such as the Apple II, the Apple III, the Atari 400 or 800, and many others, the keyboard is an integral part of the computer chassis. In other cases, a "detached" keyboard may be used. Typically, this is a box containing the keyboard, some interface circuitry, and nothing else. In still other cases, the keyboard may be one part of a *terminal* device that also includes a display screen or printer to receive the output from the computer. Regardless of its physical location, the keyboard still serves the same purpose—it allows characters to be typed and entered into the computer.

There also are functional differences between keyboards that may or may not affect the efficient use of the system as a whole. In looking at a number of different computers and peripherals, you'll quickly find that things aren't always standardized. Manufacturers' specifications use such descriptions as "ASCII keyboard," "conventional typewriter-style keyboard," and "typewriter-like keyboard." As a general rule, any two keyboards have the alphabetic keys, numeric keys, and space bar in the same relative positions, but the similarities end there. Other keys such as the Return, Control, Shift, Escape, and Backspace tend to be wherever the manufacturer happens to put them. Worse yet, often-used characters such as the plus sign, equals sign, right and left brackets, semicolon, and colon tend to be in totally different positions from one keyboard to another, and to make matters still worse, a character such as the equals sign may be uppercase on one device and lowercase on another.

This means that you may have to adjust your typing style to fit the keyboard you are using, and if you happen to configure a system with two or more keyboards, you may have considerable difficulty each time you change from one to another. Among the three systems I own and use, I have a total of four keyboards. My primary system is equipped with an ADDS® Regent 25 terminal with one keyboard pattern. My Qume® Sprint 5 printing terminal is equipped with another keyboard of a different pattern, which I use for special "off-line" operations and as a backup should I lose the use of another terminal. I also have a Hazeltine® 1500 terminal with a third keyboard arrangement, and I use it as a general backup unit. Finally, the Apple II has its own built-in keyboard different from all the others. To further complicate matters, I occasionally connect either the ADDS or the Hazeltine as an external terminal for the Apple II to bypass the Apple's built-in keyboard and gain access to the complete ASCII character set.

As a result, I'm frequently having to adjust from one key pattern to another and often find myself making a lot of typing errors during the first few hours on any one device. In an attempt to reduce those problems, I generally prefer to use the ADDS terminal for word-processing applications and program generation, the Hazeltine for numeric data entries, the Qume printer's keyboard only if absolutely necessary when the other terminals are inoperative, and the Apple II keyboard only for Applesoft and Apple Integer BASIC programming.

In addition to simple key location, a separate numeric keypad much like a calculator is featured on some keyboards. Getting into the habit of using such a keypad and then switching to a keyboard without one can be difficult. Another dissimilarity is in the repeat function for the keys. The Hazeltine terminal automatically repeats when a key is held down. The ADDS terminal repeats automatically for all keys except the New Line (Return) key, which must be struck separately for each new line. Both the Qume and the Apple II keyboard require that a separate Repeat key be held down to repeat a character. Such differences not only are annoying but can lower efficiency, especially when moving from one keyboard to another.

The Apple II keyboard deserves some special attention. First, it does not normally have any provision for lowercase letters and hence is known as an "uppercase keyboard." The Shift key functions only to access a few special characters and the symbols provided by the uppercase numeric keys; it does not switch between upper- and lowercase letters. Adding one of the available lowercase adapters may or may not be much of an improvement because most do not employ the Shift key but instead use either the Escape or the Right Arrow key to change from upper- to lowercase and back again. My biggest problem with the Apple II keyboard is that it does not offer the full set of ASCII characters; in particular, it omits some of the nonprinting control characters often required by specialized software. While this may not be of great importance in some cases, it does tend to hinder some programming applications. Again, I frequently end up connecting an external terminal device to gain access to those characters and easy case-shifting capabilities.

The other item of note on an Apple II is that the Reset key is located immediately above the Return key, where it can easily be hit by mistake. The problem is that hitting the Reset key aborts a program being run and may or may not cause the loss of a program being developed. Since my Apple is fairly new, it does have an internal switch under the keyboard that allows me to change the Reset function to require pressing both the Control and Reset keys simultaneously. Since these keys are at opposite ends of the keyboard, this is a two-handed operation and usually cannot be done without deliberate intent. The instruction sheet provided for this feature recommends that the option be activated only by experienced system users, but I found it an advantage to establish the double-key reset pattern as soon as I set up the system.

The Output Devices. The two most common types of output devices found on personal and small business computers are the video display and the printer. The first generally is used for interactive purposes so that you can see what you have entered at the keyboard, examine program lines, check data outputs, and so on. The second is used to obtain *hard-copy* printouts, such as complete program listings or program results. While it's common to find a small computer system without a printer, it's a very rare system that does not have some type of video-display capability.

In talking about computer memory earlier in this chapter, I briefly touched on memory-mapped video. Typically, there are two ways in which a computer system may handle its video displays to the user. The simplest method involves transmitting a character or character "stream" to a "dumb" terminal that simply displays those characters on the screen. This is very much like transmitting the characters to a printer that outputs the characters exactly as they are received. With a typical device such as a cathode-ray terminal (CRT), the character appears on the screen at a position immediately following the preceding character, and special control characters are used to reposition the cursor to overwrite or change that character.

Normally, a CRT device offers few if any graphics capabilities and, on small computer systems, allows only the simple presentation of alphanumeric characters in either light printing on a dark background or dark printing on a light background. While a CRT device typically requires some special controlling software known as a *device driver*, that software generally is invisible to the user and consumes fairly little memory.

On the other hand, some systems, such as the Apple II, the Vector Graphics models, and other popular brands, map the contents of the video screen in a reserved area of the RAM memory. By periodically scanning the memory map and transmitting its contents to the display screen, individual characters, patterns, or dots on the screen can be turned on and off anywhere on the screen according to the contents of the corresponding memory locations. This constant scanning and updating of the display provides many useful and attractive features, including the ability to devise elaborate graphics, utilize full-color displays, and perform other operations that can be achieved only with dot-by-dot manipulation and continuous screen updating from memory. However, the feature is costly in terms of computer memory lost to other uses.

In the Apple II computer, text display and the primary and secondary low-resolution graphics displays use 2,048 bytes of RAM, while the secondary and primary pages of high-resolution graphics use another 16,384 bytes. That's a total of 18,432 bytes of RAM consumed just to map the video displays, and it comprises a large chunk of memory typically unavailable for other program uses. On some systems, part of the memory used for mapping the various displays may be reclaimed and used for other purposes if the particular display mode is not used. However, all memory-mapped video systems will cost some memory just to maintain the text displays.

Since memory mapping does reduce the amount of RAM available for other things, it also reduces the size of the programs that can be written and the amount of data that can be handled on an in-memory basis at any one time. Therefore, it also limits the effectiveness of the computer, since a shortage of memory may require splitting a program or set of data into smaller parts, using the parts separately, and slowing down the computer's overall *throughput.*

Video displays are very transient things that allow you to look at a few lines of a program or set of data at one time. The information usually can be accessed quickly and without a lot of fuss and bother. However, it's desirable and often necessary to have a more permanent record of data, programs, and computed outputs. The *hard-copy* paper printout that provides such a record is obtained from a separate peripheral known as a printer.

Here again, there are many possible choices that can be made from an almost limitless collection of printout devices. There are character printers, line printers, dot-matrix printers, thermal printers, graphics printers, and others. Each has its own characteristics in terms of printout speed, readability of the printed page, interfacing requirements to the computer, and so on. In choosing a printer, it's necessary to make some compromises or tradeoffs, usually between printing speed, printing quality, and price.

Perhaps the single most popular printer type for personal and small-business use is the dot-matrix variety. The individual characters are formed as patterns of tiny dots resulting from small pins striking the ribbon and transferring dot images to the paper in specific arrangements. For the user of a small computer system, this style offers two advantages, namely availability in versions at a price as low as about $450 (1981 dollars) and a fair degree of printing speed. Even inexpensive versions are capable of printing speeds ranging from 50 to 80 characters per second. The overall readability of the printout is a direct function of the number of pins or wires used to construct the characters. In general, the more wires available, the more readable the output. A 9×9 dot matrix will produce sharper and more readable outputs than a 5×7 matrix, and an 18×9 matrix will produce a better output than either of the others.

Different dot-matrix printers offer different frills and different advantages. Among the features that may be found within a price range of about $450 to $1,150 are proportional spacing, expanded typefaces, special graphics characters, bidirectional or unidirectional printing, and text justification (flush right margins). Some reach printing speeds that exceed 200 characters per second. Given the relatively low price, the number of available features, and an acceptable printing speed, dot-matrix printers have become quite popular among microcomputer users and serve quite well for general-purpose printing. They may not, however, be well suited to specialized printing tasks.

High-speed printers such as ballistic line printers or ink-jet printers are used only occasionally with microcomputers and then only for special applications. Their cost often runs to many thousands of dollars, and they are designed specifically for high-volume use where printing speed is the chief concern. A ballistic line printer that prints out entire lines of information at one time is capable of reaching speeds of several hundred lines per minute, far exceeding the printing speed of any character-by-character printer. However, their cost, complexity, and specialized application keeps these printers from being a major factor in the market for microcomputers.

Character or letter-quality printers often are used on small-business computers but less frequently on personal computers. These machines all operate on the principle of positioning a type element over a location on the page and then striking that element against a ribbon to print a single, contiguous image of the character. The style of type element may by a spinning daisy wheel, a rotating ball, or a turning thimble, but the principle remains the same: every character typed on the page is a single and distinct character on the type element. Typically, these printers are both slower and more expensive than the dot-matrix variety. The speeds range from as low as 12 to as high as 55 characters per second. They also offer many standard or optional frills such as proportional spacing, bidirectional printing, interchangeable type elements for different printing styles, and the use of either inked fabric ribbons or carbon ribbons. However, their prices typically range from a low of about $1,200 to $4,000 or more (1981 dollars), so they may be beyond the budgets of many small businesses and most personal-computer users. In fact, it's possible for the cost of a good letter-quality printer to exceed the combined cost of all other components in a computer system.

Speed, printing quality, price, and fancy frills or options all have to be weighed in choosing a printer. Furthermore, the choice of a printer can have a direct influence on the effective use of the computer system as whole. Selecting a slow device like a 12- to 25-cps character printer may result in almost interminable waiting periods when the application involves mostly printed outputs. In addition, the entire computer system probably will be unavailable for other uses while a printing process is underway. Selecting any type of letter-quality printer may cause serious problems when most of the printouts are graphics such as bar charts or line graphs. Although most daisy-wheel, ball, and thimble printers do have graphics capability, it's usually quite slow and difficult to use.

Choosing a printer for a specific application requires careful thought. As just one example, selecting a dot-matrix printer for word-processing applications may be a serious mistake. That statement needs a little more discussion. Nearly every microcomputer available today has the capability of being a word processor; all you have to do is buy a software package that the programmer claims is a word processor. Right? No, wrong! It's not uncommon for a writer or the executive of a small business to buy a microcomputer to have word-processing capabilities for preparing manuscripts, writing letters, typing reports, and so on. All too often, price is weighted too heavily in the assessment of the system components, and a dot-matrix printer is selected because of the apparent difference between its $400-to-$1,000 price and the $2,000-to-$4,000 tag on a professional letter-quality printer.

Writers who buy such systems will have difficulty selling their work. I have talked to quite a number of editors recently and found considerable resistance to writers who use dot-matrix printers. Some of the editors indicated that the writers' work would get less than preferential treatment, and many others said that they wouldn't read the manuscripts at all. This means that writers who buy dot-matrix printers may spend a lot of time on books or articles that they will be unable to sell because the editors to whom they submit the manuscripts won't read dot-matrix printing.

The small business typically faces another problem, particularly when the word processor is used to prepare letters and other materials for distribution to customers and others outside the company. Quite simply, most dot-matrix printouts are clearly recognizable as machine-generated and usually are considered "junk mail." Since such items are viewed as mass-produced, they have little effective impact on potential clients or customers and may even create a rather negative image.

A Panoply of I/O Devices. Peripheral devices for input to and output from a computer are not limited to keyboards, video displays, and printers. There are hundreds, even thousands of devices from which to choose, and a computer user quickly can become a gadgeteer with analog/digital converters, telephone modems, digitizers, graphics pads, speech synthesizers, display enhancers, digital clocks, plotters, printing "spoolers," and other miscellaneous devices that may or may not prove useful in a given application.

The important thing to remember in adding any I/O device to a computer system is that the device's purchase price alone is not its entire cost. Every I/O device must be controlled by the computer, and that takes some kind of programmed *device driver* to instruct the computer as to what it should do with the connected device. Even when the programming is provided by the device's manufacturer or some other source and doesn't require a lot of programming effort on your part, it still costs you in terms of memory and overall computer capabilities. The drivers for the I/O devices reside in RAM memory; therefore, each driver reduces the amount of memory available for your use in other applications that may not make use of the device. If you become involved in writing large programs such as those for accounting use, text processing, statistics, or even sophisticated games, committing RAM to an unnecessary I/O device's drivers may mean that you have insufficient memory for your own program.

Mass-Storage Devices

The final element of the system diagram in Figure 1-1 is the mass-storage device. On today's small computer systems, this typically is either a cassette tape, one or more *floppy disks*, a "hard" disk, or a combination of these. The devices provide some means for permanently storing information, such as programs, data, and text, by recording it on a magnetic surface, as does an audio-tape recorder or video recorder.

It's easy to take modern mass-storage devices for granted, but they result from as much technological evolution as microcomputers. While computers were shrinking in size and increasing in capabilities and speed, mass-storage techniques were being modified and revised to keep pace with the newer, smaller, and faster computers. In two decades, microcomputers that fit on top of a desk have evolved to take the place of room-size giants that were slower, less capable, and vastly more expensive. Similarly, mass-storage devices have changed from slow, cumbersome paper-oriented machines to extremely fast and efficient magnetic recording devices.

When I had my first contact with a computer in 1963, the popular form of storage for data and programs was punched 80-column cards. That meant that every line of a program and every group of data items had to be *keypunched* onto its own card and that those cards had to be maintained in very strict sequential order. A fair-sized computer program might involve a stack of computer cards several feet high and weighing more than was convenient to carry around. If a box of cards happened to tip over and spill, it meant having to re-sort the entire collection before they could be used as input to the computer. It also meant that if an error was made in keypunching, the entire card had to be replaced. Since that situation might not be found until the program was loaded into the computer, it would mean stopping the run, punching a new card, reloading the entire program, and hoping that another error wasn't encountered elsewhere. The whole process of getting a single program punched onto cards and then getting it up and running in the computer could take days or even weeks.

By the late 1960s, high-speed card punches and readers were quite popular for the larger computers. By that time, a computer could be equipped with a peripheral machine that would read 1,500 or more cards per minute, and the computer also could output data to a machine that would punch the 80-column cards at the rate of 100 or more every minute. These devices were vast improvements over earlier machines, which could read only 200 or so cards a minute, but they were still slow by today's standards.

During the early 1970s, when I first became involved with minicomputers, punched paper tape was the state of the art for those machines. Instead of going onto several thousand separate cards, the data could be keypunched onto a continuous strip of paper that could, in turn, be read by another machine and transmitted into the minicomputer. However, the standard Teletype® paper-tape reader could transmit only 10 characters per second to the computer, and even the high-speed paper-tape readers transmitted only 150 to 300 characters per second—hardly a high-speed operation compared to what is available today, although it was quite an accomplishment at that time.

As minicomputers gained a foothold in the marketplace, two other forms of data storage and retrieval gained popularity. One was reel-to-reel magnetic tape, which could receive or transmit data at a rate of about 1,600 characters per second. The other was a *hard-disk* system that could transmit and receive data at rates of 100,000 to 200,000 characters per second. The machines were, however, quite costly. Magnetic-tape devices were priced right around $8,000 to $9,000 with an interface for the computer, and the hard disk was priced at about $8,100 with its interface (all in 1972 dollars).

By the mid-1970s, microcomputers were beginning to expand, first as a sort of novelty for hobbyists and later as a serious tool for business and personal use. Along with the gain in the microcomputer's acceptance and popularity came a gain in the popularity of the tape cassette and the floppy disk as mass-storage media. Both offered the ability to store large amounts of data, and both could be sold at more reasonable prices than the larger devices used on larger computers. As the microcomputer industry boomed, efforts were made to incorporate other types of mass-storage devices such as magnetic-card readers, paper-tape devices, large magnetic-tape units, hard disks, and so on. But none proved as popular or as readily accepted as the cassettes and floppy disks. Today, new hard-disk technologies are making these devices more popular, but their prices remain prohibitive for many users.

Most of the micros for personal and business use were first introduced with only the ability to record ("write") and play back ("read") from a tape cassette. Even as late as 1981, many new brands of micros were making their first appearances in the stores with only the capability of using a cassette for data and program storage. The cassette itself cannot be distinguished from an ordinary audio cassette, and most small computers are equipped with what is essentially a standard audio-cassette recorder. While tape cassettes serve very well for simple recording and for loading programs and data that can be handled in strictly sequential order, they are relatively slow and don't allow information to be accessed as easily as might be necessary or desirable.

For example, it's common practice to store only one computer program on a cassette. If two or more programs are on the same tape, locating the second or subsequent one is somewhat difficult and always frustrating. To get at the second program, it's necessary to advance the tape past the first one, either by reading the tape and ignoring the output or by using a fast-forward to move the tape. Since there's no absolutely reliable indication of exactly where to stop the tape and then resume reading, finding the start of the second program can take quite some time.

Similarly, data on tape are useful only if the entire set of data is needed at once or if sequential reading of the entire set can be tolerated to locate a single item. Suppose you have a *file* of 1,000 English words on a tape and want to use only word number 840 in a program. Your two choices are to read all of the words into the program and store them in memory or to read words and count them until you reach number 840, disregarding any words read while the count is less than that desired.

The floppy diskette essentially eliminates the problems encountered with tape cassettes. The diskette is a flat disk of plastic-like material coated with a magnetic substance and enclosed within a flexible plastic jacket. When inserted into a disk drive, the disk spins at high speed inside the jacket, and a read/write *head* in contact with the disk surface can either record data onto it or play back data from it. Its advantages over the tape cassette include the ability to hold more data than the cassette, a much higher rate of data handling, and, most importantly, the ability to store and retrieve data to and from separate disk areas in a random manner.

The ability to randomly access information on a diskette is vital to effective computer use. First, it means that numerous programs can be stored on a single diskette and retrieved without having to read the entire diskette or read past unwanted programs. Second, it allows data written to the diskette to be verified and rewritten if necessary, thus preventing data errors that later may interfere with the computer's operations. Third, it allows data files to be set up in such a fashion that one item can be retrieved from a list of hundreds or thousands without the delays and inconvenience of reading each item in sequence. It is my opinion that no computer can be an effective tool without such random-access capabilities. Computer time costs money, and data retrieval usually is the most time-consuming operation, so anything that can be done to reduce the time and cost of data handling is critical to the efficient and effective use of the machine.

Disk systems do cost a lot more than cassette systems, but they usually are well worth the price difference when considering the amount of time and frustration they can save. A computer like the Apple II can be equipped with two mini-floppy drives for just a little less than the cost of the computer itself (about $1,000 to $1,100 in 1981). Of course, different computers have different diskette drives and different prices. An 8-inch floppy-disk drive costs considerably more than the drive for a 5½-inch mini-floppy. A double-density drive costs more than a single-density drive but offers twice the data storage per diskette. A double-sided diskette drive costs more than a single-sided drive but is like having two drives on line at the same time. A very nice installation would be "dual quads" consisting of two double-sided double-density disk drives, which would be equivalent to eight single-sided single-density drives. Although dual quads are expensive, in the 8-inch variety they put 2.2 to 2.5 million bytes (megabytes) of data storage on line at any time.

In addition to the initial purchase cost of a disk drive and its interface, there is a hidden cost to the computer user. As with any other peripheral device, programming is needed to operate the disk drive, and that programming consumes valuable computer memory. In the case of a disk system, the programming is known as a *disk-operating system* or *DOS* and includes the instructions to the computer concerning the handling of all disk-related tasks, such as writing data, reading data, cataloging file names, assigning disk space, deleting previously recorded files, verifying the data read from or written to the disk device, and so on.

Disk-operating systems take many forms, including the CP/M® (*C*ontrol *P*rogram for *M*icroprocessors) package available for many computers and developed by Digital Research. Other operating systems include DOS 3.3 for the Apple II and MSDOS for the IBM Personal

Computer and several others. The TRS-80 alone offers TRSDOS, NEWDOS, and LDOS. With the exceptions of CP/M and MSDOS, operating systems generally are unique to the machine for which they were designed, so they aren't transferrable from one machine to another. Each sets up its own disk formats and performs its data-handling operation according to the whims of its programmers. However, they all have one thing in common: they consume a significant portion of a computer's RAM memory.

In the case of the Apple's DOS 3.3, about 10.5K of RAM is devoted to the operating system and is unavailable for other uses. The memory area occupied by DOS must not be overlaid by any other data or programs. Otherwise, DOS itself is destroyed and so are the abilities to use the disk drives, creating a situation in which you can't store or save a program under development or the results of a program run. In the worst case, having memory used by one of your programs collide with memory used by DOS will destroy both your own program and DOS, necessitating retyping or reloading your program.

The memory lost to a disk-operating system is cumulative with the memory lost to other system features such as memory-mapped video and any number of special locations reserved for system use. If a system uses 10.5K for its DOS and another 18K to map multiple pages of graphics displays, it's possible to reduce a 48K system to less than 20K of memory space directly usable by a program. When it comes time to write a lengthy and complex program of your own, you'll probably find that 20K of memory really isn't a lot to work with, and you may run headlong into an "out of memory" error message. That's why I recommend you know exactly how much usable memory is available in a particular system after accounting for all the miscellaneous overhead items and that you know this before you buy the system.

Much of what I'll be presenting later in this book relates directly to reducing the amount of memory consumed by your programs. I've found that memory conservation and programming efficiency go hand in hand; I'll be comparing different techniques in terms of speed, memory utilization, or both so you can see the impact on each when the same operation is done two or more different ways.

From Hardware to Software

The preceding sections of this chapter have dealt with the physical components of a small computer system, components known collectively as the *hardware*. But it takes more than hardware to make any computer operational. The computer must be told exactly what operations it is to perform on specific items of data. Providing those instructions in a language that the computer can use is the process called programming.

The set of instructions provided to the computer is known as a program, with all programs grouped collectively under the term *software*. For all practical purposes, the words "program" and "software" are interchangeable. When a programmer or computer user talks about software, the reference is to one or more programs. Similarly, when the programmer talks about a program, the reference is to a "piece" of software.

For convenience, software can be separated into two general categories, namely the *system software* and the *applications software*, with the latter group sometimes called *user software*. The distinction between the two is largely a matter of function, with system software consisting of the programs necessary to make the computer operational, and applications software being the individual programs prepared to perform specific tasks such as word processing, calculating statistical analyses, playing games, and so on.

As a further distinction, system software normally is provided with the computer system at the time of purchase, while applications software either must be purchased separately or must be developed by the user. Typically, the system software includes the disk-operating system and the high-level languages, of which BASIC is only one possibility. Often, the system software includes certain *utility programs* for highly specialized uses such as copying information from one diskette to another, examining the contents of a diskette, creating and editing disk files, assembling programs, or debugging programs.

On the other hand, something like a word-processing package, a general-ledger accounting package, or a game would be purchased separately, usually isn't obtained from the computer-system manufacturer, and isn't required for the computer's overall operation. Instead, it performs a specific function directly related to how the computer is used. By establishing a use or application for the machine, such software falls into the category of applications software. Similarly, you as a computer user can expect to be developing some of your own programs for purposes as diverse as income tax calculations, making address labels for mailings, determining equipment depreciation, and so on. Again, the programs you create are not essential to the operation of the computer system but only to the particular application you have in mind, so they are considered applications software.

There's always a bit of a question as to the classification of a high-level programming language like BASIC. Is it system software? Is it applications software? The question can be argued either way with about equal success; after all, the high-level language is not strictly required to make a computer operational but only to provide an element of convenience for the system user. Nevertheless, I prefer to view programming languages as system software since they allow the computer to be programmed for other functions in a language I can use, usually are designed to come up and running without any deliberate intervention on my part, and are purchased as a standard feature and integral function of the system as a whole.

At this point, I've established that hardware is the physical machinery of the computer system while software consists of the programmed instructions that make the hardware "do its thing." But there's a third category that creates a gray area between the two, namely *firmware.* In very simple terms, firmware is nothing more than a hardware device in which a particular piece of software resides permanently.

To clarify, I'll refer back to a minicomputer of the early 1970s. It was not the kind of machine that would be ready for use as soon as it was switched on. Before that computer could be used, it had to be *loaded* with a program each time it was switched on. Here was a bit of a paradox. In order for a program to be loaded, the computer must be programmed to perform the loading operations. The problem, then, was how to get a program designed to load other programs into a computer that contained no program to allow loading anything in the first place. In terms of the hypothetical hotel analogy, all of the pigeonholes were empty, including the ones that would contain the instructions on how to fill the pigeonholes.

Originally, the only solution to this circular problem was to load certain memory locations with some very basic instructions manually. To do this, it was necessary to use an array of front-panel switches to "toggle in" or enter individual coded instructions into specific memory locations. Since those instructions had to be coded as lengthy "words" of binary digits (on/off switch settings) and had to be loaded into memory "addresses" also coded in binary, quite a few switch operations were necessary to enter all the instructions needed. The process often was viewed as one of "pulling the computer up by its bootstraps," so the short program became known as a *bootstrap loader,* and the process of toggling it into the computer's memory was called *booting* the computer.

Once the bootstrap loader had been toggled in, it provided the raw instructions that enabled the computer to activate a paper-tape reader and accept another, more sophisticated, *loader* program into memory. In its turn, that loader provided the more sophisticated instructions that would allow the computer to accept other programs. As a result, getting the computer ready to do something useful was a long, complex, and error-prone procedure requiring the manual toggling of the bootstrap loader, the loading of a general-purpose loader, the loading of the system software, and then the loading of any applications software. All in all, the process could take many minutes and, in the event of an error, might have to be repeated several times.

Shortly thereafter, the manufacturer introduced a plug-in device known as a *bootstrap circuit board.* Essentially, this provided a way to skip over the switch-toggling operation by "coding" the bootstrap instructions into a hardwired device. With that card plugged into the computer, turning power on automatically loaded the hardwired instructions into the correct memory locations so the user could progress directly to the more elaborate loader program without playing around with a lot of switch settings. That bootstrap circuit card was a simple piece of firmware—a hardware device that contained the programmed instructions or software of the bootstrap loader.

Early microcomputers faced the same problems, and a number of them were first introduced without automatic start-up provisions. Those relatively primitive machines still required that the booting be done by toggling front-panel switches to enter the appropriate instructions. But with increasing popularity came increasing sophistication. A major step forward has been the so-called *turnkey* machine, which lacks the array of front-panel lights and switches found on earlier machines. Instead, it has a key-operated power switch and a "start switch," and it is equipped with an internal turnkey module. When power is switched on or the start switch is pressed, the turnkey module automatically boots the system and loads all necessary loading instructions. Those instructions then cause the computer to load BASIC or some other program from disk automatically. The turnkey module that causes all this is the system's firmware.

A computer like the Apple II Plus is even more sophisticated in that it has both automatic start-up and Applesoft BASIC in firmware—specifically in read-only memory (ROM) devices. With it, I can switch power on and have Applesoft (without the disk-operating system) up and running faster than I can move my hand from the power switch to the Reset key. If I want the disk-operating system and Apple's integer BASIC loaded into memory from disk storage, the process takes a little longer—about 18 seconds.

Converting often-used software such as the BASIC language into firmware offers several advantages. First, there is the benefit of speed; with the Apple II Plus, Applesoft in ROM is accessible almost instantly upon powering up the computer as compared to a relatively long delay of several seconds to load Applesoft or Integer BASIC from disk. Second, programs in ROM are nonvolatile; turn power to a microcomputer off and the contents of RAM memory are lost and must be reloaded from scratch, but the contents of ROM devices still are there when power is reapplied. Third, firmware doesn't consume valuable RAM locations needed for other uses; in the Apple II Plus, Applesoft is available with no appreciable loss of RAM space while disk-loaded BASICs for some machines may consume 20K or more of memory. Fourth, firmware is safer than disk-stored software; a disk can be destroyed relatively easily by a mechanical failure in the drive, a defective diskette, poor handling techniques, exposure to a magnetic field, or operator error.

It is worth noting that, given the time, money, equipment, and inclination, almost any software can be converted to firmware. With access to the proper equipment or sufficient funds to pay someone else, it's not particularly difficult to take a piece of applications software such as an accounting package or word-processing system, have it programmed into a PROM (programmable read-only memory), install the PROM into a computer, and have the computer come up and running that application each time power is switched on.

Programming Languages

At this point, I recommend that you read or at least skim Appendix B. That appendix contains information about the structure of numerical systems, numerical conversions, and number handling. At the very least, be sure you understand the terminology of bits, bytes, and the hexadecimal and binary systems before proceeding. To demonstrate the pros and cons of high-level computer languages, it will be necessary to examine briefly the differences between approaches. As we work up from raw binary coding through hexadecimal coding and assembly language, the advantages and disadvantages of high-level forms eventually become quite evident.

Binary Machine-Language Programming

Deep inside a modern computer are thousands of microminiaturized circuits and electronic components, each performing a specific task. But circuits exist only in one of two states—on and off. Relays may be either closed or open. Switches may be set or not set. Electrical currents may be flowing or not flowing. Through the magic of electronic design and engineering, a computer is made to perform its tasks as a direct function of the components and combinations of components that are on or off at any given instant.

Given only two possible states of any component, a computer's total vocabulary is limited to the two "numbers" zero and one, which correspond to the off and on conditions respectively. Imagine what it would be like if you had to go through life with a vocabulary limited to the words "no" and "yes." In order to communicate even the simplest messages, you would have to devise and define specific patterns of those two words, with each pattern having a different meaning. For example, a hamburger might be given a descriptive pattern of a yes and seven no's, while french fries might be given a yes, six no's, and another yes. Ordering a burger and fries from the local fast-food joint would be quite a chore, since you would have to order "yes no no no no no no [pause] yes no no no no no yes." Make even the smallest error or pause at the wrong moment, and you could wind up with a fish fillet and onion rings instead of a burger and fries.

Of course, people aren't restricted to such a small vocabulary, so communication isn't that cumbersome or time-consuming. However, the CPU of any computer is limited to exactly that two-word vocabulary of yes and no, with all instructions, input data, and output data presented in patterns of zeros and ones. The resulting numerical system is known as *binary* numbering, and the individual zeros and ones are *bits* (*b*inary dig*its*).

For now it suffices to know that computer CPUs are designed to recognize and respond to instructions coded as specific sequences of bits. You also should be aware that different computers recognize different bit patterns or "words" for equivalent instructions. In larger computers, 16, 32, or more bits may be needed to make up a recognizable word, while most of the common and popular microcomputers for personal and small-business use are based on a system of eight bits.

Because the binary system is inherent to electronics and computer technology, a computer works with binary-coded instructions very quickly and efficiently. However, the human mind has considerable difficulty in dealing with lengthy series of zeros and ones. To illustrate, consider the following three-instruction program for a 6502 microprocessor contained in an Apple II computer:

```
10101101 10100000 00001111
01101101 10101010 00001111
10001101 10100100 00001111
```

The complexity of this format is misleading. One might expect the little program to perform some great feat, but all it does is take two numbers from memory, add them together, and store the result back into memory. The 6502 microprocessor recognizes the eight-bit words in the leftmost column as specific instructions, while the second and third columns represent the memory addresses containing the data operated upon by those instructions.

In this case, the first line fetches the value from memory location 4000 and loads it into an internal holding and working area known as an *accumulator*. Don't worry about the terminology. Words like "fetch," "accumulator," "register," and "flag" all are features internal to the computer and are of concern only to those who program at the machine level. Here you need be concerned only with the overall function, not the individual details. The second line fetches the value from memory location 4010 and adds it to the accumulator. The third line takes the result of the addition from the accumulator and stores it back into location 4020.

It should be quite obvious that coding programs in binary is difficult, tedious, and prone to a great many errors. It took 72 bits to tell the computer to add two numbers together. A mistake in any one or any combination of those bits would have yielded an erroneous program. And remember that this is a very simple little program using only 3 of the 56 possible instructions in a 6502 microprocessor and only three of the tens of thousands of memory locations that may be available. To further complicate matters, 22 of the 56 instructions for a 6502 microprocessor have one or more alternate forms (addressing modes) that must be coded as parts of the instructions.

There has to be an easier way to program, and, in fact, there are several. Progressing toward easier programming methods is like climbing a ladder. The higher you go, the easier it becomes for you to write a program, but the farther removed you become from the binary language the machine can understand. At each rung above ground level, new procedures have to be devised to convert your program into the code the computer can use, so the translating methods become quite complex by the time you reach the top of the ladder.

Hexadecimal Machine-Language Programming

The first step up from binary coding is relatively easy to accomplish. It involves nothing more than a "shorthand" method of representing the binary code. It happens that eight bits can be divided into two groups of four and treated as a single digit in the *hexadecimal* numbering system. Most microcomputers are designed to accept inputs and report outputs in hexadecimal, with the machine performing its own internal conversions quickly so that they are not obvious to the programmer. Personally, I don't know of any microcomputer currently on the market that actually allows direct binary coding in ones and zeros—they all rely on the shorthand method even at the level of *machine-language* programming. Without going into the details at this time, the little program for adding two numbers on the 6502 microprocessor would be represented thus in hexadecimal:

```
AD AØ ØF
6D AA ØF
8D B4 ØF
```

In this case the AD, 6D, and 8D are recognized by the computer as the load, add, and store instructions respectively. The numbers following each instruction are the memory addresses. Incidentally, if you try to convert the hexadecimal addresses to binary using the techniques to be found in Appendix B, you won't get 4000, 4010, and 4020 because the 6502 microprocessor requires that hex addresses have the first two and last two number pairs transposed. The assembly-language hex address A00F actually represents RAM address 0FA0.

It's apparent that writing hex code is far simpler than writing binary code. For one thing, there are fewer items to be handled; in this example only 18 hex digits were needed to represent 72 binary digits. For another, hexadecimal instruction codes are more distinctive, easier to recognize, and easier to remember than lengthy strings of zeros and ones. But hexadecimal coding still poses problems to all but experienced programmers in that it bears no resemblance to a person's everyday experiences. There are no words similar to conventional written English, letters from A through F are used to represent numerical values, and everything is counted in groups of 16 rather than the groups of 10 everyone has used since childhood.

Assembly-Language Programming

The next higher level of programming is *assembly language*, which involves replacing hexadecimal instruction codes with easily remembered three-letter codes called *mnemonics*. It's a first step toward using something akin to English in programming a computer, and it serves to speed the programming process considerably. Most software packages for handling assembly language also allow the programmer to reference other instructions with a name or label instead of with a memory location, provide the ability to relocate a program to different areas of the computer's memory, and offer a number of special aids.

However, assembly language cannot be understood by the computer in the form in which the programmer writes it. Instead, a *source program* written by the programmer must be processed by an *assembler* software package to create an *object program*. The assembler package converts the source program into machine code that can be loaded into and run by the computer; the computer is incapable of running the source code directly.

Any particular computer often has a number of different assemblers available, each with its own approaches to making life easier for the programmer and each with its own requirements for formatting and entering the source code. While all assemblers enable the programmer to spell out operations with mnemonics rather than numeric codes, there are differences in the way assemblers handle data, memory addresses, labeling, and so on. For example, one assembler may allow memory addresses and numeric data to be entered as decimal numbers, another may require hexadecimal numbers, and still another may allow a choice of either form by adding a character or combination of characters to designate one numerical system or another.

To illustrate, the sample program for adding two numbers might appear in one of the following assembly-language forms, with hexadecimal notation in the one on the left and decimal notation in the one on the right:

```
LDA $FAØ        LDA 4ØØØ
ADC $FAA        ADC 4Ø1Ø
STA $FB4        STA 4Ø2Ø
```

These programs are functionally identical to the binary and hexadecimal programs already described, and they consist of instructions to load a value from one memory location (LDA), add the value from a second location (ADC), and store the result in a third location (STA). When assembled into object code, the instructions and addresses would be converted to their hexadecimal or binary equivalents and would be directly usable by the computer.

In such a simple example, the advantages of assembly language are not immediately apparent. However, I don't want to delve deeply into assembly language because that would deviate from the main direction of this book. Therefore, I'll leave it to you to investigate assembly language on your own if you're so inclined or simply to take my word that it is a significant improvement over straight binary or hex machine-language programming. What you do need to recognize is that assembly language relieves the programmer of some, but not all, of the details. An assembly-language programmer still has to be very aware of the internal workings of the CPU and memory, the memory locations already used and those still available, the memory addresses used to store data, and the individual formatting requirements of the assembler software being applied.

While assembly language is a significant step up from machine language, it still causes problems for anyone not thoroughly familiar with a computer, and it isn't particularly easy for the novice to learn. Therefore, still further language development is needed.

High-Level-Language Programming

At the top of the programming ladder are the *high-level* languages. These are the languages designed to be the easiest to program because of their similarity to already familiar terms and approaches, but they also are the farthest removed from the language the computer understands and therefore require the most "conditioning" to be made usable.

There are literally dozens of high-level languages in existence at any given time, with some surviving over long periods and others appearing one day and disappearing the next. Of the long-term survivors, five languages immediately come to mind: COBOL (*Co*mmon *B*usiness-*O*riented *L*anguage), FORTRAN (*For*mula *Tran*slation Language), UCSD Pascal, "C," and BASIC (*B*eginner's *A*ll-purpose *S*ymbolic *I*nstruction *C*ode).

Of these languages, COBOL is designed specifically for business-oriented applications and has been set up so that programmers with a background in accounting, bookkeeping, and similar occupations can adapt their vocabularies and formulas both quickly and efficiently. FORTRAN is quite popular among the members of the scientific and technical community because it is oriented heavily toward complex numerical processing and the easy entry of scientific formulas and data. BASIC, although designated a beginner's language, has become a general-purpose programming language that is easily learned and applied across a wide range of computers and computational requirements. BASIC is particularly popular on microcomputers for both personal and small-business use because it is both versatile and comparatively easy to learn.

Both Pascal and "C" are growing in popularity and claim important advantages over BASIC. Among the features are high speed, "structured" programming, and portability from one computer to another. Yet neither can be expected to displace BASIC as a "standard" microcomputer language in the forseeable future.

In dealing with high-level languages, there is, as the joke says, "some good news and some bad news." First the good news: high-level languages make it very easy to program a computer in comparison with the lower-level languages, and they relieve the programmer of much of the burden involved in keeping track of memory locations, labels, mnemonics, and so on. Through the abbreviated descriptions of the lower-level languages, I've been using a simple addition problem to trace the changes from one level to another. In a language like BASIC, that same addition is represented by a single, simple statement of the form "LET Z=X+Y". Most BASICs don't even require the "LET," so the statement becomes "Z=X+Y". No fuss! No bother! It's a simple algebraic expression easily handled by anyone with a fundamental knowledge of elementary arithmetic and algebra.

Notice that the BASIC statement doesn't reference memory locations. The programmer neither knows nor cares where the values of X, Y, and Z are stored. The tedious little details like making memory assignments are handled by the language itself and are invisible to the programmer. In assembly or machine language, the programmer has to know exactly where those values are kept in memory; if the value of Z is needed later in the program it must be retrieved from the same location in which it was stored. In a high-level language, the value is returned automatically anytime it's called.

All in all, a high-level language serves to make life much easier for a computer programmer. But now the bad news: some high-level languages are notoriously inefficient and waste a tremendous amount of computer time. As I've said, such languages are far removed from the raw binary codes the computer needs. Therefore, the programs written at the high level must somehow be converted down to those binary codes by either of two general techniques, namely *compiling* and *interpreting.*

A language such as FORTRAN is compiler-oriented. It parallels assembly language in that the compiler program operates on source code written by the programmer and produces object code usable by the computer. Once reduced to machine-language object code, the program gains the full speed and efficiency of the computer's inherent capabilities. However, getting from the source code to executable object code can be a bit of a problem. First, compilers are designed to detect common errors such as mistyping a command, leaving out a punctuation mark, and so on. When the compiler detects such an obvious error, it notifies the programmer (or system operator) of the fact. The error or errors then must be corrected in the source code and followed by recompilation. Sometimes this procedure has to be repeated a number of times before a successful compilation is achieved.

Even then, there may be errors, particularly errors in logic or problems in misnaming an item. In fact, there are many types of errors that are not detected by the compiler. When the object code is run on the computer, a few types of errors may force the machine to abort the run, but many others show up only as discrepancies in the output, garbage on the printed page, and so on. Again, the programmer has to go back to the source program, isolate the problem and correct it, have the program recompiled, and attempt another run of the object code. Correcting one problem may lead to finding others, and it can take quite a bit of effort to achieve a truly successful program run. Once the program is successful, however, the compiled object code can be maintained in mass storage and used over and over again without further delays. At that point, and only at that point, full computer efficiency is achieved.

A language such as BASIC uses the interpretive approach. As an interpreter, BASIC does not provide object code that can be loaded directly into the computer. Instead, the interpreter resides in memory and translates or interprets each character, statement, function, constant, variable, or expression as it is encountered during the run. Suppose you have a set of instructions that execute in a "loop" and have to be performed 10,000 times during a single program run. With an interpreter, every element of the program must be reinterpreted for the computer's use every time the loop is executed. The process of interpreting takes time.

BASIC also constructs things like a variable table, array tables, and a "stack" to keep track of the values, memory locations, and return addresses needed for the program. Just as a single example, every time the program calls for the value of Z, the variable table must be searched before the value can be found—which, again, is time-consuming.

In fact, a BASIC interpreter performs many thousands of different operations the programmer never sees, but each operation consumes a certain amount of the computer's time and decreases the overall speed with which a problem can be solved. Since every interpretive step associated with each programmed operation must be performed every time the need for it is encountered, a great deal of computer time is "wasted" by purely internal operations. Furthermore, a BASIC interpreter resident in RAM rather than ROM decreases the amount of memory available for the user's programs. The larger and more sophisticated the interpreter, the larger the memory loss; a simple, stripped-down BASIC may fit into 4K or 8K, but a fully expanded interpreter may require 20K or more. When the reduction of memory space reaches a point where it's necessary to break a large program into two or more parts, the loss of efficiency is compounded by the time required to transfer data from one part to the next.

In return for all this inefficiency, the BASIC interpreter delivers an element of convenience. One useful feature is that interpreters typically are *interactive*—that is, they allow the programmer direct and immediate access to the program elements so they can be modified to alter the operations or correct an error. There is no need to wait for a compiler's error report, return to the source program to search and correct the problem, and then wait for a recompilation. In general terms, a compiler-oriented language takes longer and makes it more difficult to develop and perfect a program but provides faster and more efficient execution after the program has been perfected. An interpreter-based language takes less time and effort during the development stages but sacrifices the subsequent efficiency of execution.

It must be noted, however, that BASIC compilers now are available for many of the microcomputer systems. Microsoft offers a compiler called BASCOM® and a linking loader called LINK-80® that run on CP/M-based systems. Several companies, including Hayden Book Co., Inc., offer compilers for Applesoft. And many more compiler offerings can be expected in the future. With a BASIC compiler, a programmer can have the best of both worlds. The interactive interpreter is available to develop, test, and perfect a program with moderate ease. The compiler then can be used to obtain a machine-language "command program" that runs quite efficiently and with a large speed increase over the interpretive form.

The Language Called "BASIC"

The high-level languages that every computer user now takes for granted weren't always available. There was a time when even minimal programming required an individual who could combine the skills and talents of a mathematician, a logician, and a programmer all at the same time. The typical programmer of the day faced the dual task of first formulating a workable solution to a given problem and then converting that process into computer steps. Developing the formula or *algorithm* to arrive at a problem's solution was difficult enough, but the programmer also had to worry about manipulating the internal workings of the computer with complex instructions written in machine or assembly language.

Learning to program a computer was a tremendous chore in itself, particularly when most programming was being done in either raw machine language or assembly language. Problems in advanced calculus, particle physics, quantum mechanics, and other exotic fields all had to be reduced to simple additions, subtractions, multiplications, and divisions, and then they had to be programmed in a language completely foreign to an individual's everyday experiences. Even the early versions of FORTRAN required a lot of work and a considerable knowledge of the computer. As a result, a programmer could end up spending more time trying to manipulate the computer than was spent in formulating the solution in the first place.

To teach the fundamentals of problem solving on a computer without becoming bogged down in the details of internal operations, there was a need for a simplified programming language that would emulate the overall functions without involving the user in matters of allocating memory locations, shifting data in and out of registers, structuring multiple-step machine language routines for basic arithmetic, and so on.

When Thomas E. Kurtz and John G. Kemeny developed BASIC in 1964, that need was met. In its original form, the language was extremely simple, consisting of only a few instructions and the four arithmetic operations of addition, subtraction, multiplication, and division. The programming instructions essentially imitated the internal workings of a computer in allowing numbers to be compared, allowing program control to be passed from one set of instructions to another (often on the basis of a comparison between two numbers), and allowing specified operations to be repeated or *looped* as many times as necessary.

With BASIC, someone starting to learn about computers could concentrate on the task of developing algorithms and problem-solving approaches without knowing or caring about how the computer was performing individual operations and manipulations. To do a simple addition of two numbers, the user had only to use a simple algebraic equation, and the language software would take care of setting up the multiple-step data manipulations between the computer's memory and internal registers. The language offered other advantages including program instructions using conventional English words such as DATA, READ, LET, IF...THEN..., and GOTO. It also allowed data to be entered as conventional decimal numbers rather than less familiar binary codes or other numbers developed from odd numeric systems and methods of counting. All in all, it provided a familiar, almost comfortable working environment for the novice programmer.

Over the following years, computer technology advanced rapidly. The size of practical machines began to shrink, prices were reduced, and computers began to appear in more and more business offices, research labs, manufacturing facilities, financial institutions, hospitals, and commercial facilities. With the expansion of the market came a shift in programming requirements. Manufacturers of the smaller computers soon realized that the number of machines they could sell was related to the ease with which customers could apply them to specific and frequently unique problem-solving tasks. That in turn necessitated providing a means by which computers could be programmed by people without extensive backgrounds in mathematics and programming. Essentially, the process of learning to program was shifting from the strictly academic world into the real world of commerce and industry.

To enable accountants, business executives, laboratory technicians, and others to use computers without extensive training, it was necessary to provide a programming language that was simple to learn but still could be utilized effectively in generalized problem solving across a broad range of applications. BASIC turned out to be the logical choice. A license to use the language could be obtained from the trustees of Dartmouth College, and the language could be configured for and implemented on small computers with comparative ease and minimal expense.

When the minicomputer manufacturer for which I worked in 1971 first announced the availability of BASIC on its machine, it was just one of many companies to do so across a span of just a few months. It was almost as if there had been a common agreement that BASIC would be made available on all minicomputers at the earliest possible date. Within a little less than a year, BASIC was being treated as the "standard" language for minis, although no two versions were identical.

In many ways, the development of microcomputers followed the same general pattern. Although the early micros were essentially hobby machines, the potential for a vast and untapped market in homes and small businesses was recognized quite quickly. But the same old problem popped up again—providing a simple yet powerful language that could be learned and used quickly by people with no prior experience with computers. Again, the attributes of BASIC made it an ideal choice. Although modern BASICs are far different from and much more complicated than the early versions, they retain the important features of using conventional decimal numbers as data, using familiar English words as instructions, and providing rapid interaction with the user to allow immediate detection and correction of errors.

As a result, BASIC has become a standard feature of micro-computers for both personal and small-business applications. Today it's hard to imagine a computer of any kind that doesn't provide one version or another of BASIC. Other languages may or may not be available on a particular machine, but BASIC usually is the first language provided by the manufacturer, generally is the first language employed by a new computer owner, and often remains the principal language over the entire life of the machine. Despite its flaws—and it does have numerous flaws such as comparatively slow execution times—BASIC provides relative ease of learning, ease of use, and a broad range of applicability that combine to make it the language of choice for a great many people.

As I've said, today's versions of BASIC are significantly different from the early versions, incorporating a variety of *enhancements* designed to adapt the language to different machines, allow use with disk-based mass storage, and provide special operations and commonly used functions as a part of the language rather than a part of a program written in the language. Compared side by side, a fully enhanced version such as Microsoft's BASIC-80 makes a typical 1971 version look very crude indeed, even though that earlier version was the state of the art at the time.

To illustrate how far the evolution has progressed, one 1971 version of BASIC offered 18 program statements, four arithmetic operations, a few logical comparisons, and no built-in or *intrinsic* functions. Its entire set of programming instructions was limited to the statements CALL, DIMension, END, FOR, GOSUB, GOTO, IF...THEN..., INPUT, LET, NEXT, PAGE, PRINT, READ, REMark, RESTORE, RETURN, and STOP. It could perform the fundamental comparisons between numbers to determine if one was less than, greater than, equal to, or not equal to the other, but it lacked the more elaborate logical comparisons or Boolean operators involving AND, OR, NOT, EOR, and so on. It allowed numbers to be added, subtracted, multiplied, and divided, but it had no preprogrammed internal functions for calculating square roots, exponents, sines, cosines, tangents, and the numerous other values commonly required in data processing. It lacked any provision for manipulating *string data* consisting of quoted literal letters and other characters; its data-processing abilities were limited strictly to numerical data.

In comparison, Microsoft's BASIC-80, running under the Digital Research CP/M system, provides some 46 program statements, 52 intrinsic functions (including 17 for manipulating literal strings), and 18 arithmetic and logical operators. BASIC-80 also provides the ability to handle four types of variables (string, integer, single-precision, and double-precision), is equipped with extensive editing facilities for correcting and altering programs, has a large set of direct system commands, and provides a great many specialized statements for formatting outputs, handling disk files, and so on.

Perhaps the most important enhancements made to BASIC over the years involve the intrinsic functions that allow a programmer to access particular calculations without knowing the details of how those calculations are performed. For instance, suppose a programmer needs to determine the square root of a number. Under the 1971 version of BASIC, there were no built-in functions, so a separate routine had to be supplied in every program requiring a square root. Under BASIC-80, a single statement serves the same function without the programmer having to know exactly how to calculate or approximate a square root.

Consider the following two examples showing how to calculate square roots of all integers from 1 to 500 using the two different approaches. To provide a reasonable comparison, I ran both versions under the same version of BASIC. To avoid complicating the timing, I didn't do anything with the square roots after they were calculated, thereby eliminating delays for printing, displaying, or storing them in discrete memory locations. The PRINT CHR$(7) function served simply to sound a "bell" signal at the conclusion of the calculations as an audible indication to halt the stopwatch.

```
1ØØ FOR X1=1 TO 500
2ØØ GOSUB 1ØØØ
3ØØ NEXT X1
35Ø PRINT CHR$(7)
4ØØ END
1ØØØ IF X1<Ø THEN 1Ø7Ø
1Ø1Ø IF X1=Ø THEN 1Ø8Ø
1Ø2Ø X9=.5*(1+X1)
1Ø3Ø X2=X9
1Ø4Ø X9=.5*(X2+X1/X2)
1Ø5Ø IF X9<X2 THEN 1Ø3Ø
1Ø6Ø RETURN
1Ø7Ø PRINT "SQR ERROR",X1
1Ø8Ø X9=Ø
1Ø9Ø RETURN
```

[81.6 seconds]

```
1ØØ FOR X1=1 TO 5ØØ
2ØØ X9=SQR(X1)
3ØØ NEXT X1
35Ø PRINT CHR$(7)
4ØØ END
```

[25.1 seconds]

At this point, you need not be concerned with the workings of the two sample programs, only with their memory consumptions and execution times. Calculating 500 square roots with the program on the left uses 202 bytes of memory to hold the program and requires 1 minute 21.6 seconds to execute. Calculating the same 500 square roots with the program on the right uses only 52 bytes of memory for the program and requires only 25.1 seconds. Enhancing BASIC to provide the SQR() function reduces both memory consumption and execution time significantly, eliminating 150 bytes and saving 56.5 seconds. Extending this same technique to the numerous other functions inherent in modern BASICs further improves program performance, reduces memory requirements, and makes it simpler for the user to write an effective program.

While today's BASICs are more capable than the early versions, they also are considerably more complex. Each added feature and enhancement has meant more instructions to remember, more rules to apply, more pages of descriptive text in books and manuals to define and describe the elements, and a longer learning process. Still, BASIC remains a comparatively easy and painless way to approach programming and to perform the day-to-day functions we've come to expect from our computers. The language is firmly entrenched in everyday computer use and will continue to be in widespread use for many years.

Chapter 2

Getting Down to "BASICS"

"BASIC"—Some Pros and Cons

As a programming language, BASIC is under constant fire by software companies, programmers, and individual users alike. Pick up almost any issue of any popular magazine for users of small computers and you're likely to find at least one article or editorial that criticizes BASIC and advises you to use one or another of the many available languages in its place. This is especially true right after a software-development company launches the marketing effort for a new or improved language that it claims is "perfect" for microcomputers.

"BASIC is too slow to be effective." "Too much memory is wasted." "The capabilities are too limited." "BASIC doesn't force the programmer to use 'structured' programming techniques." "It's strictly for beginners." These are just a few of the comments you can expect to encounter.

Yes, BASIC is slow, at least in comparison with some other languages. As I pointed out in Chapter 1, BASIC is about as far removed from the computer's binary machine language as you can get. Furthermore, the usual form of the language is an interpreter, which means that every line, statement, function, expression, and character in a program must be translated into appropriate machine instructions every time it is encountered. Yet the problem of excessively slow execution can be minimized by applying special "tricks" and good programming techniques to make the application program as efficient as possible.

By eliminating unnecessary operations and program statements that waste computer time, choosing and using available features and functions carefully, setting up a good algorithm, and other procedures, the BASIC programmer can cut wasted time significantly. Given a compiler to convert a BASIC program into permanent machine code, the execution speed can be improved enough to make the language quite competitive with other languages.

Yes, BASIC does waste memory space. As an interpreter, the language must reside in either RAM or ROM, and this means that certain portions of the computer's overall memory space are not available to the programmer. Furthermore, BASIC consumes memory to maintain working tables, for return addresses of subroutines, for a memory stack, and for other special purposes. The interactive nature of the language allows you to enter, execute, modify, list, and observe the execution of a program, speeding the process of developing and perfecting a program but costing you additional memory to house the editing, error-checking, and error-reporting functions required. Those memory locations also are lost to the programmer's direct use, and total losses may combine to limit severely the size of the program that can be written and executed under BASIC.

Even compilation of a program into machine language may be inefficient in terms of memory space because compilers don't always code the most memory- or speed-efficient routines possible. However, it is possible to program around limited memory. Writing a "tight" program that doesn't waste storage for things like unnecessary spaces, nonexecuted remarks, unused variables, and other program "frills" frequently solves some of the problems.

The matter of limited capabilities under BASIC relates directly to the implementation of the language in use on any particular computer. As I'll demonstrate later, there are many BASICs, each different and each having its own set of features and capabilities. Very simple BASICs with few enhancements beyond the original Dartmouth BASIC are quite limited and require considerable ingenuity to achieve even some of the simplest objectives.

On the other hand, the fully expanded and enhanced BASICs available for most small computers (sometimes at extra cost) improve the utility of the language to the point where most applications can be programmed with relative ease but at the cost of slower execution and increased memory consumption. Remember that BASIC is an all-purpose language and, as such, was never intended to compete in highly specialized applications. While it may be possible to write a BASIC program for some very complex scientific calculations, you really can't expect BASIC to perform them as well as a language such as FORTRAN that is intended specifically for those uses.

The criticism that BASIC doesn't force the use of "structured" programming is valid only if you happen to advocate such a style. In my mind, the absence of such requirements is a point in BASIC's favor. Being forced into a particular program structure rather than being allowed to free-form a program makes the process too much like machine- or assembly-language programming and eliminates the ease of learning and programming that is characteristic of BASIC. In addition, those who advocate structured programming often do so because the result is easily read by the human eye. They even insist on wasting space through excessive use of remark statements, spaces, indented subroutines, and other costly approaches, all intended to make the program easily read but all to the disadvantage of the computer that has to execute the program. While some elements of structured style such as positioning of subroutines within a mainline program may be useful, others can just as easily prove detrimental.

Later in this chapter, I'll be giving more attention to the space and execution-speed losses incurred with "dressing up" a BASIC program. For now, it suffices for you to know that there are going to be such costs, that the concepts of programming efficiency and rigid structuring for ease of readability are fundamentally incompatible and often mutually exclusive, and that you are going to have to make some compromises. You are going to be faced with deciding between writing a program for maximum efficiency within the computer, maximum readability by a human being, or some level between those two extremes. You'll have to remember that I am emphasizing the importance of "runtime" efficiency, so you'll have to interpret, temper, and apply many of my remarks in the context of the uses to which your programs will be put, the number of different people who will have access to those programs, and whether you will be marketing the program to others or using it strictly for your own purposes.

Classifying BASIC as strictly a beginner's language may have been appropriate 10 or 15 years ago, but it is not appropriate today. While it's true that the majority of computer users and programmers learn BASIC as their first language and later may find another language more suitable, BASIC still has become the language of choice for ongoing use in many business, industrial, technical, and personal applications. BASIC offers the capabilities necessary to program sophisticated games, information-management systems, personal finance and budgeting, business accounting, inventory control, and mailing lists, to name just a few.

As the single most widely used language on small computers, BASIC receives considerable attention from software designers, business executives, accountants, engineers, and others. The language also offers an element of compatibility and portability from one brand of computer to another so software can be developed on one machine and adapted to other machines. Note that I said "an element of compatibility and portability." I will soon demonstrate that the process of moving software from one machine to another isn't as simple as it sounds, even with a "universal" language like BASIC.

All in all, BASIC does provide numerous advantages to novice, intermediate, and advanced programmers alike. However, all programmers need to be aware of both the pros and the cons of using the language, and they have to take special care to use the language properly. It's all too easy to misuse BASIC and suffer serious consequences in slowed execution times and increased memory requirements for any program.

Learning BASIC

I've been stressing the fact that BASIC is both easy to learn and easy to use. It's not my purpose to go through the fundamentals in order to teach you programming, and there's little point in my doing so beyond the material necessary to define and describe important terms. If you visit any bookstore or computer store, or if you follow the articles in any computing magazine, you'll find a wealth of information on the fundamentals of BASIC and how to construct simple programs.

Books published on the subject fall into either of two rather broad categories. First, there are machine-specific books such as the *Applesoft Tutorial*, which supports one version of BASIC as implemented on the Apple II and Apple II Plus computers. Second, there are general books such as *BASIC for Home Computers*, written by Bob Albrecht, LeRoy Finkel, and Jerald R. Brown (New York: John Wiley & Sons, Inc., 1978). If you're just learning BASIC, I recommend that you obtain at least one book in each category. Using the programming manual that comes with your computer to resolve any problems or differences, work page by page through the machine-specific book first and then the general book. The whole process shouldn't take more than a week, and you should have a pretty good feeling for the fundamentals by the time you're done.

Since BASIC is so popular and so widely used on small computer systems, it has received considerable attention from software designers who make the results of their work available as packaged programs at a price. For most common computer applications, such as inventory control, accounting, word processing, mailing lists, and so on, working programs for nearly every brand of computer system can be purchased right "off the shelf." Whether written in BASIC or some other language, such packaged software provides you with sophisticated programs that can be used without the tedious and time-consuming tasks of actually designing the procedures, typing the programs, and going through all the necessary testing and *debugging* operations that may be needed to make the program operational.

However, purchased applications software may fall short of your particular needs or may not be available at all for your application. Even if prepackaged software is available, it may be too costly for your budget, or you may just prefer to write your own. In any case, you're faced with the problem of either modifying a purchased package or devising your own programs from scratch. But even then you don't have to be totally on your own. Again, the popularity of BASIC has made available many books that contain *listings* of programs to perform specific functions. By simply keying those programs into your computer and sometimes making a few modifications to adapt them for a specific machine, you have them available for your use anytime you need them. Once saved on a mass-storage medium such as a diskette, those programs may be used by themselves or as individual routines contained within other larger programs you write yourself.

Typical of the many useful books for this approach are *Some Common BASIC Programs* by Lon Poole and Mary Borchers (Berkeley, Calif.: Adam Osborne & Associates, Inc., 1978); *BASIC Computer Programs for the Home* by Charles D. Sternberg (Rochelle Park, N.J.: Hayden Book Co., Inc., 1980); *BASIC Computer Programs for Business*, also by Charles D. Sternberg (Rochelle Park, N.J.: Hayden Book Co., Vol. 1, 1980; Vol. 2, 1982); and *Calculating with BASIC* by Raymond Guido (Milford, Conn.: Scelbi Publications, 1979). The list of such books is nearly endless, and every computer owner should keep several on hand as reference material and as sources of individual program routines.

In fact, there seems to be an unlimited supply of such books containing different programmers' concepts of the best ways to solve given problems with computers. Their contents range from programs for simple home menu planning and game playing to those that perform computations in advanced calculus and particle physics. It's even possible to obtain a complete accounting system with general-ledger, accounts-payable, accounts-receivable, and payroll facilities in a single book.

You should be aware that there are some interesting "hybrids" available, specifically the "book-software" packages now being offered by many book and software publishers. With these, you purchase both a descriptive book and either a diskette or a cassette that has the programs prerecorded. The book contains the instructions for using the programs and usually includes the program listings, while the magnetic media are intended to be used in direct "machine-readable" form by your system. The initial purchase price for these combination packages is higher than for the book alone, but you may find the increased cost worthwhile because it saves you many hours of keying or typing programs or data, and it theoretically provides you with "clean" programs that have been checked, tested, debugged, and fully prepared for an "insert-and-run" operation. In short, you have access to the programs without the tedious task of copying them from print to computer. You should also eliminate the unavoidable "typos" that sneak into any transcription from a printed page to a computer.

A note of caution is necessary, however. When considering a combined book-and-software package, make certain that the magnetic medium is compatible with your system. It does you no good to buy a package recorded for an Apple II if you are running a TRS-80, Atari, Commodore, Osborne, or some brand other than the one for which the cassette or diskette is specifically recorded. **Read the labeling of the magnetic media—it will identify the usable systems and any special equipment you need to have.**

The ready availability of reference books doesn't relieve you totally of the problems inherent in doing your own programming, however. You may have to write a larger program that uses the published programs as individual routines, modify the programs written for one machine or one version of BASIC to run on your own facilities, or improve the programs by reducing their memory requirements or increasing their execution speeds. It's an essential truism of computer programming that any program can be improved, no matter how well it was written in the first place. With programs published in books, this is compounded by the author's having to generalize the program enough to make it as *portable* from one system to another as possible. The result is that a given program lifted from a book, or even one purchased off the shelf, may not be as efficient or effective as it could be. When I've had occasion to lift programs from published listings, I've found that I usually can halve the memory consumption and as much as triple the execution speed by applying relatively simple programming concepts.

Given any small computer system, getting into BASIC programming at one time or another and learning how to manipulate and handle that language is virtually unavoidable. But the whole point of the language is that its similarity to English and algebra makes it almost ridiculously easy to learn. If you want to enter or input data to a program, it's no problem to remember that BASIC uses an INPUT statement. If you want to print the results of a calculation on the screen, BASIC provides a PRINT statement. If you want to compare two values, there's an IF...THEN... statement. If you want to calculate a value, you write it as an algebraic statement, as you would on a hand-held calculator.

Some simple programs can be written within a few hours by even the most inexperienced people. In fact, many useful programs can be written with only five BASIC statements. As an example, a simple program to balance a checkbook can be written using PRINT to output to the screen, INPUT to accept data from the keyboard, LET (or implied LET) to perform calculations, IF...THEN... to test values and *branch* or transfer program flow accordingly, and GOTO to force an immediate unconditional branch in program flow. The program could be something like this:

```
100 PRINT "A PROGRAM FOR CHECKBOOK BALANCING"
110 PRINT
120 PRINT "ENTRY", "CREDIT", "DEBIT", "BALANCE"
130 LET B=0
140 PRINT ,,,B
150 PRINT
160 INPUT "ENTRY";E
170 IF E=0 THEN END
180 PRINT "ENTRY","CREDIT","DEBIT","BALANCE"
190 LET B=B+E
200 IF E<0 THEN 230
210 PRINT E,E,,B
220 GOTO 150
230 PRINT E,,E,B
240 GOTO 150
```

This simple program allows you to type an amount in dollars and cents with the decimal point, adds the amount to the previous balance, and displays the numbers in appropriate columns. If the entry is negative, it's treated as a debit. If the entry is positive, it's a credit. If the entry is zero, the program is terminated.

At this point, I could take the next 30 pages or so to define all the terms common to BASIC programming, pointing out applications of the more common ones in the checkbook program. However, that information is readily available in any reference manual for the language, and I'd only be duplicating material out of context. Instead, I advise you to refer to your other books and manuals, read the introductory chapters therein, and refresh your memory on the meaning of terms such as constant, string, integer, fixed-point, floating-point, real-precision, single-precision, double-precision, variable, array, expression, logical operator, relational operator, and functional operator. I'll be using those terms throughout the remainder of this book, so it's important that you know what they mean for your particular computer and its implementation of BASIC.

Instead of defining all those terms, I'll use the rest of this chapter to describe the general concepts of employing a computer's power, recognizing and compensating for the differences between BASICs implemented on various machines, and some overall programming practices and habits that facilitate a computer's execution of your programs. In Chapter 3, I'll go into more detail on the differences between BASICs, including a comparison of features between some widely used versions. In Chapter 4, I'll begin to present individual techniques that can be applied to specific programming statements to enhance the computer's performance. There I'll deal with the things you may be able to do to compensate for differences between language implementations. I'll also be including some routines that should be useful if your version of BASIC lacks certain functions. Chapters 5 and 6 will expand on individual approaches and "tricks" designed to avoid costly delays in execution time.

Computer Power and Computer Errors

When you acquire a computer, you acquire a very powerful tool. You have to remember that the system, complete with its software, is exactly that—a useful tool—no more and no less. Just as a lever gives your muscles more power in moving an object, a computer gives your mind more power in moving data and solving intellectual problems. Without your weight and muscles to push it, a lever can do no work; it's a worthless piece of metal. Without your brainpower behind it, your computer can do no work; it's a worthless pile of scrap parts. While the mechanical efficiency of a lever is a function of where you place its fulcrum, the operational efficiency of your computer is a function of how well you provide its instructions and data.

Regardless of the programming language in use, a computer offers numerous capabilities that give you a tremendous advantage in solving complex problems and handling detailed procedures. Of all the advantages, four are worthy of special attention: (a) the ability to manipulate large amounts of data, (b) the ability to perform repetitive operations over and over again very quickly, (c) the ability to alter program flow according to conditions encountered, and (d) the ability to do the computations without making errors.

Handling Data

Consider a situation in which you are handed 500 scraps of paper, each containing either a single word randomly selected from the dictionary or some random number between 1 and 10,000. Your task is to sort those papers into order, either alphabetical order for words or increasing value for numbers. It's reasonable to assume that sorting the 500 items could take several hours, and you would have several choices of procedure, such as re-sorting the paper scraps themselves, writing the numbers on a separate sheet, and so on. In any event, it will take quite a bit of time to get the words or numbers correctly ordered.

In comparison, a computer can do the same sorting job in just minutes or seconds, depending upon how the operations are programmed. If the task is expanded to include hundreds of such sets of items or individual sets numbering thousands, tens of thousands, or hundreds of thousands of items, the computer's advantage in handling large amounts of data becomes even more apparent. Work that could take many days by hand can be reduced to just a few hours.

It happens that many of my own computer applications involve just such sorting of words into alphabetical lists. It's quite common for me to face the task of alphabetizing 50 or 60 lists, each with about 250 words, several times a week. At other times, I may have to sort through 20,000 words to locate all the ones that contain a particular letter combination such as "AT." Before I acquired my first computer, I did those tasks by hand, and I hate to think about the thousands of hours I spent doing nothing but searching word lists. With the computer's assistance, I now can sort the same 50 or 60 lists in well under an hour, and I can locate all the words with a particular letter combination from a list of up to 20,000 words in only a few minutes.

In commercial, industrial, and scientific applications, a computer's ability to handle large data bases is critically important. A single scientific experiment might require the processing of many hundreds of thousands of measurements and instrument readings. A business office might require that mailing lists with thousands of names and addresses be maintained and later sorted according to features such as particular postal zip codes, individual cities, selected employment titles, or other distinguishing attributes. Even accounting departments in the smallest businesses have to keep careful track of receipts, expenditures, taxes, payrolls, unpaid bills, closed accounts, and other entries, all of which combine as a *data base* of thousands of individual items.

Thus, the first advantage of computerization can be summarized by saying that *a computer provides a means of handling large quantities of information and data.*

Performing Repetitive Operations

All computer languages, including BASIC, provide some facility for performing repetitive operations. A *program loop* is nothing more than a sequence of instructions that are executed over and over again until a predetermined condition or combination of conditions is satisfied. A computer may be instructed to perform certain operations a thousand times until a certain variable has a specified value or until a particular set of conditions has been met. To many programmers and computer users, this is the single most important feature of any computer.

To cite a simple example, assume you have the need to determine square roots of all the integers from 1 to 10,000. Some of them you probably know without calculating, such as 3 being the square root of 9, 5 being the square root of 25, and 10 being the square root of 100. Others you have to calculate. To do the calculations by hand is a long and tedious process. With a pocket calculator, using the square-root-function key

10,000 times still is a long procedure. But even with a relatively slow programming language such as BASIC, a computer can calculate those same 10,000 answers in just minutes. To test this, I ran the following program under several BASICs and timed it with a stopwatch as it calculated the square roots:

```
10 FOR F1=1 TO 10000: F9=SQR(F1): NEXT F1
```

On an S-100 type computer with several different BASIC interpreters and the Apple II Plus with Applesoft, the program took approximately the same amount of time—an average of 8 minutes 15 seconds for each of five trials conducted on each machine. This means that the square roots were computed at an average rate of 20.2 per second. I then tried a compiled version of the routine in machine language on the S-100 computer, and it finished in 4 minutes 38 seconds for an average rate of 35.97 computations per second. Just try matching either of those rates on your trusty pocket calculator.

One of the nicest things about computer programming is the ability to *nest* loops inside other loops. The result is much like an automobile's odometer, in which the inside loop goes through a specific number of cycles to increment the next loop. That one in turn goes through a number of cycles to increment still another. Usually such nesting can be carried out to as many levels as needed, limited only by the total memory available. However, some languages place a definite limit on the number of nested loops that may be used. Applesoft, for example, limits nested FOR...NEXT loops to a maximum of 10 levels; exceeding that limit generates an "out of memory" error whether or not available memory really is exhausted.

Once you get into complex programming chores, you'll find that the ability to program loops and nest them in different ways becomes a very valuable tool indeed. It means that you can perform complex and interdependent operations with a minimum of programming effort. If it weren't for the ability to use and nest such loops, writing a program would require writing lines of code for each individual operation in sequence. Imagine trying to program the simple square-root computation if it had to be 10,000 separate instructions. Any kind of complex applications would require a computer with such massive amounts of memory that the machine wouldn't be practical or affordable. And in such a case, computer calculations probably would require more time to program than to work out by hand, so the whole advantage of the computer would be lost anyway.

Therefore the second advantage can be summed up by saying that *a computer is a practical solution to performing repetitive operations.*

Altering Program Flow

Although a computer isn't intelligent, at least not by any accepted standards and with the present state of the art, it does provide certain "decision-making" capabilities that are vital to successful programming. The ability to perform a *conditional branch* to redirect program flow and subsequent operations is of paramount importance in nearly every programming task. Using conditional branching, a computer can be directed to perform one set of operations if particular conditions exist, another set of operations for different conditions, and still another set of operations under other conditions. In fact, much of programming involves setting up the instructions that detect specific conditions and redirect program flow accordingly.

Assume that you are driving your car along an east-west freeway and encounter an exit sign that reads something like "North to Cheyenne—Next Right/South to Colorado Springs—Second Right." You have reached a conditional branch. *If* you want to go to Cheyenne, you have to take the first turnoff on the right. *If* you want to go to Colorado Springs, you have to pass the first turnoff and take the second. *If* you don't want to do either, you have to pass both turnoffs and continue heading in the original direction.

You have a decision to make, and you make it based upon certain conditions. When you want to go to Cheyenne or Colorado Springs—perhaps you have a meeting in one of those cities—you make the appropriate turn based on knowing where you have to end up. You might also choose to take one turnoff or the other if you know that somewhere along that route is another turnoff (another conditional branch) that can redirect your travel to a different city not even listed on this first exit sign. Make the wrong decision or base the decision on erroneous information, and you'll find yourself in a place other than where you want to be.

When programming in BASIC, you actually construct your own turnoffs and direction signs with statements such as IF...THEN..., ON...GOTO..., and ON...GOSUB.... A program statement such as IF X=1 THEN 1000 is telling the computer to examine the value of X, continue in the same direction (with the statement following this one) if X has a value other than one, or turn off and execute statements starting at line 1000 if and only if X has a value of one. Knowing the condition that must be met, the computer then has its instructions as to whether or not to deviate or branch from the *mainline* program flow.

By using conditional branching, a programmer gains total control over all computer operations performed. Without such branching, there's no control and thus no possibility of writing a program. In the simple checkbook-balancing program listed earlier in this chapter, two conditional branches are used. The one in line 170 determines whether or not the keyboard entry is a zero; if it is, the program ends immediately; if it is not, the program accepts the value and calculates a new balance. The branch in line 200 determines whether the nonzero entry is positive or negative; a negative entry is printed in the debit column, and a positive entry is printed in the credit column.

There are many creative and sometimes ingenious ways of writing conditional branches in a given program. The preceding illustrations are the simplest cases, but conditions and directions may be specified in very complex patterns. For example, a series of numerous IF...THEN... statements can be used to detect any one of many different conditions and branch to varying locations depending upon which condition is statisfied. A single IF...THEN... statement may contain a series of conditions, all of which have to be satisfied before branching is allowed. The ON...GOTO... and ON...GOSUB... statements allow a condition or combination of conditions to be examined for any one of several possibilities, with branching to subsequent operations determined by which one of the possibilities is found.

Incidentally, the FOR...NEXT loop also contains an inherent conditional branch. The FOR statement sets the condition to be satisfied before starting the loop, and the NEXT statement examines the condition to see whether it has been met. If not, program control branches back to the beginning of the loop; otherwise the loop ends, and program flow continues with the next statement following the loop. This is somewhat analogous to being forced to drive a car around a city block until you find a parking space. As long as you haven't found a parking space, you have to keep going around and around. When you do find a space, you can stop, park the car, get out, and continue about your business.

So the third advantage of computers can be summarized by saying that *computers can perform decision-making operations provided the programmer stipulates the conditions and the possible directions from which to choose.*

Computer Errors

"It must be a computer error!" How many times have you heard or read that statement? You receive a package in the mail, and it doesn't contain what you ordered, or part of the order has been omitted. The supplier claims, "Computer error!" The utility company fails to credit last month's payment and threatens you with a collection agency. But you have a canceled check, so it's another "computer error"! You receive a paycheck for $5.78 instead of the usual $578.00, and the payroll personnel tell you, "Computer error!" The bank loses your deposit or your entire account, and once again it's a "computer error"!

That poor computer. It's the scapegoat for just about every type of mistake imaginable. And it's convenient to blame the computer because most people accept the statement at face value. After all, computers are mysterious and formidable things to most people, and the average individual assumes that the people and businesses using the machine must know a lot about them and must know where the blame for the mistake lies. It's also useful to blame the computer because people have heard about so many such errors that they tend to accept them as a normal part of life. Many people who complain about some mistake or another may just shake their hands and go away when they hear that familiar "computer error" statement.

Near my own computers I keep a sign that reads, "People make mistakes—computers don't." It's a constant reminder to me not to blame the machine for my own errors and to remember that computers are incapable of making mistakes. That rather broad statement needs some additional consideration. Always remember that a computer does exactly what it has been told to do. It can't deviate from the instructions given to it by human programmers and operators, and it can't make decisions unless it's been instructed as to how to make them and what to do after they've been made.

Most of the errors blamed on computers actually are clerical errors on the part of the people who use them. The individual entering data at the keyboard gets a bit fumble-fingered and misplaces the decimal point in a number. That same person's eyes get bleary, and entire lines or blocks of data are omitted from the input. A piece of paper logging orders or receipts slips unnoticed from a desk to the floor and is swept away by the cleaning crew. All of these and many more result in what eventually will be called a computer error so that blame doesn't fall where it really belongs—on the humans employed to operate and use the machine. I'd venture to guess that some 90 to 95 percent of so-called computer errors fall into this category—pure human carelessness or misuse.

Another prevalent area of human error is found in the computer programming. It's easy for a programmer to overlook a set of conditions that may occur only a few times in many thousands of processing operations. As a result, the computer may encounter a poorly defined set of conditions not previously anticipated. For example, it may be possible to have a program that branches on the simultaneous detection of three different conditions, while there may be a rare instance of some data set being differentiated from all others only by a fourth condition not covered in the programming. In such a case, that one occurrence may still meet the three programmed conditions and be treated accordingly. The result is an item treated as a member of a larger set of items when it actually should have been treated separately. The error isn't in the computer; it's in the program written by a human.

Outright programming blunders are fairly common as well. These aren't just oversights; they are the direct result of a programmer's telling the computer to do something it shouldn't be doing at all. I've seen an instance of a general-purpose accounting program in which all functions performed quite well handling general and special ledgers, accounts payable, accounts receivable, and so on. In fact, they functioned perfectly right up to the point of using the program to obtain a quarterly summary of expenditures in one specific category. At that point, everything went haywire and massive areas of data stored on disk simply disappeared. It turned out the programmer had mistakenly instructed the computer to open a disk file and *write* data instead of opening it and *reading* the data. On this particular system, opening an existing file to write data automatically erased the entire contents of that file.

The real problem in this case occurred because nobody had bothered to check the summary-preparation routine for each and every category. Instead, the program was "spot-checked" and tested only on the basis of a few "normal" conditions and occurrences. The supplier's headaches really began when it was discovered that many of the defective software packages had been shipped to end users, all of whom eventually encountered a "worst-case" condition and found the problem the hard way through massive losses of data.

When an error results from a defect in the programming, that error is of human origin. The computer is sometimes blamed, but it's not at fault.

Other causes of supposed computer errors include design or manufacturing errors as well as unpredictable external influences on the machines' operation. There are such things as equipment failures. A circuit chip may fail. A disk drive may go down. Wiring connectors may work loose. The equipment may overheat. The list goes on and on, but all these things may appear either as complete-system failures or as errors in the results obtained by executing a program. For example, a defective disk drive (or a defective diskette) may show up not as a total failure that halts the system but as erroneous data either read as input to the computer or stored from the output. The problem is compounded by interruptions to the main power line, static-electric discharges, and other disturbances that originate outside the computer. Regardless of which situations cause what appear to be computer errors, they cannot legitimately be blamed on the computer. Usually they can be traced directly to human factors in design omissions or mistakes, manufacturing flaws, testing inadequacies, and so on. In other cases, deliberate manufacturing shortcuts to reduce costs may be at fault.

When I first acquired my original S-100 type system, I spent most of the first four months with the equipment "down" for repair. Most of the problems were centered around the disk drives; at various times they either halted the system entirely by making it impossible to load a program or merely resulted in thoroughly butchered outputs. In the latter case, it looked as though I had encountered what might be a true computer error. However, eventually two external causes were found, and fixing them remedied the errors.

The first problem was defective diskettes, 180 of them in three shipments of 60 from the same manufacturer. The magnetic surfaces were contaminated by foreign material that would detach from the diskette, stick to the read/write heads, and destroy the remainder of the disk. But before the diskette would fail completely, I'd encounter data errors as individual bytes would be misread. Within anywhere from an hour to a week, the entire diskette would fail and, as often as not, "crash" the drive heads and necessitate major equipment repairs. The cure was abandoning the entire brand of diskette and upgrading to premium-grade media. Even though the out-of-pocket diskette cost more than doubled, the changeover was well worthwhile because of the immense improvement in data reliability.

The second problem became obvious only after the first had been cured. Up to that point it had been camouflaged by the more frequent occurrence of magnetic media failures. Over a period of about two months, I noticed increasing rates of failures to read data from the diskettes and errors in the data that had supposedly been read successfully. Eventually, the service technician found the problem. A ribbon cable had been partially severed during the manufacture of the disk drives, and the cut portion was concealed inside a connector where it wasn't visible but was just ahead of the pin contact. Constant normal vibration of the machine had caused further deterioration in what already was a poor connection, and continued vibration was making and breaking contact on some of the signal lines. It wasn't enough to cause a total failure, but only to give an intermittent loss of operation or loss of data.

Hardware failures such as these cannot be classed as computer errors. They may be traced back to the person who assembled the part, the engineer who designed a circuit, the quality-control inspector who passed the unit, the supplier who failed to test the unit thoroughly enough, and other human causes not under the control of the computer. Similarly, the computer cannot control nearby lightning strikes or surges in or interruptions to the power-supply lines. Nor can it control a static discharge after someone walks across a shag carpet and touches the keyboard. Once again, blaming the computer for making an error as a result of such circumstances is misplacing the blame.

In the years that I've been working with computers, I've yet to see anything that I would consider a true computer error. That is, I have never encountered a situation in which the computer was in good working order, was properly programmed, received accurate data, and yet provided erroneous data. So the fourth advantage of a computer can be summarized by saying that *a computer is incapable of making mistakes.*

Using a Computer's Power

Having briefly described some of the aspects of computer power and having exorcised the mythical monster known as a computer error, it's necessary to give some consideration to when and how computers may be put to the best use. To state it simply, there are times when you want to use a computer and other times when you don't. Recognizing what should and what should not be programmed is a basic prerequisite to using your time and your computer's time effectively.

To achieve the best possible utilization of either a personal or a small-business computer, it's necessary to examine a proposed programming task critically. In doing so, you have to determine whether or not using a computer to perform that task will actually gain you anything. It's all too easy to waste valuable computer time on trite, essentially useless programs that don't save you time, don't make life easier, and don't provide better results or better efficiency than you can achieve by other means.

Now I don't want to imply that writing simplistic programs or computer games is a total waste. Such things can be quite useful in learning how to program your machine, checking machine outputs against known or expected results, and so on. However, unless you are in the business of writing and selling simple programs and games, such pursuits eventually should be abandoned in favor of more useful ones. If you can find an advantage to chasing a glowing dot around a video screen or computerizing checkbook balancing and income tax preparation, fine. But most people actually would be losing by programming such procedures.

Program those tasks that make maximum use of your computer's inherent power. In particular, strive to utilize the machine's abilities fully in handling large amounts of data and performing repetitive operations.

The checkbook-balancing routine presented earlier in this chapter for illustrative purposes is a prime example of poor program selection. To put it bluntly, balancing a checkbook by computer gains you absolutely nothing. If you write 50 checks a month, you're using your checkbook more than most people do, and 50 or even 100 checks hardly constitute a large amount of data. Furthermore, the calculations are nonrepetitive. For each number entered, only one addition and one printout operation are necessary. As a result, the most important facets of computer power remain unused in this application. Since each number has to be entered individually from the keyboard, as much time is required with the computer as would be needed to do the same thing on a $9.95 pocket calculator. Your gain: nil!

Programs for maintaining various types of inventories may or may not be good candidates, depending upon the number of items to be listed. Listing the description, serial number, identifying markings, purchase date, and purchase price of every item in your house on a room-by-room basis may involve hundreds of items. In this case, you'd want to keep the entire list stored on magnetic media so you could retrieve it, add items, and delete items without having to retype entire pages by hand. Although such a program might not make use of repetitive operations, it would enable you to manage a fairly large data base and could offer additional advantages in permanently storing the information on cassette or disk, allowing easy searches for a specific item or all items in a particular category, and rapid access anytime you need the information.

I happen to use the facilities of a purchased word-processing package for this. Since I had to buy the software for other uses anyway, it didn't cost me anything or take a lot of time to set up. If I need to know something, say the price of a desk lamp purchased three years ago, it takes only seconds to retrieve the information instead of hours to locate the old receipts and claw my way through them to find the right one.

Similar applications might include a filing system for collections such as 35-mm photographic slides kept in carousel-style trays. With several thousand slides in a collection, it's always a major chore to locate the one slide or group of slides of interest. If you have a computer program that records the carousel number, subject matter, date, exposure information, and slot number within the carousel, it becomes relatively simple to search a disk file for all shots on a given subject, all shots in a given year, and so on. While the element of repetition enters into the searching procedures, especially if your program reorders random data entries into carousel sequence, date, and alphabetical subject files, you also have the advantages of mass storage, easy access, and the manipulation of a large number of individual items.

Of course, programs to utilize computer power can be as sophisticated as you care to make them. As just one example, many common business and scientific pursuits require some form of statistical analysis. In the business world, statistical breakdowns may affect sales forecasting, profit and loss predictions, and salary guidelines. In scientific pursuits, it's advantageous to analyze statistically measurements and instrumentation readings taken over a period of time or under varying conditions. It is characteristic of statistical calculations that large data bases are needed; the larger the sample used, the more accurate the analysis. In addition, the calculations themselves are rather long, complex, and tedious, and they often must be repeated over and over and over again for individual data items and various combinations of those items. Obviously, this is a near-perfect candidate for computerization.

As a college freshman in 1963, I experienced what it was like to do analyses of physics experiments without the aid of pocket calculators or computers. At that time, the closest things to a computer available to freshmen were slide rules and a few big, mechanical, lever-operated calculators in one of the labs. Analyzing the data collected during 2 hours in the lab commonly required upwards of 12 hours of pushing buttons and pulling levers on those calculators and was a tedious, error-prone process. Recently, I located some of my old laboratory notebooks and tried the same analyses on the same data with my 1978-model S-100 bus computer. After about 45 minutes of entering data, the entire analysis could be completed by the computer in less than 10 minutes.

Program tasks you have to perform frequently. Computer programs are meant to be run time and time again, doing the same basic things at different times or with different data. Writing or purchasing a piece of software you will use only a few times or will use once or twice a year is definitely not to your advantage.

In the first place, it takes many times longer to write a program initially than it does to perform the operations by hand. This includes setting up the procedures in a logical order that can be programmed, coding the program statements, keying the statements into the computer, and testing and debugging the program until it operates properly. One figure I've seen mentioned indicates it takes an experienced programmer who's both fast and good at his job at least three times longer to prepare the program than to solve the problem. A relatively inexperienced programmer can reasonably expect that number to increase by a factor of ten or more. In some cases, it may even take hundreds of hours to program a task that can be done by hand in less than hour.

I've run into that last situation on several occasions, usually with programs I develop for the creation of word puzzles that are sold to magazines. The very first one I programmed was for a puzzle I could do by hand in an hour. Writing the first program and debugging it to the point of being operational took over 200 hours. Perfecting the program so it was efficient enough for high-speed, unattended commercial production of the puzzles required an additional 1,400 hours, spread out over a period of a year and half and including some 40 major program revisions. If I didn't use that program from 50 to 100 times a day, it wouldn't have gained enough to justify the time spent on it.

It's also important that you perform the tasks often enough to be thoroughly familiar with the operations and approaches required. If you can't solve a problem by hand, you can't write a computer program to solve it. Even if you *could* write a program without solving the problem manually, you would have no means of knowing whether or not the machine's output was accurate unless you had first worked the same problem correctly yourself. Writing error-free programs is one of those unreachable goals that nobody ever achieves, at least not all the time. Without exception, every program must be tested carefully and thoroughly. Output results must be checked against solutions known to be correct. Even single-pass checking doesn't suffice for most applications, and dozens of successive runs may have to be checked with different sets of data before isolated errors occurring under specific conditions can be eliminated.

Sometime between January 1 and March 30 of any given year, nearly every owner of a small computer system gets bitten by the same bug: an irresistible urge to write or buy a program to prepare income tax returns. Unless you're an accountant providing a tax service to others, you'd better fight that temptation. Trying to program your individual income tax return into your computer is a classic example of how not to use the machine effectively.

First, it's going to take you longer to prepare the program than to complete the forms by hand with the aid of an inexpensive calculator. Second, you still have to work the taxes yourself in order to check the accuracy of your program, and you may have to work them many times to be sure your program functions correctly. If you have to work them anyway to check the computer, where's the advantage in using the computer at all? You don't even have the advantages of a large data base or the need for repetitive operations in the program. Most personal tax returns, and many of those for small businesses, just don't require that many entries. Besides, the IRS and Congress keep changing the rules of the game from year to year, so what you program one year may be largely inapplicable the next. With only one or two tax returns required in any year, there simply isn't enough use of the program to justify the effort.

Well, if it's not a good idea to write a tax program, how about buying one or lifting one from a book or magazine? *Let the buyer beware!* Purchased and published software packages do not come with any guarantee of accuracy. It's your name that's signed at the bottom of the tax form, under penalty of perjury, so you can't afford to accept the output of a purchased program without checking it thoroughly. Most commercial software and many programming books contain a disclaimer such as, "This program is sold 'as is' with no warranty as to performance or fitness for a particular purpose; the responsibility for its quality and performance is assumed by the purchaser." Again, you wind up having to work the taxes yourself, just to check the computer output. Having worked them by hand, you've only wasted your money in buying the software.

Programs in magazine articles may be even less reliable. A couple of years ago, I happened to find an article and program listing for calculating equipment depreciation—just what I happened to be doing with a calculator at that time. Since I had several hundred depreciable items to be handled plus yearly acquisitions and disposals of equipment, the program appeared to be useful and to satisfy my selection criteria. So I keyed it into my computer, spent some time correcting typing errors, and tried it out on the same sample the author included in his article. The results—perfect! I got the same answers that the author had for the data used in the article.

I then tried the program out on one of my own depreciable items and came up with totally different results than I had calculated by hand. It didn't work! It didn't even come close! I immediately went to my own calculations, checking them half a dozen times without finding an error. So I tried the program on some samples published in an IRS tax guide. Again, the computer and the IRS results differed sharply! Finally, I examined the program line by line and statement by statement.

What I found was that the author had allowed the purchase date (month and year) to be entered but then failed to use pro rata values for partial-year depreciations. As a result, an item purchased in November and entitled to one-sixth of a year's depreciation was being treated as if purchased in January and entitled to a full year. The discrepancy could have been more than enough to cause an IRS audit of the return. Continued examination revealed even more problems: (a) only two of the three popular methods of depreciation were included, with one of them misnamed as the missing one, (b) the provision for an additional first-year depreciation allowed by the IRS had been omitted, and (c) the calculation of investment tax credit was completely wrong. As far as I could tell, the author of the program had no knowledge of the subject, was working under a total misconception of what was involved, and certainly hadn't bothered to check his results against known answers such as those in the IRS literature. Using the program as written, without checking it, would have been a disaster.

As it happened, I had to rewrite the entire program. After several days of testing, I finally got it to the point where its outputs agreed with the IRS examples and with my own hand-worked samples. Although it's saved me time in subsequent years, it cost a lot of extra time and effort when I originally set it up.

Program tasks that will save you time. This is closely tied to utilizing a computer's power and programming things you already know how to do. As long as the machine can save you time, it's to your advantage to use it. But if the machine starts to cost you more time than it returns, it hinders you and no longer is an advantage. I've already pointed out that things like checkbook balancing and income tax preparation aren't practical uses of a computer because they just don't offer a time advantage. Yet getting ready to prepare income taxes can be practical, particularly for small-business types such as writers, artists, photographers, accountants, and others who have to account for a considerable number of income and expense items in determining their profits.

I happen to be one of those people, running my own small consulting and writing business as a sole-proprietorship rather than as a corporation. During an average year, I have thousands of little bookkeeping tasks to keep track of, ranging from the purchase of a single postage stamp to large expenditures for computers and peripherals. Yet my needs are not exotic enough to require a general-ledger accounting package, the number of receivables and payables at any one time doesn't justify purchasing such specialized software, and a lack of employees keeps me from needing a payroll system.

Essentially, I need only a single-entry bookkeeping system that categorizes 40 types of expenses and allows the listing of dates of transactions, the names of people who were paid or who paid me, the type of payment (check number, credit card, and so on), and the running totals for credits, debits, and balances through the previous week, for the current week, and to the current date. I also need weekly printouts, monthly summaries, quarterly summaries, and a final year-end tabulation that interrelates all the different income and expense categories.

For several years, I used one of the many printed bookkeeping records available in any office-supply store. Eventually, closing the week's books every Saturday got to be a major chore, particularly if I'd forget to enter an item and have to go back and rework several weeks' calculations. Eventually, I converted the manual process to a computer program, closely following the record book I already was using. It took about 23 hours to prepare the program, but it reduced my Saturday accounting time from 5 hours or more to around 30 minutes. Saving an average of 4.5 hours a week, 52 weeks a year, over the past three years has freed up some 700 hours since I implemented the system.

A fringe benefit appears at income tax time, when the final yearly report obtained from the computer provides all the numbers I need to plug into the tax forms for my small business. I merely distribute them into the proper "holes" on the form, use a calculator to add them up, and proceed directly from the business taxes to personal taxes with a savings of about 35 hours a year in comparison to what I had been doing before.

Program tasks you can run without intervention. For one reason or another, most people assume that they have to sit right by the computer in order to use it. If a program takes a half hour or more to run to completion, it would be better to write the program so that it can restart itself without having to be instructed to do so.

Naturally, many computer applications do require continuous attention. Word-processing systems don't do very well if nobody is at the keyboard to enter the words. In fact, any program that requires direct keyboard entry of data also requires that someone be there to make the entries. However, it's possible for many applications to be *batched* so program parameters for many consecutive runs are input all at once from the keyboard, data are drawn from mass storage (tape or disk) as needed, and the computer progresses from one pass to another without further intervention on the part of the system operator.

I took that approach in devising the programs for the many types of word puzzles I free-lance. Each was set up so that it accepts a series of parameters including puzzle size, disk identification of the desired word list, number of words needed, and so on. As each complete set is entered from the keyboard, it's stored in a series of arrays, and a counter variable is incremented. Every time the program completes one output, it decrements the counter variable, retrieves the next set of parameters from the arrays, and branches back to start a new puzzle. The cyclic process continues until the counter variable reaches zero.

With that technique, I load the parameters for eight to ten hours of continuous computer operation and then walk away. While the computer is busy doing its "grunt work," I'm free to sleep, read, mow the lawn, attend business meetings, write letters, work on other programs, or do anything else I wish. It's even gotten to the point where the computer runs 24 hours a day—as a word processor when I need it, as a general-purpose number cruncher when I need that, and as a puzzle crafter whenever it might otherwise be idle.

One obvious result is that the machine has become more cost-effective. Even sitting idle, a computer costs money because the purchase price has to be spread over the number of hours of ownership; the more hours the machine works, the cheaper it is by the hour. The other result is that I have created a sort of electronic clone that saves time, generates income, and relieves me of tedious and routine tasks. I'm free to pursue other matters and don't have to be a slave to the computer console.

Creating Your Programs

As you begin to program your computer, whether in BASIC or in any other language, you'll find that the job breaks down into six distinct stages, namely (a) identifying and evaluating the problem, (b) devising a workable solution to the problem, (c) flowcharting the method of solution as steps that can be programmed, (d) coding the individual instructions into the language being used and entering that code into the computer, (e) testing and debugging the program, and (f) running the program.

Identifying and Evaluating the Problem

Naturally, the first step in writing any program is to identify the problem and evaluate it in terms of possible advantages that may result from using a computer. Before you can solve any problem, you first must know exactly what it is that you want to solve.

The task you choose may range from very simple to ultra-complex. At various times, you'll find yourself involved with a variety of problems from simple invoice preparation to multifaceted hybrid accounting systems, from playing tic-tac-toe on the screen to the preparation of commercial-quality crossword puzzles, from drawing a single color picture on a screen to total and realistic animation of a sophisticated simulation-style war game.

As a general rule, the problems you want to solve probably will be related to your personal background and experience. As a physicist, you might want to examine something like the behavior of gas molecules under the influence of a magnetic field. As a biologist, you might choose to develop model studies of genetics and inherited characteristics in a particular life form. As an electrical engineer, you might tackle circuit design and analysis. As the owner of a business, you might want to devise a hybrid accounting or inventory system for your own special method of doing business. As a computer hobbyist, you might be interested only in computerizing games or general household chores.

Regardless of what types of tasks you set yourself, you have to define them before you can solve them. It's never been particularly difficult to find uses for computers in commercial, industrial, and scientific fields. Those areas always have enough specialized applications to make extensive use of computers a real advantage. Since their needs are constantly changing to keep pace with the economy, changing markets, new methods, and new technologies, there is an unlimited supply of problems that have to be faced and solved on a day-to-day basis.

The home user or hobbyist buying a personal computer faces more of a challenge. Most people simply don't have much need for computer power. An individual working on a factory assembly line isn't likely to need a simulation of the behavior of subatomic particles. A construction worker may not be impressed by the fact that a computer can be programmed to predict a corporation's profits based on past years' performances. A taxi driver can't be expected to get excited over the idea of programming a study of the flight dynamics of a spacecraft. Obviously, people's experiences and backgrounds affect the way they view a computer and the types of things they may want to do with one.

This is an ever-present dilemma with home and personal computers. The manufacturers are hard pressed to find enough useful applications to justify the machines to someone without a definite and specialized need. It's easy to sell a computerized word-processing system to writers or lawyers, who have real and specific needs. Similarly, it's easy to sell a computer with graphics capabilities to artists, illustrators, or designers. But it's much harder to sell that same machine on the basis of what it can do for an average household. There is, after all, a limit to the uses for turning lights on and off, planning menus, addressing Christmas cards, calculating the interest on a mortgage, and the like.

When they first appeared on the market, many of the microcomputers were machines targeted for electronic hobbyists and "tinkerers." You'd go into the local computer store and order a kit that you'd have the fun of assembling and testing. But there was little software support, so once the machine was assembled and operating, you'd be on your own. The market for the machines was limited to those people having some electronic or mechanical inclination combined with the desire to play around with fancy circuitry and components.

Then someone had a real brainstorm. Put a computer in every home, and you have an untapped and almost unlimited market. At that point, there was a noticeable shift in manufacturers' philosophies. The kit-style computers began to fade away, and they were replaced with assembled units that could be purchased as complete packages at relatively low costs. Some supporting software, crude as it was, became available, and the computer manufacturers were off and running with the modern wonder machine. You could now buy a computer to handle your household budgeting, turn your appliances on and off, balance your checkbook, manage your family menu planning, prepare shopping lists, and play glorified games in full color on your own television.

But home computers, while gaining in popularity, didn't do as well as was hoped both because people were leery of these new contraptions and because there was little day-to-day need for computer power. The machines were a novel luxury, but they were not a necessity. Again, manufacturers shifted tactics. Although home use of computers remained an important consideration, more and more of the machines began to appear in configurations advertised as useful for small businesses. With declining prices, increasing computational capabilities, and the availability of sophisticated software for special purposes, even the smallest one-person businesses could afford to buy a computer that would help fulfill specialized needs.

Today, most of the machines are being promoted as small-business computers rather than as home computers, at least in all of the computer stores near where I live. And the term "personal computer" has come to mean both types. In eavesdropping on conversations between salespeople and interested buyers, I've noticed that the sales emphasis is on fairly sophisticated applications, usually in business. Home uses seem to be played down, except for the ever-present computer games. But there's one bothersome point that often creeps into the sales pitch—an implied or even bluntly stated sales "kicker" that the computer can give the purchaser a source of income.

The point is that the ultimate purpose of the software you design affects how you go about defining and evaluating the problems. There typically are two choices. The first is to write programs exclusively for your own use, whether in your home or in some business enterprise you have going. The other is to write programs or use a computer with the intent of making a direct profit from the software or the computer itself. What you have to realize is that the computer is only a tool. Just going out and buying one doesn't mean you'll be able to use it for profit. While a writer may benefit from acquiring a word-processing system, buying such a system doesn't make you a writer. You probably won't benefit from the word processor unless you already have your points of sale well established.

Similarly, buying a computer won't guarantee that you can sell the software you develop. One of the most common misconceptions is that having a personal computer automatically enables you to write programs for the constantly expanding games market. Defining your programming tasks as including the production of salable and profitable games could very well be a mistake. That's a highly competitive market, filled with ingenious and innovative programmers all looking to make a fortune. While it's easy to write a mediocre game, those don't sell well anymore, and it requires both sophisticated gaming techniques and advanced programming methods to compete with much of what's already been done.

While writing this chapter, I received a telephone call from a man who had just purchased a $4,000 personal-computer system. He contacted me because he had seen some publicity on my puzzle-crafting enterprise and wanted to buy my software packages. I couldn't sell the software because rights to it already had been purchased by a publishing house, but we talked extensively about his plans. He had purchased his system "to find a way to make money with it." That was his only justification! Several pointed questions proved quite revealing. Did he have prior experience with microcomputers? No! What programming languages did he already know? None! Did he already have some money-making enterprise going? No! Had he investigated the salability of computer software? No! Did he have any real idea of what to do with his system? No!

This individual is not untypical of many computer buyers. They purchase a machine without any prior experience in the field, without any clear-cut goals or objectives, and without appraising the marketability of computer-oriented products. They haven't defined and evaluated their problems, yet they intend somehow to find a way to make money with the machine and cash in on the field.

What I'm really saying in all this is that you have to be careful in defining your programming objectives. If you set out to make a buck with the computer, and you aren't already making money doing the same things in other ways, you're likely to be disappointed. If, however, you set out simply to improve your capabilities, free up some time, and gradually learn what can and cannot be done with your machine, you'll get immense satisfaction from it. And if you're especially lucky, you just might happen to stumble across some use for the computer that will make money, and then you can utilize it.

Once you have an idea of what you want the computer to do, you have to decide whether or not it's to your advantage to use a computer. This goes back to the earlier sections of this chapter on utilizing a computer's power. Your primary concerns have to be whether or not a particular program is going to save you time, make effective use of the computer's operating time, and provide a practical and useful program you can run again and again. If developing the program would take more time than doing the tasks by hand, or if the program is going to be of limited usefulness, its best left unprogrammed. As I've already pointed out, there's little or nothing to be gained, and sometimes a lot to be lost, by wasting time on programs for checkbook balancing, tax preparation, menu planning, and so on.

Devising a Workable Solution

After you have defined your problem and any limitations you wish to impose on it and have evaluated its use of your computer's power, you can proceed to devising a solution. In the process, you'll be formulating your approach and developing an *algorithm* or method of solution that can be converted into an actual computer program. As I indicated earlier, you must know how to solve the problem before you can program a computer to do it. First, the computer can do only those things you tell it to do, so you have to state every step and every operation explicitly within the body of the program, in terms that the computer language such as BASIC can understand and use. Second, you absolutely must have several completed examples against which you can check the computer results once you have a working program.

If you intend to write a program to handle the accounting needs of your small business, you first have to know what those needs are. Then you have to determine what you need in the way of weekly, monthly, quarterly, and annual reports. You have to analyze IRS and state tax requirements and restrictions and determine how they will affect the way you represent your finances and tax obligations. You also have to know about such things as single- and double-entry bookkeeping, IRS record-keeping requirements, allowable deductions, and allowable depreciation over several years of useful life.

Once you know all that, you have to investigate the peculiarities of your computer. You may find that your computer and the language you intend to use do strange things when dealing with decimal numbers. Some systems will round off numbers in an undesirable manner; others will truncate them and lose the decimal fraction under particular circumstances. You may even find it necessary to handle all numbers as integers (without decimals) to get the accuracy you want, reinserting the decimal points when the value is printed out in the final reports.

Once all of those things have been identified and included, you have to set up a systematic approach under which accepted accounting practices are used to calculate total receipts and expenditures, mileage allowances, equipment depreciations, tax credits, and so on. In many cases, the methods are expressly defined by the IRS or in books on accounting, but you have to know those methods before you can apply them to your program.

With your algorithm or approach put together, you have to test it out by hand, working out the numbers for transactions over several weeks, months, or even years until you are positive that you've included all imaginable circumstances and that the approach works for any situation that's likely or unlikely to occur. Then and only then are you ready to begin the process of putting together a computer program.

It doesn't make any difference what problems you want to solve. You still have to devise the algorithms in your own mind and work the solutions by hand. You'll find it rather difficult to simulate the operation of a coal-fired power plant if you don't have a working familiarity with power plants, combustion boilers, steam generators, control panels, and so on. It won't be any easier to write an effective Dungeons and Dragons™ style game if you don't know the gaming principles, some classical mythology, and the state of the art in computer games; you also have to know how to play and beat the game in order to devise a playable and eventually beatable computer version.

Even simple tasks require thought and planning. Assume that you need to know all the numbers between 1 and 10,000 with integer square roots. For example, 81 would be such a number because 9 is its square root and is an integer. However, 82 would not qualify because its square root is 9 plus a fraction. Two approaches or algorithms are apparent. In one, take every integer from 1 to 10,000, compute the square root, and test the root to see if it is an integer. In the other, just take numbers from 1 up, square them, and print the results until the square equals or exceeds 10,000. The real tricks are to know which way is faster and more efficient for the computer and to know which provides the more reliable results. To show how this works, the following two programs illustrate the methods and compare the times required using the two algorithms.

```
10 X=1
20 Y=X*X
30 PRINT X,Y
40 X=X+1
50 IF Y<10000 THEN 20
60 END
```

[4.8 seconds]

```
10 FOR Y=1 TO 10000
20 X=SQR(Y)
30 IF INT(X)=X THEN PRINT X,Y
40 NEXT Y
50 END
```

[529 seconds]

The two tests were run under ROM Applesoft (without DOS modification) on a 48K Apple II Plus. As you can see, there is a tremendous time difference, with the program on the right taking 110 times longer than the program on the left. In addition, a major problem occurs with the program on the right: the algorithm fails to provide the correct results. Because of the way the computer handles real numbers internally, the square root of 9 turns out to be not an integer 3 but some other number with a fractional part. In fact, this program under Applesoft detects only 17 of the 100 numbers actually required and totally misses those having square roots of 3, 5, 6, 10, 12, 13, 15, 17-31, 33-63, 64-68, 70-90, and 100.

The cause of the error is not immediately apparent with simple tests. Asking Applesoft to PRINT SQR(9) results in an integer 3 being displayed on the screen and looks exactly like asking it to PRINT INT(SQR(3)). Therefore, it appears that the square root and the integer of that square root should be identical. However, checking the equality with the statement IF SQR(9)=INT(SQR(9)) THEN PRINT "OK" should display "OK" on the screen if the numbers are equal; it does not, so the computer is differentiating internally between the two values that it displays on the screen as being the same number.

Remember that the decimal numbering system is a foreign language to a computer and that all values are handled internally in binary. During the translation processes performed by the interpreter, some very strange things can happen to numerical values as decimal fractions seem to appear out of nowhere or disappear into some primeval void. Furthermore, different computers using different versions of a language such as BASIC tend to handle the problems in different ways. Using the SQR() function, Applesoft lost 83 of the 100 desired answers, but some other computer might lose more or less than that number, depending upon exactly how the square roots are calculated and handled internally.

Looking back at the square-root example on the left, you'll notice that I simply multiplied the number in variable X by itself in statement 30 where Y=X*X. It also appears possible to use the exponentiation function in the statement Y=X^2, but two things happened when that approach was tested. First, the execution time increased to 9.3 seconds, nearly doubling that of the listed program because exponentiation involves calling a subroutine that takes that much longer. Second, some of the computed squares picked up a small additional fraction, so something like the square of 91 was printed out as 8281.0001 instead of the 8281 needed. Meanwhile, other values are printed out as integers. Again, this reflects on the way this computer and its version of BASIC perform numeric operations internally.

There are at least two ways to correct the problem and strip off the meaningless fractional portion. Both involve making an integer out of the computed results, and both have little impact on the overall execution time. On the left is a method that simply prints the integer portion of the computed square; on the right, a method that forces the value into an integer variable (declared by the "%" symbol):

```
1Ø X=1
2Ø Y=X^2
3Ø PRINT X,INT(Y)
4Ø X=X+1
5Ø IF Y<1ØØØØ THEN 2Ø
6Ø END
```

[9.4 seconds]

```
1Ø X=1
2Ø Y%=X^2
3Ø PRINT X,Y%
4Ø X=X+1
5Ø IF Y%<1ØØØØ THEN 2Ø
6Ø END
```

[9.3 seconds]

The lesson to be learned here is that the method of solution for any given problem must be designed carefully. In one example, a completely unusable algorithm was applied, with errors that could be quite serious if it were part of a larger and more complex program relying on using only numbers with an integer square root. In another, using the exponentiation function instead of simple multiplication resulted in both a significant loss of time and the computation of undesired fractions.

Interestingly, I've tried to find a point at which Applesoft exponentiation would have a time advantage over successive multiplication. In doing so, I've run similar loops to calculate the powers of each integer from 1 to 100, and I've gone up to the twelfth power (Y=X^12) with multiplication always retaining a significant speed advantage. Of course, other factors such as line length, memory space, and programmer convenience also must be considered, and tradeoffs have to be made. It's not always the best idea to multiply a variable by itself twelve times if only a single resulting value is needed. Outside of repetitive operations, the time increase for exponentiation would hardly be noticeable and could be tolerated. In a repeating loop, that may not be the case.

Flowcharting a Program

Flowcharting a program usually is an integral part of devising a workable solution to a problem. It consists of diagramming the logical progression through the procedures so individual steps may be encoded later as program instructions. Some people advocate extremely complex and detailed flowcharts with different symbols for keyboard input, magnetic-media input, screen display, hard-copy printed output, decision-making steps, and processing functions, all interconnected with a system of lines and arrows that show how any one symbol receives program control from or transfers control to any other symbol. Yet an adequate job of flowcharting can be done simply and easily with two symbols: a rectangle for general-purpose operations and a diamond for a decision point.

There are programmers who are adamant about the need for thorough and detailed flowcharts, and there are those who advocate the simplified forms or even no formalized flowcharting at all. Much depends on how the program is to be used and for whom it is being prepared. Programmers working inside a corporation such as a research company or a software house may find the employer requires detailed documentation on all programs, including extensive flowcharting. The principal reason is that the employer assumes the programmer will leave the company sooner or later, and someone else should be able to assume responsibility for the software without having to spend days, weeks, or months trying to figure out how the original programmer approached the problem.

The end use of the program also affects the amount of flowcharting programmers are requested to provide. Software houses providing custom programs for outside clients often are required under contract to supply the buyer with complete documentation so the user can assume responsibility for maintaining and updating the programs. Software developers putting out proprietary programs they don't wish duplicated, copied, or infringed sometimes relax requirements because flowcharts are intended to be read only by in-house personnel and not by outsiders.

On commercial, industrial, and scientific levels, flowcharting is common practice, but the subject often is ignored at the level of personal and small-business microcomputers. Often it seems that drawing the charts is an unnecessary step that keeps a person away from the keyboard, and many users just prefer to hack away at a program until they get something that seems to work.

In his book on assembly-language programming for the 6502 microprocessor, Dr. Rodnay Zaks states the situation in a manner applicable to all programming languages:

> Flowcharting is a highly recommended intermediate step between the algorithm specification and the actual coding of the solution. Remarkably, it has been observed that perhaps 10% of the programming population can write a program successfully without having a flowchart. Unfortunately, it has also been observed that 90% of the population believes it belongs to this 10%! The result: 80% of these programs, on the average, will fail the first time they are run on a computer. (These percentages are naturally not meant to be accurate.) In short, most novice programmers seldom see the

> necessity of drawing a flowchart. This usually results in "unclean" or erroneous programs. They must then spend a long time testing and correcting their program. . . . The discipline of flowcharting is therefore highly recommended in all cases. It will require a small amount of additional time prior to the coding but will usually result in a clear program which executes correctly and quickly. Once flowcharting is well understood, a small percentage of programmers will be able to perform this step mentally without having to do it on paper. Unfortunately, in such cases the programs that they write will usually be hard to understand for anybody else without the documentation provided by flowcharts. As a result, it is universally recommended that flowcharting be used as a strict discipline for any significant program.[1]

The points Dr. Zaks makes are quite important. Flowcharting may take more time during the preparation stages, but it can save considerable time and aggravation later. First, drawing a flowchart helps clarify the algorithm itself and often serves to isolate errors in logic or planning that could cause difficulties in running the program. Second, the finished charts provide a step-by-step sequence for the program coding, making the job of writing the program instructions much simpler than simply hacking away at them. Third, charts are a valuable aid in testing and debugging the program because they indicate exactly what is being done when and where. Fourth, charts are useful as permanent documentation of the program, particularly when it's necessary to go back into the programming at some later date to modify, update, or add to the instructions.

I don't happen to subscribe to the idea of making all programs easily readable and understood by others unless the program is being written either under contract to someone else or with the intent of having it published or sold. Since most of the heavy use of my computers is to generate word-puzzle manuscripts for sale, the numerous programs I've written for them have been considered proprietary. Therefore, I not only don't want anyone else reading them, I deliberately omit any form of documentation and make them as convoluted as possible. If someone happened to get hold of a readable diskette or listing despite my best efforts to prevent it, he or she would have a lot of trouble trying to analyze the algorithms and program structures I used—enough trouble, I hope, to discourage the would-be program thief.

However, the very devices I use to protect my programming approaches and concepts cause trouble even for me. Each time I go to

[1]Rodnay Zaks, *Programming the 6502*, 3d ed. (Berkeley, Calif.: SYBEX, Inc., 1980), pp. 9-10.

make a program improvement, I have to spend time reanalyzing the existing program and refreshing my memory as to what I did where. And when, despite my original intent, I had those puzzle programs published in book form, I had to modify them significantly for publication, mostly to eliminate some of the contorted structure and to alter the output forms to make them more versatile. Of the time spent in writing the book containing those programs, 80 percent was for analyzing and restructuring the programs, and many weeks were spent going back through old programs just to trace their long-forgotten operation.

As a result, I now look more favorably on the process of drawing flowcharts, though I still don't do it in every case. When I do draw flowcharts, I make them as simple as possible, limiting the contents to overall functions rather than the details of each routine. For some of the simplest programs, the flowchart might be nothing more than a simple block diagram such as the one shown in Fig. 2-1. In a case such as this, I have standard routines stored on a "library" disk for operations such as entry of parameters from the keyboard, reading data from a disk file, various construction modules such as cryptogramming techniques, and generalized printing formats to drive my printer. As I develop a program, I simply attach preprogrammed and pretested "modules" as subroutines to a short mainline program and then proceed to make whatever minor alterations are necessary in those modules to accommodate the unique features of the data being handled.

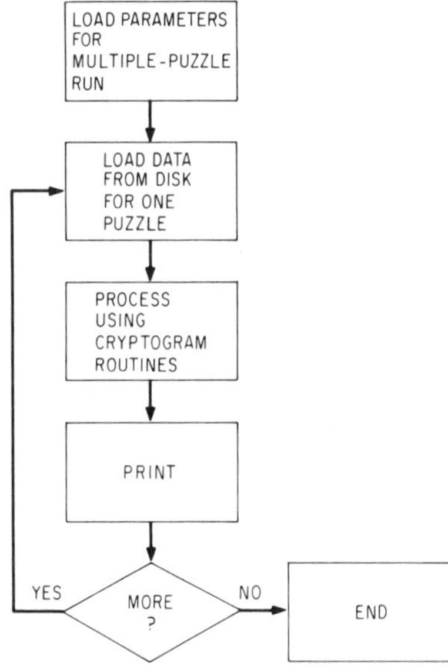

***Fig. 2-1.* Simplest Form of a Program Flowchart**

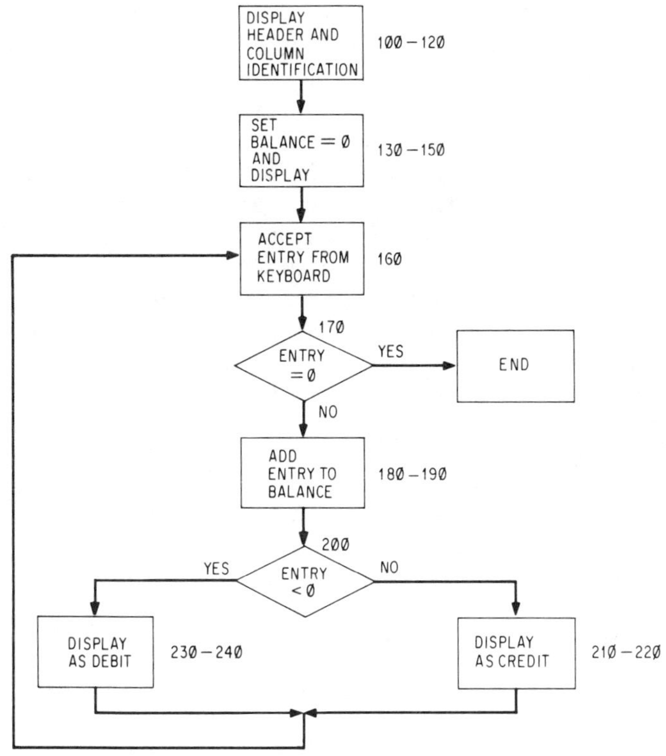

Fig. 2-2. **Typical Decision-Style Program Flowchart**

Flowcharts can be as complex as you care to make them, and some programmers try to chart each step and each line of a program. Figure 2-2 illustrates a moderately complex chart for the simple checkbook-balancing program presented earlier. As you can see, nine blocks represent the 15 program lines. Incidentally, note the numbers outside each block. They denote the corresponding line numbers in the program. I find that if I'm taking the trouble to do a chart in the first place, it's convenient to add those line numbers immediately after I've tested and accepted the program. This little trick makes the chart considerably more useful when a complex program has to be reexamined months or years later. However, you have to be careful to renumber the flowchart if you renumber the program lines; alternatively, you also might choose to keep a copy of the original listing that shows the line numbering as recorded on the chart.

To summarize, drawing flowcharts on paper or in your head is a highly recommended practice and can be of great benefit in writing and later changing programs. But the amount of detail you put into those charts has to be a purely personal decision based upon your programming experience, preferences, and overall needs.

Coding a Program

Once you've developed your algorithm and have a paper or mental flowchart of the program, it's time to encode the specific instructions that comprise the actual program. Too many novice programmers tend to view this as a purely mechanical task—something to be done and disposed of as quickly as possible. But the whole process of coding instructions happens to be a task worthy of considerable attention, because there are many ways of encoding any given sequence of operations.

In later chapters, you'll see that different versions of BASIC offer various sets of usable instructions and that many combinations may be available to perform any one task. However, one combination of instructions may not be as efficient as another. Earlier in this chapter, I demonstrated that a difference as simple as that between the statement Y=X*X and Y=X^2 can double the time required to execute the operation. There are many more such considerations that have to be weighed carefully as you sit down to write the program.

Before you can encode a single program line, you first must know the details of your programming language, in this case BASIC. You also must be aware of the way in which your version of BASIC implements and handles various instructions and statements considered "standard." Chapters 4 through 7 describe some of these details in far greater detail, but at this point it's necessary for you at least to recognize the fact that there may be differences in the ways BASICs use the random-number generator, evaluate FOR...NEXT loop controls, handle decimal fractions, manipulate string data, and so on. All of those differences and many more have to be accommodated in your program.

Given the algorithm, flowchart, and knowledge of your BASIC, you have to choose between writing the program on paper for later typing or keying into the computer and doing your coding right at the keyboard. When I first began to work with my own microcomputer, I followed old habits, coding the entire program on paper, typing the whole thing in one continuous session, and then testing and debugging the finished program. That was a carry-over from the days when I would have to prepare a program on special coding forms, submit them to a keypunch operator, examine the returned printout for errors, and correct and resubmit changed versions as necessary before I could finally submit the program to the computer operator for a run.

However, there are a number of problems with that procedure, one of which is that it takes a lot of time to test and debug the program. Finding blatant errors that halt the computer operation (things like a syntax error, "out of memory," or an improper variable type) isn't very hard, but finding logical errors that result in "butchered" data can be a frustrating experience in a long program. I've had situations in which only half of the expected results were output because a "counter" variable had been altered inadvertently so that it no longer indicated the actual count of data items or operations to be performed. Locating that in a long program of several hundred lines can be difficult, and it usually involves stopping the program at various points and checking the value of the suspect variable. Eventually, the error can be narrowed down to a small portion of the code, but it does take a while to get there.

One of the principal advantages of BASIC is that it is interactive. Therefore, the program can be controlled from the keyboard. A run can be stopped at any time, and a direct command can then be entered from the keyboard to print the present value of one or more variables. The language also provides an immediate indication of the type and exact location of errors in program syntax, such as mistyped instructions, codes that aren't a part of BASIC, and so on. Some versions go directly to an *edit mode* upon detection of certain errors, allowing the line to be corrected immediately.

Making use of the interactive nature of the language, I find it beneficial to do all of my coding right at the keyboard. By stopping every 20 lines or so and running the program to that point, I can eliminate major errors that halt the program almost as soon as I type them. Furthermore, I can determine the desired results for a given set of data at any point in the program and compare them with the values polled from the keyboard. If they match, the odds are that I don't have a logical or procedural error to that point. If an unexpected result does pop up, I already have narrowed the possible cause to the limited number of lines typed since my previous halt.

Although this technique does take longer during the initial entry phase, it saves a lot of time in later debugging operations. By writing the programs at the keyboard and testing each operation as I key it in, I find I can reduce subsequent testing and debugging by at least 75 percent because most of the errors are caught long before they become buried in page after page of code.

Testing and Debugging a Program

Very few, if any, programs run perfectly the first time. The nature of programming provides far too many opportunities for error to allow anyone to write a perfect program every time. Transposing letters or numbers is a common problem when keying a program into a computer, and simple typographic errors are the major cause of program failures. Confusing a numeric "0" with an alphabetic "O" or a numeric "1" with a lower case "l" is another source of errors. Those and other things of a similar nature are all mechanical mistakes, many (but not all) of which are easily found under BASIC because program operation halts with an error message displayed upon encountering an instruction, expression, or even a punctuation mark that can't be interpreted.

Misunderstanding or misusing an instruction in the language is a far more serious mistake because the program may run without detecting the error and provide outputs that are partially or totally wrong. For example, you might assume that your version of BASIC has a random-number generator that returns a value between 0 and 1 (including the whole number one). If you need to choose a number from 0 through 10 as the value of a variable, you could do so with the statement X=INT(RND(1)*10). In such a case X equals 0 if the random-number generator returns a value from 0 through 0.099999, X equals 10 only if the random-number generator returns a 1, and all integers between 0 and 10 are available, though not necessarily in an even distribution.

However, most BASICs have a random-number generator that returns a value from 0 through something less than 1, typically a maximum value of 0.999999. Since 10 times that maximum value is 9.99999, the truncated integer value is 9, and the value 10 never can be obtained by the program. Changing the program statement to read X=INT(RND(1)*10)+1 may gain variable values of 10, but it loses all values of 0 by virtue of the added number. To get the full range of values from 0 to 10 under such a BASIC, it may be necessary to use statements such as X=INT(RND(1)*11) or X=INT(RND(1)*10+.5). However, those statements may in turn cause problems in running the program under a BASIC that does return random numbers including the whole number 1 or performs a rounding function; they could set X equal to 11 so it is outside the desired range.

Problems like that are fairly common in BASIC, and they affect numerous instructions including the FOR...NEXT loop. Too often, they are not clearly defined in the instruction manuals that accompany the language package, and they can catch an unwary programmer by surprise. I'll be providing much more information on this subject in later chapters, but I want to alert you to the possibility of such differences' affecting your programming in what often are very subtle ways.

In addition to the misuse of instructions, errors in the algorithm or the conversion of the algorithm may sneak into a program. Again, they may show up not as an outright error that halts the execution but as major or minor deviations from expected results. Slipups like forgetting to compensate for decimal placement or the handling of real numbers are typical of this type of error.

Basically, then, the debugging operation can be divided into two segments. First, the code must be cleaned up so that the program can get past errors in syntax, out-of-range subscripts, "NEXT without FOR" errors, missing operands, and so on. Most of these errors are due to carelessness in coding the program, either through mistyping a character or omitting something like a closing parenthesis after an expression. Typically, any error of this type stops the program execution immediately, displays an identifiable error message, and identifies the line in which the error has occurred. With that assistance, it's easy to correct the mistakes and rerun the program. By the time execution reaches a normal, error-free program termination, most of the obvious errors should have been eliminated. Be alert, however, for errors that may be contained in a routine or subroutine that happens not to have been used during a particular run and that may show up later.

It's much harder to isolate and correct the errors that arise when a statement is used incorrectly or when the algorithm itself is defective. Since these usually allow the program to run to completion, you get no computer identification of the problem and have to work the entire program step by step by hand to check your logical procedures. Even then, a misunderstanding of something like the random-number generator may not be detected easily. In such cases, the most effective debugging procedure involves halting the program at various points and using direct commands from the keyboard to poll the current values of the different variables. Checking those values against what you calculate they should be at any given point often is the only way to identify the problem and locate the program section in which it occurs.

Never assume that a program is executing properly just because it runs to completion. You must, in all cases, check the outputs carefully against known results, and you must do so many times before you accept the program as accurate. No program has been adequately debugged until you've run every combination of "worst-case" data you can imagine. Even then, a few nasty little pests may get by you.

Running the Program

After all the work that's put into the preliminary stages, actually starting a "production run" of the program seems a bit of an anticlimax. But that is the point at which all your efforts pay off. If you've been writing a fancy game program, you finally can sit down to play it—provided you can face it again after a long debugging session. If you've been working on something like a program to produce word games, you can turn the computer over to unattended operation and go work on the next one.

From this point on, anytime you want to use the program, all you have to do is load it from your mass-storage media into the computer's memory and instruct the machine to run it. If you've done your job well, you shouldn't have to make any further changes unless you think of something you want to add, modify, or improve, at which time you have to go back through the whole evaluation, solution, algorithm, flowchart, and debugging procedure one more time.

Program Readability versus Efficiency

Before jumping into the next chapter, which finally gets into specific details, there's one more general area that warrants consideration. Over the past few years, there's been an increasing emphasis on the importance of program readability. Magazines and books for programmers and computer users continually advise that every program should be written for maximum readability *by the human eye.* Among the almost universal recommendations are thorough internal documentation of every program, extensive use of spaces to improve clarity, a separate line number for every program statement, frequent use of spaces and tabulations to indent subordinate lines of loops and subroutines, and the use of meaningful names for variables.

To provide the internal documentation of a program, those who promote this idea demand the frequent use of remark ("REM") statements that fully define and describe virtually every step of the algorithm and the program's execution. The intent seems to be the incorporation of both the program and its instruction manual into one entity. The justifications used to support internal documentation make it sound like a pretty good idea. After all, this makes the program easier for others to read and understand, much simpler to debug because every step is clearly identified, and more easily modified or expanded at a later date. Supposedly, it relieves people other than the original programmer from having to spend a lot of time analyzing the approach, and it relieves the programmer of having to reanalyze the program should changes be needed. For a few dishonest souls, it also makes stealing the program or the idea behind it much less difficult.

The same people also advocate separate program lines for every statement or instruction and placing a space after every element of a program line—whether or not the language requires those extra line numbers and spaces and contrary to the speed hints contained in almost every BASIC manual. Again, the ability of a human being to read the program is given preference, with separate lines and extra spaces enabling the eye to separate the various elements into discrete units. As a typical example, a comparison might be made among three ways of writing the same routine:

```
100 FOR X1=1 TO 500
200 X9=SQR(X1)
300 NEXT X1
400 PRINT CHR$(7)
500 END
```

or the more common version:

```
100 FOR X1=1 TO 500 : X9=SQR(X1) : NEXT X1 : PRINT CHR$(7) : END
```

or, where the version of BASIC allows:

```
100 FORX1=1TO500:X9=SQR(X1):NEXTX1:PRINTCHR$(7):END
```

Obviously, the first version is easier to read than the second, and the second is easier to read than the third. But I'll soon show that readability is achieved at a price—possibly too high a price. I will concede, however, that the third version may look a lot like gibberish to a novice programmer, but anyone who works with that form should learn to read it as quickly and easily as the others with only a few days' practice.

To carry the process forward another step, the advocates of readability also like indentation of lines that are subordinate to other lines. Once more they point out that the program listing is easier to decipher—besides, it's prettier. So they'd have you write a subroutine for something like a "bubble sort" of a string array thus:

```
1000 REM ******* BUBBLE SORT TO ALPHABETIZE ARRAY A$(.) *******
1002 PASS=1 : REM FORCE ONE PASS THRU SORTING LOOP
1004          IF PASS=0 THEN 1016 : REM EXIT IF NO SWAPS
              OCCURRED
1006                    PASS=0 : REM ZERO THE LOOP CONTROL
1008                    FOR X=1 TO Y-1
1010                              IF A$(X) > A$(X+1) THEN
                                  SWAP A$(X),A$(X+1) : PASS=1 :
                                  REM RESET CONTROL IF SWAP OCCURS
1012                    NEXT X : REM NEXT ARRAY ELEMENT
1014          GOTO 1004 : REM BRANCH BACK TO CONTROL TEST
1016 RETURN:REM GO BACK TO MAINLINE PROGRAM ****************
```

This example is exaggerated, carrying the use of internal documentation (remark statements) to an unlikely extreme, but it serves to illustrate just how far you could go in trying to satisfy all the requirements for making it easy to recognize, easy to read, and easy to understand. To see how much readability you gain, compare it against a partially compressed form of the same subroutine:

```
1000 PASS=1
1002 IFPASS=0THENRETURN
1004  PASS=0:FORX=1TOY-1:IFA$(X)>A$(X+1)THENSWAPA$(X),A$(X+1):
     PASS=1
1006 NEXTX:GOTO1002
```

The benefits of the first form over the second are obvious. Or are they? I'll delay the answer to that question a little longer.

The two samples also illustrate the use of a "meaningful" variable name, specifically the one called "PASS". Again, it's obvious that such a name gives the routine an element of familiarity. However, most BASICs recognize only the first two letters of any variable name, so the program recognizes only "PA" as the name, wasting the two letters "SS" and two memory bytes each time it's encountered. You also should be aware of the fact that such BASICs do *not* differentiate between such variable names as PASS1, PASS2, PASS3, and so on. Each of those is treated as variable PA, so the unwary programmer could easily destroy the value of a variable that should be retained for use elsewhere in the program. If this same subroutine were compressed fully, it would be written thus:

```
1000 P=1
1002 IFP=0THENRETURN
1004 P=0:FORX=1TOY-1:IFA$(X)>A$(X+1)THENSWAPA$(X),A$(X+1):P=1
1006 NEXTX:GOTO1002
```

Readable programs do carry a price, however. Habitually using such techniques wastes memory space, slows program execution, wastes storage space on magnetic media, lengthens the time required to load a program into memory, and increases the number of keyboard operations necessary to enter the program.

Imagine for a moment that you are a pharaoh in ancient Egypt and have a slave labor force working on your pyramid. As you go to the site to inspect the work, you find most of the workers laboring heavily to move large stones into position. But a quarter of the work force is scurrying back and forth carrying baskets, supposedly to move supplies and support the other workers. Being of a curious nature, you stop one of the carriers and look into the basket, only to find that it is empty. Suddenly you realize that all the basket carriers are scurrying around, looking very busy, but have empty baskets and are not contributing anything to the construction job. As a result, you are being cheated—you need a larger work force and more time to complete your pyramid.

In programming, spaces, excess line numbers, remark statements, and meaningless letters in variable names all are empty baskets. Every time you use a meaningless and unnecessary character in a program you are forcing the BASIC interpreter to scurry around in identifying the item and dismissing it. Ultimately, this requires both extra memory space and extra time. As an Egyptian pharaoh, you can eliminate baskets from the kingdom—then nobody has such an object to conceal his idling. As a programmer, you have the same option—eliminate the waste by eliminating the useless items.

I support the view that the actual *running* programs should be as "tight" as possible, with no wasted characters of any kind. In making that statement, I also have to differentiate between what I choose to call the "record" program and the "running" program. The difference is that the first is the version used during development, to generate copies for sale, trade, or publication, and to facilitate future revisions and modifications, while the latter is the "workhorse" version that is run on a day-to-day basis.

The point is, *efficient programs are written for computers, not for people,* and that's what this book is all about—preparing efficient programs. In order to gain maximum efficiency, it certainly seems logical to treat anything that doesn't contribute directly to the function of the program as "garbage" to be purged from the running version without hesitation. As I will soon demonstrate, it's a simple fact of life that human readability and computer efficiency are essentially incompatible concepts, and that *steps or procedures serving only to improve readability most often have an adverse effect on efficiency.*

Don't misunderstand me! Readability has its place, and that place is in the record version of the program where internal documentation and ease of readability are important during development, during subsequent changes, and for the use of anyone else who has access to the program. Of course, that means having two versions stored for every program and the necessity of updating both whenever a change is necessary. Yet the dual approach gives you the best of both worlds, with a fully documented and formatted program on one hand and an optimum-efficiency program on the other.

The creation of the compressed version from the record copy isn't really very difficult or time-consuming. There are compression programs commercially available from numerous sources. And some word-processing packages such as Micropro's WordStar® are capable of searching entire programs for all occurrences of REM statements, spaces, specific variable names, and so on. I happen to prefer the word-processing method because it gives me direct control over the compression process.

Even when lifting programs and routines from published listings found in books and magazines, it often is worthwhile to put some effort into eliminating unnecessary spaces, shortening variable names, striking remark statements, and combining as many instructions as possible on a single program line. The result is a cleaner program consuming less memory and disk space while executing in less time.

To demonstrate just how important these considerations are, I first compared the memory consumptions of the first and third bubble-sort routines already presented by entering each from the keyboard and checking the remaining free memory space. Subtracting the free space with the routine in memory from the free space with the computer cleared and no program in memory gave me a reliable count of the number of bytes used just to "house" each routine without executing it or allocating string space. The first version (fully compressed) used only 80 bytes. This was a savings of 490 memory bytes, which indicates that 86 percent of the memory used by the first version could be eliminated. That's quite a savings.

Next, I used the first and third versions of the bubble-sort subroutine to alphabetize a list of 200 four-letter words. Although the content of the list taken directly from my data base stored on disk isn't important, the words were totally randomized. The same list was applied for both programs, and it provided 35,422 iterations of the FOR. . . NEXT comparison and swapping loop as determined by a separate run with a counter variable incrementing each iteration. This assured an execution time long enough to provide meaningful timing measurements and a good comparison between the two approaches.

To input the word list into a string array, a three-line main program was used, halting execution with a STOP instruction (line 200) just before entering the subroutine so that timing was based only on the sorting routine and not on the data-input operation. In line 300, a PRINT CHR$(7) instruction was used to sound an audible tone on the CRT when the operation was completed. The following listings are for two test sequences under different interpreters. The tests designated 1A and 1B were conducted under Microsoft BASIC Revision 4.51, with Test 1B using full compression without any spaces. Tests 2A and 2B were performed under Microsoft BASIC Revision 5.2 (BASIC-80), with test 2B using only those spaces absolutely necessary for that interpreter.

Test 1A (Microsoft 4.51)

```
100 CLEAR 20000 : DIM A$(200)
200 OPEN"I",1,"A:ID#1":FOR X=1 TO 200:INPUT#1,A$(X):NEXT:Y=200:
    STOP
300 GOSUB 1000:PRINT CHR$(7):END
1000 REM ******* BUBBLE SORT TO ALPHABETIZE ARRAY A$(.) *******
1002 PASS=1 : REM FORCE ONE PASS THRU SORTING LOOP
1004          IF PASS=0 THEN 1016 : REM EXIT IF NO SWAPS
              OCCURRED
1006                    PASS=0 : REM ZERO THE LOOP CONTROL
1008                    FOR X=1 TO Y-1
1010                              IF A$(X) > A$(X+1) THEN
                                  SWAP A$(X),A$(X+1) : PASS=1 :
                                  REM RESET CONTROL IF SWAP OCCURS
1012                    NEXT X : REM NEXT ARRAY ELEMENT
1014          GOTO 1004 : REM BRANCH BACK TO CONTROL TEST
1016 RETURN : REM GO BACK TO MAINLINE PROGRAM ****************
```

[10 minutes 58 seconds (658 seconds)] *[657 bytes]*

Test 1B (Microsoft 4.51)

```
100 CLEAR 20000:DIM A$(200)
200 OPEN"I",1,"A:ID#1":FOR  X=1  TO  200:INPUT#1,A$(X):NEXT:Y=200:
    STOP
300 GOSUB 1000:PRINT CHR$(7):END
1000 P=1
1002 IFP=0THENRETURN
1004 P=0:FORX=1TOY-1:IFA$(X)>A$(X+1)THENSWAPA$(X),A$(X+1):P=1
1006 NEXTX:GOTO1002
```

[8 minutes 23 seconds (503 seconds)] *[172 bytes]*

Test 2A (Microsoft 5.2)

```
100 DIM A$(200)
200 OPEN"I",1,"A:ID#1":FOR X=1 TO 200:INPUT#1,A$(X):NEXT:Y=200:
    STOP
300 GOSUB 1000:PRINT CHR$(7):END
1000 REM ******* BUBBLE SORT TO ALPHABETIZE ARRAY A$(.) *******
1002 PASS=1 : REM FORCE ONE PASS THRU SORTING LOOP
1004          IF PASS=0 THEN 1016 : REM EXIT IF NO SWAPS
              OCCURRED
1006                    PASS=0 : REM ZERO THE LOOP CONTROL
1008                    FOR X=1 TO Y-1
1010                              IF A$(X) > A$(X+1) THEN
                                  SWAP A$(X),A$(X+1) : PASS=1 :
                                  REM RESET CONTROL IF SWAP
                                  OCCURS
1012                    NEXT X : REM NEXT ARRAY ELEMENT
1014          GOTO 1004 : REM BRANCH BACK TO CONTROL TEST
1016 RETURN : REM GO BACK TO MAINLINE PROGRAM ****************
```

[11 minutes 9 seconds (669 seconds)] *[661 bytes]*

Test 2B (Microsoft 5.2)

```
100 DIM A$(200)
200 OPEN"I",1,"A:ID#1":FOR  X=1  TO  200:INPUT#1,A$(X):NEXT:Y=200:
    STOP
300 GOSUB 1000:PRINT CHR$(7):END
1000 P=1
1002 IF P=0 THEN RETURN
1004 P=0:FOR X=1 TO Y-1:IF A$(X)>A$(X+1)THEN SWAP A$(X),A$(X+1):
     P=1
1006 NEXT X:GOTO 1002
```

[8 minutes 32 seconds (512 seconds)] *[166 bytes]*

In these test sequences, the B version always ran faster than the A version—Test 1B required 155 seconds less than Test 1A, and Test 2B required 157 seconds less than Test 2A. This means that, under either BASIC interpreter, the expanded form wasted 23.5 percent of its time interpreting useless characters and remark statements. By eliminating some 86 percent of the memory space required and 23.5 percent of the execution time, program compression provided considerably more efficiency and much better use of the computer's time. If the same techniques are used in large programs with many such repetitive routines, the gains can be quite substantial, and some programming efforts can show gains in terms of hours rather than just minutes.

A little caution is necessary, however. "Reserved" words must not be constructed inadvertently. In a BASIC that requires no spaces at all between program elements, there is a statement FIELD . . . AS . . . used in random-file handling. If the line FIELD10ASC$ is used to field 10 spaces for variables C$, a syntax error occurs because the function ASC() has been called without an argument. In such a case, the separating or delimiting space between AS and C$ would be necessary. Applesoft also has some interesting peculiarities. For instance, it will not accept an A before THEN in an IF . . . THEN . . . conditional branch. In that case, the program line would be "parsed" as IF AT HEN . . . rather than IF A THEN. . . .

So you're faced with another decision. Do you want to program for readability or efficiency? For small programs, it probably does no harm to use the expanded and fully documented style, as long as your computer memory is large enough to support the wasted space and you don't get involved with a lot of lengthy repetitions. For large programs involving more than 50 or 60 program lines and many loops, you're probably better off if you compress as much as possible regardless of memory size. If your machine has only 16K or 32K of memory, you might be forced into compression to avoid constant occurrences of an "out of memory" error.

However, if you are writing programs for publication, you'll probably have to use the expanded approach to have it accepted by an editor. Since the objective then is to make the program easily understood by other readers, emphasis usually is placed on readability over efficiency. Leave it to the publication's reader to compress the program as he or she sees fit. In such cases, it's essential to keep both an expanded and a compressed version on separate diskettes, with the latter being the one you actually use on a day-to-day basis.

For my own programming purposes, I sometimes use a compromise method that I've yet to see applied to commercial software packages, although it minimizes wasted memory space and execution time while allowing a form of self-documentation. Essentially, it involves "footnoting" a program much as book chapters often are footnoted at the end rather than on each page. Many of the commercial software packages contain something like a "README" file used to hold revisions or updates to the manual and thus minimize the costs of reprinting manuals every time a change is made to the program. With that as an acceptable practice, it's just as easy to segregate remarks and explanations from the body of the program by using a separate text file recorded on a program diskette.

The program still would have REM statements, but only as footnote indicators to the separate text file. For example, lines 1000 and 1002 of the earlier example for Text 1A in this chapter might be written as:

```
. . .
1ØØØ REM 1
1ØØ2 PASS=1 : REM 2
. . .
```

Then a word processor, text editor, or similar program would be used to set up a text file such as "FOOTNOTE" that would contain the lines:

```
1. BUBBLE SORT TO ALPHABETIZE ARRAY A$(.)
2. FORCE ONE PASS THRU SORTING LOOP
```

This eliminates 84 characters from the program for Test 1A, reducing memory requirements and speeding execution accordingly. Yet the internal documentation is still available, though the bulk of the comments have been externalized and are no longer in the computer's way. Of course, the program still contains the REM statements, which have to be interpreted, so there remains some loss in execution time, but at least the amount of "working" program code can make the best use of the machine's available memory or even be increased beyond otherwise limited capabilities.

One final note concerning the REM statement. If you elect to use it in your programs, don't make it the object of a control transfer. I've deliberately done it that way in the preceding example, but it's frustrating to someone who wants to strip down a program. If you have a GOSUB 1000 in the program and line 1000 contains only a REM statement, removing the line results in an "undefined line number" error. It's far better and slightly more efficient to make the transfer to the first executable line following the remark. I can only urge you to do some of your own memory and time comparisons with your own programs and on your own machine. Try to be aware of how many bytes or how much time you lose by adding an extra line number, an unnecessary remark, or even a space.

Pay attention to small details. Saving a total of 0.1 second in a loop may not seem like much, but that loop may be nested several levels deep within other loops and have to execute tens of thousands of times per program run. Over 40,000 iterations of a 0.1-second saving, the total reduction mounts up to 4,000 seconds (1 hour 6 minutes), which is well worth the loss of a little readability or the effort to make some changes in the loop.

Chapter 3

A "BASIC" Understanding

In order to use BASIC effectively, you first must have at least a partial understanding of how your particular version of the language may or may not differ from other versions. In preceding chapters, I've frequently qualified my use of the name BASIC with either "version" or "implementation," and I've done so for a very specific reason. In the simplest terms, the BASIC interpreter that runs on your machine may be considerably different from the versions that run on my machines. I have 15 BASICs among three machines, all different and all requiring special attention whenever I move from one to another.

In this chapter, I intend to define the critical differences and begin to show you how to get around difficulties that may arise as a result of not having a particular instruction, having a version of BASIC that differs from another in some subtle feature of a particular statement, or trying to adapt programs written under one BASIC so they will run on your machine. Much of this relates directly to the concept of program *portability*—that is, the capability of transferring a given program from one system to another. As you'll see, achieving total portability among all systems is at worst impossible and at best difficult. At the very least, it's often necessary to sacrifice program efficiency to make the program easily adaptable to other machines.

The information herein is applicable to the conversion of virtually any program from one system to another and should prove quite valuable as you work on programs taken from sources such as the popular computing magazines. I must point out that you shouldn't shy away from any program just because it requires a little work to adapt. Although the procedures may look difficult at first glance, appearances are deceiving.

A little practice will enable you to work back and forth between BASICs with a minimum of effort. There are very few cases where every consideration presented in this chapter will be applicable to one version of BASIC, so you need only recognize and use those that affect your machine.

At the same time, the material I'll be covering also has a direct effect on the efficient use of your machine. Several subjects are "hidden" from you in the documentation normally furnished with BASIC language packages or are skimmed over lightly in the literature. As a result, misunderstanding the exact function of a program statement may lead to erroneous or inefficient programs.

As an added fringe benefit, I'll be providing routines and short programming steps in this and subsequent chapters to compensate for functions missing from a particular BASIC. For example, some BASICs provide string-handling functions that are not available in other implementations but are very convenient when you have to handle quoted literal data. In most cases, a short subroutine can be used to take the place of the missing function, although the resulting program may not be as efficient.

When I present a routine, you'll find that I usually don't follow my own advice in Chapter 2 about compressing program lines and stripping "garbage" characters and statements. Since these routines are for publication, readability is given preference. If you use the routines in your own programming, just remember to strip and compress them to achieve minimum memory usage and maximum execution speed.

BASIC-Language Implementation

I've said it before, and I'll say it again. The manner in which a particular system implements its BASIC language demands a considerable amount of attention before any programs can be keyed into the system. Although Shakespeare said, "A rose by any other name would smell as sweet," BASIC by any name at all may not always be basic.

Considered generically, BASIC probably is the single most popular and widely used language for small computers, but its popularity contributes directly to the modern-day programmer's headaches. The extensive evolution the language has undergone since its first development at Dartmouth College has resulted in refinements and extensions that have given it greater and greater computational powers. Today, BASIC has reached a level where some versions are extremely versatile and eminently suitable for many applications. Many of the early versions of BASIC lacked intrinsic functions for such elementary procedures as determining the sine or tangent of an angle, but modern versions nearly always have these and numerous other functions already built into them.

The problem now is that too many people have meddled with the language, each with his or her own ideas of how it should be improved. During its evolution, BASIC ran headlong into a very serious problem—a lack of standardization. Since there were no standards on how a computer language should be written, every computer manufacturer who was licensed to use the language imposed idea's of how it ought to work. Even today, nearly every company that begins manufacturing a new computer tries to reinvent the whole world of BASIC programming, so there are about as many versions of the language under similar names as there are brands of computers. To make matters worse, there often are several versions of BASIC for the same computer, since it may be provided in a stripped-down version to save memory and in various "extension" levels that add features but require additional memory.

As just one example, the Apple II allows you to choose Integer BASIC with or without a disk-operating system (DOS); floating-point BASIC, known as Applesoft, with or without DOS; and two versions of Microsoft BASIC (with an added plug-in card). You can even transfer other versions of Microsoft BASICs into the Apple II from other machines. The newer Apple III maintains an emulation mode to give you access to the Apple II Integer and floating-point BASICs and goes a step farther to add a whole new "business" BASIC of its own. In 1982, CP/M became available on the Apple III, giving it access to still more BASICs. Similar considerations allow almost any personal or small-business microcomputer to operate with a choice of BASICs.

Therein lies the single biggest headache for the user or programmer of any small computer system. The sheer number of BASIC versions and implementations available for modern machines makes it impossible to write any but the most elementary programs and still have them 100 percent compatible from one computer system to another. Some BASICs provide good routines for handling literal alphanumeric data (strings); others do not. Some BASICs provide a large number of intrinsic functions and operations, and others require that those same functions be programmed out individually. Some BASICs are very fast and efficient, while others are slow and cumbersome.

Combine the number of different BASICs with the number of different terminals, printers, data-storage devices, the use or nonuse of memory-mapped video, and other variable features of computer systems in general, and the number of programming possibilities quickly becomes unmanageable. In trying to establish a definite set of rules for BASIC, one arrives at the point where there are more exceptions to rules than there are valid rules. Nothing seems totally universal, including much of what I'll be presenting throughout the remainder of this book.

No matter how skillful a programmer is or how much effort is put into making a program portable from one system or one BASIC to any others, the best that can be achieved is minimizing the difficulties that may be encountered by other users and selecting a BASIC language implementation that has been widely distributed and is likely to be around for a while. The individual details for special cases then must be left to the person using the program on a specific machine.

To illustrate just how complicated this can become, the MITS 300/25 system (Altair 8800b computer and peripherals) I had used since 1978 supported nine implementations of BASIC—five obsolete versions specific to the machine and four Microsoft BASICs available under CP/M. Each of the nine functioned differently from the others, and each had its own quirks and peculiarities. Furthermore, each BASIC interpreter required a slightly different amount of memory to hold the language itself.

In mid-1982, I had to face yet another complication. The old Altair system "died" for good, with continued maintenance no longer available frequently enough to allow me to continue using that machine. As a result, I had to replace it with a new Morrow Designs Decision 1™ unit, which kept me within the highly expandable and versatile S-100 bus technology. Although the Decision 1 provided me with far superior operating capabilities, the acquisition of the new machine has caused numerous problems. All those problems have revolved around trying to salvage the software and associated data I had developed over the years. For one thing, I lost the ability to run the older Altair BASICs, both because the interpreters themselves wouldn't run on the new machine and because there was a radical change in disk formats. This meant a sudden flurry of activity to get the materials moved from the old Altair disk formats to the newer CP/M formats within the Altair system itself, upgrade them to the Microsoft BASIC-80 interpreter common to both the modified Altair and the Morrow Designs units, and get them transferred from machine to machine across an interface so I wouldn't have to spend years retyping the program lines and data files.

It proved to be a lot of work, and I did run into a few of the old Altair BASIC programs that wouldn't transfer well at all. Ultimately I have had to rewrite and reenter those programs from scratch. Yet it's been worth the effort because the resulting programs now are compatible with current standards and are portable from one system to another if both run the CP/M operating system and support Microsoft BASIC-80. Overall, I've seen a significant improvement in capabilities, speed, and convenience as a result of moving to the new machine. I still miss the availability of the older BASIC interpreters, but the gains have far outstripped any inconveniences or difficulties I've encountered.

I should note, however, that the system change occurred after the benchmarking tests in this book were completed and book production was underway. As a result, the Microsoft BASIC-80 and Microsoft BASIC 4.51 timings presented reflect operation under the older 8080a microprocessor and not the newer and faster Z-80 machine. However, since any differences in timings that would be seen between the two machines are in magnitude and not in relative proportions, all noted trends and interrelationships remain valid regardless of the machines' characteristics.

All the versions I've used, including the obsolete Altair versions, essentially employ the Microsoft approach to BASIC and come as close as possible to being the same programming language. Yet each version and each revision functions differently, and a given program is not always transported easily from one BASIC to another. Incidentally, the old Altair BASICs generally are close to Microsoft Revision 4.51 in terms of features, approaches, and programming style, though not in speed.

To further complicate matters, the 48K Apple II Plus system I also use is equipped with a Microsoft SoftCard and an additional 16K Microsoft RAMCard. It adds five more BASICs unique to that system, including Apple Integer BASIC loaded into the 16K RAMCard from disk, Applesoft without DOS, Applesoft with DOS, Microsoft BASIC-80 (MBASIC) with low-resolution graphics only, and Microsoft BASIC-80 (GBASIC) with both low- and high-resolution graphics.

As if coping with those BASIC implementations on the two machines were not enough, I have the three systems interfaced together for program and data exchange. Operating under CP/M, I can transfer programs written in BASIC back and forth. I can transfer the Microsoft BASIC interpreters (Revisions 4.51, 5.1, and 5.2) without graphics from either the MITS or Morrow Design systems to the Apple. I can transfer compiled programs with the MITS and Morrow Designs to and from the Apple. I also have provisions for transferring programs in any BASIC from the CP/M-equipped machines to Applesoft, where they can be edited and modified to run under that interpreter. Finally, I can transfer programs back and forth between the Apple's MBASIC or GBASIC and Applesoft, again with the appropriate modifications. In the near future, I plan to add even more computer brands, with each machine interfaced to every other machine.

The real problem with all of this is that the BASICs are not totally compatible. For example, programs written for Apple's Integer BASIC require a lot of work to adapt for Applesoft and even more work to adapt for the Microsoft CP/M BASICs running on the Apple. Even on the Altair machine, each revision of its specific BASICs is slightly different in relatively minor ways, while major program modifications may be required to adapt them to Microsoft's BASIC-80 running under CP/M. As a result, I can achieve a degree of partial portability in a given program, but never total portability in even one machine.

The closest I get to an element of true portability is between BASIC-80 on the S-100 machines and BASIC-80 (MBASIC or GBASIC) on the Apple II, but even there I have to account for differences in display formats, external terminals, keyboard characters, and so on. I also have to make sure that graphics capabilities are not used because the S-100 machines don't support them. The same considerations hold true for compiled "command" programs transferred from one machine to the other, further complicated by the fact that a file compiled for an 8080a microprocessor will run on a Z-80 microprocessor, but Z-80 code won't run on the 8080a. Incidentally, Microsoft's BASCOM compiler can generate either 8080 or Z-80 code on command, but other than a 5 to 10 percent reduction in disk space, I've seen no advantage to Z-80 code. In fact, 8080 code sometimes runs faster than Z-80 code on the Z-80 microprocessor.

I should also mention that I've observed an odd pattern as I've progressed upward through newer and newer BASIC interpreters. After mid-1978, each successive interpreter I acquired operated more slowly than its predecessors, particularly in the area of literal alphanumeric string handling. At each level, I gained new programming capabilities and important new features, but I found that upgrading my programs usually slowed them down noticeably. When I moved up to Microsoft's BASIC-80 (Revisions 5.1 and 5.2) in early 1981, I had great expectations, but in my particular applications involving very large programs and almost pure string handling, it turned out to be the slowest of all. From the standpoint of overall "throughput" in a program run, it seems that the improvements to BASIC interpreters during recent years tend to be made at the cost of reducing string-handling efficiency. At the same time, the efficiency losses noted in string handling often do not affect numerical processing and sometimes can be avoided in short programs, but they can be a real inconvenience when it's necessary to deal with large, complex, string-intensive programming.

Because the Altair computer is obsolete and is no longer supported even by its original manufacturers, I don't want to dwell on that system. However, I do need to point out one fact that may be of interest in this particular context and that will show up again in Chapter 5 of this book when I benchmark string-handling capabilities. Simply stated, that computer offered the best string-handling BASIC I've found on any machine or under any operating system. Altair BASIC Revision 5.0, released in July of 1978, offered very fast string-handling capabilities with very little time lost to internal memory operations normally required in those applications. Although it's almost identical to Microsoft BASIC Revision 4.51, available under the CP/M operating system, at least in terms of overall operating features and performance, I've never been able to match its string-handling speed. In fact, the availability of that one interpreter is the primary reason I hadn't scrapped the Altair system long ago.

The point of all this is to illustrate one fact of life that applies to programming in BASIC. With such substantial differences among BASICs of the same general family, from the same original source, and running on the same hardware, it follows that there can be even greater differences among BASICs of different families, from different sources, and running on different hardware. The problems of transcribing any program from one system to another are inescapable, but they are not insurmountable. Meanwhile, you also have to give due consideration to the efficiency of your BASIC in relation to that of other versions. When you run headlong into a version that is inherently slow and inefficient for a particular application, you may be able to minimize some of the problems, but others will remain no matter how much you massage your programs.

BASICs Side by Side

Perhaps one of the best ways to introduce the differences between language implementations is to compare several versions side by side, showing some of the features each makes available to its users. Once that's been done, attention can be devoted to the specific differences in certain statements, functions, and commands—differences that affect the way you are going to be using the language.

Table 3-1 is a partial list of the BASIC statements available in Microsoft and Apple BASICs. Table 3-2 lists some of the notable intrinsic functions of each, and Table 3-3 lists some of the direct commands that may be issued from the keyboard. Some BASICs allow certain direct commands to be used as program statements or certain program statements as direct commands, so that there is a gray area of items that belong to both categories. Literature for the Apple differentiates between "deferred" and "immediate" commands, which correspond to program statements and direct commands respectively. The tables are intended for informational purposes only and do not include every possible statement, function, or command, especially those that serve special purposes for one interpreter. You might want to go through this table, compare it with the index of your own BASIC manuals, and check off the items that you have available.

As you can see from Tables 3-1, 3-2, and 3-3, there are substantial differences between the various BASICs on just these machines—certainly enough differences to give you a lot of programming headaches when switching from one to the other. And the tables don't even tell the whole story. First, not all of the available statements, functions, and commands have been included. Second, different statements and commands are available for BASIC-80 running under operating systems other than CP/M. Third, there are variations in meaning and use when the "same" item is used as a program statement or as a direct command from the keyboard. Fourth, the tables don't reflect the differences in the way numbers are handled, truncating versus rounding functions, statement and command syntax, and so on. Instead, the tables

Table 3-1

Side-by-Side Comparison of BASIC Program Statements

	S-100 CP/M System			Apple II Plus System				
Statement	CP/M Microsoft BASIC, Revision 4.51	CP/M Microsoft BASIC-80, Revision 5.2	CP/M Microsoft BASCOM Compiler	Apple Integer BASIC (with DOS)	Applesoft (with DOS)	CP/M Microsoft MBASIC, Revision 5.2	CP/M Microsoft GBASIC, Revision 5.2	Your System
BEEP				†	†	X	X	
CALL*	X	X	X§	X	X	X	X	
CHAIN*		X	X§	X¶	†¶	X	X	
CLEAR*	X	X		X	X	X	X	
CLOSE	X	X	X	X¶	X¶	X	X	
COLOR				X	X	X	X	
COMMON*		X	X§			X	X	
CONSOLE	†	†		†	†	†	†	
DATA	X	X	X		X	X	X	
DEF FN*	X	X	X		X	X	X	
DEFINT/SNG/DBL/STR	X	X	X§			X	X	
DEF USR*	X	X	X	†	†	X	X	
DIM*	X	X	X§	X	X	X	X	
DRAW					X			
END	X	X	X§	X	X	X	X	
ERASE	X	X				X	X	
ERROR*	X	X	X			X	X	
FIELD**	X	X	X	†¶	†¶	X	X	
FLASH				†	X			
FOR...NEXT*	X	X	X§	X	X	X	X	
GET*	X	X	X	X*	X*	X	X	
GOSUB...RETURN*	X	X	X	X	X	X	X	
GOTO*	X	X	X	X	X	X	X	
GR*				X	X	X	X	
HCOLOR					X		X	

Table 3-1

Side-by-Side Comparison of BASIC Program Statements (continued)

	S-100 CP/M System			Apple II Plus System				
Statement	CP/M Microsoft BASIC Revision 4.51	CP/M Microsoft BASIC-80, Revision 5.2	CP/M Microsoft BASCOM Compiler	Apple Integer BASIC (with DOS)	Applesoft (with DOS)	CP/M Microsoft MBASIC, Revision 5.2	CP/M Microsoft GBASIC, Revision 5.2	Your System
HGR*					X		X	
HIMEM:					X			
HLIN				X	X	X	X	
HOME				†	X	X	X	
HPLOT					X		X	
HSCRN							X	
HTAB				X	X	X	X	
IF...GOTO...	X	X	X	X	X	X	X	
IF...THEN...[ELSE]*	X	X	X	X	X	X	X	
INPUT*	X	X	X	X	X	X	X	
INPUT# **	X	X	X			X	X	
INVERSE				†	X	X	X	
KILL or DELETE*(file)	X	X	X	¶	¶	X	X	
LET (or implied LET)	X	X	X	X	X	X	X	
LINE INPUT	X	X	X			X	X	
LINE INPUT# **	X	X	X			X	X	
LOMEM:				†	X			
LPRINT*	X	X	X	†	†	X	X	
LPRINT USING*	X	X	X			X	X	
MID$ (as command)	X	X	X			X	X	
NORMAL				†	X	X	X	
ON ERROR...GOTO...*	X	X	X§		X	X	X	
ON...GOSUB...	X	X	X	†	X	X	X	
ON...GOTO...	X	X	X	†	X	X	X	
OPEN*	X	X	X	¶	¶	X	X	

Table 3-1

Side-by-Side Comparison of BASIC Program Statements (continued)

	S-100 CP/M System			Apple II Plus System				
Statement	CP/M Microsoft BASIC Revision 4.51	CP/M Microsoft BASIC-80, Revision 5.2	CP/M Microsoft BASCOM Compiler	Apple Integer BASIC (with DOS)	Applesoft (with DOS)	CP/M Microsoft MBASIC, Revision 5.2	CP/M Microsoft GBASIC, Revision 5.2	Your System
OPTION BASE		X	X			X	X	
OUT*	X	X	X					
PLOT				X	X	X	X	
POKE	X	X	X	X	X	X	X	
POP				X	X	X	X	
PRINT*	X	X	X	X	X	X	X	
PRINT USING*	X	X	X			X	X	
PRINT# **	X	X	X	†¶	†¶	X	X	
PRINT# USING**	X	X	X			X	X	
PUT**	X	X	X			X	X	
RANDOMIZE		X	X			X	X	
READ	X	X	X		X	X	X	
REM	X	X	X	X	X	X	X	
RESTORE*	X	X	X		X	X	X	
RESUME*	X	X	X§		X	X	X	
ROT					X			
RUN*	X	X	X§	X	X	X	X	
SAVE*	X	X	X	X	X	X	X	
SCALE					X			
SHLOAD					X			
SPEED					X			
STEP	X	X	X	X	X	X	X	
STOP*	X	X	X§		X	X	X	
SWAP	X	X	X			X	X	
TEXT*				X	X	X	X	

Table 3-1

Side-by-Side Comparison of BASIC Program Statements (continued)

	S-100 CP/M System			Apple II Plus System				
Statement	CP/M Microsoft BASIC Revision 4.51	CP/M Microsoft BASIC-80, Revision 5.2	CP/M Microsoft BASCOM Compiler	Apple Integer BASIC (with DOS)	Applesoft (with DOS)	CP/M Microsoft MBASIC, Revision 5.2	CP/M Microsoft GBASIC, Revision 5.2	Your System
TRON/TROFF or TRACE/NOTRACE*	X	X	X§	X	X	X	X	
VLIN				X	X	X	X	
VTAB				X	X	X	X	
WAIT	X	X	X		X	X	X	
WHILE...WEND		X	X§			X	X	
WIDTH*	X	X	X	†	†	X	X	
WIDTH LPRINT		X	X			X	X	
WRITE		X	X			X	X	
WRITE# *		X	X	X¶	X¶	X	X	
XDRAW				X	X			
XPLOT				X	X			

*Indicates program statements known to be different, either in major or minor ways, from one BASIC to another.
†A corresponding function is available by other means.
§Special provisions must be observed when using the compiler.
¶Available on the Apple II only with DOS.
**Unique to the Microsoft method of handling disk files.

merely provide a starting point for your own analysis of the BASIC employed by your machine.

BASIC Commands, Statements, and Functions

This section summarizes many of the common commands, statements, and functions provided by modern BASIC interpreters. Because Microsoft BASIC-80 is an ANSI (American National Standards Institute) standard version and is available on many computers, emphasis is placed on its instruction set and the definitions used in that version.

The list of items in the following paragraphs is not intended to be all-inclusive; certain commands, statements, and functions are omitted because their meanings are obvious and easily obtained from manuals, while others are omitted because they are unique to one particular system. Of particular note are the graphics commands—these are omitted because it's not my purpose to define graphics approaches and because the graphics instructions and techniques vary widely from machine to another. Instead, I put my emphasis on those items known to require special attention in nongraphic applications or commonly used for numerical or string data handling.

The definitions and syntax formats herein are abbreviated and are not intended to describe the items fully but only to define them. This section is not a replacement for the BASIC instruction manuals furnished with your system; instead, it provides a means of introducing some of the important differences in the ways BASICs "do their thing." In the descriptions, brackets shown in the form of the item denote optional entries and features.

Table 3-2

Side-by-Side Comparison of BASIC Intrinsic Functions

	S-100 CP/M System			Apple II Plus System				
Statement	CP/M Microsoft BASIC Revision 4.51	CP/M Microsoft BASIC-80, Revision 5.2	CP/M Microsoft BASCOM Compiler	Apple Integer BASIC (with DOS)	Applesoft (with DOS)	CP/M Microsoft MBASIC, Revision 5.2	CP/M Microsoft GBASIC, Revision 5.2	Your System
ABS()	X	X	X	X	X	X	X	
ASC()	X	X	X	X	X	X	X	
ATN()	X	X	X		X	X	X	
BUTTON()				X	X	X	X	
CDBL()	X	X	X			X	X	
CHR$()	X	X	X		X	X	X	

Table 3-2

Side-by-Side Comparison of BASIC Intrinsic Functions (continued)

	S-100 CP/M System			Apple II Plus System				
Statement	CP/M Microsoft BASIC Revision 4.51	CP/M Microsoft BASIC-80, Revision 5.2	CP/M Microsoft BASCOM Compiler	Apple Integer BASIC (with DOS)	Applesoft (with DOS)	CP/M Microsoft MBASIC, Revision 5.2	CP/M Microsoft GBASIC, Revision 5.2	Your System
CINT()	X	X	X			X	X	
COS()	X	X	X		X	X	X	
CSNG()	X	X	X			X	X	
CVI()/CVS()/CVD()†	X	X	X			X	X	
EOF()	X	X	X			X	X	
ERR	X	X	X	¶	¶	X	X	
ERL	X	X	X			X	X	
EXP()*	X	X	X		X	X	X	
FIX()	X	X	X			X	X	
FRE()*	X	X	X		X	X	X	
HEX$()	X	X	X			X	X	
INKEY$		X	X			X	X	
INP()	X	X	X					
INPUT$()		X	X			X	X	
INSTR()	X	X	X			X	X	
INT()	X	X	X		X	X	X	
LEFT$()	X	X	X		X	X	X	
LEN()	X	X	X	X	X	X	X	
LOC()*	X	X	X			X	X	
LOF()*	X	X	X			X	X	
LOG()	X	X	X		X	X	X	
LPOS()*	X	X	X			X	X	
MID$()	X	X	X		X	X	X	
MKI$()/MKS$()/MKD$()†	X	X	X			X	X	

Table 3-2

Side-by-Side Comparison of BASIC Intrinsic Functions (continued)

	S-100 CP/M System			Apple II Plus System				
Statement	CP/M Microsoft BASIC Revision 4.51	CP/M Microsoft BASIC-80, Revision 5.2	CP/M Microsoft BASCOM Compiler	Apple Integer BASIC (with DOS)	Applesoft (with DOS)	CP/M Microsoft MBASIC, Revision 5.2	CP/M Microsoft GBASIC, Revision 5.2	Your System
OCT$()	X	X	X			X	X	
PDL()				X	X	X	X	
PEEK()*	X	X	X	X	X	X	X	
POS()*	X	X	X		X	X	X	
RIGHT$()	X	X	X		X	X	X	
RND()*	X	X	X	X	X	X	X	
SCRN()				X	X	X	X	
SGN()	X	X	X	X	X	X	X	
SIN()	X	X	X		X	X	X	
SPACE$()	X	X	X			X	X	
SPC()	X	X	X		X	X	X	
SQR()*	X	X	X		X	X	X	
STR$()*	X	X	X		X	X	X	
STRING$()	X	X	X			X	X	
TAB()*	X	X	X		X	X	X	
TAN()	X	X	X		X	X	X	
USR()*	X	X	X§		X	X	X	
VAL()	X	X	X		X	X	X	
VARPTR()*	X	X	X			X	X	
VPOS()						X	X	

*Indicates intrinsic functions known to be different, either in major or minor ways, from one BASIC to another.
†Unique to the Microsoft method of handling disk files.
§Special provisions must be observed when using the compiler.
¶A corresponding function is available by other means.

Table 3-3

Partial Side-by-Side Comparison of BASIC Direct Commands

	S-100 CP/M System			Apple II Plus System				
Statement	CP/M Microsoft BASIC Revision 4.51	CP/M Microsoft BASIC-80, Revision 5.2	CP/M Microsoft BASCOM Compiler	Apple Integer BASIC (with DOS)	Applesoft (with DOS)	CP/M Microsoft MBASIC, Revision 5.2	CP/M Microsoft GBASIC, Revision 5.2	Your System
AUTO	X	X		X	†	X	X	
CONT	X	X		X	X	X	X	
DELETE or DEL (lines)	X	X		X	X	X	X	
EDIT*	X	X		§	§	X	X	
FILES or CATALOG	X	X		X	X	X	X	
LIST	X	X		X	X	X	X	
LLIST*	X	X		§	§	X	X	
LOAD*	X	X		X	X	X	X	
KILL or DELETE (file)	X	X		X	X	X	X	
MERGE	X	X			†	X	X	
NAME or RENAME (file)	X	X		X	X	X	X	
NEW	X	X		X	X	X	X	
NULL	X	X						
RENUM	X	X			†	X	X	
RESET (files)	X	X				X	X	
RUN	X	X		X	X	X	X	
SAVE*	X	X		X	X	X	X	
SYSTEM	X	X				X	X	

*Indicates direct commands known to be different, either in major or minor ways, from one BASIC to another.

†A corresponding function is available by means other than BASIC itself such as the Apple's DOS Toolkit software package.

§The general function is available, but not as the single direct command typical of a Microsoft BASIC.

Commands and Statements

CALL < address >[(< arguments >)] is one of the methods of accessing an assembly-language subroutine; the USR() function is another method. The address usually is a variable name and is the starting memory location or *entry point* for the subroutine. The arguments are the values passed to the subroutine for its execution. With Apple Integer BASIC or Applesoft, the most common use is to call a specific subroutine "built into" the computer's system software with a simple CALL < address > such as CALL -936 to clear the screen and home the cursor. With either MBASIC or GBASIC and the Microsoft SoftCard in the Apple, CALL%... accesses 6502 subroutines, and CALL... without the "%" symbol accesses Z-80 subroutines. Each user must study the system documentation carefully for the proper use of this statement under any given BASIC.

CHAIN [MERGE] < program >[,< line >][,ALL][,DELETE < range >] is used with disk systems and allows multiple programs to be run in sequence, with all or some of the variables passed from the first program to the second. It also allows the merging of two programs, the deletion of lines from a program, and transfer to a specific line number—all depending upon the implementation of the language. The statement is valuable when limited memory space forces the use of short programs run in sequence. Not all BASICs provide a CHAIN statement, and not all of those that do provide it allow for all the options. In one revision of Microsoft's BASCOM compiler, the CHAIN statement is recognized as a means of accessing the next program, but variable transfer is not allowed, so it may be necessary to store variables as a disk file and read them back from disk at the start of the next program segment. Again, individual system manuals must be studied carefully.

CLEAR [,[< n >],[< m >]] sets all numeric variables to zeros and all string variables to nulls. Under BASIC-80, optional expression < n > sets the highest memory location available, and optional expression < m > sets aside stack space; the number of bytes set aside for the stack determines the depth of subroutine nesting that will be allowed before an "out of memory" error occurs. CLEAR cannot be used in BASIC-80 to allocate string space; the allocation is performed dynamically as needed.

Microsoft Revision 4.51 BASIC uses the form CLEAR [< n >], in which a simple CLEAR serves to set all variables to zeros or nulls, while the optional expression < n > designates the number of memory bytes allocated or reserved for string storage. It does not allow the use of a CLEAR statement to set the highest memory location or to allocate string space. Applesoft does not allow any optional expression, so CLEAR serves only to set all variables to zeros and nulls. Finally, many BASICs allowing optional expressions also allow them to be variables, but some BASICs may require the expressions to be integer constants.

CLOSE[[#]<f>[,[#]<f>]...] terminates all disk-file transfers, where <f> is the number under which the file was opened originally. Not specifying a number closes all open files. Under the Apple II DOS, the form is simply CLOSE [<f>], without the "#" symbol. Since the CLOSE operation typically forces the contents of an output buffer to be written to the disk file, closing files is an important step to prevent loss of data, particularly when a program is interrupted from the keyboard. Note that most BASICs close files automatically upon encountering an END or a NEW statement, but *not* a STOP statement. Users must check the instruction manuals.

COMMON <variable list> passes variables between "chained" programs and must be executed before the CHAIN statement transfers control. It is used only when a portion of the variables are required and a CHAIN ALL statement is unsuitable, making it useful as a means of clearing unused variable space when transferring control from one program segment to another. The <variable list> contains the names of all variables to be transferred, both array and nonarray. Variables no longer needed simply aren't included in the list. Note, however, that at least one revision of the BASCOM compiler does not recognize the COMMON statement and, in fact, has no provision for passing variables between compiled machine-language programs using the simple technique available to the BASIC-80 interpreter.

CONT is a direct-execution command entered from the keyboard to resume program execution after a halt. On most systems, a Control-C keystroke or the STOP and END statements cause an immediate halt, and CONT may be typed to resume from the point of interruption. It never is used within a program. The most frequent application of this command is after a Control-C or STOP has been employed during debugging to allowing intermediate values to be examined from the keyboard; CONT then resumes normal execution from the point of interruption. However, CONT may not provide a normal or accurate continuation if the variables had been "clobbered" by an END statement (or a system RESET on the Apple II). Program execution may not be CONTinued if a program line is edited or changed during the interruption. In some instances, an interruption occurring while a nested loop is being processed will not CONTinue. Applesoft may refuse to execute any further disk-access commands after a CONT directive.

DATA <constant list> stores numeric and string constants for access by READ statements. DATA statements are not executed, and most BASICs allow them to appear anywhere in a program. The most common practice is to locate all DATA statements at the end of a program where they are readily located and changed whenever necessary. Numeric data may be integer, fixed-point, or floating-point; string data must be enclosed in quotes. Any number of DATA statements may be used in a program, and any one DATA statement may contain as many constants as will fit on a line, with all constants separated by commas.

DEF FN< name >[(parameter list)] = < function definition > both names and defines a single-line function written by the user in BASIC (not assembly language). The name of that function then is the < name > preceded by FN. The parameter list must correspond one to one with the parameters passed to the function when called from the program. DEF FN must be executed *before* the function it defines may be called from the program. Establishing user-defined functions for common operations occurring again and again within a program may save a significant amount of memory space but may or may not speed program execution, depending upon the efficiency of the individual BASIC in accessing and processing such functions.

DEF< type > < letter range(s) > predefines the variable types as integer, single-precision, double-precision, or string, depending upon whether the statement takes the form DEFINT, DEFSNG, DEFDBL, or DEFSTR. This relieves the programmer of the burden of explicitly declaring every variable with a %, !, #, or $ character at each appearance of the variable name in the program. By eliminating the type-declaration characters from each name, a significant amount of memory may be gained, but execution speed seems to be either unaffected or only slightly slowed. These statements are not available under Apple Integer BASIC or Applesoft, so explicit variable-type declaration is necessary, and it may "eat up" available memory very quickly on a small system of 32K or less, thereby contributing to a need for splitting large programs into segments and chaining them.

DEF USR[< n >] = < address > defines the starting address (beginning memory location) of an assembly-language subroutine. The optional < n > is an integer from 0 through 9 that defines the user's subroutine, and the < address > is an integer expression that evaluates to the starting memory address for that subroutine which later will be called by the USR( ) function. A given USR number may be defined and redefined as often as necessary, so there is no limit to the total number of subroutines that may be used; the only limit is that there may be only 10 subroutines "currently" defined at any one time. On the Apple II, the DEF USR statement is not available, but its function is simulated by "poking" the starting address into memory location $0A_H$ through $0C_H$.

DIM < subscripted variable list > specifies the maximum values for array-variable subscripts and allocates memory space accordingly. A subscript of zero normally is valid, but BASIC-80 provides an OPTION BASE statement that may be used to set the minimum subscript to one, thereby saving some memory if you don't like to use zero subscripts. Most BASICs automatically will dimension an array variable for 10 elements if a subscripted variable is encountered without a DIM statement having been executed for that variable. This can cause a "redimensioned array" error if a DIM statement for the variable is encountered later in the program. Under most interpreters, variables and expressions may be used to designate the subscript size, but the BASCOM compiler demands that all dimensioning be done with integer constants.

Some interpreters such as Apple Integer BASIC require that strings be dimensioned before they can be used. The maximum length of each and every string variable must be defined in a DIM statement even though the string variable may not be subscripted. Other differences also necessitate some caution in dimensioning. Consider a statement DIM A(15); in some BASICs, 16 variables A(0) through A(15) are valid, while others allow only 15 variables A(0) through A(14). Some, such as Applesoft, allow multiple dimensions and subscripts such as DIM A(20,10), while others, such as Apple Integer BASIC, permit only a single dimension or subscript. Furthermore, some BASICs "zero" or "null" all arrays upon executing a RUN or CLEAR statement, but others such as Apple Integer BASIC require that variables be zeroed or nulled with a separate program loop. Check your manuals!

END terminates program execution immediately, *closes all disk files*, and returns control to BASIC's command level. Its use normally is optional, and it may be placed anywhere in the program, though it's usually positioned at the end of the mainline program to prevent accidental "runover" into subsequent subroutines. Under some BASICs, an END statement may "clobber" values assigned to some variables, making the subsequent use of a CONT command inadvisable. If the program is written so that the last executable statement is on the last numbered line and there is no danger of "runover" into following subroutines or DATA statements, program execution stops after the last line even when the END (or STOP) statement is omitted. One exception is Apple Integer BASIC, which displays an error message if the program is not terminated with an END statement, though the error doesn't affect the program already executed.

ERASE < array-variable list > eliminates arrays from a program, freeing the memory space for other uses and allowing the variables to be redimensioned. It differs from the CLEAR statement in that it removes only the specified arrays, while CLEAR zeros or nulls *all* array and nonarray variables. ERASE is not supported by the BASCOM compiler, and the function is not provided by Apple Integer BASIC or Applesoft. When present in the language, ERASE is a handy way of clearing unused variables to allow memory and names to be reused for other purposes. It's also a rather neat way to "zero" a numerical array or "null" a string array by erasing and immediately redimensioning the arrays. In the absence of an ERASE statement, clearing an array usually must be done with a FOR...NEXT loop or, under a few BASICs, with a MAT statement. Microsoft BASIC-80 interpreters allow erasing and redimensioning, but the BASCOM compiler does not, so programs running under the interpreter will fail to compile unless all ERASE and subsequent redimensioning statements are purged.

ERR and **ERL** are special variables used in "error-trapping" routines to identify the error code and the line number causing the error. ERR, ERL, or both may be used in an IF...THEN... statement of the trapping routine to direct or redirect subsequent program flow according to what error is detected and/or what line number causes the error. On Apple II systems, there is no equivalent function to the ERL variable, but the function of the ERR variable may be simulated by examining the contents of decimal memory location 222 with a PEEK(222) statement to identify the error code. Note that error trapping can become quite complex with some BASICs and may even slow program execution, particularly under a compiler.

ERROR< n > is a special statement used in a program or issued directly from the keyboard for either of two purposes. First, it may function to simulate a specific error and print the error message (useful in identifying types of errors and testing a program for the conditions under which an error may occur). Second, it may be used to define new error codes to accommodate anticipated errors not normally indicated by the "built-in" BASIC error messages. This statement commonly is found in Microsoft-based languages but is not provided by Apple Integer BASIC or Applesoft.

FIELD[#]< f >,< field width > AS < string variable >,... is used only with a random-access disk file (never a sequential-access file) and allocates space for variables in a random-file buffer. All GET and PUT statements used to transfer data to and from a random-access disk file do so through the buffer, and that buffer must be properly "fielded" before the data exchange can be made. Fielding variables can become complex, and the appropriate Microsoft or other instruction manual should be studied carefully before attempting to use random files. The FIELD statement as such is not available under Apple Integer BASIC or Applesoft, but its function is simulated by the "length parameter" specified in the OPEN statement for a random-access disk file.

FOR <var>=<x> TO <y> [STEP <z>]...NEXT [<var>] [,<var>...] comprises a common FOR...NEXT loop that executes instructions in the loop a specified number of times. The variable < var > serves as a counter whose value changes with each iteration of the loop from the value of expression < x > to the value of expression < y >. The

STEP size and direction are optional and are assumed to be +1 if not otherwise specified. Loops may be "nested" inside each other, usually with no specific limit on the number of loops that may be so nested. Applesoft does, however, impose a 10-level limit on the depth of nesting.

Every user needs to be aware of a difference in the way a loop is handled from one BASIC to another. Under BASIC-80 (Microsoft Revisions 5.1 and 5.2), the control variable is checked *before* executing the loop, so the body of the loop is skipped whenever the initial value < x > times the sign of the step < z > exceeds the final value < y > times and sign of the step < z >. Under Microsoft BASIC Revision 4.51, Apple Integer BASIC, and Applesoft, the control variable is not checked until *after* the loop has been executed, meaning that a FOR...NEXT loop *always* must execute at least one time regardless of the initial values of < x > and < y >. In Chapter 4, I'll be describing this in more detail, since the variation can spell the difference between a successful and an unsuccessful program execution.

Another difference of note is that Apple Integer BASIC requires the use of the variable name after the NEXT statement while Microsoft and Applesoft BASICs allow the variable name to be omitted under certain circumstances. That omission is recommended for both memory conservation and speed increase.

GET [#]< f >[,< r >] under Microsoft BASICs reads a record from a random-access disk file into the random-file buffer. The < f > is the integer number under which the disk file was opened, while the optional < r > is any record number within that file. Data in the random-file buffer are accessed with subsequent statements such as an implied LET for string data or CVI( ), CVS( ), and CVD( ) functions for numeric data. Again, the reader is referred to the system instruction manuals for details on random-access disk files. Under Apple Integer BASIC and Applesoft, a GET statement generally has a completely different function, being used much like an INPUT statement to "get" a single character from the keyboard or, with DOS, to "get" characters from *either* sequential- or random-access disk files. Special attention must be paid to the GET statement when moving back and forth from regular Apple BASICs to the Microsoft BASICs with the SoftCard because this statement has totally different meanings.

GOSUB < line >...RETURN causes a branch to and subsequent return from a subroutine. Subroutines may be called any number of times from the mainline program or from other subroutines. "Nesting" of subroutines usually is limited only by available memory (or the stack size set for BASIC-80), although Applesoft does impose a fixed limit of 25 levels. The return from the subroutine is to the statement, not the line number, immediately following the GOSUB; therefore, multiple GOSUBs may be used on one program line, with each causing its own branch. Multiple RETURN statements may be used in a subroutine at different points if logic so dictates. One notable difference in implementation is that Apple Integer BASIC allows the GOSUB to be followed by an expression or arithmetic variable as a "computed" GOSUB, while Microsoft and Applesoft BASICs allow only a line number expressed as an integer. In the latter case, computed GOSUBs are not available, and the ON...GOSUB...RETURN statements must be used instead.

GOTO < line > unconditionally transfers program control to a specified line number, and execution continues from that point. As with the GOSUB... statement, some versions such as Apple Integer BASIC allow the use of a computed GOTO..., while others such as the Microsoft and Applesoft BASICs do not. GOTO... also may be used as a direct keyboard command to enter a program at a specific line number, most often after a program interruption to check intermediate values.

IF < expression > THEN [GOTO] < line or statements > [ELSE < line or statements >] facilitates decisions affecting program flow and the operations to be performed. Those decisions are based upon the evaluation of the < expression > and may involve a branch to a new line number, the execution of particular program statements, or both. The IF...THEN... statements also provide an alternative method of constructing program loops without the use of the FOR...NEXT statements, although the method that proves most efficient may vary from one BASIC to another and must be determined by testing both on the specific system. The statements may be nested, with the depth of nesting usually limited only by the length of the program line. If the conditions of the statement are not met, program execution proceeds with the next line number in the program.

The IF...THEN... statement requires additional consideration because there are several distinct implementations available. First, neither Apple Integer BASIC nor Applesoft allows the use of the ELSE option. Under Integer BASIC, a "syntax error" message is displayed as soon as a line containing ELSE is typed. Under Applesoft, no error message is displayed, not even when the program is executed—the ELSE portion of the statement simply is ignored, and the desired program branch never is achieved. This causes a "logical" error very difficult to isolate during program debugging.

Second, some BASICs allow three separate forms, namely the IF...THEN..., IF...GOTO..., and IF...THEN GOTO... statements. The three are functionally equivalent. Some users advocate the IF...GOTO... form as executing faster than the IF...THEN... form, but that's a matter that needs to be tested for each version of BASIC. At times, I've found the IF...GOTO... form slightly slower, at other times slightly faster. However, the IF...THEN GOTO.. form is redundant and wasteful. It wastes extra memory locations for the GOTO, which serves no function and does tend to slow execution. If you're lifting a program from a published source and you encounter the IF...THEN GOTO... form, I suggest you change it to IF...THEN....

Third, there are differences in the ways BASICs handle the THEN... portion of the statement. With the Microsoft and Applesoft versions, a "false" or "zero" evaluation of the expression being tested causes *all* statements following the THEN on the same program line to be ignored with execution proceeding directly to the next line. With Apple Integer BASIC, the same condition causes only the first item of the THEN portion to be ignored. For example, the statement IF X=1 THEN PRINT "TRUE":GOSUB 1000 would execute differently. If X=0, Applesoft would neither print nor branch to the subroutine; Apple Integer BASIC would not print, but it would branch to the subroutine.

INPUT[;][<"prompt">;]<variable list> accepts input from the terminal keyboard during program execution. Execution pauses until the variables specified in <variable list> have been typed at the keyboard. If <"prompt"> is omitted, a question mark is displayed at the terminal to request the input, or <"prompt"> may be used to have the terminal print a message that identifies the needed input. Under BASIC-80, replacing the semicolon after <"prompt"> with a comma suppresses the question mark display. Variable values typed at the keyboard must be of the same type and number as those specified in the <variable> list, or an error message will be displayed.

Typically, commas and semicolons entered at the keyboard in response to an INPUT statement are treated as delimiters, so a single statement of the form INPUT A$,B$,C$ would seek three string inputs, each separated by a comma. Under BASIC-80, supplying fewer or more than the number of inputs required causes an error message and requires that all inputs be reentered; other BASICs may allow each item to be entered and terminated with its own carriage return or may select only the first items from a list of many items when more are entered than are needed.

The syntax for an INPUT statement varies widely from BASIC to BASIC, and even Apple Integer BASIC and Applesoft use different approaches. Considerable care is required in structuring the INPUT statements for any given implementation, and examples in the instruction manuals for a particular system should be followed precisely.

INPUT#<f>,<variable list> reads data from a sequential disk file that has been opened for input, assigning the data read to the variables in the <variable list>. The <f> is the integer file number assigned when the file was opened, and the variable list must relate one to one to the items read from the file. The variable types must also match;

for example, an integer cannot be read for a string-type variable name in the < variable list >. The data items in the file should appear exactly as they would if they were being typed at the keyboard in response to an INPUT statement.

Under DOS, both Apple Integer BASIC and Applesoft use an INPUT statement without the "#" symbol, and they have special provisions for differentiating between disk input and keyboard inputs. Normally those and similar BASICs define a point after which all INPUT statements are treated as disk-oriented until another point is reached at which subsequent statements are redefined as being keyboard-oriented. The use of disk operations is a direct function of the disk-operating system employed by any machine, so an Apple functions differently than a CP/M system, which is different from a TRS-80 system, which is different from another system, and so on.

KILL < file name > deletes the named file from the disk under CP/M-based operating systems. Under the DOS used by an Apple II, the equivalent command is DELETE < file name >. With most operating systems, if that file is open when the KILL command is executed, an error message is displayed and the file is not deleted—the file must be closed before it can be deleted from the disk.

[LET] < variable > = < expression > assigns the value of the < expression > to the named < variable >. It's common practice to use an implied LET statement of the form < variable > = < expression >, and many programs never contain the LET statement as such. In general, programs are more efficient when the implied form is used, needing less memory and executing faster if the LET is omitted. There are a few versions of BASIC around that allow multiple statements of the form A=B=C=3, but most prohibit that structure and require an equivalent A=3:B=A:C=A format to accomplish the same thing. Incidentally, using an unacceptable A=B=C=3 form may or may not generate an error message. Neither Applesoft nor Apple Integer BASIC displays such a message; instead, they merely ignore the operation and don't change the values assigned to the variables.

LINE INPUT[;][< "prompt" >;]< string variable > inputs an entire line of as many as 254 characters as a single string variable. Delimiters are not used, so all characters typed at the keyboard up to the Carriage Return are assigned to < string variable >, including commas, semicolons, and spaces. Under most BASICs, a question mark is printed *only* if it is part of the quoted < "prompt" >, which must be a literal string and not a string variable.

Under Apple Integer BASIC and Applesoft, there is no LINE INPUT statement. Applesoft requires that a string entered from the keyboard and containing commas or semicolons be enclosed in quotation marks; the quotes are not treated as part of the string. In Apple Integer

BASIC, the INPUT statement functions like LINE INPUT and will accept any characters including commas, semicolons, and quotes, with the quotes being treated as a part of the literal string. Also note that Integer BASIC requires a comma and not a semicolon after <"prompt">.

LINE INPUT#<f>,<string variable> is the Microsoft equivalent of LINE INPUT used for disk inputs. It reads an entire line of up to 254 characters from a sequential disk file opened for input and assigns that line to the <string variable>. The statement reads all characters up to a Carriage Return or the end of the line, whichever occurs first. Commas, semicolons, and quotation marks are all considered a part of <string variable>. Again, Apple Integer BASIC and Applesoft lack this program statement, and the operation must be simulated by other means with the INPUT statements as modified by DOS.

LIST is a direct command issued from the keyboard and not used within the body of a program. Depending upon the language implementation, the command may be used as LIST to output the entire program in memory to the screen, as either LIST [line]-[line] or LIST [line,[line] to output a designated portion of the program, or LIST [line] to output a single program line. Many BASICs also provide equivalent LLIST forms to output the listings directly to a hard-copy printer, but others require special action such as a CONSOLE command followed by LIST or a PR#. . . command followed by a LIST for Apple Integer BASIC and Applesoft. Attempting to use a LIST or LLIST as a statement within the body of a program normally halts execution, lists the program, and returns BASIC to its command level—execution cannot continue from the point of interruption after a LIST or LLIST.

LOAD<program>[,R] loads a program from a disk file into memory. Without the optional R, the program does not execute; with the R, the LOAD command is equivalent to a RUN command, so program execution begins immediately. Various BASICs and operating systems provide several variations, including the method of defining which drive holds the program file. For example, under BASIC-80 and CP/M, the drive is defined in the file name so LOAD "B:PROGRAM" loads PROGRAM from drive B. Under a "standalone" BASIC, the same program might require a LOAD "PROGRAM",2 to retrieve the file on drive 2. Apple BASICs have their own syntax of the form LOAD f [,Ss] [,Dd] [,Vv] where file f is loaded from the diskette with a specific (optional) slot, drive, and volume number. Apple BASICs also differentiate a binary program file from other files and require a special BLOAD command for those.

LPRINT [<expressions>] outputs data to the printout device (line printer). If the list of expressions is omitted, a blank line is printed as a

Carriage Return/Line Feed sequence. BASIC-80 assumes a 132-character print width, although that may be altered with a WIDTH LPRINT statement. An LPRINT USING form also is widely available to allow printouts in a specified format, but the variations between methods are so great that they cannot be covered adequately in this book—refer to your programming manuals for details. The LPRINT statement has many of the same limitations as the LLIST already mentioned. With a BASIC not supporting a serial line printer, it may be necessary to use CONSOLE and PRINT statements. With Apple Integer BASIC and Applesoft, it's necessary to use a PR#... followed by a PRINT statement.

LSET and **RSET** statements take the form LSET <string variable>=<string expression> and RSET <string variable>=<string expression>. These are used by Microsoft BASIC to move data from memory to the "fielded" random-file buffer in preparation for a PUT statement. They differ in the way they "justify" the data in the buffer, and the reader is referred to the BASIC manuals for further assistance. Apple Integer BASIC and Applesoft operating under DOS have no equivalent functions, and none are required for random-file disk access with those implementations.

MERGE <program> is available under Microsoft BASICs as a direct command from the keyboard to combine two programs into one. It is not used as a program statement since execution of a MERGE command returns BASIC to its interactive command level. To use the command, one program is loaded into memory, and the second program (stored as an "ASCII file") is merged from disk. As the merge is performed, lines are inserted as appropriate; if the program being merged contains a line number between numbers in the original program, that line is inserted between the original lines. If the merged program contains the same line number as one already in the original, the line is overlaid (replaced) by the program being merged. This command is particularly useful in constructing a library of common routines and subroutines that can be merged into a mainline program, thus saving a lot of unnecessary typing time. Under Apple DOS, there is no MERGE command as such, and the operation must be performed by separate software such as the "Applesoft Programmer's Assistant" contained in the Applesoft Tool Kit software package that can be purchased separately.

**MID$(S$,<n>[,<m>])=S1$** used as a program statement replaces a portion of one string with another string. The characters in string S$, starting at character position <n>, are replaced with the characters in string S1$. The optional <m> value specifies the number of characters from string S1$ to be used in the replacement; if <m> is omitted, all of S1$ will be used. However, the replacement never can go beyond the original length of string S$. Note that MID$() used as a program statement in this form is not the same as MID$() used as a function, described later in this chapter, and some BASICs such as Apple Integer and Applesoft do not provide the "statement" form. In such cases, replacing a portion of a string requires multiple operations to separate out the needed portions of two strings and then combine or *concatenate* those portions back into the final string.

NEW is a direct command from the keyboard that immediately deletes any program in memory and clears all variables. This command should be issued before starting to type or key any new program to make certain no lines are still in memory from a previous program. It need not be used to load or run a program from disk because the NEW operation is implied and performed automatically upon a LOAD or RUN command that references a file name.

ON ERROR GOTO <line> transfers program control to an error-trapping routine when an error is encountered. Individual BASIC instruction manuals should be consulted for additional details on the use of this statement and the programming of subsequent error-trapping routines. There is considerable variation in the way different BASIC implementations handle error trapping, and caution is necessary. I will point out, however, that error trapping sometimes can lead to problems, particularly if the trapping routine is not reset upon interrupting or ending a program run, which allows subsequent keyboard errors to be transferred to the trap where they may cause the machine to "hang" or resume execution unexpectedly. Apple Integer BASIC does not provide the ON ERROR GOTO... statement.

ON <expression> GOSUB <line numbers> and **ON <expression> GOTO <line numbers>** are conditional multiple-line branches in program execution that depend upon the evaluation of <expression> to direct the branch. If the value of the expression is, say, three, the branch will be to the third line number specified in the list. If <expression> evaluates to zero or greater than the number of line numbers in the list, most BASICs allow execution to continue with the next executable statement following the ON...GOSUB... or ON... GOTO... statement. If <expression> evaluates to a negative number or a number greater than 255, most BASICs display an error message, usually "illegal function call." Apple Integer BASIC does not provide these two statements; instead, it uses "computed" GOSUBs and GOTOs.

OPEN<mode>,[#]<f>,<file name>,[<reclgth>] is the BASIC-80 syntax to "open" a disk file for output to or input from that file. The <mode> is "O" for a sequential output file, "I" for a sequential input file, or "R" for a random-access input/output file. The <f> is an integer expression from 1 to 15 that remains associated with the particular file for all other disk operations until the file is closed. The <file name> is a string expression that must conform to the individual system's requirements for naming disk files. The optional <reclgth> is an integer expression that sets the record length of random files and has a default value of 128 bytes.

The syntax of the OPEN statement is different for virtually every BASIC implementation. Apple Integer BASIC and Applesoft impose completely different requirements on the OPEN statement and all disk operations, so users of those and other systems need to follow the examples in the manuals as closely as possible until a good working familiarity with the methods and approaches is achieved.

OPTION BASE <n> is a rather useful statement available under BASIC-80 but is not provided by other Microsoft or Apple BASICs. The value of <n> can be set to either zero or one, thereby setting the lowest value of the subscripts for all array variables. When using array variables, a statement such as DIM A(20) actually allows 21 variables from A(0) through A(20). With the option base set to one, only variables A(1) through A(20) are allowed, freeing some memory for programmers who prefer not to use the zero element of an array.

POKE I,J writes or "pokes" the integer value J into memory location I (also an integer value). This is particularly useful in passing values back and forth between a BASIC program and an assembly-language subroutine, as well as for loading such subroutines, storing data in an efficient manner, and so on. Whether I or J is decimal, hexadecimal, or octal is a function of the BASIC implementation in use, but the overall function and syntax remain the same. Under Apple Integer BASIC and Applesoft, POKE statements are used quite frequently to set parameters for tone-generating routines, set game-control outputs, switch graphics pages, move back and forth from text to graphics, and so on. While it's possible never to use a POKE statement on some machines, it's almost unavoidable on the Apple II.

PRINT [<expression list>] outputs data to a terminal display. PRINT and LPRINT function identically except for the destination of the output. If the <expression list> is omitted, a blank line is printed; if it is included, the values are printed in the format specified. BASIC-80 divides a line into "print zones" of 14 characters each, and a comma between items of the <expression list> forces an automatic tab to the start of the next print zone. A semicolon between items causes them to be printed one after another without tabbing or spacing (unless a space is a part of the expression). If the <expression list> ends with a comma or semicolon, the next PRINT statement encountered continues printing on the same line, spacing or tabbing as appropriate. The defined print zones and subsequent tabbing may differ from one BASIC to another. Many BASICs also provide a PRINT USING statement to format displayed outputs, but, like the LPRINT USING, the details of the formatting vary so widely that attempting to define them in this book would be futile.

Many BASICs allow a convenient shorthand keyboard entry for PRINT, namely a question mark (?). For example, typing ?A is equivalent to typing PRINT A. When listed, a program will show PRINT, not the ? symbol, so it's a fast and easy way to enter a complete command with a single keystroke. Many BASICs also allow things like L? for LPRINT, ?# for PRINT#, and so on.

PRINT#<f>,<expression list> under Microsoft-style BASICs is the opposite of INPUT# and writes data to a sequential disk file already opened for output. The <expression list> must contain both the data and the formatting characters necessary to assure proper data retrieval from the disk at a later time. An "image" of the data is written just as it would be displayed on a terminal screen, so care is needed to "delimit" individual items. Numeric items generally are delimited by semicolons or commas (commas write extra spaces). String items must be separated by semicolons in the list and, in some cases, explicitly delimited by printing separating commas or even quotation marks as part of the data stream. Apple Integer BASIC and Applesoft operating under DOS impose other requirements on printing data to a disk file with a simple PRINT statement, such as no "#" symbol and procedures to define the points at which such statements refer to disk or display printouts.

PUT[#]<f>[,<record number>] is provided by Microsoft BASICs to write a record from the random-file buffer to a random-access disk file. The buffer must have been fielded and the data must have been loaded into that buffer by an LSET or RSET statement. Once again, it is essential that the BASIC instruction manual for the individual system be consulted for the details on handling random-access files. Apple Integer BASIC and Applesoft, as modified by Apple DOS, do not have an equivalent statement; their procedure for writing data to a random-access file is substantially different from that employed under Microsoft implementations.

RANDOMIZE [<n>] "reseeds" the random-number generator so it doesn't return the same sequence of random numbers each time the program is executed. Since this statement normally is used with expression <n> omitted, program execution is suspended until a seed value is input from the keyboard in response to a displayed prompt. Under BASIC-80, reseeding with the same number for different program runs results in the same random-number sequence. Many BASICs do not have a RANDOMIZE statement, but its absence can be remedied easily with a few simple program statements as described in Chapter 5. Some BASICs reset the random-number generator to the start of the same sequence each time a RUN or LOAD is executed; others allow the generator to continue from the point of last interruption. This affects the way programs function in that the first method allows outputs to be duplicated, while the second prevents exact duplication unless the entire procedure from machine start-up is repeated exactly.

READ <variable list> reads the values from DATA statements and assigns those values to the specified variables. The assignment is on a one-to-one basis, so there must be as many values in DATA statements as there are variables in READ statements to avoid an "out of data" error message. READ statements access DATA statements in sequential order, and multiple READ statements resume accessing data where the previous read stopped. Refer to the RESTORE statement for additional information.

REM <remark> allows explanatory remarks to be inserted in a program. REM statements are not executed, but they are included in program listings. Anything typed on a program line following a REM statement is ignored during program execution. As was pointed out in Chapter 2, however, REM statements consume a lot of memory space and may contribute significantly to a slowdown in program execution because they have to be interpreted as nonexecutable statements. At least one byte is used for the REM, plus an additional byte for each character of the remark, including spaces. While remarks do aid later readability of program listings, their cost in terms of space and speed makes it advisable to avoid or at least minimize REM statements in a program. Incidentally, some versions of BASIC allow another character such as the apostrophe (') as an abbreviated form of the REM statement.

RENUM [[<new>][, <old>][, <increment>]], is a direct command issued from the keyboard and is not used as a statement within a program. Depending upon the version of BASIC and the syntax required, the command reassigns line numbers for all or part of any program. Typically, it allows both the new starting number and the increment to be specified, and it defaults to line numbers beginning with 10 and increasing by 10 when no parameters are assigned. I've found this particularly useful in checking a program for GOTO, GOSUB, THEN, and other transfers not matched to line numbers by storing a copy of the program on disk, giving a RENUM 1,,1 command, and allowing the interpreter to print a list of lines containing an unreferenced transfer. Upon reloading the original program version from disk, I can edit the lines affected to provide proper transfer destinations. Once again, the form, syntax, and availability of the command may vary from one BASIC to another, while Apple BASICs require running a separate renumbering program.

RESTORE [<line>] allows DATA statements to be reread from a specified line number. If used, the <line> must be that of a DATA statement. If the <line> is omitted, the restoration defaults to the first DATA statement in the program. In either case, the next DATA item read will be the first item on the line in question. Not all BASICs allow a line number to be specified; in those that do not, the RESTORE statement always resets to the first item of the first DATA statement. That situation forces the user to structure DATA statements carefully so that the program can "read past" unwanted data items with a FOR...NEXT loop after a RESTORE. BASICs not providing a DATA statement (such as Apple Integer BASIC) obviously do not provide a RESTORE statement.

RESUME continues program execution after an error-trapping routine has been performed. This statement usually can take one of four forms, namely RESUME, RESUME 0, RESUME NEXT, and RESUME <line>, depending upon where the program execution is to continue from the point of the error condition. Like the ON ERRR GOTO... statement and the ERR and ERL variables, the use of this statement depends upon the way a specific version of BASIC handles error-trapping routines. Special care is necessary when using the BASCOM compiler because any RESUME <line number> statement in the program increases the size of the compiled file (to add line numbers) and slows the overall execution of the machine-language program. Additional caution may be needed if the detected error is in a FOR...NEXT loop; Applesoft, for example, requires that the loop be restarted at the FOR... statement, not in the middle or at the NEXT statement.

RUN <program>[,R] loads a program file from disk and runs it. The <program> name must be exactly the same as the name used when the file was saved on the disk and must comply with the requirements of the individual computer system. The current contents of memory are deleted before loading the new program. If the optional R (BASIC-80 only) is omitted, all disk files are closed; if the R is specified, the disk files remain open. An alternative to this command on certain systems and under certain conditions is the CHAIN statement, with or without a COMMON statement to transfer variables from one program to another.

BASICs handle the definition of the disk drive in the same ways already described for the LOAD command—as part of the <program> name under CP/M, as a separate added entry under other BASICs, or as part of the slot, disk, drive, and volume specification under Apple Integer BASIC and Applesoft. Apple DOS also provides a BRUN version with slightly different syntax for binary files.

SAVE <program>[,A][,P] is the opposite of LOAD or RUN, serving to save the program named by <program> on disk. Under

BASIC-80, the optional A denotes that the file is to be saved in ASCII rather than compressed form, and the P denotes that is to be encoded in "protected" form so that it cannot be listed at a later time. Like LOAD and RUN, the <program> name must be one that is acceptable to the individual system. The syntax of the SAVE program may differ from one system to another. Specifying the drive number on which to save the file also parallels the LOAD and RUN commands, with the drive being a part of the name under CP/M, a separate item under some other BASICs, and part of the slot, drive, and volume parameters under Apple versions. The Apple versions also provide a BSAVE version for binary files with still another syntax to specify the starting memory location and the length of a machine-language program.

STOP prints a "break at line..." message on the terminal, immediately terminates program execution, and returns control to BASIC's command level. Unlike the END statement, STOP does not close disk files. Because the disk-file handling differs, STOP and END statements are not totally interchangeable, even though many programmers often treat them as being the same. Apple Integer BASIC does not provide a STOP statement; an END statement must be used to avoid an error message.

SWAP <variable>,<variable> exchanges the values of two variables. Both variables must be of the same type, such as integer, string, and so on. When a particular BASIC doesn't provide this statement, the function is easily accomplished by using an intermediate "holding" variable. For example, assume that variables A(1) and A(2) are to be swapped and that variable B is unused. The exchange of values can be accomplished with a simple B=A(1):A(1)=A(2):A(2)=B sequence equivalent to SWAP A(1),A(2).

WAIT <address>,I[,J] provides a means of halting program execution until a certain condition is met. For instance, it could be used to pause until a key is pressed on the keyboard or until a certain response is received from a printer. Essentially, the <address> is an I/O port number on some computers or a memory address in an Apple II and must contain a specific value or the statement loops back on itself. Refer to the manuals on specific systems for descriptions of the logical comparisons being made. The nature of this instruction makes it quite easy to enter an "infinite" loop from which the machine never can escape; the only way out is to reset or restart the entire system with the loss of any program or data in memory. This instruction should be used with extreme caution, and any program containing a WAIT statement should be saved on disk *before* any attempt is made at execution so that restarting the system won't cause complete loss of the program.

WHILE <expression>...<loop statements>...WEND executes a program loop as long as a specified condition is true. The WHILE...WEND loop is similar to a FOR...NEXT loop except in the way that its iterations are controlled. Usually used in sorting and similar operations, the WHILE...WEND loop seems to have a slight speed advantage over a FOR...NEXT loop, but it can be replaced easily by a FOR...NEXT loop or even an IF...THEN... conditional branch in any BASIC that does not support WHILE...WEND. Like the FOR...NEXT loops, these usually can be nested to any desired level, limited only by available memory.

WIDTH [LPRINT] <expression> sets the printed line width to the specified number of characters. If the optional LPRINT is omitted, the statement sets the width of the terminal device; if it is included, the width is set on the printout device. In BASIC-80, if the integer <expression> is 255, the line length is "infinite" and long strings may be printed without having extraneous Carriage Returns or Line Feeds generated by the BASIC interpreter. Not all BASICs offer the WIDTH LPRINT option, and many of them make it extremely difficult to set printer width from within a program; others have different restrictions on the width that may be set and may or may not allow infinite strings. Apple Integer BASIC and Applesoft do not provide a WIDTH statement at all; they require that a "text window" be sized by completely different means.

WRITE#<f>,<expression list> writes data to a sequential disk file opened for output. The <expression list> may contain string or numeric expressions, but the items must be separated by commas. This statement differs from PRINT# in that WRITE# does the formatting tasks automatically—commas are inserted between the items as they are written to the disk file, and strings are delimited by quotation marks. BASIC-80 also offers a WRITE[<expression list>] statement without the "#" symbol or file number <f> to output to the display terminal; with numeric outputs it functions like a PRINT statement, but with string outputs it adds commas and delimiting quotation marks. Under Apple DOS, only the disk-file version is available, with a slightly different syntax and some differences in the operation.

Intrinsic Functions

ABS(n) returns the absolute value of n, where n is either a constant or an evaluated expression. The absolute value always is a positive number, so ABS(n) returns n if n is positive and –n if n is negative. To illustrate, ABS(15*(2)) and ABS(15*(–2)) both return the value 30. Two easy substitutions for ABS(N) are the statements IF N<0 THEN N=–N and IF N<0 THEN N=–1*N.

ASC(S$) returns the numeric ASCII value (an integer) of the *first* character of string S$. As an example, ASC("A") and ASC("ABCDEF") both return decimal 65, which is the ASCII code for the letter "A." While S$ may be a quoted literal string, a string variable, or an evaluated string function, S$ must not be null if an error message is to be avoided.

ATN(n) returns the arc tangent of n, where n is expressed *in radians* and may be either a constant or an evaluated expression. Most BASICs require that the arc tangent always be a single-precision number, never double-precision or integer. Since Apple Integer BASIC allows only integers, the ATN() function is not provided. Arc tangent values always are in the range from −pi/2 to +pi/2.

CDBL(n), CINT(n), and CSNG(n) all convert the value of n from one "data type" to another. CDBL(n) converts n to a double-precision number, CINT(n) converts it to an integer, and CSNG(n) converts it to single precision. The argument n may be a constant or an evaluated expression. Given a single-precision variable N! with the value 3.14159, the statement N#=CDBL(N!) might set N# equal to 3.141589879989624, while N%=CINT(N!) sets N% equal to an integer 3. On many BASICs, it's possible to duplicate the functions with simpler statements such as N#=N! or N%=N!, but there may be cases in particular BASICs where the result may be other than that desired. In years of programming, however, I've yet to encounter a situation where I gained any advantage in using the CDBL(), CINT(), or CSNG() functions instead of a simple equality statement between variables of two types.

CHR$(n) returns a single-character string having the numeric ASCII code n. For example, CHR$(65) returns the string "A". This function is used most often to send special characters to either the terminal or the printer, and to evaluate certain string relationships. For instance, LPRINT CHR$(8) sends a Backspace character to the printer, while PRINT CHR$(7) "rings the bell" on the terminal device. Typically, BASICs don't accept direct keyboard entry of "nonprinting" characters, including all those having ASCII codes from decimal 0 through 31, so the CHR$() function is the only method available to use those characters within a program.

An exception is Apple Integer BASIC, which does accept nonprinting characters as part of a string but does not display them on the screen; it also has no CHR$() function. Under Apple Integer BASIC and Applesoft, particular codes have special meanings, such as Control-D (ASCII code 4), which is used as a directive to DOS as part of the disk-handling operations. To set a string variable D$ equal to a Control-D, Applesoft would use D$=CHR$(4). Apple Integer BASIC would use D$="", where the nonprinting character does not display but is present as D$="[Control-D]".

COS(n) returns the cosine of the angle n, where n is expressed *in radians* and may be either a constant or an evaluated expression. Most BASICs perform the cosine computation in single precision. Since Apple Integer BASIC does not allow real numbers, cosine calculation is impossible and the function is not provided.

CVI(S$), CVS(S$), and CVD(S$) convert strings to numeric values. Under Microsoft BASICs, all data stored in random-access disk files is in string form, and those strings must be converted to retrieve the numeric data. CVI() returns an integer, CVS() returns a single-precision value, and CVD() returns a double-precision value. To illustrate, a literal string might be stored as "501" on disk. It would be retrieved from disk as a string variable, say A$, and the integer value 501 then could be set into variable A% by A%=CVI(A$). BASICs providing these functions also specify the size of the string; under BASIC-80 it takes a two-byte string to hold an integer number, a four-byte string to hold a single-precision number, and an eight-byte string to hold a double-precision number. Those string sizes have a direct effect on both memory and disk-space utilization, with integer equivalents requiring much less space than other numeric types. The reverse functions to set numeric values into packed strings are performed by MKI$(), MKS$(), and MKD$().

EOF(<f>) is used under Microsoft BASICs, to return a true (−1) value when the end of sequential file number <f> is reached while reading data. The function tests for end-of-file to avoid attempting to input data past that point. Assume you have a disk file with 180 data items and use a loop to read those items. On the 181st read attempt, you'll get an error message and your program will halt. However, if you precede the reading loop with a statement like IF EOR(1) THEN..., the program will branch to the destination of the THEN immediately upon reaching the end of the file. If that destination is the next executable line following the reading loop, you avoid the error message, and program execution continues normally.

EXP(n) returns the value of e to the power of n, where e is the base of natural logarithms and has an approximate value of 2.71828. Under Applesoft, EXP(1) yields 2.71828183 as e^1, EXP(2) yields 6.3890561 as e^2, and so on. BASICs differ in the way they handle "overflow" (a number too large) in this function. Under Applesoft, X=EXP(100) will yield an overflow error message and halt program execution. Under Microsoft's BASIC-80, X=EXP(100) will display the overflow message but will continue program execution with X having "machine infinity" (the largest number possible) as its value. Again, the EXP() function requires real numbers, so it is not available with an integer-only language such as Apple Integer BASIC.

FIX(n) returns a value that is the truncated integer portion of n equivalent to SGN(n)*INT(ABS(n)). The function is not available under Apple Integer BASIC or Applesoft. When dealing with positive numbers only, FIX() and INT() operate identically. When dealing with negative numbers, INT() may return the next lower number, but FIX() does not. To illustrate, consider the following statements and their returned values under BASIC-80:

```
PRINT FIX(59.88)       returns  59
PRINT FIX(-59.88)      returns -59
PRINT INT(59.88)       returns  59
PRINT INT(-59.88)      returns -6Ø
PRINT CINT(59.88)      returns  6Ø
PRINT CINT(-59.88)     returns -6Ø
```

FRE(n) or **FRE(S$)** returns the number of memory bytes not being used by BASIC and the program under execution. Although n and S$ are dummy arguments, using a string as the argument, such as FRE("A"), forces a garbage collect before the number of free bytes is returned by some BASICs. Although many instruction manuals recommend the frequent use of a FRE() statement to force the string-space garbage collection, this can lead to real trouble and a major loss of computer efficiency. I'll be presenting considerably more information on this subject later. The FRE() function is not allowed at all under Apple Integer BASIC. Under Applesoft, BASIC-80, and some other BASICs, both FRE(n) and FRE(S$) return the same number. Under Microsoft BASIC Revision 4.51 and other BASICs allowing string-space allocation, FRE(n) returns only the free nonstring space, while FRE(S$) returns the free string space remaining in the memory "block" specifically allocated by a CLEAR <n> statement.

HEX$(n) returns a *string* representation of the hexadecimal equivalent to decimal n. On BASICs providing this function, n usually is rounded or truncated to an integer value before computing the hexadecimal equivalent. To illustrate, the statements PRINT HEX$(15) and PRINT HEX$(15.2) both return the string "F" that is the hex representation of decimal 15, while PRINT HEX$(16) or PRINT HEX$(15.9) both return the string "10". Like so many others, this function is not available with Apple Integer BASIC or Applesoft.

**INKEY$** is available in BASIC-80 to accept a single-character string from the keyboard (or a null if no character is pending). The character is not echoed to the display. This function is roughly equivalent to the GET statement in Applesoft except that GET halts program execution pending a response, while the INKEY$ function assumes a null and continues execution. The following two routines serve identical purposes, with the one on the left being for Applesoft and the one of the right being for BASIC-80. Both display the word "DONE" when any key is struck.

```
100 GET A$
200 PRINT "DONE"
```

```
100 A$=INKEY$: IF A$="" THEN 100
200 PRINT "DONE"
```

INPUT$(n[,[#]m]) is available under BASIC-80 to return a *string* of n characters from the keyboard or from a disk file. For example, INPUT$(20,#1) returns a 20-character string from the sequential disk file previously opened for *input* as file #1. INPUT$(1) returns a single character typed at the keyboard without echoing it on the display. It happens that INPUT$(1) under BASIC-80 functions very much like the Applesoft GET statement, halting program execution until a key is struck. Its advantage over the GET statement is that more than one character may be required, so an INSTR$(5) halts execution until five characters have been typed. The following routines illustrate ways to suspend a program temporarily until a key is struck; Applesoft routines are on the left, and equivalent BASIC-80 routines are on the right.

```
100 PRINT"PRESS ANY KEY"
102 GET A$
. . .

100 PRINT"<C> TO CONTINUE"
102 GET A$
104 IF A$<>"C" THEN 102
. . .
```

```
100 PRINT"PRESS ANY KEY"
102 A$=INPUT$(1)
. . .

100 PRINT"<C> TO CONTINUE"
102 A$=INPUT$(1)
104 IF A$<>"C" THEN 102
. . .
```

INSTR([n,]S$,S1$) returns the numeric position at which string S1$ is found within string S$. The optional n, which must be between 1 and 255, specifies the starting position in string S$ at which the search starts. If S1$ is not found in S$, a zero is returned. S$ and S1$ may be string variables, string expressions, or string literals depending upon what is necessary in the program. A number of BASICs do not provide this function, and it will receive considerably more attention in Chapter 4. When available, the function is quite useful in programs requiring a lot of string handling and sorting. For example, to search a long list of words in array S$(.) for those containing only the letter combination "AW", it's only necessary to construct a loop containing the statement IF INSTR(S$(X),"AW") THEN PRINT S$(X) to obtain the necessary list.

INT(n) returns the largest integer less than or equal to n. When negative numbers are involved, the "largest integer" is the next *lower* number, so some care is required. For example, INT(112.34) returns 112, but INT(−112.34) returns −113. If negative numbers are expected and the next lower number is not desired, it will be necessary to use the FIX() function (if available) or to devise your own procedure.

LEFT$(S$,n) returns a string consisting of the leftmost n characters of S$, where n is an integer constant, variable, or expression. The value of n must be within the range of 0 to 255; if n is greater than the length of S$, the entire string is returned, *without* any additional spaces being added. If n is set equal to zero, it specifies a zero-length string, so the function returns a null string. To illustrate, assume S$ is the string "ABCD". The function LEFT$(S$,2) returns "AB", a LEFT$(S$,6) returns "ABCD" *not* "ABCD␣␣" or "␣␣ABCD", and a LEFT$(S$,0) returns the null string "". Compare this to the MID$() and RIGHT$() functions.

LEN(S$) returns the number of characters in string S$, including all nonprinting characters and spaces. For example, LEN("ABC␣DEF␣GHI") returns a value of 11 for the nine letters and two spaces. Most BASICs will not allow the length of any string to exceed 255 characters, and it's often important to determine the length of individual strings to prevent exceeding that maximum during concatenation or other handling techniques. Some BASICs may impose a maximum string length even shorter than 255 characters.

Apple Integer BASIC does not provide a LEN() function and handles strings differently than many other implementations. In that version, every string variable must have a length equal to or shorter than the length specified in a DIM statement. An Apple Integer BASIC program with a DIM A$(10) statement generates an error message if you try to set A$ to a string of more than 10 characters. Furthermore, with no DIM statement for the particular string-variable name, Apple Integer BASIC will not allow the variable to be assigned a string of any length.

LOC(f) is available under Microsoft BASICs to locate the next record number that will be used in a random-access disk file if a GET or PUT statement is executed. When applied to a sequential-access disk file, LOC() returns the number of sectors read or written since the file was opened. The file number f must be an integer constant that corresponds to the number under which the file was opened for data transfers.

LOF(f) is used by Microsoft BASICs to determine the last record written to a random-access file. Note that this differs from LOC(), which determines the next record to be written or read. LOF() may not be used on a sequential file, or an error message and program halt result. Again, f must be an integer constant matching the file number under which the random-access file was opened for data transfer.

LOG(n) returns the natural logarithm of n, where n may be a real constant, a single- or double-precision variable, or an expression. However, n must be greater than zero to avoid an error message. Since Apple Integer BASIC does not allow real numbers, it contains no LOG() function and is incapable of computing logarithms.

LPOS(n) returns the position of the printing "pointer" within the *line printer buffer*, which may but usually doesn't correspond to the physical position of the printhead of the line printer. The argument n is a dummy constant, variable, or expression that must be provided in the program but isn't used by the function. Since the Apple II has no specific provision for a line printer, no LPOS() function is provided by Integer BASIC or Applesoft; however, it is available under CP/M and BASIC-80 as provided with the SoftCard. Thus far, I've never found a practical use for this function and have chosen to ignore it altogether in my own programming.

MID$(S$,n[,m]) returns a string of length m that is taken from string S$ starting at position n. Both n and m may be integer constants, variables, or expressions, but the values must be between 1 and 255. If m is omitted or is greater than the number of characters from position n to the end of the string, all of the rightmost characters starting at position n are returned. If n is greater than the length of S$, a null string is returned. Assume S$ contains "ABCD". The functions MID$(S$,2), MID$(S$,2,3), and MID$(S$,2,10) all return the string "BCD". Meanwhile, MID$(S$,2,1) returns "B", and MID$(S$,2,2) returns "BC". Note that when used as a function, MID$() differs from the MID$() used as a program statement and defined earlier in this chapter. In one case, a string is returned; in the other, a string is altered. Compare this function with the LEFT$() and RIGHT$() functions.

MKI$(<integer>), **MKS$(<single-precision>)**, and **MKD$(<double-precision>)** convert numeric values to strings for transfer to a random-access disk file through the random-file buffer utilized by Microsoft BASIC. Any numeric value to be stored in such a file must be converted, using one of these functions as part of an LSET or RSET statement. MKI$() uses a two-byte string for integers, MKS$() uses a four-byte string for single-precision real numbers, and MKD$() uses an eight-byte string for double-precision numbers. These functions are the complements of the CVI(), CVS(), and CVD() functions described earlier.

OCT$(n) functions in the same manner as HEX$() except that it returns a *string* representing the octal equivalent of the decimal n. The value of n is rounded or truncated (depending upon the BASIC) before computing the octal value.

POS(n) returns the numeric horizontal position of the display-screen cursor. The (n) usually is required, but it is a dummy argument and may have any value. Horizontal screen positions, corresponding to column numbers, range from one at the leftmost edge to the maximum width of the screen. This function is useful to keep successive print operations from exceeding a specified partial- or full-screen width, and a statement such as IF POS(1) > 40 THEN PRINT CHR$(13) forces a carriage return if the cursor position is at or beyond column 40.

RIGHT$(S$,n) returns a string consisting of the rightmost n characters of S$, where n is an integer constant, a variable, or an expression. The value of n must be within the range of 0 to 255; if n is greater than the length of S$, the entire string is returned, and that string is *not* "padded" or filled with spaces. If n is equal to zero, it specifies a string of zero length so a null string is returned. Assuming that S$ contains "ABCD", the function RIGHT$(S$,2) returns "CD", and RIGHT$(S$,6) returns "ABCD" and *not* "˽˽ABCD" or "ABCD˽˽". The function RIGHT$(S$,0) returns the null string "". Compare this with the LEFT$() and MID$() functions.

RND[(n)] returns a random number between 0 and 1. There are considerable differences among different BASICs in the way the random-number generator is reseeded and the range of values returned. Under BASIC-80, unless the random-number generator is reseeded by a RANDOMIZE statement or if it is reseeded with the same value, the same sequence of numbers is returned each time the program is run. If n is less than zero, the same sequence always is used regardless of the reseeding. If n equals zero, the last number generated is repeated. If n is greater than zero or is omitted, the next random number in the sequence is generated. Under BASIC-80, the (n) is optional, so a simple RND performs the same function as RND(1); most other BASICs require the complete RND(n) form to avoid a "syntax error" message and program halt. Earlier, I mentioned the problems that may result when one BASIC can return a value of 1.0 while another can return only values less than 1.0, or when one does numerical rounding and another does truncating. I'll be giving this function even more attention later.

SGN(n) returns a numeric value representing the sign of the constant, variable, or expression n. If n is greater than zero (positive), SGN(n) returns a 1. If n equals zero, SGN(n) returns a 0. If n is less than zero (negative), SGN(n) returns a −1. While this function provides a shortcut for program branching based on the sign of a number rather than its value, I usually prefer to use IF . . . THEN . . . comparisons against a zero value to achieve the same thing. To illustrate, the following two program statements perform exactly the same branches:

```
1000 ON SGN(A)+2 GOTO 2000,2010,2020
1000 IF A<0 THEN 2000 ELSE IF A=0 THEN 2010 ELSE 2020
```

SIN(n) returns the sine of angle n, where n is a constant, variable, or expression that expresses the angle *in radians*. For most BASICs, the SIN( ) function is calculated as a single-precision real number, and the absence of real numbers under Apple Integer BASIC and some other "stripped" BASICs prevents the implementation of this function or the computation of any trigonometric functions.

SPACE$(n) returns a string of n spaces. Whether a constant, a variable, or an expression, the value of n is rounded or truncated to an integer and must range from 0 to 255 or the maximum string length of the BASIC being used. The program statements S$="‸", S$=CHR$(32), and S$=SPACE$(1) are equivalent methods of setting S$ as a string containing only a single space. With short strings of six or fewer spaces, the memory-space and speed advantage seems to lie with the first method without the SPACE() function. However, when long strings of spaces are needed, the SPACE$( ) function offers a significant advantage in memory savings and a slight edge in execution speed. The function also is useful where the number of spaces to be printed is dependent upon the value of some variable, say within a FOR. . . NEXT loop.

SPC(n) prints n spaces (blanks) and may appear only in PRINT and LPRINT statements. The number of spaces, n, may be specified as a constant, a variable, or an expression, but the value of n must be in the range of 0 to 255. If a given BASIC limits maximum string length to less than 255 characters, n also is limited to the same maximum. Like the SPACE$() function, the SPC() function offers no real advantage in memory savings or execution speed unless more than six to eight spaces are being printed. The statement PRINT SPC(2);"ABLE" offers no advantage over the statement PRINT " ABLE".

SQR(n) returns the square root of n, where n is an integer or real constant, variable, or expression having a value equal to or greater than zero. Generally, the square root is a single-precision number, so the computation is unavailable on Apple Integer BASIC or any other BASIC not providing real numbers. Computers are incapable of handling "imaginary" roots, so an error message and program halt occur if n is negative.

STR$(n) returns a string representation of the value of numeric n. This function is the complement of the VAL() function. The numeric n may be a constant, a variable, or an expression and may evaluate as an integer or real number. Under Microsoft BASIC, the string representation has a leading space, so STR$(A) where A=10 returns " 10". Under Applesoft, there is no leading space, so STR$(A) returns "10". When a leading space is provided, some care must be exercised in using the STR$() function, particularly in printing values to the display screen or the line printer, where the leading space may not be desirable. One way to eliminate the problem is with a program statement of the form S$=MID$(STR$(N),2) instead of S$=STR$(N). However, do not attempt that with Applesoft, or you will lose the first digit in the string.

STRING$(n,m) or **STRING$(n,S$)** returns a string of n characters, each of which either has ASCII code m or is the first character of string S$. For example, STRING$(3,65) and STRING$(3,"ABC") both return "AAA". This function is particularly useful for printing long strings of the same character such as a row of asterisks (ASCII code 42) across the width of an 80-column screen, where PRINT STRING$(80,42) would do the job nicely and quickly.

TAB(n) spaces (tabulates) to print position n, where n is a constant, variable, or expression rounded or truncated to an integer value. This function may appear only in PRINT and LPRINT statements. The value of n must be in the range of 1 to 255 or the maximum string length for the BASIC being used. If it is greater than the maximum printing position, a TAB(n) causes the device to print on the next line. "Overtabbing" to the next line sometimes produces unexpected results, with the beginning of the next printed item being somewhere other than the left margin, so some caution is required when formatted outputs are desired.

Be careful when using the TAB() function on an Apple II running BASIC-80. Tabbing beyond column 40 causes some strange printouts. The problem is aggravated by setting an infinite line length with a WIDTH 255 or WIDTH LPRINT 255 statement. For example, the line LPRINT TAB (20); "A"; TAB(70); "B" might print "A" at position 20 and "B" at position 91, summing the desired tab position with the printheads prior position on the line.

TAN(n) returns the tangent of angle n, where n is a constant, variable, or expression that evaluates as an integer or real number and represents the angle *in radians*. Most BASICs calculate the tangent as a single-precision number, and the unavailability of real numbers under Apple Integer BASIC and some other BASICs prohibits the use of the TAN() function or any equivalent computation. BASICs differ in the way they handle "overflow" of the tangent. Some display an overflow message and halt program execution; others display the message but continue execution using "machine infinity" as the requested value.

USR[< n >](x) calls a user's assembly-language subroutine defined elsewhere in the program with the DEF USR. . . statement. The < n > is a single digit from 0 to 9 that indicates which user subroutine is being called (a USR0 is assumed if < n > is omitted). The argument, x, is used to pass a parameter to the subroutine by means of a constant, variable, or expression. As already indicated in the description of the DEF USR statement, Applesoft uses the form USR (x), where x passes the parameters, and the jump to the starting address of the subroutine must be contained in hexadecimal memory addresses 0A through 0C. Typically, a programmer might set up several subroutines and store them in an otherwise unused area of memory. Under a Microsoft BASIC, each would have a numerical designation and could be called as USR0 through USR9. Under Applesoft, the programmer has to "poke" the jump to the starting address into the three memory locations before calling any given subroutine.

VAL(S$) returns the numeric value of string S$ and is the complement of the STR$() function. VAL() strips any leading spaces, tabs, and linefeeds from the string before evaluating it, so the leading space added by the STR$() function in some BASICs need not be a concern in converting the string back to a numeric value. If the first nonblank character encountered in the string is other than a numeric character, VAL() returns a zero as the value. For example, X=VAL (" 1.234") returns with X equal to 1.234. However, X=VAL("ABCD") returns with X equal to zero. The numeric value of a null string also is set to zero.

VARPTR(< variable >) gives the decimal memory address of the first data byte associated with a specific < variable >. Most often, this is used to obtain the memory location of a variable or the start (zero element) of an array so that address may be passed as a parameter to an assembly-language subroutine, which can, in turn, access the data beginning at the specified address. As an example, the program statement Y=USR1(VARPTR(A(0))) could be used to obtain a value for Y calculated by subroutine USR1 from the contents of array A(.); upon calling USR1, the starting address of the array is passed, and the subroutine then can access all necessary elements of the array from that starting address. To avoid an illegal function error, the < variable > must have been assigned a value prior to calling VARPTR( ). Furthermore, no new variables should be assigned between calling VARPTR() and using the address returned because such assignments change array addresses.

This function also has a second form, namely VARPTR(#<f>), in which the value returned when <f> is the number of a sequential file provides the starting address of the disk I/O buffer assigned to that file. When <f> is the number of a random-access file, the function returns the starting address of the "field" buffer assigned. There are some variations from BASIC to BASIC in the operation of this function, usually associated with the type of disk-operating system involved, so the user must pay special attention to the instruction manuals for the proper use of the VARPTR( ) function.

VPOS(n) functions much like POS(), except that it returns the current vertical position of the cursor on the screen. Although (n) must be present, it is a dummy argument and may have any value. When available, the function makes it easy to back up the cursor and erase the previous line since that line is always VPOS(0)–1 after any "completed" print statement. The POS( ) and VPOS( ) functions may be used together to keep track of the position of any printed item on the screen, allowing immediate return to that position at a later time for overwriting a new printout.

The "BASIC" Choice

In this chapter, I've tried to demonstrate that there are a great many differences among BASICs used on various machines. In doing so, I've covered only those versions currently available on my own machines, and I have not included all of the commands, statements, functions, and operational differences even among those. There are two points that must be repeated.

First, read your manuals carefully, especially when you go to bring up a new machine or a new version of BASIC. While it's easy to find gross errors such as an unrecognizable statement, the subtle differences in the ways languages handle numbers, statements, and functions can be very difficult to isolate. Semantics in the manuals can mean the difference between a successful program run and an unsuccessful one. For example, a manual that says a function returns a value "between" two numbers may handle the function differently from one that says the value is "from" one number "to" or "through" another number. If in doubt, construct a simple test loop and try it out before you incorporate the item into a larger program.

Second, remember that the simplest form of a program statement may or may not be the most effective in terms of execution time or memory consumption. If you'll recall, I've already pointed out that the statement X=Y*Y*Y is more effective than X=Y∧3, but that S$="∧∧∧" is more effective than S$=SPACE$(3) or S$=STRING$(3,32). Again, test your approaches carefully before you build them into large programs. It's far easier to avoid using an ineffective approach than it is to correct it once it has become an integral part of a program.

In the next chapter, I'll be taking several of the individual statements and functions I've introduced in this chapter and explaining them in far more detail. I'll be showing you some of the more common and costly misuses of particular items, alternate ways of doing the same things, and some alternatives you may have if a given item is not available under your particular version of BASIC.

Some "BASIC" Techniques

Chapter 3 was devoted to brief descriptions of the ways in which BASIC languages may differ from one computer system to another. It pointed out some of the more common problem areas and promised further details and amplifications of questionable items. In this chapter, I will provide many more of those details in my attempt to give you a better understanding of the language and the things you can do to squeeze more computing power and efficiency from it.

As I've already explained, Microsoft's BASIC-80 interpreter is promoted as an ANSI standard version of BASIC. It's available on a number of different computers, although obtaining it may require adding special hardware such as the Microsoft SoftCard on the Apple II. Quite often, a disk containing BASIC-80 also has Microsoft Revision 4.51, sometimes called either OBASIC or MBASIC. Therefore, I'll use the general Microsoft approach to BASIC as the baseline from which I will be developing procedures and comparisons. While the comparisons I will present are applicable to many different BASICs, the execution times and percentages of change may vary from one to another.

You do have to be aware that other implementations such as Apple Integer BASIC, Applesoft, or the BASICs provided by other popular computers such as the TRS-80, Atari 800, or various Commodore models may or may not resemble the Microsoft versions and may or may not necessitate varying degrees of program modification to accommodate functional and operational differences. I'll have to leave it to you to interpret the information herein in terms of your own system capabilities. I remind you that, although the contents of this and subsequent chapters may appear intimidating at first, you probably will not have to apply each and every item to any one BASIC or any particular system. I have no way of knowing what system and what BASIC you are using, so I have to approach the subjects of program efficiency and program conversions from a "worst-case" point of view.

If you have a reasonable familiarity with your system and its BASIC, it should not be difficult to apply the information in these chapters. I hope that you'll find the material a valuable aid in writing your own programs and adapting programs from published sources so they run quickly and effectively. My aim is to provide you with the means of identifying and modifying commands, statements, and functions as necessary and developing alternative approaches when your system lacks a "standard" feature of some other system. I also want to get you into the habit of thinking in terms of programming efficiency; with the background I present, you then can proceed beyond the points at which I leave off.

Number-Handling Methods

The best place to begin considering the details of BASIC operation is with the way the language handles numbers. This book doesn't allow space for an exhaustive study of numerical handling and manipulations, but it is important for you to know that *different BASICs handle both numeric constants and variables in different ways.* The manner in which numbers are handled and the way a program is written to use those features directly affect the accuracy and efficiency of a program. Therefore you must be constantly aware of the requirements, restrictions, and limitations imposed by your particular system.

A Matter of Precision

In general, numeric constants and variables can be classified into either of two overall categories, namely *integers* and *real numbers.* To oversimplify the matter, a real number is one containing a decimal point, while an integer is a whole number with no decimal point. For example, the number 12 is an integer, but the number 12.0 is a real number. If you perform simple arithmetic operations in your head or with pencil and paper, you usually don't differentiate between 12 and 12.0—as far as you're concerned, the values are identical and the decimal portion of the latter one can be dropped without affecting the operations. However, a computer does differentiate between the two numbers, storing them differently in memory and using different arithmetic processes when manipulating them.

There are BASICs such as Applesoft that differentiate only between integers and real numbers. Some don't even allow it to go that far; Apple Integer BASIC allows the use of integers only and does not permit any real numbers or decimal points anywhere in its operations. Under Integer BASIC, no functions are provided for arithmetic operations requiring decimal values, and it is impossible to compute sines, cosines, tangents, square roots, logarithms, and similar values.

On the other hand, some BASICs subdivide real numbers for both constants and variables into *fixed-point, floating-point, single-precision,* and *double-precision* numbers. Microsoft versions, including BASIC-80, do exactly that. Yet all BASICs don't necessarily define the subgroups in exactly the same manner. Typically, a fixed-point number is a positive or negative number within a defined range of values, containing a decimal point, but not so large as to require representation in an exponential form similar to scientific notation. On many systems, fixed-point constants and variables may be specified as single-precision for one range of values and double-precision for a larger range of values. A floating-point number is a positive or negative number represented in an exponential form and usually beyond the value range that can be achieved with a fixed-point number. Both single- and double-precision values usually can be specified for floating-point numbers.

To illustrate how this works, consider the following examples applicable to Microsoft BASICs:

1. A simple constant such as 378 is an integer, a number within a predefined range of values and not having a decimal point.

2. Constants such as 402.5, 2.8, and 1.789 are fixed-point numbers, again within a predefined range of values but having a decimal point. However, single- and double-precision considerations enter into the representation of fixed-point numbers and may be defined within the body of a program. Take, for example, the square root of 2. A single-precision representation of that value as a computer output might be printed as 1.41421, while a double-precision output might be printed as the value 1.414213538169861 with the fraction carried to more decimal *places* to indicate greater precision but not necessarily greater accuracy.

3. A constant such as 1E−04 is a floating-point number equivalent to 0.0001, with single precision denoted by the "E" form of exponentiation. A constant such as 1.56789D−06 is a floating-point number equivalent to 0.00000156789, with double precision denoted by the "D" form. Just as in scientific notation, the *sign* of the exponent denotes the direction to move the decimal, with a negative sign meaning to move the decimal the stated number of positions to the *left* and a positive or missing sign meaning to move *right.* Therefore, −1.56E6 denotes the number −1560000, while −1.56E-6 denotes −0.00000156. Both "E" and "D" forms merely indicate a power of 10.

Variables are subject to the same considerations and are assigned "data types" that indicate the degree of numeric precision. Therefore, variables may be of the same types as the numeric constants under the particular BASIC. With Applesoft, the only distinction allowed is between integer and real-precision variables. Integer-variable names always are followed by a percent symbol "%" and take the form C%, B1%, and so on. Applesoft uses no explicit type declaration and no appended symbol for real-precision variable names, so variables designated C, B1, and so on would be real-precision. It's important to note that variables C and C% may be used in the same program and are *not* the same variable name—C% might be assigned an integer value of 20 while variable C has a real-precision value of 55.34. Thereafter, both variable names may be used independently and without any correlation. Apple Integer BASIC uses no type designations for numeric variables and treats all of them as integer variables.

Under BASICs such as those from Microsoft, numeric variables may be integer, single-precision, or double-precision types, and each is designated by its own appended symbol. Integer variables use the percent symbol ("%") as does Applesoft, so variable names like C% and B1% have integer values. Single-precision variables either use an exclamation point ("!") as the type designation or are undesignated, so C!, B1!, C, and B1 all have single-precision values. Double-precision variables use a pound symbol ("#") designation, so C# and B# have double-precision values.

Just as Applesoft allows variables C% and C to be used within the same program as completely different and independent names, the Microsoft BASICs allow C%, C!, *and* C# to be used separately and independently—they are not the same variables. However, the variable names C and C! are the same single-precision variable, are not independent, and always have the same value. If you use the statement LET C!=2.2222 in a program, *both* C! and C have the value 2.2222, but C% and C# do not.

Data-type designations also may be used with numeric constants. By matching or mixing data types in a computation, the results can be made to differ dramatically. Consider the following series of examples in which the division operations on the left were entered to BASIC-80 from the keyboard using various combinations of precision levels and the results to the right were printed as the outputs.

```
PRINT 12.2/5.2       2.34615               (single-precision)
PRINT 12.2!/5.2!     2.34615               (single-precision)
PRINT 12.2#/5.2#     2.346153846153846     (double-precision)
PRINT 12.2/5.2#      2.346153809474065     (mixed-precision)
PRINT 12.2#/5.2      2.34615393221026      (mixed-precision)
PRINT 12.2%/5.2%     DIVISION BY ZERO      (invalid operation)
```

The foregoing examples show how precision affects computations, even with constants. Pay particular attention to the difference between single- and double-precision computations, and then to the differences between double and mixed precision. Actually, the third example, marked double-precision, is the most accurate; the division does indeed result in an infinitely repeating series. The final line shows a "division by zero" error because entering a single-precision number (with a decimal) and an integer type ("%") returns a zero value so that 12.2%/5.2% is equivalent to zero divided by zero. A 12.2%/5.2# would be equivalent to zero divided by a number and would return a value of zero.

The same types of differences are encountered if either or both the dividend and divisor are variables. This points up the importance of carefully matching variable and constant types in a program to avoid problems with excessive precision, possible data inaccuracies, or invalid operations.

Since BASIC interpreters are interactive, some unexpected things can happen as you key a program into the system. If you type a constant that is beyond the defined limits for a particular data type, the interpreter will adjust the format or data type as necessary. Often this means that listing the program on the display terminal or the printer shows a different constant from the one originally typed. Consider the following examples; the lines typed on the keyboard under BASIC-80 are shown on the left, and the listed program lines are shown on the right:

Keyed In	*Listed Out*
1Ø LET A=1ØØØØ	1Ø LET A=1ØØØØ
2Ø LET B=1ØØØØØ	2Ø LET B=1ØØØØØ!
3Ø LET C=1ØØØØØØ	3Ø LET C=1E+Ø6
4Ø LET D=1ØØØØØØØ	4Ø LET D=1ØØØØØØØ#
5Ø LET E=.ØØØØØØ1	5Ø LET E=.ØØØØØØ1
6Ø LET F=.ØØØØØØØ1	6Ø LET F=1E−Ø8
7Ø LET G=1.2345	7Ø LET G=1.2345
8Ø LET H=1.23456	8Ø LET H=1.2346
9Ø LET I =1.234567	9Ø LET I =1.234567#

Some unexpected difficulties may arise. For one, rounding occurs in line 80. There is no easy way to determine if the value is being rounded strictly for the listing while retaining the unrounded value internally or if the rounding affects internal operations as well. With undeclared variable types, each variable name is assumed to be single-precision, but the constants in lines 40 and 90 have been set to double precision because they exceed the single-precision range for this BASIC—a situation that may or may not cause problems with later computations performed by the program.

Just to keep life interesting, the rules governing constant and variable types are not the same from one BASIC to another. First, consider Applesoft. An integer is any number in the range from −32767 to +32767 and not containing a decimal point. A real-precision number is any number containing a decimal *or* any number outside the integer range. Furthermore, the range of real-precision numbers is limited to nine decimal digits with an exponent from −38 to +38. The largest number Applesoft can handle without an "overflow" error is about 1.7E+38 (that's 17 followed by 37 zeros).

Meanwhile, Microsoft BASICs define an integer as any number in the range of −32768 to +32767 and not containing a decimal. Note the difference at the lower end compared to Applesoft. Single-precision numbers are those having a decimal point, those not having a decimal point but outside the integer range and having seven or fewer digits, those with the exponential form using "E", and those indicated by a trailing exclamation point ("!"). Double-precision numbers are those having from 8 to 16 digits, those with the exponential form using "D", and those indicated by a trailing pound symbol ("#"). Exponent ranges for both single and double precisions are limited to −38 to +38, so the notations "E−38" to "E+38" and "D−38" to "D+38" are valid.

What does all this nice, confusing information mean? Well, it means you have to be careful! I've been leading up to a description of the effects numerical type designations can have on the programs you write and run under BASIC. As I'll soon show, these considerations do influence the results you can expect from a program and the speed with which you can obtain those results.

As an initial example, consider determining the square root of a number. First, the SQR() function is not available under Apple Integer BASIC, and the computation involves real numbers, which also are unavailable. Under Applesoft, you could execute the following lines and get the indicated results:

```
10 A%=SQR(2): A=SQR(2)
20 PRINT A%, A
```

[Results: A%=1   A=1.41421356]

The A% is an integer-variable name, so its value is truncated under Applesoft to set the value to the integer portion of the computed square root. The variable A is a real-precision name, so the result is reflected to the nine-digit limit of a real-precision number.

Under Microsoft BASICs, you have three options, and you could execute the following lines:

```
10 A%=SQR(2): A!=SQR(2): A#=SQR(2)
20 PRINT A%, A!, A#
```

[Results: A%=1   A!=1.41421   A#=1.414213538169861]

Variable A% is an integer variable, so its value automatically is rounded under BASIC-80 or truncated under other BASICs to set the value as the integer portion of the computed result. Variable A! is a single-precision name, and the value is printed to the limit of six digits; some BASICs will store the value internally with seven digits but output one less digit than is stored. Variable A# is a double-precision name with its value output to the full 16-digit limit for that type.

Now consider the computation of the fraction 1/10,000, which is 0.0001 in decimal form. Remember that an integer variable may have only an integer value, and consider the case for Applesoft:

```
10 A%=1/10000: A=1/10000
20 PRINT A%, A
```

[Results: A%=0   A=1E−04]

Now, do the parallel operations under BASIC-80, and the results are somewhat surprising:

```
10 A%=1/10000: A!=1/10000: A#=1/10000
20 PRINT A%, A!, A#
```

[Results: A%=0   A!=1E−04   A#=9.999999747378752D−05]

The results for A% and A! are pretty much as expected, but the one for A# seems a little odd for such a simple problem in arithmetic. Worse yet, A# is not "correct." What's happening is that the program is performing a division with two single-precision numbers and converting that single-precision value to a double-precision result for A#. The command LET A#=CDBL(.0001) gives equally wierd results, though not necessarily the same result as LET A#=1/10000. To "correct" the little program, it would be necessary to write it thus:

```
10 A%=1%/10000%: A!=1/10000: A#=1#/10000#
20 PRINT A%, A!, A#
```

[Results: A%=0   A!=1E−04   A#=1D−04]

Now the results are technically "correct," and consideration can be given to other aspects of numeric handling. Specifically, when is it or is it not an advantage to use one level of precision over another? I've already shown that mishandling precision levels can lead to unexpected and possibly erroneous results. In the next two sections, I'll be showing other reasons why increased precision may not be desirable for any but the most unusual computations. First, every increase in precision level consumes more memory for variable and constant storage. Second, every increase in level also increases the execution time for the program.

A Matter of Memory Consumption

Many instruction manuals furnished with BASIC interpreters for personal and small-business computers provide little if any information on the relative memory consumption for numbers of different precisions. But whether they clearly state it or not, a single-precision number requires more memory storage than an integer, and a double-precision number requires more memory than a single-precision number. Under a language like Applesoft, a real-precision number requires more memory than an integer.

In order to give a general feeling for the relationships involved, I'm going to pluck some information from older BASIC manuals that did define the memory requirements for each numeric type, and did so quite explicitly. Although the exact number of bytes may vary slightly from one system to another, the descriptions I've chosen serve very well to illustrate the general trends. Yet even among those manuals, there are differences in the actual numbers of bytes stated for a given precision level; however, the overall interrelationships remain the same despite the individual differences. You should view this information as "typical" or "nominal," not necessarily as cast in concrete for a particular system.

One BASIC manual indicates that simple (nonarray) integer variables require five memory bytes each, nonarray single-precision variables require seven bytes, and nonarray double-precision variables require 11 bytes. That same manual also defines the memory space for array variables according to a specific formula for each type. The equations used to calculate array space are:

Integer arrays:
no. bytes = [(no. elements) × 2] + 6 + [(no. dimensions) × 2]

Single-precision arrays:
no. bytes = [(no. elements) × 4] + 6 + [(no. dimensions) × 2]

Double-precision arrays:
no. bytes = [(no. elements) × 8] + 6 + [(no. dimensions) + 2]

Applying those equations when setting up a 20 × 20 numeric array of 400 elements in two dimensions, a DIM A%(20,20) statement allocates 810 bytes, A DIM A!(20,20) allocates 1,610 bytes, and a DIM A#(20,20) allocates 3,210 bytes. Each increase of precision level drastically increases the memory consumption.

Another manual gives a somewhat different indication of memory consumption. It states that an integer number in the allowable range of −32768 to +32767 is represented in binary in a two-byte field. Floating-point numbers are represented as a decimal fraction or *mantissa* and a power of 10 or *exponent.* With that breakdown, a single-precision number with up to seven significant digits in the allowable range of 2.9387×10^{-38} to $1.70141 \times 10^{+38}$ requires three bytes for the mantissa plus one byte for the exponent. A double-precision number with up to 17 significant digits in the same allowable range requires seven bytes for the mantissa and one byte for the exponent. Graphically, the memory requirements are shown in Fig. 4-1.

Most of the newer manuals furnished with today's interpreters omit the memory-consumption data, and many don't even indicate that there are such differences. Regardless of whether or not the manuals address the subject at all and regardless of the actual number of bytes involved, it is a fundamental assumption that integer variables and constants require the least memory, while double-precision variables and constants require the most memory. Therefore, maximum memory conservation is achieved by using integers whenever possible, using single precision when necessary, and avoiding double precision except under the most unusual circumstances where you simply can't perform the computations any other way.

A Matter of Execution Speed

Throughout the bulk of programming literature, you'll encounter a couple of "glittering generalities" concerning the use of variables and constants. One "speed hint" often recommended is to use integer

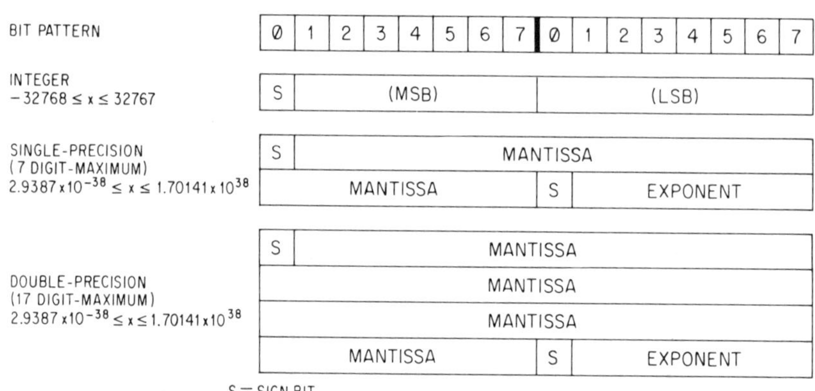

Fig. 4-1. **Typical BASIC Memory Consumptions**

variables whenever possible. Another is that integer arithmetic is faster than real-precision arithmetic and that single-precision manipulations are faster than those for double precision. The question then becomes, *just how much execution time can you save in a program?*

To answer that question, it's necessary to compare techniques using several different BASIC interpreters with a routine that can run on any of the versions, can be systematically modified to test a single feature at a time, and requires enough time for execution to allow the times to be checked with a stopwatch. I'm going to do exactly that to demonstrate the effects of numeric precision on FOR...NEXT loop control and the effects of integer versus real-precision arithmetic. The times I'll be citing are the averages of five trials timed against a stopwatch. While they may not have a great deal of statistical validity, the differences are great enough to identify efficient and nonefficient techniques despite the ±0.5-second timing error I consider probable in starting and stopping an electronic stopwatch.

Effects of Numeric Precision on Loop Control. Because the FOR... NEXT loop is one of the most useful programming tools available and is, therefore, one of the most common programming structures, attention has to be given to the way in which the loop is controlled. That is, what effect is seen when the control variable is an integer as compared to a real number?

With many BASICs, the manuals advise you to use integer-type control variables in the FOR...NEXT statements to speed execution, but they rarely tell you just how much speed you might expect to gain. Remember that keeping track of precision matching in arithmetic operations is important in maintaining accurate results, as I've already shown. But doing that takes a lot of conscious effort, and you need to know whether the speed gain you get in one way is worth the time lost to create the program and manipulate precision levels properly.

I must point out that some BASICs don't allow certain levels of precision for the FOR...NEXT control variable. For example, Applesoft displays a syntax error anytime you try to use a declared integer variable as the control, so you can't use something like FOR X%...NEXT X%. This means that all loops in Applesoft *must* be controlled by real-precision variables. Microsoft BASICs allow either integer or single-precision loop-control variables, but not double-precision variables. Therefore, those BASICs will allow loops of the integer form FOR X%...NEXT X%, the declared single-precision form FOR X!...NEXT X!, and the undeclared single-precision form FOR X... NEXT X. They do not allow the double-precision form FOR X#... NEXT X#.

An easy way to test the speed variations in FOR...NEXT loop control is to perform 15,000 arithmetic operations in such a manner that exactly the same arithmetic is performed in every test. The two "nonsense" programs that follow do just that, performing a simple integer multiplication 15,000 times and differing only in that the loop control in the first is an integer while the second is in single precision.

```
10 FOR X%=1 TO 15000
20 Y%=(2*3*4*5)*(2*3*4*5)
30 NEXT X%
```

[Microsoft Rev. 4.51 (CP/M): 233.0 seconds]
[Microsoft Rev. 5.2 (CP/M): 209.7 seconds]
[Compiled Microsoft (CP/M): 1.2 seconds]
[Microsoft Rev. 5.2 (Apple II MBASIC): 206.3 seconds]
[Microsoft Rev. 5.2 (Apple II GBASIC): 206.1 seconds]

```
10 FOR X!=1 TO 15000
20 Y%=(2*3*4*5)*(2*3*4*5)
30 NEXT X!
```

[Microsoft Rev. 4.51 (CP/M): 244.7 seconds]
[Microsoft Rev. 5.2 (CP/M): 222.5 seconds]
[Compiled Microsoft (CP/M): 21.9 seconds]
[Microsoft Rev. 5.2 (Apple II MBASIC): 218.1 seconds]
[Microsoft Rev. 5.2 (Apple II GBASIC): 218.0 seconds]

If the compiled versions are disregarded for a moment, the time comparisons show that integer control was faster than single-precision control for each interpreter. The differences range from 11.7 seconds for Microsoft Revision 4.51 to 12.8 seconds for Microsoft Revision 5.2 on a CP/M-based S-100 bus machine, with an average difference of 12.04 seconds. Another way of viewing this is to say that integer control saves from 4.8 percent to 5.8 percent of the execution time required by single-precision control for the BASICs being tested.

The results in the compiled form, showing 1.2 seconds for one method and 21.9 seconds for the other, were quite surprising, and I had to recompile and retest over and over again before I'd accept that much difference. Every recompilation and retest came up with the same results for the programs processed by Microsoft's BASCOM compiler and loaded with the LINK-80 relocating loader. This example serves to demonstrate that improved efficiency in writing a program under the interpreter can result in drastic speed increases when compiled into machine code. The numbers also reflect the immense speed advantage gained by compilation.

Two other trends are worthy of special note. First, Microsoft Revision 5.2, runs considerably faster than Revision 4.51 for this type of numerical processing. Later in this chapter, however, I'll show that it runs much more slowly for string processing. Second, there is no significant difference in the execution speed under Microsoft Revision 5.2 when compared between the S-100 bus machine and the Apple implementations. This means that the Z-80 microprocessor on the Apple's SoftCard is no more efficient in this application than the 8080A microprocessor in the S-100 computer.

To complete this comparison, it's also necessary to take a look at the timing for the same operation under Applesoft and Apple Integer BASIC. The following are the programs run and the times obtained, with Applesoft on the left and Integer BASIC on the right. Remember that integer loop controls cannot be used with Applesoft and that Integer BASIC offers only integer loop control *and* arithmetic.

```
10 FOR X=1 TO 15000
20 Y%=(2*3*4*5)*(2*3*4*5)
30 NEXT X
```

[Applesoft: 282.3 seconds]

```
10 FOR X=1 TO 15000
20 Y=(2*3*4*5)*(2*3*4*5)
30 NEXT X
```

[Integer BASIC: 141.0 seconds]

In this test, Applesoft runs considerably more slowly than any of the other BASICs tested. Integer BASIC runs considerably faster than any of the others, though its strictly integer arithmetic probably accounts for most of its efficiency.

Another "space and speed hint" offered by many manuals is to eliminate the variable from the NEXT statement of a FOR...NEXT loop, thus saving a small amount of memory and presumably speeding execution. I tested that for the integer version of the same loop control and did, indeed, find a speed increase. The test program and results obtained were:

```
10 FOR X%=1 TO 15000
20 Y%=(2*3*4*5)*(2*3*4*5)
30 NEXT
```

[Microsoft Rev. 4.51 (CP/M): 226.9 seconds]
[Microsoft Rev. 5.2 (CP/M): 203.8 seconds]
[Microsoft Rev. 5.2 (Apple II MBASIC): 200.7 seconds]
[Microsoft Rev. 5.2 (Apple II GBASIC): 200.6 seconds]

By eliminating just the one variable name from line 30, I was able to reduce the execution time by between 5.5 and 6.1 seconds. On the average, each test routine using the variable after the NEXT statement was wasting 2.7 percent of its execution time on a useless operation. Similarly, under Applesoft, eliminating the X from line 30 reduced the execution time from 282.3 to 278.5 seconds, saving 3.8 seconds or 1.3 percent of the execution time. The variable cannot be eliminated under Apple Integer BASIC.

All of this adds up to a potential time savings of between 7 and 8 percent, depending upon the individual program, the BASIC involved, and so on. That doesn't sound like much, but remember that the effects are cumulative throughout a long program run and with other techniques used to increase a program's efficiency. But even by itself, 7.5 percent of an hour is 4.5 minutes, and 7.5 percent of 24 hours is 1.8 hours, so the savings can be significant for large programs and long or repetitive program runs.

Furthermore, the sample program is not in its most efficient and compressed form. Under virtually any BASIC, I can write the program as a single line and eliminate the overhead of up to five bytes per line number. Under Microsoft Revision 4.51, I can eliminate the spaces. Fully compressed under Microsoft Revision 4.51, it takes only 224.1 seconds (a savings of another 2.8 seconds or 1.2 percent from the preceding time) to run the single-line program:

```
10 FORX%=1TO15000:Y%=(2*3*4*5)*(2*3*4*5):NEXT
```

Effects of Numeric Precision on Arithmetic Speed. When the manuals tell you to do as much arithmetic as possible using integer variables and numbers, they don't tell you just how much time you're going to lose by not following that advice. It happens to be rather easy to check that out, using the same multiplication routine I've been demonstrating. In showing you the single-line version of the routine that runs in fully compressed form under Microsoft Revision 4.51, I used integer loop controls and an integer arithmetic operation to obtain an execution time of 224.1 seconds.

Now, by eliminating the percent symbol from the Y variable name, I force integer multiplication with conversion of the results to single-precision memory storage, effectively forcing a CSNG() operation with the evaluation of Y but without using the CSNG() program function explicitly. The program now appears thus:

```
10 FORX%=1TO15000:Y=(2*3*4*5)*(2*3*4*5):NEXT
```

Under Microsoft Revision 4.51, the execution time increases by 5.3 seconds to a total of 229.4 seconds. That's an increase of 2.4 percent over the integer version. I further modify the program so all constants in the multiplication are in single precision and test it again. This time, the program is written as:

```
10 FORX%=1TO15000:Y=(2!*3!*4!*5!)*(2!*3!*4!*5!):NEXT
```

In this case, execution time increases to 268.7 seconds, adding 44.6 seconds or 19.9 percent to the time required to perform the computations with integers alone. Once again, I modify the routine to force the arithmetic computations into double precision:

```
10 FORX%=1TO15000:Y#=(2#*3#*4#*5#)*(2#*3#*4#*5#):NEXT
```

This double-precision version requires 700.7 seconds, taking more than three times (313 percent) longer than the purely integer version. Clearly, the efficiency of arithmetic operations is a function of the numeric precision, and efforts to handle those operations at the lowest possible level of precision will pay off handsomely in time saved.

The examples just cited all involve the multiplication of numbers, a moderately complex operation for a computer. Simple addition and subtraction operations also show parallel speed changes from one precision of arithmetic to another, although the differences are not as dramatic as those for multiplication. However. division poses an interesting situation, particularly with Microsoft BASICs that offer two methods for division. These interpreters allow you to specify a normal, real-precision division by using a forward slash ("/") character or an integer division by using a backward slash ("\") character. Apple Integer BASIC and Applesoft do not offer the two types; with Integer BASIC, all arithmetic must be in integer form, and Applesoft allows only a single type of division whether using integers or real-precision numbers.

The manuals for BASICs providing both real and integer division usually recommend the integer form as a means of increasing execution speed, but once again they fail to quantify the impact. While it seems logical to assume that dividing integers is faster than dividing real numbers, the question is, by how much? From the usual literature, you don't know whether the speed gain amounts to 1 percent, 10 percent, or 100 percent.

To pin this down and provide some valid comparisons, I've again set up a little nonsense program that performs the same division operation 15,000 times. In each case, the loop is under integer control, the variable being calculated is an integer, and the constants used for the division both are integers. The only difference tested is, therefore, the difference between the forward-slash real division in the first example and the backward-slash integer division in the second example. For these tests, only Microsoft BASIC Revisions 4.51 and 5.2 (BASIC-80) on the S-100 bus computer are reported. I've already shown that MBASIC and GBASIC on the Apple's SoftCard closely parallel the times achieved with BASIC-80 on the S-100 system under test, and any difference is so small as to be negligible for my purposes.

```
10 FOR X%=1 TO 15000
20 Y%=1500/100
30 NEXT
```

[Microsoft Rev. 4.51: 128.1 seconds]
[Microsoft Rev. 5.2: 132.0 seconds]

```
10 FOR X%=1 TO 15000
20 Y%=1500\100
30 NEXT
```

[Microsoft Rev. 4.51: 72.2 seconds]
[Microsoft Rev. 5.2: 66.3 seconds]

As you can see, there is a great difference, with Revision 4.51 gaining 55.9 seconds or 43.6 percent for integer division and BASIC-80 gaining 65.7 seconds or 49.8 percent. Also take note of the relative timing between the two versions. I've already pointed out that Microsoft Revision 5.2 showed a speed advantage over Revision 4.51 in multiplication operations, but division operations appear to give it the speed advantage only with the integer division denoted by the backward slash. For normal division denoted by a foward slash, the speed advantage is with Revision 4.51.

In comparison, the only division allowed under Applesoft runs in 156.8 seconds for the following program on the right, and the only one allowed under Integer BASIC runs in 49.7 seconds for the program on the left. This shows that Applesoft has the slowest division speed of all the interpreters tested, while Apple Integer BASIC has the fastest division operation.

```
10 FOR X=1 TO 15000          10 FOR X=1 TO 15000
20 Y%=1500/100               20 Y=1500/100
30 NEXT                      30 NEXT X
```

The next logical step is to try the same arithmetic with greater precision. The following two programs show the results for single-precision constants and variables under the Microsoft BASICs in the first example and with real precision under Applesoft in the second example:

```
10 FOR X%=1 TO 15000
20 Y=1500!/100!
30 NEXT
```

[Microsoft Rev. 4.51: 115.0 seconds]
[Microsoft Rev. 5.2: 113.3 seconds]

```
10 FOR X=1 TO 15000
20 Y=1500.0/100.0
30 NEXT
```

[Applesoft: 240.1 seconds]

The results under Applesoft are pretty much as expected, with a time increase of 83.3 seconds when the dividend and divisor are forced to real-precision numbers. But the results under the Microsoft BASICs are somewhat surprising, with times between those obtained for regular division of integer constants and integer division of integer constants. This apparently indicates that Microsoft BASICs provide a built-in speed advantage when using single-precision constants with regular division as compared with using integer constants with the same division.

Since those results did seem a little odd, I proceeded to test some variations of the same operation using double precision. In the three programs listed, the leftmost divides integer constants but sets the result into a double-precision variable. The center one divides single-precision contants and sets the result into double precision. The rightmost example does all arithmetic in double precision. Indicated execution times are under Microsoft BASIC Revision 4.51.

```
10 FOR X%=1 TO
   15000
20 Y#=1500/100
30 NEXT
```

[123.3 seconds]

```
10 FOR X%=1 TO
   15000
20 Y#=1500!/100!
30 NEXT
```

[116.5 seconds]

```
10 FOR X%=1 TO
   15000
20 Y#=1500#/100#
30 NEXT
```

[743.6 seconds]

Of these three examples, only the rightmost, with all double-precision numbers in the division, shows the expected results—an extremely large time increase over all other methods, with the execution time fully 10.3 times longer than the 72.2 seconds required for integer division with integer constants. The other two cases, however, took surprisingly little time, and again the deviation seems to be attributable to an improved efficiency for real division of integer and single-precision numbers despite the presence of the double-precision variable name.

The discrepancies between what I expected to see and what I actually received prompted still other division tests in an attempt to identify a valid pattern. The following programs and times are those found for the first set of tests on 15,000 division operations using a variable in place of a constant for the dividend. Stepping through the loop in increments of two assures an evenly divisible number and the use of integer values throughout the computations.

```
10 FOR X%=2 TO 30000 STEP 2
20 Y=X%/2
30 NEXT
```

[Microsoft Rev. 4.51: 123.0 seconds]
[Microsoft Rev. 5.2: 133.4 seconds]

```
10 FOR X%=2 TO 30000 STEP 2
20 Y=X%\2
30 NEXT
```

[Microsoft Rev. 4.51: 80.3 seconds]
[Microsoft Rev. 5.2: 69.3 seconds]

Once again, integer division demonstrates a clear speed advantage over regular division. Furthermore, Revision 5.2 retains the advantage over Revision 4.51 only for the integer division, as I've already demonstrated when constants are used. The timing differences between divisions using one variable and one constant compared with the divisions using two constants is extremely small, but it may not be strictly valid. These last samples incorporate a STEP statement that may have some small effect on the overall speed of the loop (more on that subject later).

On the other hand, Applesoft but not Apple Integer BASIC demonstrated a significant change in speed when using a variable to replace one of the constants. Using the following routines, Applesoft (on the left) ran to completion in 80.2 seconds compared with 156.8 seconds for the all-constants version presented earlier. That nearly cut the execution time in half. Integer BASIC (on the right) ran to completion in 51.5 seconds, requiring almost two seconds longer than the all-constants version.

```
10 FOR X=2 TO 30000 STEP 2        10 FOR X=2 TO 30000 STEP 2
20 Y=X/2                          20 Y=X/2
30 NEXT                           30 NEXT X
```

The small increase required by Apple Integer BASIC may be attributable, at least in part, to the added STEP statement in line 10. However, I can offer no clear-cut explanation for the extreme speed gain obtained under Applesoft other than to suggest that it might have something to do with that particular language's handling of real-precision variables. The discrepancy was so great in comparison with other tests that I went back to it several times, typing and retyping the programs, timing and retiming the runs, and checking and rechecking—always with the same results.

As a final series of tests, I decided to try the division with two variables. The test programs and the results obtained were as follows:

```
5 A%=2
1Ø FOR X%=2 TO 3ØØØØ STEP 2
2Ø Y=X%/A%
3Ø NEXT
```

[Microsoft Rev. 4.51: 130.0 seconds]
[Microsoft Rev. 5.2: 139.8 seconds]

```
5 A%=2
1Ø FOR X%=2 TO 3ØØØØ STEP 2
2Ø Y=X%\A%
3Ø NEXT
```

[Microsoft Rev. 4.51: 87.1 seconds]
[Microsoft Rev. 5.2: 75.8 seconds]

In all four tests, using two variables instead of one variable and one constant caused an increase in execution time. For Revision 4.51, the increase was 6.8 to 7.0 seconds (5.7 percent to 8.4 percent). For Revision 5.2, it was 6.4 to 6.5 seconds (4.7 percent to 9.4 percent). Since most manuals recommend using variables instead of constants as a memory-saving technique, these results show that you have to be cautious, particularly with integer values. You may wind up unintentionally trading a memory gain for a speed loss or vice versa.

When I performed a parallel test on the Apple, I noted an extension of the discrepancy. The Applesoft version shown on the left ran in 75.3 seconds for a gain of 4.9 seconds (6.1 percent) over the previous version, while the Integer BASIC form ran in 56.1 seconds for a loss of 6.4 seconds (12.4 percent).

```
5 A=2                              5 A=2
1Ø FOR X=2 TO 3ØØØØ STEP 2         1Ø FOR X=2 TO 3ØØØØ STEP 2
```

20 Y=X/A	20 Y=X/A
30 NEXT	30 NEXT X

By now, it has probably occurred to you that the Applesoft test isn't an exact parallel to the Microsoft tests since it uses all real-precision values while the others use integer values. So the question now is, *can the Applesoft speed increase be duplicated by using single-precision variables in the Microsoft divisions?* No such luck! I tried it by changing the variable names from A% and X% to A and X, thereby forcing them to single precision. The Microsoft test ran in 128.6 seconds for a gain of only a few seconds.

Despite some of the details and the occasional discrepancies from expected behavior, the overall trend is clear. First, integer arithmetic generally has a considerable speed advantage over real-precision operations, especially when the BASIC offers an integer division operation. Second, the use of double precision in an arithmetic procedure can cause a very large increase in the required execution time. As a result, program efficiency can be improved by using the lowest possible level of precision at all times.

However, such approaches as substituting preassigned variables for constants may or may not achieve a speed increase, depending upon the specific BASIC in use. Therefore, it is necessary for each user to test his or her own system to determine its behavior under different circumstances, incorporating the results of those tests into future programming efforts. *Don't take an instruction manual's word for anything, and don't assume that what works well on one system will work equally well on another.*

Rounding versus Truncating

Probably the majority of BASIC interpreters convert real values to integers by simply truncating the numbers. That is, they drop the fractional portion and retain the integer portion. This is equivalent to performing an INT() operation. However, Microsoft Revisions 5.1 and 5.2 (BASIC-80) perform a rounding operation that can lead to surprising results when a program relies on truncating numbers. For example, the program statement A%=1.51 would give A% an integer value of 1 under Microsoft Revision 4.51 or Applesoft but an integer value of 2 under BASIC-80. The expression A%=1.495 would set A% equal to an integer 1 under either method. In effect, a *truncating* BASIC always rounds *down,* while a *rounding* BASIC rounds *up or down* depending upon the value of the least significant digit(s).

For most BASICs, the difference between rounding and truncating will not affect conversions between single- and double-precision numbers, only conversions from real numbers to integers. That is, setting A# equal to the double-precision 1.555555555 and then using the statement A!=A# will set A! equal to 1.55556 with either type of BASIC. Similarly, setting A# equal to 1.555549999 and performing an A!=A# will set A! equal to 1.55554 under either type. Just for the fun of it, try typing the direct command A#=1.555544 into a BASIC with double-precision capability. If you happen to use something like Microsoft Revision 4.51 or either revision of BASIC-80 and type the command PRINT A#, the number you see displayed should be something odd like 1.555544157954712 with 16 digits—this doesn't happen for every number, but it sure can catch you by surprise when it does.

Anyway, it's important that you know whether you're dealing with a truncating or a rounding BASIC when you do your programming. The procedure affects not only simple conversions from floating-point to integer numbers in assignment statements but function and expression evaluations as well. For example, a formatted print statement containing a TAB(A) function where A evaluates to 9.57 would tab to the ninth print position in a truncating BASIC but to the tenth position in a rounding BASIC. In fact, any function relying on an integer argument can prove to be a bit of a problem if it is moved from one BASIC to another without accommodating the difference between truncating and rounding operations.

Variable subscripting is affected in the same way. Suppose your program contains the statement X=Y(A), where A is evaluated by some preceding computation to be 4.7. With a truncating BASIC, X would be set equal to the value of Y(4), but a rounding BASIC would set X equal to Y(5). Dimensioning an array according to an evaluated variable or expression runs the same risk. If you use a DIM X(A) statement where A evaluates to 15.8, one version would give you a valid subscript range from X(0) through X(15), while the other would allow X(0) through X(16).

Even the operation of the random-number generator is affected. For example, RND(A) where A equals 0.5 would cause an RND(0) function under truncating and an RND(1) function under rounding. It happens that on Microsoft BASICs, RND(0) returns a value the same as the last one obtained from the generator and RND(1) returns the next number in the random sequence. The result is two totally different commands. In Chapter 5, I'll be showing that even stranger things can happen when the number returned is used to define a range of integers to be applied in later computations.

Misusing or misunderstanding the truncating and rounding features of the language can contribute to some errors that are extremely hard to diagnose in a finished program. Worse yet, the errors may be intermittent and show up only as occasional discrepancies in the outputs. As long as your program deals only with integers, rounding versus truncating will be no problem. However, once you start dealing with real numbers, including those output by the random-number generator, you do need to exercise some caution in handling your variables. Of course, you could go to using functions such as TAB(INT(A)) instead of TAB(A) or statements like X=Y(INT(A)) instead of X=Y(A) to get around the problem, but those techniques impose an extra overhead in increased memory consumption and reduced execution speed.

A Practical Hint

Numerical techniques can have a considerable impact on the programs you write in terms of memory space consumed, execution time required, and the accuracy of the results obtained. One area where this becomes particularly important is in accounting applications, where it's necessary to deal with dollars and cents—real numbers complete with decimal points and fractional components. The novice programmer is apt to approach the entire procedure in terms of single-precision computations. After all, $99.99 is a single- or real-precision value and should be handled accordingly. Or should it?

Sooner or later, a program dealing with decimal fractions is bound to run headlong into "rounding" errors, particularly where division operations are required for determining percentages, prorating values, and so on. When these are first encountered, many programmers decide to improve the accuracy of their computations by switching over to double-precision numbers and arithmetic. The result: even more of the same or worse errors and a drastic reduction of computer efficiency.

Instead, the problems can be eliminated by working the computations in integer form, as long as the values are within the defined integer range. When a value is entered in dollars and cents as a decimal fraction, it is multiplied by 100 and converted to an integer. All arithmetic, data storage, and other internal program operations then proceed with the integer values. When an output is needed, the values are divided by 100 to return them to dollars and cents, and the results are printed to only two decimal digits (a handy function here is a PRINT USING statement). This eliminates rounding or truncating errors throughout the data-handling operations to yield improved accuracy. It also speeds up all calculations, enhances the overall operation of the program, and allows the computer to operate with a minimum of wasted time.

The same techniques can be applied to any numerical processing task where the absolute limit of decimal accuracy is known beforehand. Multiply the data by the appropriate number to make an integer, perform all operations with integers, and then convert the integer results back into decimal fractions at the time of printout.

However, caution is necessary. In most computers, the largest integer that can be entered or computed without generating an error message is +32767. If, for instance, you are in an accounting program and enter the amount $328.00 to be handled by multiplication to an integer, you will get an error message because 32800 is beyond the acceptable range for integers. Obviously, an accounting system limited to a maximum amount of $327.67 is of little use in the real world. In such cases, you will have to do your arithmetic in real numbers, live with an overall slowdown and loss of efficiency, and incorporate some other method of eliminating rounding and arithmetic errors. Appendix C of this book presents some effective rounding and formatting algorithms for just these types of applications, but you have to remember that their use further slows program execution.

String-Handling Methods

A *string* or *string literal* is nothing more than a series of one or more characters enclosed in double quotation marks and input or output exactly as it appears. The characters within the string may be alphabetic letters, numeric digits, punctuation marks, and, in some cases, special nonprinting characters that don't appear on the display screen or hard-copy printout but are contained within the body of the string. Most BASICs limit the length of a string to 0 to 255 characters, with a zero-character string known as a *null string.* As with numeric items, strings may be handled as either constants or variables, and certain manipulations may be performed on them.

Some examples of valid string literals include "PROGRAM", "$105.95", and "Copyright (c)". Since the double quotation marks are used to enclose or *delimit* the string, BASICs do not allow a double quotation mark to be a part of the string itself, so "THIS PROGRAM IS "ALPHABET SORT"" would not be a valid string and would generate a syntax or other error message. However, the single quotation mark or apostrophe is allowed, so that same string can be written as "THIS PROGRAM IS 'ALPHABET SORT'", which is perfectly acceptable.

In dealing with string variables, the variable type must be specifically declared as part of the variable name by appending a dollar sign ("$"), just as integer variables append a percent symbol ("%"), single-precision variables append an exclamation point ("!"), and double-precision variables append a pound symbol ("#"). Failure to declare the data type for a string variable results in either a "syntax error" or a "type mismatch" error message and an immediate program halt. The following are some examples of both valid and invalid uses of strings:

```
A$="PROGRAM"        [valid variable and literal]
B1$="$123.45"       [valid variable and literal]
J$=""               [valid variable and null string literal]
YP$=$10.95          [type mismatch—no quotes]
XX$=9876.5          [type mismatch—string and numeric]
```

A%="854"	[type mismatch—numeric and string]
B!="412.3"	[type mismatch—numeric and string]
C#="STRING"	[type mismatch—numeric and string]
D="SUM"	[type mismatch—numeric and string]

Probably the most common use of string constants and variables is to provide headers and text information to accompany and identify numeric data printouts or displays. After all, computers are designed for "number crunching" and not for extensive string manipulation. However, string data can be manipulated directly and quite effectively using statements and functions provided by most modern BASICs. I've personally spent several years writing nothing but programs for string-handling techniques required to produce commercially salable word games. Those programs are provided and described in my book *Create Word Puzzles with Your Microcomputer*, published by Hayden Book Company in 1982. Readers having a specific interest in complex string-handling techniques will find more information in that book than I could fit into this one.

The important thing to remember is that handling string data is not the same as handling numeric data. First, you can't add, subtract, multiply, divide, or exponentiate string constants or variables. Second, you must use special functions such as MID$(), LEFT$(), RIGHT$(), LEN(), and others provided by the language to perform "special" operations on the strings. However, BASICs differ widely in the number of special functions and the handling techniques they allow for string data. The following sections are devoted to a description of some of the more important functions and techniques. As you get into programming that makes heavy use of string-handling features, you'll find that efficiency considerations become even more critical than they were for numeric operations. You'll also find that differences between BASICs become even more apparent, both in the features offered and in the speed with which they can be performed.

Storing Strings in Memory

Like numeric data, strings have to be stored in a computer's random-access memory, often in a section of memory specifically set aside or allocated for string storage. That section of memory generally is designated "string space" and sometimes must be allocated as part of a CLEAR program statement before strings are assigned. Incidentally, most BASICs that allow fixed string-space allocation also provide two nasty error messages. One is the "out of memory" message and the other is the "out of string space" message. Both are "fatal" errors and halt program execution immediately. It's quite possible to run out of string space while you still have plenty of memory available or vice versa, but most BASICs make it impossible to reallocate additional memory to string space without totally destroying the values already stored.

As a general rule, a simple string constant requires one byte of memory for each character, so the string "THIS IS THE DATA" would require 16 bytes to store the 13 letters and 3 spaces. Obviously, long strings require considerably more memory than short ones, so long strings used for input prompts, printout formats, and other frivolous internal operations can eat up a lot of memory very quickly. Similarly, long descriptive explanations used in nonexecuting REM (remark) statements consume a lot of memory without performing any useful function in the program, so their lengths should be held to absolute minimums whenever they have to be used. If you doubt this, refer back to the description of readability versus efficiency in Chapter 2.

When manipulating strings, it's definitely an advantage in both memory conservation and speed of execution to assign a variable name and then use that variable to call the string whenever it's needed more than once or twice. Typically, the variable name would require from three to six bytes of memory each time it appears in a program, depending upon the version of BASIC being used, and it would be more efficient than multiple appearances of strings having more characters than that number. However, using a variable for repetitive appearances of strings having fewer characters than the variable name would be inefficient. To illustrate, setting a six-byte variable name A$ equal to "PROGRAM LOOP" and using it 20 times in a program would save 120 bytes when compared to repeating the literal string each time. Conversely, setting A$ equal to a null string and using it 20 times would waste at least 100 bytes.

Many BASICs allow the use of string-variable arrays, providing for subscripted string variables just as they provide for subscripted numerical variables. However, string arrays increase memory consumption dramatically. Earlier, I presented typical equations for calculating the memory space required for numeric arrays. The typical formula for a string array is:

String arrays:
no. bytes = [(no. elements) × 3] + 6 + [(no. dimensions) × 2]

This means that a DIM A$(20,20) statement would require 400 elements in a two-dimension array, thereby consuming 1,210 bytes of array space. However, there is a critical difference in the way string arrays and numeric arrays are handled. In numeric arrays, the actual values are stored in the array space itself. In string arrays, only a *pointer* to another memory address is stored in the array space.

In accessing an element of a string array, BASIC goes to the array storage, locates the value of the pointer for the element required, and then retrieves the actual string data from sequential memory addresses beginning at the address designated by the pointer. Therefore, the actual string space required is the size of the array space *plus* one byte for every character in the string. Using the same DIM A$(20,20) statement and assuming that each of the 400 strings contains 10 characters, the required string space would be the 1,210 bytes for the array of pointers plus another 4,000 bytes for the strings themselves. Totaling more than 5,200 bytes, that one string array consumes a hefty piece of available memory—10.5 percent of 48K or 7.9 percent of 64K.

Allocating String Space

A BASIC such as Microsoft Revision 4.51 requires that memory space be allocated for string variables at or near the beginning of the program. BASIC-80 (Microsoft Revisions 5.1 and 5.2), Applesoft, and Apple Integer BASIC do not require such an allocation and don't even provide a means of setting aside a specified amount of string space.

In those BASICs that do require string-space allocation as a separate operation, it generally is accomplished through the use of a CLEAR <n> command, where <n> is an argument that sets the amount of memory reserved strictly for string storage. For example, the command CLEAR 10000 in Microsoft Revision 4.51 sets aside 10,000 bytes of memory for string storage. Should the program require more than that number of bytes, an "out of string space" message, which is totally separate from and independent of the "out of memory" message, is displayed—there may be a lot of free memory remaining, but it hasn't been allocated to string storage, and a reallocation may be necessary for the next program run.

The "out of string space" message indicates a fatal error from which there usually is no recovery without restarting the program. However, I have encountered situations in which a recovery was possible. One of my own applications is a rather large program that takes lists of randomly entered words, alphabetizes them, and then sorts them to eliminate duplications, words contained inside other words, and so on. To prepare lists of some 200 words on a specific topic for later use in the computerized construction of word games, it works with numerous parallel string arrays and consumes very large quantities of string space. There have been occasions when, for one reason or another, I've used larger string arrays than normal and encountered the "out of string space" message just before the program completed its half hour or so of sorting.

In that situation, I could not execute a new CLEAR <n> command without destroying all the work to that point, but I had written the program with many long, descriptive strings assigned to variables for printed prompts, on-screen progress reports, and so on. By using direct keyboard commands to set those message variables to null strings, say with a B$="" command, and then executing a CONT or GOTO... command, I sometimes could free up just enough string space to allow the program to finish. As long as I didn't actually edit a program line, alter the arrays themselves, or perform a CLEAR command, the contents of the data arrays would remain intact and usable upon return to the program. This is, however, a tricky operation, and it's far better to have enough string space allocated before running the program.

Conversely, overallocating string space can result in an "out of memory" error when there's still a lot of unused space in the string area. I've never found a good, reliable way around this error; it has almost always proved immediately fatal to the program run with no possibility of recovery. Again, a CLEAR command would destroy all work up to the point of failure. Unlike string space, unallocated memory cannot be freed up by setting a numeric variable to a zero because the zero value still occupies the same number of bytes as the original value. Besides, an "out of memory" error often occurs at a point where even a direct command involving a numerical operation can't be executed from the keyboard.

There is only one possible way out, which I have been able to use on rare occasions. When the "out of memory" error occurred on a BASIC featuring an ERASE statement and at a point in a program beyond which several numeric arrays were no longer to be used, I was able to issue an ERASE command from the keyboard for the arrays in question, return their space to available memory, and then continue the program with a GOTO... command. But that's far too rare an occurrence to rely upon for salvaging program runs on a regular basis.

With those kinds of problems, the question is, *how do you determine how much string space must be allocated?* Regrettably, this is no sure-fire formula and no truly reliable way to make that determination before running a program. If you do enough programming with strings, follow similar procedures from program to program, and use similar string-array sizes each time, you eventually may develop a "feeling" for the amount of string space required. Otherwise, "sizing" a CLEAR <n> statement is a matter of trial and error. Many BASICs using allocated string space, including Microsoft Revision 4.51, boot up with a predetermined amount of space, something like 200 bytes, allocated for string storage, just as though a CLEAR 200 command had been executed. While this may be adequate for storing the input prompts, formatting messages, and a few other miscellaneous printouts, it's far from enough for any serious string-handling programs. It won't even allow you to execute a DIM A$(15,15) statement without an immediate "out of string space" error.

You also must recognize that the amount of memory allocated to strings directly affects the string-space "garbage-collection" function of a BASIC interpreter, which I'll be describing in more detail in the next section. In turn, this affects the efficiency of a string-intensive program as a whole and can have serious effects on the overall execution time. Whenever the interpreter runs out of available string space, it performs the garbage collection to free any space not currently in use and rid itself of extraneous string data. If little string space is allocated, this must be done frequently; the frequency decreases as the amount of allocated space or the amount of unused space increase. At the same time, larger space allocations take longer to free up when the procedure is performed, so a balance between frequency and duration of the garbage collection must be achieved.

In general, I've seen the best overall execution times achieved when large memory areas are allocated so that garbage collection is performed as few times as possible. Therefore, it's often an advantage to allocate as much memory as possible to string space while allowing only sufficient unallocated memory to hold the program and any nonstring variables. For a BASIC requiring separate allocations, I recommend loading the program, determining the amount of total free memory space remaining, and then executing a CLEAR <n> command for that amount less 1,000 bytes. This provides a good starting point, and successive tries can be made to reduce the CLEAR statement by 1,000 bytes each time until a successful execution without an "out of memory" message is achieved. For my own applications I then reduce the allocation by another 750 to 1,000 bytes and set that final value into the CLEAR <n> statement at the start of the program.

Just remember that for those BASICs requiring memory allocation, the amount of memory must be determined experimentally; there is no fixed rule of thumb for determining the value to be used in the CLEAR statement. The allocated space must be at least large enough to avoid the "out of string space" message, yet not so large as to result in an "out of memory" error.

BASIC-80 (Microsoft Revisions 5.1 and 5.2) operates in an entirely different way. This interpreter allocates string space dynamically as needed. No CLEAR command is used to make a string-space allocation, and a CLEAR command with any argument serves an entirely different purpose. Under BASIC-80 the command takes the form CLEAR,n,m where n sets the highest memory location available for use by BASIC-80 and m sets aside stack space. The CLEAR command with no arguments simply sets all numeric variables to zero, sets all string variables to nulls, and defaults to maximum memory and a preset stack size.

In handling string data, this interpreter apparently starts off with a small amount of memory automatically designated for strings. When that space runs out, the interpreter performs a garbage collect and sets aside a little more string space. The procedure repeats over and over again as long as new string storage is required. As result, there is no "out of string space" error message with BASIC-80, only an "out of memory" message when all memory has been used up by any combination of string and nonstring storage. On the surface, this sounds like a good approach, but it's costly in terms of execution time for string applications, and, as I will soon show, it makes BASIC-80 the least desirable of all the implementations I've tried using for string-intensive programming.

Applesoft incorporates string pointer arrays into memory space shared with numeric arrays (refer to the memory maps furnished in the Applesoft manual). Its CLEAR statement may be used only without arguments and only for the purpose of setting all variables to zero and all strings to nulls. There is a notable "bug" that allows string storage to overrun the space used by high-resolution graphics screens and machine-language subroutines, so special steps such as the frequent use of the FRE() function have to be incorporated into an Applesoft program to prevent this from happening.

Incidentally, the Applesoft manual makes a point of the fact that unused strings are not removed from memory automatically. For example, if you have A$ assigned to the word PROGRAM and then execute the statement A$="RESULTS", the word RESULT does not overlay and replace PROGRAM. PROGRAM is retained in memory until removed by a garbage-collection operation such as that forced by a FRE() function.

Apple Integer BASIC differs again. Like Applesoft, it does not provide a CLEAR <n> command to allocate string space, but it also lacks a FRE() function to determine the amount of unused memory or force a string-space garbage collection. Unlike Applesoft or the Microsoft versions, Apple Integer BASIC does not allow subscripted string variables (no string arrays). Where the statement DIM A$(20) under Applesoft would indicate a 21-element array with any element from A$(0) through A$(20) having up to 255 characters, it indicates a single variable A$ with a maximum string length of 20 characters under Integer BASIC. Furthermore, every string variable used in an Integer BASIC program must be dimensioned in that manner prior to its first use in any other program statement.

Whether or not it acts to allocate string space that is separate from nonstring space, bear in mind that any CLEAR statement used by any version of BASIC as a part of the program or as a direct command from the keyboard clears all variables immediately. It is not possible to interrupt a program, issue a CLEAR command, and then continue execution from the point of interruption—the program must be restarted.

Free-Space Determinations and String-Space Garbage Collects

Many BASIC instruction manuals, including those for Applesoft and BASIC-80, recommend frequent use of the FRE() function within the body of a program to force the interpreter to clear unused memory space.

Under Applesoft, FRE() is supposed to prevent string storage from overrunning memory assigned to the graphics screens and machine-language subroutines, so it might serve a useful function. Under other BASICs or under Applesoft operating without high-resolution graphics, it may not serve a useful purpose, and it wastes execution time. There is no real gain in forcing a string-space garbage collection more frequently than is absolutely necessary. In fact, the time lost in garbage collections forced unnecessarily can convert a fast, efficient, and practical string-handling program into a slow, inefficient, and impractical one.

Applesoft offers only a FRE(< n >)syntax where the dummy argument <n> may be any numeric constant, variable, or expression. In response, the computer performs a garbage-collection operation to clear unused strings from memory and return all possible memory locations to "available" status before reporting the amount of free space. According to the Applesoft manual, this is the only way available to eliminate "old" and unused strings, and it is mandatory to prevent string space from overrunning and destroying or damaging the contents of "high-res" graphics pages and machine-language subroutines.

Microsoft BASICs offer two forms of the function. The FRE(<n>) function with a numeric dummy argument returns an immediate indication of free space without forcing a string-space garbage collect. On all but BASIC-80 this number does *not* include the space allocated for string storage. The second form FRE(S$) with a string argument does force the string-space garbage collection before reporting space availability and, except for BASIC-80, returns only the free memory remaining in the area allocated for strings.

For Microsoft Revision 4.51, the values returned by FRE(S$) are not the same as those returned by FRE(<n>) since they apply to separate areas of the memory. For BASIC-80 (Microsoft Revisions 5.1 and 5.2), FRE(S$) and FRE(< n >) return the same value because string space is allocated dynamically as needed and is a part of normal memory until actually used. However, the FRE(S$) form still forces the garbage collection under BASIC-80, and that operation requires a significant amount of time.

By way of illustration, I've used Control-C commands to interrupt programs being tested and performed FRE() commands from the terminal keyboard. In so doing I've used a FRE(0) for Applesoft and a FRE("A") for Microsoft BASICs to force the string-space cleanup. Under some older BASICs, the system would have responded within a few seconds, but BASIC-80 and Applesoft both suffered delays of numerous minutes; sometimes the program even appeared to have "hung" because a Control-C command to terminate execution is ineffective while a garbage collect is under way.

The manual for BASIC-80 contains some interesting statements under the description of the FRE() command:

> BE PATIENT: garbage collection may take 1 to 1½ minutes. BASIC will not initiate garbage collection until all free memory has been used up. Therefore, using FRE("") periodically will result in shorter delays for each garbage collection.

While this may be true for programs that don't do a lot of string handling, it has proved quite troublesome in string-intensive programming where as much memory as possible is devoted to string storage and where long lists of lengthy words are being manipulated.

Back in Chapter 3, I mentioned that string handling was one area in which I would have to include some consideration of the old Altair BASIC that I used extensively for several years before upgrading to the CP/M operating system and CP/M-based Microsoft BASICs. For the most part, the disk-extended Altair BASIC, Revision 5.0, released in 1978, looks identical to Microsoft BASIC Revision 4.51, which has been used extensively for samples presented thus far. However, it was a "standalone" language, booting directly from disk without going through a separate operating system such as CP/M. It provided essentially the same set of commands, statements, and functions as Microsoft Revision 4.51, and the two BASICs were almost completely compatible outside of a handful of changes to accommodate the differences between disk control for a standalone language and disk control for a CP/M-based language.

In most applications, both Altair BASIC 5.0 and Microsoft BASIC 4.51 function almost identically, with execution times for particular operations being within approximately 5 percent of each other. However, there is one important exception: string handling. For programs making use of most available computer memory and performing large amounts of string handling and manipulating, there is a tremendous difference in performance between Altair BASIC 5.0 and Microsoft BASIC 4.51, as I will demonstrate in subsequent paragraphs. I realize that most of you who read this do not have access to the old, obsolete Altair systems, but I include that one "oddball" BASIC in these discussions for historical, comparative, and informational purposes and because it shows a radical departure from what seems normal for the popular BASICs available today.

The first noticeable difference between the Altair BASIC and the CP/M-based Microsoft BASICs concerns the performance of string-space garbage-collection operations. Under the Altair BASIC, the string-space garbage-collection delays were noticeable only as an occasional pause of a few seconds—more like a quick "hiccup" in the execution. Converting or "uploading" the same programs to Microsoft BASICs created some new problems completely unrelated to the tasks of altering syntax, substituting instructions, and so on.

In the process of converting the programs from their original Altair BASIC lexical standards to the CP/M-based Microsoft standards, there often was a considerable difference in execution time that could not be accounted for within the body of a program. Typically, Microsoft Revisions 4.51, 5.1, and 5.2 took considerably longer to do the same string handling than did the older Altair BASIC, even though tremendous speed increases were being gained by compiling and linking the programs under Microsoft's BASCOM compiler and LINK-80 linking loader. In some cases, a program that had run in a few minutes under the Altair BASIC would take an hour or even several hours under the Microsoft interpreters.

It soon became obvious that one difference resulted from the way BASIC-80 performed its dynamic memory allocation and string-space garbage collection. To verify and quantify the impact, I wrote a small string-handling program and used it as a benchmark to test the overall execution times of different BASIC versions performing exactly the same programmed operations. The following paragraphs summarize the results of those tests in terms of comparative running times for the benchmark program. I won't claim that the results are statistically valid or in accordance with any standard testing procedures, but they indicate disparities significant enough that simple timing and testing errors would not account for the differences. As usual, timing was done by stopwatch, the watch being started when the Carriage Return was pressed to execute a RUN command and stopped when the audible buzzer sounded as a result of the PRINT CHR$(7) in line 50.

To conduct the tests, three versions of a program were set up, differing from each other in the frequency with which string-space garbage collects were forced by FRE("A") program functions. The three versions of the benchmark program are designated Version A, Version B, and Version C. All three store 800 long strings or "words" in a string array dimensioned for 1,000 elements. To avoid odd results, which sometimes occur when the same string is used over and over again, each array variable is given a slightly different string by adding STR$(X) to the end of a standard test string during each iteration of a FOR...NEXT loop. Version A forces a garbage collect after every 100 words. Version B forces a garbage collect only when all 800 words have been stored. Version C does not force any garbage collects other than what the BASIC interpreter may require as a result of its internal operations. The listings are as follows:

Version A Benchmark

```
5 CLEAR 31ØØØ:DEFSTR P:DEFINT A-O:DEFINT Q-Z:DIM P(1ØØØ)
1Ø P="ABCDEFGHIJKLMNOPQRSTUVWXYZ":Y=1:Z=1
2Ø FOR X=Y TO Y+99:P(X)=P+STR$(X):NEXT
3Ø PRINT FRE("A"),Y
4Ø IF X<8ØØ THEN Z=Z+1ØØ:Y=Z:GOTO 2Ø
5Ø PRINT CHR$ (7)
```

Version B Benchmark

```
5 CLEAR 31ØØØ:DEFSTR P:DEFINT A-O:DEFINT Q-Z:DIM P(1ØØØ)
1Ø P="ABCDEFGHIJKLMNOPQRSTUVWXYZ":Y=1:Z=1
2Ø FOR X=Y TO Y+99:P(X)=P+STR$(X):NEXT
3Ø PRINT Y
4Ø IF X<8ØØ THEN Z=Z+1ØØ:Y=Z:GOTO 2Ø
5Ø PRINT FRE ("A"),CHR$(7)
```

Version C Benchmark

```
5 CLEAR 31ØØØ:DEFSTR P:DEFINT A-O:DEFINT Q-Z:DIM P(1ØØØ)
1Ø P="ABCDEFGHIJKLMNOPQRSTUVWXYZ":Y=1:Z=1
2Ø FOR X=Y TO Y+99:P(X)=P+STR$(X):NEXT
3Ø PRINT Y
4Ø IF X<8ØØ THEN Z=Z+1ØØ:Y=Z:GOTO 2Ø
5Ø PRINT CHR$(7)
```

The CLEAR 31000 statement in line 5 was used only for the Altair BASIC and Microsoft Revision 4.51 tests to allocate memory to string space. Since BASIC-80, including MBASIC and GBASIC on the Apple with a SoftCard, allocates string space dynamically as needed, no CLEAR statement was used when running those tests. Otherwise, the programs were identical. The Altair BASIC was even configured to provide the same 35,035 free bytes of memory before program loading as was provided by Version 5.1 of BASIC-80 on the 64K Altair 8800b computer used for the test. Table 4-1 summarizes the test results.

For the Applesoft tests, the DEFSTR and DEFINT statements were removed from line 5, and variables P and P(.) were changed to P$ and P$(.) respectively. Numeric variables X, Y, and Z were allowed to default to real-precision types because this BASIC doesn't allow declared integer variables such as X%, Y%, and Z% to be used for the control of FOR...NEXT loops. The test results also are summarized in Table 4-1.

The comparisons in Table 4-1 illustrate two things. First, the garbage-collect operations performed by the CP/M versions of the Microsoft BASIC interpreters consume a considerable amount of execution time. Notice that the single garbage collect forced by program Version B adds more than a minute and a half to the execution time of program Version C. Second, the use of the FRE( ) function in a program to force unnecessary garbage collections is extremely costly in terms of execution time as illustrated by the prolonged intervals required for program Version A under all but the Altair BASIC.

Surprisingly, the Applesoft tests all ran considerably faster than the BASIC-80 tests for the 64K Altair machine, but they also ran much more slowly than Altair Revision 5.0 BASIC. Problems were encountered in

Table 4-1

Comparative String-Handling Execution Times

BASIC Implementation	Version A*	Version B*	Version C*
Altair BASIC, Revision 5.0, Disk-Extended Version	12.5 sec.	11.6	11.4 sec.
Microsoft BASIC (OBASIC), Revision 4.51, CP/M Version	412.0 sec.	111.0 sec.	8.6 sec.
Microsoft BASIC (BASIC-80), Revision 5.1, CP/M Version	414.0 sec.	111.0 sec.	8.6 sec.
Microsoft BASIC (BASIC-80), Revision 5.2, CP/M Version	415.0 sec.	112.0 sec.	9.0 sec.
Applesoft Basic running on 48K Apple II Plus with DOS	236.8 sec.	66.0 sec.	11.4 sec.
MBASIC (BASIC-80) running on 56K Apple II Plus with CP/M	581.5 sec.†	370.1 sec.†	370.1 sec.†

*All times are averages of at least five trials.
† "Out of memory" error occurred at time indicated upon attempting to set up P$(780).

running the tests under the MBASIC version of BASIC-80 with a 56K CP/M installed in the Apple II. In all cases, the benchmark programs ran out of memory upon attempting to set P$(780). But look at the amount of time it took to reach the error condition. For Version C of the program, the first 700 array elements were set up in under 20 seconds, and the balance of the time was required by the frequent garbage collects performed as available memory decreased below 2,000 bytes.

In an attempt to get Version C to finish under the Apple's MBASIC, I first changed the DIM P$(1000) to DIM P$(802) in line 5, freeing up some memory previously consumed for unused string-array pointers. The program then took 343.0 seconds to reach the "out of string space" error message, and that message occurred upon my attempting to set P$(800). Leaving the DIM P$(802) statement intact, I then changed string P$ to eliminate only the letter "A" at the beginning of the string. This would make each stored string exactly one character (one byte) shorter. In this case, the program did run to completion in 85.1 seconds, but with only 512 bytes of free memory remaining.

This serves to demonstrate the interaction of available memory, the number of strings being used, and the string-space garbage-collection operation. Simply stated, as available memory decreases, the incidence of garbage collection increases. With less and less memory available to store new strings, more and more time has to be spent cleaning up unused space.

To see what would happen with more extensive string handling but without forcing unnecessary garbage collects, a fourth version of the test program was derived from Version C. This one makes multiple passes through the routine without ever calling a FRE() function. Again, the Altair BASIC was configured to provide the same free memory as BASIC-80 Revision 5.1, and the CLEAR 31000 statement was used in line 5 for Altair BASIC but not for BASIC-80. This fourth program revision was as follows:

Version D Benchmark

```
5 CLEAR 31ØØØ:DEFSTR P:DEFINT A-O:DEFINT Q-Z:DIM P(1ØØØ)
1Ø P="ABCDEFGHIJKLMNOPQRSTUVWXYZ" Y=1:Z=1
2Ø FOR X=Y TO Y+99:P(X)=P+STR$(X):NEXT
3Ø PRINT Y,
4Ø IF X<8Ø0 THEN Z=Z+1ØØ:Y=Z:GOTO 2Ø
5Ø PRINT CHR$(7):GOTO 1Ø
```

Program Version D was run with both Altair BASIC Revision 5.0 and Microsoft BASIC (BASIC-80) Revision 5.1. It was allowed to repeat for five complete passes under each interpreter. The only string-space garbage collects performed were those required by the BASIC interpreter itself; none were forced from the test program itself. The results were dramatic! The Altair BASIC completed the five passes in 84 seconds (1 minute, 24 seconds). Revision 5.1 of BASIC-80 required 1,477 seconds (24 minutes, 37 seconds) for the same five passes.

Version D also was modified for Applesoft, with the CLEAR, DEFSTR and DEFINT statements removed and the P$ and P$(.) used in place of P and P(.). The five repetitions in this case took 600 seconds (10 minutes). Again, the time was longer than for Altair BASIC but shorter than for BASIC-80.

Attempting to run Version D under MBASIC with 56K CP/M on the Apple proved impossibly tedious, even with the modifications made for the earlier tests. Once the first pass had been completed, the garbage collects were performed so frequently that it seemed to take forever to get through a hundred string assignments; the test eventually was abandoned with no time consumption recorded. As a rough extrapolation from what was timed to the point of termination, my best guess is that it would have taken several hours for that test to finish—if it ever finished at all.

For still another comparison, program Version A was compiled and linked using the Microsoft BASCOM compiler and the LINK-80 linking loader. Even with the FRE() function performed every 100 "words," its total execution time in five trials averaged only 6.1 seconds as compared to nearly 7 minutes for the same program under the interpreter. That yielded a 68-to-1 speed advantage for the compiled version. Finally, program Version D was compiled, linked, and run, yielding an execution time of 4.7 seconds for a single pass and 25.7 seconds for a full five passes.

In comparison with the BASIC-80 interpreter run of over 24 minutes, the compiled version yielded a speed advantage of 57 to 1 for the more than 4,000 array insertions performed in the five passes.

This little exercise clearly illustrates that one BASIC does not necessarily perform its string-handling operations like another. As a broad generality, differences of the type noted here often are not evident in ordinary "number crunching." They become apparent only during intensive string-handling operations, and then only when a large number of strings and a large portion of the available memory are in use.

The benchmark programs I've listed can be used to check the performance of almost any BASIC. If the times are close to those indicated for the Altair BASIC, string-intensive programs should execute quickly and efficiently. If, however, the times are closer to those for the BASIC-80 interpreter, the same programs can be expected to run rather slowly and to spend most of their execution time tied up in garbage collections. I've often developed programs of my own that run well under one system but, when moved to another BASIC, run so poorly and so inefficiently that they prove nearly unusable on that system without extensive reprogramming and modification.

String Manipulations

BASIC languages usually offer a number of string-manipulation operations that allow you to combine and separate string values at will. However, not all BASICs offer exactly the same functions and features. Since string handling often is not viewed as a "normal" computer function, the features to accomplish it may be "tacked onto" the language almost as an afterthought. Nevertheless, string manipulations can prove very useful across a wide range of applications, and the following sections of this chapter are devoted to a description of the common features and functions found in a typical extended BASIC.

Of course, most BASICs do allow simple string *concatenation*, in which two strings are combined into one. Usually this is accomplished with a plus sign ("+"), though a few BASICs use the ampersand symbol ("&") to differentiate string concatenation from numeric addition. Under the Microsoft and Apple approaches, a simple string concatenation could be performed with the following program to have variable C$ contain the string "THIS IS A TEST":

```
10 A$="THIS IS ":B$="A TEST"
20 C$=A$+B$
30 PRINT C$
```

Remember that the plus sign in this case denotes concatenation, not addition. Under no circumstances may the symbols for subtraction ("–"), multiplication ("*"), or division ("/") be used in conjunction with string constants or string variables. While concatenating strings is easy to accomplish with a single symbol, separating strings is far more complex and requires a number of special functions that may or may not be inherent in any particular BASIC implementation.

The MID$() Function. In Microsoft and Applesoft BASICs, the MID$() function extracts a string or "substring" of one or more characters from another string. Note that I don't use the term "substring" in the same sense as some "substring-oriented" BASICs do; more on that subject a little later.

The function MID$(<string>,n,m) returns a second string that starts with the nth character of the original and contains m characters. If m exceeds the length of the original or is omitted, the returned string terminates with the last character of the original. Assume that the nine-character string "ABCDEFGHI" is assigned to string variable S$. A MID$(S$,2,1) returns "B", while MID$(S$,4) and MID$(S$,4,100) both return "DEFGHI". Similarly, MID$(S$,1,2) returns "AB", while MID$(S$,1) and MID$(S$,1,254) both return the original string "ABCDEFGHI". When the length is omitted or exceeds that of the original, the returned string is *not* "padded" with spaces. If, however, the starting position exceeds the length of the original string as in MID$(S$,12) for this example, the function returns a null string.

The MID$() Statement. When it's used as a function, MID$() appears on the *right* of an equals sign ("=") in a LET or implied LET statement, as the argument to another function, or as an expression in an IF...THEN... conditional branch. However, MID$() also may be used on the *left* of the equals sign in a LET or implied LET statement under Microsoft BASICs, in which case it becomes a program statement rather than a function. MID$() may not be used as a statement under Applesoft. When it takes the form of a program statement, MID$(< string 1 >,n[,m])= < string 2 > replaces all or any part of < string 1 > with < string 2 >.

Using the same example where S$="ABCDEFGHI", the statement MID$(S$,3,1)="Z" would change S$ to "ABZDEFGHI". In this case, m is the number of characters (from the left) of <string 2> to be used in the replacement; if m is omitted, all of <string 2> is used, but the length of the final string is not allowed to exceed that of the original. The value of n must be within the length of the original string to prevent an "illegal function call" error message. Some samples of possible replacements using the same S$ and assigning "MNOPQRSTU" to variable A$ would return the following value for S$:

```
MID$(S$,3,1)=A$          returns S$="ABMDEFGHI"
MID$(S$,3,3)=A$          returns S$="ABMNOFGHI"
MID$(S$,3,9)=A$          returns S$="ABMNOPQRS"
```

```
MID$(S$,9)=A$                returns S$="ABCDEFGHM"
MID$(S$,7)=MID$(A$,4)        returns S$="ABCDEFPQR"
```

The LEFT$() and RIGHT$() Functions. The functions LEFT$ (<string>,n) and RIGHT$(<string>,n) are available under Microsoft and Applesoft BASICs. They return substrings of the original string that consist of the leftmost or rightmost n characters, respectively. If n exceeds the length of the original string, the returned substring is identical to the original string. Using the same string variable S$="ABCDEFGHI", the function LEFT$(S$,2) returns "AB", RIGHT$(S$,2) returns "HI", LEFT$(S$,20) returns "ABCDEFGHI", and RIGHT$(S$,20) returns "ABCDEFGHI".

LEFT$() and RIGHT$() may be used only as functions, never as statements. That is, they may not appear on the left side of the equals sign in a LET or implied LET statement. As functions, they may appear on the right of the equals sign, as arguments to other functions, or as one of the expressions compared in an IF...THEN... statement. Some possible uses of these functions might include:

```
A%=LEN(MID$(S$,5))               A%=ASC(RIGHT$(S$,4))
IF RIGHT$(S$,1)="A" THEN...      IF LEN(MID$(S$,5)) > 10 THEN...
```

"Substring" Handling. There are a few BASICs around that are "substring-oriented," and they perform their limited string-handling operations in a totally different manner than Microsoft and Applesoft versions. Typically, these are recognizable because they have no MID$(), LEFT$(), or RIGHT$() functions. Furthermore, several do not allow string variables to be dimensioned for subscripting, using the DIM statement to specify the maximum number of characters in a given string variable instead of the number of variables in an array; in these cases, DIM S$(19) indicates a single string variable of no more than 19 characters. A few substring-style BASICs allow string variables to be dimensioned for subscripting but also force the programmer to declare the maximum string length. In such cases, the statement DIM S$(10,20) indicates a 21-variable array in which each string may be no longer than 10 characters.

Apple Integer BASIC can be classified as a substring-style BASIC of the first type; a DIM S$(20) statement would be required to set up a single string variable S$ that allows no more than 20 characters. Furthermore, Apple Integer BASIC lacks the MID$(), LEFT$(), and RIGHT$() functions (among others) for easy string manipulations.

As a general rule, these types of BASIC are good for applications in which strings are used on a limited basis. There's no problem in using strings and string variables to format printouts and displays, provide header lines, and so on. However, in programs relying on extensive

Table 4-2

Substring-Handling Conversions

Microsoft BASIC	Other BASIC
S1$=MID$(S$,n,1)	S1$=S$(n)
S1$=MID$(S$,n,m-n+1)	S1$=S$(n,m)
S$=LEFT$(S$,n-1)+S1$+MID$(S$,n+1)	S$(n)=S1$
S$=LEFT$(S$,n-1)+S1$+MID$(S$,m+1)	S$(n,m)=S1$
MID$(S$,1,1)=S1$	S$(n)=S1$
MID$(S$,n,m-n+1)=S1$	S$(n,m)=S1$

string data for such things as sorting for specific letter combinations or organizing long lists of words according to predetermined parameters, manipulations can be difficult at best.

With these BASICs, obtaining substrings follows a different procedure. Instead of the MID$(), LEFT$(), and RIGHT$() functions being used, the expression S$(n) obtains the nth character of string S$, while S$(n,m) obtains the substring of S$ that begins at position n and ends at position m. Table 4-2 summarizes some of the more common operations required to provide the corresponding string-handling functions on such BASICs.

Not all substitutions will work on every variation of BASIC, so some experimentation is required to determine which ones will work and what they will do.

The CHR$() and ASC() Functions. Two intrinsic functions are used to shift back and forth between string characters and their decimal ASCII equivalents. These functions are available in most BASICs, but not in Apple Integer BASIC. The CHR$(n) function returns a single-character string equivalent to ASCII value n. As examples, CHR$(32) returns a space, CHR$(12) returns a Form Feed, and CHR$(65) returns the uppercase letter "A".

The reverse function is performed by ASC(S$). This function returns the decimal ASCII value of the *first* character in string S$. For example, if S$ contains either the single-character string "A" or the multi-character string "ABCD", the function ASC(S$) returns the ASCII code 65. Even more complex structures can be developed in combination with other functions, such as ASC(MID$(S$,3)) or ASC(MID$(S$,3,1)), either of which returns the ASCII value 67 for the first letter of the substring starting at position three—a "C" if S$ contains "ABCD".

The CHR$() function is particularly useful for outputting one of the *nonprinting* characters in the ASCII set. Typically, these are the characters that are entered with the Control key plus another key pressed simultaneously. For example, to "ring the bell" of a line printer, you need to transmit a Control-G character. However, most BASICs will not accept Control characters as string values. In that case, the statement LPRINT CHR$(7) transmits the character having an ASCII value 7, which happens to be the Control-G character that rings the bell. Similar program statements are useful for transmitting Line Feeds and Carriage Returns to the terminal or printer, especially since the Carriage Return key is a delimiter and ends any input line being typed.

Applesoft and Apple Integer BASIC both use a Control-D character to initiate or terminate operations involving disk transfers. Under Applesoft, the Control-D normally is provided by a CHR$(4) function. Integer BASIC provides no CHR$() function, so the Control-D is typed as a two-key character, is embedded in quotation marks as a quoted string, and is *not* displayed on the screen. Therefore, a statement in Integer BASIC appearing as D$="" might very well contain a nonprinting character and might actually be something like D$="[Control-D]".

I know of no equivalents for the CHR$() and ASC() functions when they are not available in the BASIC interpreter. While a language such as Apple Integer BASIC may allow the direct entry of nonprinting characters, it still prevents a program from converting back and forth between quoted literal characters and their equivalent ASCII codes. In string-intensive programming, this can cause a bit of a problem by preventing conversions of strings into numeric forms that may be faster to manipulate. When you need such statements in a program and are limited to using a BASIC that doesn't provide them, you have no choice but to find an alternative to the entire procedure built around the CHR$() or ASC() function and to reprogram that procedure in its entirety. Either method may be very difficult and probably will destroy the efficiency of the program as a whole.

The INSTR() Function. Perhaps the single most useful string-handling function provided by an extended BASIC is the INSTR() function. This function is included in most Microsoft derivatives of BASIC including BASIC-80. The function is unavailable in Applesoft, Apple Integer BASIC, and some other popular implementations. However, the absence of the INSTR() function can be circumvented with one or more substitute subroutines that may be called as necessary.

The purpose of INSTR() is to return a number that indicates where a particular string occurs within a larger string. The function takes the form INSTR([n,]S$,S1$) and returns a numeric value indicating the character position at which string S1$ is found in string S$. The optional n indicates the starting position of the search; if it is omitted, the first character position is assumed to be the start.

As examples, assume that S$="ABCDEF", so the functions INSTR(S$,"C"), INSTR$(1,S$,"C"), INSTR(2,S$,"C"), and

INSTR(3,S$,"C") all return a numeric value of three. Meanwhile, the function INSTR(4,S$,"C") returns a zero because the "C" is in the third character position and precedes the start of the search at the fourth position. Whenever a match is not found, a zero is returned.

This function serves as a fast and easy way to test whether or not a given string contains a specified flag character or any particular character combination. Assume, for the moment, that 200 English words are stored in an array from S$(1) through S$(200). From that list, it's necessary to determine how many of the words contain the letter combination "IE". A simple way of performing the test is with the following routine:

```
1000 I%=0: FOR X%=1 TO 200
1002 IF INSTR(S$(X%), "IE")<>0 THEN I%=I%+1
1004 NEXT
```

Upon completing this little routine, I% contains a count of the words containing an "IE" letter combination *anywhere* within a word. It would not, however, include words in which the "I" and "E" were separated by any other character, so a word such as "TRIED" would be counted, but "ITEMS" would not.

When the BASIC language does not provide an INSTR() function, the same end results may be accomplished with character-by-character tests of the strings, although the procedure tends to be much slower than simple INSTR() checks. A small routine merely to test for the presence of one substring within another, with the equivalent INSTR() format to the right, would appear something like:

```
1000 FG%=0: Z%=LEN(S1$)                 1000 IF INSTR(S$,S1$) THEN FG%=1
1010 FOR X%=Y% TO LEN(S$)
1020 IF MID$(S$,X%,Z%)=S1$
     THEN FG%=1
1030 NEXT
```

In this routine, FG% is a flag that is set nonzero if the substring of S1$ is found within string S$. Variable Y% is set to a nonzero value before entering the routine, and it denotes the position in string S$ at which the search is to begin; a zero value for Y% will give an error message in most BASICs because strings do not have a zero character position. If the entire string is to be searched, Y% should be a one, or line 1010 should be changed to read FOR X%=1 TO LEN (S$). Note that substring S1$ may be a single character or a combination of several characters and that it is always handled literally. That is, searching for the presence of "ABC" in S$ is not the same as searching for "ACB".

If the actual position is needed for subsequent operations using that value, the routine is easily altered:

```
1000 FG%=0; Z%=LEN(S1$)
1010 FOR X%=Y% TO LEN(S$)
1020 IF MID$(S$,X%,Z%)=S1$ THEN
     FG%=X%: X%=LEN(S$)
1030 NEXT
```

```
1000 FG%=INSTR(S$,S1$)
```

In this case, the loop is terminated by forcing control variable X% to a value equaling the end value of the loop as soon as the first match is found. Variable FG% holds the position of the first match at the end of the loop. If no match is found, FG% has a zero value that may be tested to skip subsequent operations in the program if the string does not contain the substring.

A more complicated situation arises when a string is to be tested for the presence of one element of some other string. For example, it may be desirable to determine whether or not a given string S$ contains any one of the characters contained in the string S1$, where S1$="#$%&*+?". This requires the use of nested loops of which one is controlled by the length of S$ and the other is controlled by the length of S1$. Again, the comparable procedure using the INSTR() function is shown on the right:

```
1000 FG%=0
1010 FOR X%=1 TO LEN(S$)
1020 FOR Y%=1 TO LEN(S1$)
1030 IF MID$(S$,X%,1)=
     MID$(S1$,Y%,1) THEN
     FG%=1:X%=LEN(S$):
     Y%=LEN(S1$)
1040 NEXT Y%,X%
```

```
1000 FOR Y%=1 TO LEN(S1$)
1010 FG%=INSTR(S$,MID$(S1$,Y%,1)
1020 IF FG% THEN Y%=LEN(S1$)
1030 NEXT
```

In the left routine, both loops are terminated with variable FG% set nonzero as soon as any match is found. To terminate the loops, *both* control variables X% and Y% are forced to their maximum values at the same time FG% is set nonzero. If no match is found, the loops exit with FG% set to zero.

One of the most frequent uses of the INSTR() function in my own programs is to determine whether or not a string contains an asterisk ("*") or plus sign ("+") flag to indicate that it has been tested or used at some prior point in the program. Whenever I use or test a word, I insert the flag into the array variable with a statement such as S$(X)="*"+S$(X). Later, the test for the presence of the flag is part of an IF... THEN... statement and takes the form:

```
IF INSTR(S$(X), "*")THEN...
```

Since I always write my programs so that the flag is in the first character position of the string, the fastest and easiest substitution in the absence of an INSTR() function is to convert the program statement to:

```
IF LEFT$(S$(X),1)="*" THEN...
```

Of course, the usual question has to come up: *how much time can be saved by using the INSTR() function instead of an alternate approach?* One way of testing the relative speed consumptions is to search a list of strings, using exactly the same strings and searching for the same things with two different methods.

The two routines that follow illustrate the timing with the INSTR() function first and the timing with an alternate search method second. In each, the same list of 210 English words with lengths varying from 4 to 14 letters each is stored as array elements S$(1) through S$(210), and successive passes are made through the word list to provide separate counts of the number of words containing each letter of the alphabet at least once. In either version, variable I% holds the word count (210). CHR$(B%), the letter being sought, is incremented 26 times from ASCII 65 through 90 to make CHR$(B%) the letters A through Z in sequence. In the first test, the INSTR() function allows testing entire words at a time; in the second, each word must be searched one letter at a time until a match is detected. First, the routines are timed using Microsoft BASIC Revision 4.51 with string-space allocation limited to 10,000 bytes to avoid unexpected hangups due to the string-space garbage collections already discussed. Then they are timed with Microsoft Revision 5.2 to check the performance with dynamic memory allocation.

```
1000 FOR B%=65 TO 90
1002 A%=0: FOR X%=1 TO I%
1004 IF INSTR(S$(X%),CHR$(B%)) THEN A%=A%+1
1006 NEXT: PRINT A%
1008 NEXT
```

[Microsoft Rev. 4.51: 48.0 seconds]
[Microsoft Rev. 5.2: 45.5 seconds]

```
1000 FOR B%=65 TO 90
1002 A%=0: FOR X%=1 TO I%
1004 FOR Y%=1 TO LEN(S$(X%))
1006 IF MID$(S$(X%),Y%,1)=CHR$(B%) THEN A%=A%+1: Y%=LEN(S$(X%))
```

```
1008 NEXT
1010 NEXT:PRINT A%
1012 NEXT
```

[Microsoft Rev. 4.51: 447.6 seconds]
[Microsoft Rev. 5.2: 444.3 seconds]

As you see, both routines perform exactly the same overall function on the same data, but they do so with a tremendous difference in execution speed. Under Revision 4.51, the routine with the INSTR() function takes only 10.7 percent of the time required by the routine without the function, and under Revision 5.2 it takes only 10.2 percent. Obviously, the INSTR() function offers a great advantage for this type of string searching and should be used wherever and whenever possible.

The next matter of concern is whether or not the INSTR() function offers any advantage over simple LEFT$() and MID$() functions to detect a character appearing in a known position. The following three routines assume that words may or may not be "flagged" with asterisks ("*") in the first character positions, and it is necessary to know how many such words are so flagged. The same list of 210 words is used as in the preceding examples, but the B% control loop has been set to 20 repetitions of the test to provide an adequate period for stopwatch timing.

```
1000 FOR B%=1 TO 20
1002 A%=0: FOR X%=1 TO I%
1004 IF INSTR(S$(X%),"*") THEN A%=A%+1
1006 NEXT: PRINT A%
1008 NEXT
```

[Microsoft Rev. 4.51: 28.8 seconds]
[Microsoft Rev. 5.2: 27.8 seconds]

```
1000 FOR B%=1 TO 20
1002 A%=0: FOR X%=1 TO I%
1004 IF MID$(S$(X%),1,1)="*" THEN A%=A%+1
1006 NEXT: PRINT A%
1008 NEXT
```

[Microsoft Rev. 4.51: 37.6 seconds]
[Microsoft Rev. 5.2: 36.2 seconds]

```
1000 FOR B%=1 TO 20
1002 A%=0: FOR X%=1 TO I%
```

```
1004 IF LEFT$(S$(X%),1)="*" THEN A%=A%+1
1006 NEXT: PRINT A%
1008 NEXT
```

[Microsoft Rev. 4.51: 33.8 seconds]
[Microsoft Rev. 5.2: 32.6 seconds]

These three tests show that the INSTR() function maintains a speed advantage over both the MID$() and LEFT$() functions. The MID$() test took 30 percent to 31 percent longer than the INSTR() test, while the LEFT$() test only took about 17 percent longer. Incidentally, trying another test using INSTR(1,S$(X%),"*") in line 1004 instead of the INSTR(S$(X%),"*") function shown in the first example increased the execution time by 14 percent to 32.8 seconds under Revision 4.51 and by 12.5 percent to 31.3 seconds under Revision 5.2. As a general rule, avoid using the optional starting location for the INSTR() function whenever possible; that extra constant, variable, or expression costs you a lot of time.

Before attempting to convert any INSTR() function in any program, whether from the INSTR() to another method or from the other method to the INSTR() approach, you should study its intended purpose carefully. The INSTR() function is a quick and easy way to achieve a great many different objectives, and no one substitution is going to work in every case.

The SPACE$() Function. Taking the form SPACE$(n), this function returns a string of n spaces. That is, a statement such as S$=SPACE$(20) would set string variable S$ equal to 20 spaces. This function should not be confused with SPC(n), which is used only in PRINT and LPRINT statements to print n spaces on the terminal device. There are two possible approaches to substituting for the SPACE$() function, one using a quoted string and the other using a FOR. . . NEXT loop:

```
10 S$=SPACE$(3)      equals     10 S$="^^^"
10 S$=SPACE$(20)     equals     10 S$=""
                                20 FOR X=1 TO 20
                                30 S$=S$+"^"
                                40 NEXT
```

In general, it's best to use the first form, with a quoted string, when ten or fewer spaces are required. In fact, the SPACE$() function should never be used for just a few spaces since it requires more memory to store the function, parentheses, and argument than does a short quoted string. The FOR. . . NEXT loop approach should be used only when there is no

SPACE$() function and a long string of more than about 10 spaces is needed. In any case, building a string one character at a time is extremely inefficient if the SPACE$() function is available.

To verify the relative time advantages or disadvantages, I ran a series of tests on the SPACE$() function and its equivalents. The routines and the times obtained under Microsoft Revisions 4.51 and 5.2, deleting the CLEAR 25000 statement from line 10 for Revision 5.2, were as follows:

```
10 CLEAR 25000: DIM S$(1000)
20 FOR X%=0 TO 1000
30 S$(X%)="^^^^^^"
40 NEXT
```

[Microsoft Rev. 4.51: 4.5 seconds]
[Microsoft Rev. 5.2: 4.4 seconds]

```
10 CLEAR 25000: DIM S$(1000)
20 FOR X%=0 TO 1000
30 S$(X%)=SPACE$(6)
40 NEXT
```

[Microsoft Rev. 4.51: 5.5 seconds]
[Microsoft Rev. 5.2: 5.3 seconds]

```
10 CLEAR 25000: DIM S$(1000)
20 FOR X%=0 TO 1000
30 S$(X%)=SPACE$(19)
40 NEXT
```

[Microsoft Rev. 4.51: 5.6 seconds]
[Microsoft Rev. 5.2: 5.4 seconds]

```
10 CLEAR 25000: DIM S$(1000)
20 FOR X%=0 TO 1000
30 S$(X$)="": FOR Y%=1 TO 19
35 S$(X%)=S$(X%)+"^":NEXT
40 NEXT
```

[Microsoft Rev. 4.51: 1,164 seconds]
[Microsoft Rev. 5.2: 727 seconds]

Using the quoted short string had a noticeable speed advantage over the SPACE$() function. Under Revision 4.51, it required 1.0 second (22 percent) less time for 1001 six-space strings, while under Revision 5.2 it required 0.9 second (20.5 percent) less time. The FOR...NEXT loop approach turned out to be a real loser under either BASIC, requiring more than 200 times longer under Revision 4.51 and more than 130 times longer under Revision 5.2 to prepare 1,001 nineteen-space strings when compared with the equivalent SPACE$() function.

The great time disparities in the last test routine are due to the interpreters' running headlong into the string-space garbage-collection delays I pointed out earlier. The difference between the Revision 4.51 time of 1,164 seconds and the Revision 5.2 time of 727 seconds seems to be attributable to the difference in the amount of memory available. Remember that Revision 5.2 allocates string space dynamically, so it has more memory space available and performs the garbage collection fewer times.

This is one of those instances in which I have to refer back to the old, obsolete Altair Revision 5.0 BASIC for its comparative and historical value. Running all four test routines (complete with the CLEAR 25000 statement in line 10) on the same computer but with that BASIC, the times obtained were 4.6, 5.8, 6.0, and 157.6 seconds, respectively. For the first three routines, the times were comparable to those obtained under the CP/M-based Microsoft interpreters. But the fourth routine ran from 4.6 to 7.4 times faster under the Altair interpreter than under either Microsoft interpreter, although it still took almost 27 times longer than the equivalent operation using the SPACE$() function. Again, I make this reference just to show what can happen when programs are translated from one BASIC to another without examining the individual details of the operations. Translating a program with FOR. . . NEXT loop string constructions similar to this can cause drastic slowdowns and a tremendous loss of efficiency.

The STRING$() Function. Taking the form STRING$(n,m), this function returns a string of n characters all having ASCII code m. For example, the function STRING$(80,42) returns a string of 80 asterisks (ASCII code 42), and PRINT STRING$(80,42) is a handy way of printing a line of asterisks across the width of an 80-column display screen. Again, there are two possible approaches to substituting for the STRING$() function. Relatively short strings may be defined as a quoted string, while longer ones may be constructed by a FOR. . . NEXT loop. Typically, these approaches would look like this:

```
10 S$=STRING$(5,42)       equals     10 S$="*****"
10 S$=STRING$(80,42)      equals     10 S$=""
                                     20 FOR X=1 TO 80
                                     30 S$=S$+"*"
                                     40 NEXT
```

Alternatively, the function may take the form STRING$(n,S$). In that case, it returns a string of n characters all of which are identical to the *first* character of string S$. As examples, if S$ contains "ABCD", STRING$(10,S$) returns a single string of ten "A" characters, while STRING$(10,MID$(S$,3)) returns a string of ten "C" characters.

The same efficiency considerations affect the use of STRING$() as the use of SPACE$(). Specifically, use quoted strings when only a few characters are required, and use either the STRING$() or the FOR. . . NEXT loop, in that order of preference, when longer strings of the same character are needed. Again, I performed some comparative tests paralleling those performed for the SPACE$() function. The results and the times obtained under Microsoft Revisions 4.51 and 5.2 were as follows:

```
10 CLEAR 25000: DIM S$(1000)         10 CLEAR 25000: DIM S$(1000)
20 FOR X%=0 TO 1000                  20 FOR X%=0 TO 1000
```

```
30 S$(X%)="******"
40 NEXT
```

[Microsoft Rev. 4.51: 4.5 seconds]
[Microsoft Rev. 5.2: 4.4 seconds]

```
30 S$(X%)=STRING$(6,42)
40 NEXT
```

[Microsoft Rev. 4.51: 6.5 seconds]
[Microsoft Rev. 5.2: 6.1 seconds]

```
1Ø CLEAR 25ØØØ: DIM S$(1ØØØ)
2Ø FOR X%=Ø TO 1ØØØ
3Ø S$(X%)=STRING$(19,42)
4Ø NEXT
```

[Microsoft Rev. 4.51: 6.6 seconds]
[Microsoft Rev. 5.2: 6.2 seconds]

```
1Ø CLEAR 25ØØØ: DIM S$(1ØØØ)
2Ø FOR X%=Ø TO 1ØØØ
3Ø S$(X$)="": FOR Y%=1 TO 19
35 S$(X%)=S$(X%)+"*": NEXT
4Ø NEXT
```

[Microsoft Rev. 4.51: 1,164 seconds]
[Microsoft Rev. 5.2: 727 seconds]

The results are quite comparable to those obtained for the SPACE$() function, with the same approaches having the same relative advantages and disadvantages. Note, however, that the STRING$() function takes slightly longer than the SPACE$() function, with STRING$() requiring about a second longer for 1,001 operations. I also tested the operation with S$(X%)=STRING$(19,"*") in line 30 of the third routine and found it took 6.8 seconds as compared with 6.6 seconds for the STRING$(19,42) function under Revision 4.51 and 6.5 seconds compared to 6.2 seconds under Revision 5.2. Therefore, it would seem that a numeric ASCII code offers a slight advantage over a string constant or variable in this application.

The STR$() and VAL() Functions. These two functions are used to switch back and forth between literal strings and numeric values. STR$(n) returns a literal string representation of the number n. VAL(S$) returns the numeric value of string S$; if the first character of S$ is not "+", "–", or a digit, VAL(S$) returns a zero. For example, STR$(20) would return a literal string " 20" (note the leading space) and could be used in a statement of the form S$=STR$(20).

When the STR$() function is part of formatted outputs to the screen or to a printed page, some caution is necessary. A leading space in the returned string is provided under the Microsoft versions of BASIC but is not included in the string returned by Applesoft. Therefore, the statement PRINT "TEST"+STR$(N) where N is set to 20 would print as TEST 20 under Microsoft BASICs but as TEST20 under Applesoft.

The same difference exists when printing or outputting any number or numeric variable—some BASICs print a leading space. Thus, the statements PRINT "TEST"; 20 and PRINT "TEST";N would both print TEST 20 under Microsoft versions but would print TEST20 under Applesoft or Apple Integer BASIC. Failure to account for the presence or absence of the leading space can result in improperly formatted outputs.

One technique to get rid of the leading space in the string is to apply the MID$() function to obtain only the characters beginning at the second position. Thus, Microsoft BASICs would return " 20" for STR$(20) but would return "20" for MID$(STR$(20),2). However, the MID$() function applied in this manner under Applesoft would demolish the results since the string has no leading space. With Applesoft, MID$(STR$(29),2) would return a "9" instead of the desired "29".

To reverse the procedure, VAL(S$) with S$ being the quoted string "20" would return a numeric 20 and could be used in the statement N=VAL(S$) where N is a numeric variable. Leading spaces have no effect on the VAL() function and may or may not be present; they need not be restored if stripped off during a preceding STR() operation. However, to obtain a nonzero value for N, the first nonspace character of the string must be a numeral, a plus sign, or a minus sign. Most BASICs allow variable N to be either an integer or a real number. As a result, setting S$ equal to the string "−123.45" would result in N=VAL(S$) or N!=VAL(S$) obtaining −123.45 as the single-precision value, while N%=VAL(S$) would return −123 as the integer value.

When they are not provided by the BASIC interpreter, there are no clear-cut substitutions for either the STR$() or VAL() functions, although it occasionally may be possible to imitate part of their operation with some convoluted CHR$() and ASC() manipulations.

The LEN() Function. Taking the form LEN(S$), this function returns the number of characters or length of string S$. For example, if S$ contains "ABCDEF", LEN(S$) returns a numeric 6 as the actual count of characters. All characters including nonprinting characters and spaces are used in the determination of a string's length. Therefore, if S$ contains " ABCDEF ", LEN(S$) would return a numeric 8 for the six alphabetic characters plus the leading and trailing spaces. Constructing a substitute for this function can be a bit tricky, but one approach might be:

```
100 Z%=0
110 ON ERROR GOTO 1000
120 FOR X%=1 TO 255
130 IF ASC(MID$(S$,X%))>0 THEN Z%=Z%+1
140 NEXT
150 ON ERROR GOTO 0
. . .
1000 IF ERR=5 THEN X%=255:RESUME NEXT
```

In this routine, the value of Z% upon exiting the loop at line 140 would be the number of characters in string S$. The little error-trapping routine is necessary because line 130 yields an "illegal function call" (error code 5 under the BASIC tested) when the value of X% exceeds the length of S$. By trapping that specific error and forcing immediate termination of the loop by setting the control variable to its maximum value, the error is prevented from interfering with the operation of the program. Line 150 then cancels the particular error trap necessary for just this one loop. The maximum value of the loop-control variable is set at 255 because Microsoft BASICs limit the maximum length of any string to 255 characters.

To diverge for a moment: this routine touches on the concept of error trapping. It's important to point out that the structure shown will not work with Applesoft. That form of BASIC runs into trouble upon executing a RESUME statement to the FOR . . . NEXT loop and ends up in an infinite loop. Although you'd never need it because Applesoft has the LEN() function, the comparable routine under that language would have to be written something like this:

```
100 Z%=0: A%=0: ER%=0
102 ONERR GOTO 1000
104 IF ER%=0 THEN IF ASC(MID$(S$,A%))>0
    THEN Z%=Z%+1
106 A%=A%+1: IF A%<255 THEN 104
. . .
1000 Y%=PEEK(222): POKE 216,0
1002 IF Y%=53 THEN A%=255: ER%=1
1004 RESUME
```

In this routine, an "illegal quantity" error (code 53) is trapped at lines 1000 through 1004. The POKE 216,0 in line 1000 resets the error-detection feature to respond normally for subsequent errors. The sequential IF . . . THEN . . . tests of line 104 are necessary to prevent an infinite loop by aborting the test and transferring to line 106 when ER% is nonzero.

Now back to the subject of the LEN() function. To illustrate just how much time is saved by LEN(), consider the following two routines run under Microsoft BASIC. A list of 209 English words is stored in S$(1) through S$(209), and the length of each word is to be stored in a corresponding element of the L%(.) integer array. Variable I% contains the total number of words in the list. These routines test for all error conditions by omitting the IF ERR=5 . . . statement from line 1000; including that test would increase the time even more. The RESUME NEXT could just as easily have been written RESUME 1008 to branch directly to the NEXT statement.

```
1000 FOR X%=1 TO I%
1002 L%(X%)=LEN(S$(X%))
1004 NEXT
```

[Microsoft Rev. 4.51: 1.5 seconds]
[Microsoft Rev. 5.2: 1.4 seconds]

```
1000 ON ERROR GOTO 9000
1002 FOR X%=1 TO I%: L%(X%)=0
1004 FOR Y%=1 TO 255
1006 IF ASC(MID$(S$(X%),Y%))>0
     THEN L%(X%)=L%(X%)+1
1008 NEXT Y%,X%
1010 ON ERROR GOTO 0
1012 END
9000 Y%=255: RESUME NEXT
```

[Microsoft Rev. 4.51: 24.9 seconds]
[Microsoft Rev. 5.2: 24.0 seconds]

Both routines provide the same results, but the LEN() function certainly makes the procedure a lot easier, obviously requires fewer steps and less memory, and runs 16 to 17 times faster. Certainly, quite a few excess line numbers can be saved, an entire FOR. . . NEXT loop can be eliminated, and the need for error trapping can be avoided.

Defined Variable Types

In all preceding samples of this chapter, I've used explicit data-type declarations for variable names. As a result, I've had to append a percent symbol ("%") to indicate an integer, an exclamation point ("!") for single precision, a pound symbol ("#") for double precision, or a dollar sign ("$") for a string. At best, the only shortcut has been to leave a variable name undeclared and allow it to default to a single-precision name under Microsoft BASICs, a real-precision name under Applesoft, or an integer (the only numeric type allowed) under Integer BASIC. Personally, I find this quite cumbersome, especially when I'm using all integers for numeric values and have to use the percent symbol each and every time. It also consumes memory because each symbol has to be stored.

Microsoft BASICs all provide a special set of program statements (or direct keyboard commands) that make life a lot easier. The statements DEFINT, DEFSNG, DEFDBL, and DEFSTR provide a means by which variable types can be predefined according to the first letter of the variable name. These definitions thus relieve the programmer of the memory-space overhead and typing effort of explicitly declaring each variable type each time it is used. In a program, the statements are followed by a letter or letter range that denotes the starting letter(s) of the variables assigned as a particular type. These statements function as shown by the examples in Table 4-3.

Table 4-3

Variable-Type Definitions

Statement	Function
DEFSTR P	Variable names beginning with P are strings.
DEFINT A-O	Variable names beginning with A through O are integers.
DEFSNG Q	Variable names beginning with Q are single-precision numbers.
DEFDBL R	Variable names beginning with R are double-precision numbers.

In most of my own programming applications, single- and double-precision numbers are infrequently required, so only the DEFSTR and DEFINT statements are of major concern. I generally try to use a uniform approach to assigning variable types, with specific letters reserved for specific types. Somehow, over the years, I've become locked into a pattern of using names beginning with P (and sometimes O) as string variables, while all others are defined as integer variables. I know! That choice doesn't seem logical, and I've long since forgotten the original reason for picking P and O as string-variable names. Since I've written almost all my programs that way, it would be too difficult to go back and change them, but with a little 20/20 hindsight, it now seems I would have been better advised to set names with S and T as string variables rather than O and P.

Regardless of which letters are assigned to what variable types, predefinition does offer some significant advantages. In my applications, using the DEFSTR and DEFINT statements allows omission of the dollar sign ("$") string declaration and the percent sign ("%") integer declaration with each variable name and results in a significant memory reduction of hundreds of bytes per program. Sometimes it provides a small but noticeable reduction in execution time, but not always.

Since BASICs such as Applesoft do not provide these definition statements, those programs have to declare all variables properly or allow undeclared variables to default to the proper types. For example, I can execute a DEFINT A-O,Q-Z statement and a DEFSTR P statement at the start of a BASIC-80 program and subsequently call a string-array variable such as P(X) with an integer subscript. However, under Applesoft, I would have to call the same variable as P$(X%), or I could get away with P$(X) if I wanted to use somewhat slower real-precision subscripts.

As you lift programs from published sources or examine the sample routines presented in the remainder of this book, be sure to pay close attention to any type definitions in the first few lines. You also should be aware that a defined type has no effect on a variable name declared explicitly as a different type later in the program. That is, a DEFSTR P statement defines variable names beginning with P as strings, but it has no effect on variables P%, P!, or P#. In this situation, at least four variables may be named "P", with P being a string, P% being an integer, P! being a single-precision number, and P# being a double-precision number. Under some unusual versions, P$ could be used as a separate fifth variable name, but most BASICs would treat P and P$ as being one and the same. An easy test would be to type the following list of direct commands at the keyboard (without line numbers):

```
DEFSTR P      [response should be OK or cursor]
P="A"         [response should be OK or cursor]
P%=1          [response should be OK or cursor]
P!=2.Ø        [response should be OK or cursor]
P#=3.Ø        [response should be OK or cursor]
PRINT P       [response should be A]
PRINT P%      [response should be 1]
PRINT P!      [response should be 2]
PRINT P#      [response should be 3]
PRINT P$      [response may be A or a blank line]
```

If the final response to the PRINT P$ command is the letter "A", you can assume that variables named P and P$ are one and the same. If the response is a blank line, P$ contains a null string and is completely independent of the predefined string variable P. You should expect the explicitly declared variable and the predefined variable to be the same for each variable type—it would be an unusual BASIC that allowed them to be independent. The DEFINT, DEFSNG, and DEFDBL statements then can be tested in the same manner.

An interesting feature has been incorporated into this scheme that I've used occasionally and with good results where a small portion of a program requires all single-precision numbers. It's possible to start off a program with a DEFINT A-N statement and have variables beginning with the letters A through N defined as integers. Later in the program, I can use DEFSNG A-N to redefine variable names beginning with A through N as single-precision numbers. The original integer variables are not lost; they can be recalled after the second definition by explicitly declaring the integer type as part of the variable name.

For example, suppose that DEFINT A-N is executed at the start of a program, variable BB is set to an integer 25, and DEFSNG A-N is executed later in the program. A new variable BB then can be set to a single-precision value such as 32.98, but the original value of integer BB can be recalled by using BB% as the variable name. As many redefinitions as desired can be applied to the variable names as long as you remember what variables were used under what definition and later call for them by explicitly indicating the type under which they were set during an earlier definition.

In an attempt to verify the overall advantages of predefined variable types in terms of memory savings and execution speed, I again conducted a series of tests. The results, however, were surprising:

```
10 FOR X%=1 TO 5000
20 Y%=((2+3+4+5)+(2+3+4+5))*5
30 NEXT
```

[Microsoft Rev. 4.51: 63.8 seconds]
[Microsoft Rev. 5.2: 56.1 seconds]

```
5 DEFINT A-Z
10 FOR X=1 TO 5000
20 Y=((2+3+4+5)+(2+3+4+5)) *5
30 NEXT
```

[Microsoft Rev. 4.51: 64.1 seconds]
[Microsoft Rev. 5.2: 56.5 seconds]

In this case, I had expected to see a slight speed difference in the opposite direction. I then tried two other routines using variables in place of constants.

```
10 A%=2:B%=3:C%=4:D%=5
20 FOR X%=1 TO 15000
30 Y%=((A%+B%+C%+D%)+(A%+B%+C%+D%)) *D%
40 NEXT
```

[Microsoft Rev. 4.51: 254.5 seconds; 85 bytes (no spaces)]
[Microsoft Rev. 5.2: 225.7 seconds; 85 bytes]

```
5 DEFINT A-Z
10 A=2:B=3:C=4:D=5
20 FOR X=1 TO 15000
30 Y=((A+B+C+D)+(A+B+C+D))*D
40 NEXT
```

[Microsoft Rev. 4.51: 263.5 seconds; 79 bytes (no spaces)]
[Microsoft Rev. 5.2: 233.5 seconds; 79 bytes]

In these two tests, the use of the DEFINT A-Z statement actually slowed execution by 9 seconds for Revision 4.51 and by 7.6 seconds for Revision 5.2, thus adding 3.3 percent to 3.5 percent to the faster version. This result was totally unexpected, particularly since I've tested lengthy programs with and without predefinition and have experienced a time advantage with the predefinitions. But I'm unable to find a single, *short* operation that can be presented within the scope of this book to verify what I generally see on long programs of several hundred lines.

A memory savings of 6 bytes is achieved between the last two examples. If line 5 is removed, the consumption for the second example is only 70 bytes, or a savings of 15 bytes by removing the explicit declarations. Since line 5 would probably appear only once at the start of a program, its 9 bytes are added one time only, and the savings continue to mount up as the length of the program increases.

Because of the unexpected discrepancy in execution times, I suggest you try your own tests on your own system. If you consistently see an increase in execution time when you use the predefinitions, you'll have to decide on a tradeoff between memory consumption and execution speed. One way to approach it would be to use explicit declarations as part of the variable names when programs are short and there's no chance of exhausting available memory. Then use predefinitions when memory space is at a premium and saving a few thousand or even a few hundred bytes might be critical to the program's successful completion.

For uniformity in my own programming, I prefer to use the predefinition approach whenever the BASIC allows it and then to make up for any lost time with other program-compression and speed-enhancement techniques.

Handling Techniques Revisited

This chapter has served to illustrate and quantify a number of considerations affecting the way you can handle numeric and string data under BASIC. Some of the most important points can be summarized thus:

1. There are significant differences among versions of the BASIC language. Those differences must be isolated, identified, and incorporated into your individual programming techniques for your particular system.
2. The precision of numeric constants and variables has very distinct effects on both memory consumption and execution time. As a general rule, integers are more efficient than real numbers, and single precision is more efficient than double precision. Furthermore, the availability in some BASICs of integer division as compared to regular division provides some real advantages.
3. Using variables in place of numeric constants may gain some memory but at the cost of execution speed, particularly when dealing with integer values.

4. BASICs that perform numerical rounding and those that perform truncating operations can provide different results for what should be identical operations. Attempting to modify a program written with one approach to run with the other approach requires special attention.

5. Eliminating unnecessary characters reduces memory requirements and usually speeds program execution. This includes spaces, remark statements, formatting tabulations, unnecessary line numbers, and the variable name for the NEXT statement when closing a FOR...NEXT loop.

6. String-handling efficiency varies widely from BASIC to BASIC and requires special attention, particularly concerning the performance of garbage-collection operations and their effect on overall execution time. String handling typically requires more memory and longer execution times than numeric manipulations.

7. Individual string-handling features and special functions also differ from one BASIC to another. In some cases, it will be necessary to devise alternate programming approaches when a function that is needed is not provided. In other cases, the relative advantages or disadvantages of multiple approaches must be examined and tested. In general, some string-handling functions built into the language are better left unused when only short strings are involved.

More "BASIC" Techniques

In the preceding chapter, I devoted most of my attention to those items that directly affect the numeric- and string-handling techniques employed with various versions of BASIC. In this chapter, I'll move on to considerations of some of the fundamental programming operations and statements. I will include descriptions of the random-number generator and its operations, defined user functions, loop construction with IF...THEN... and FOR...NEXT statements, and a number of other items that have a broad impact on the way you write your programs.

As usual, my emphasis is on those specific things that can cause problems in writing programs or transferring programs from one system to another, as well as considerations affecting either the memory consumption or execution speed for a given program. Again, you need to view the information I present as general guidelines that you'll have to confirm or refute for your own system and its BASIC; you should not view these things as cast in concrete or as a bible of conversion and programming information. I strongly suggest that you take the benchmark routines presented and try them. Time them for yourself and see if you get the same results or find the same overall trends.

Random Numbers

One subtle difference among BASICs is in the way they use their random-number generators. I first noticed that there was a bit of a problem when I began converting programs from other BASICs to the BASIC-80 interpreter for compilation. Programs that had been running perfectly for years suddenly began to fail, sometimes in very odd and unpredictable ways. Some programs failed with any one of several different and unexpected error messages such as "illegal function call," "subscript out of range," and so on. Still others ran to completion but gave erroneous results and improperly prepared printouts.

It took a while to run down the cause of these problems, but many eventually were traced to the random-number generator and the use of the RND() function. What I was running into was a difference in the range of values being returned for a given RND() call.

Random Numbers Returned

The random-number generator and the RND() function used to access it are employed extensively in most of my programs, frequently within loops that execute the RND() function thousands or even tens of thousands of times in a single program run. My most frequent use is to return an integer value within some limited range. For example, assume that a list of words held in a string array contains N entries as P$(1) through P$(N%). To pick one word at random, it's necessary to use the random-number generator to derive a number from 1 through N with no possibility of a zero, a number greater than N, or a fraction. An IF...THEN... test on the returned value is not desirable because of the time lost to perform the test several thousand times during the run.

Under the Microsoft or Applesoft BASICs, the function RND(1) returns a single-precision number between zero and something less than 1.0. It might return 0.99999, but never 1.0. Thus, a simple method of randomly selecting an integer value might be to use a program line such as:

```
100 X%=RND(1)*N% + 1
```

I expected that the one simple equation could never return an integer less than 1 or a value greater than N%. Given N% equal to 10, the largest number possible for the right side of the equation is 10.9999, which the X% would force to be *truncated* as an integer 10. The lowest value for the equation would be 1.0, which would be truncated to an integer 1. Indeed, that does prove true for Microsoft Revision 4.51 and Applesoft, both of which return values limited to a minimum of 1 and a maximum of N%.

Under BASIC-80, however, the values when converting to an integer are rounded instead of truncated. The highest expression evaluation of 10.9999 would be *rounded* to 11. So the same expression could return integer values from 1 to N%+1, the highest of which was beyond the range limitations desired. That spelled trouble!

In referencing an array, element P$(N%+1) might not be dimensioned, which would cause a "subscript out of range" error. If, on the other hand, the array element is included in the dimensioned-array size, there would be no error message, but the element probably would contain a null string or other erroneous information that would make the program results wrong. To avoid either an error condition or erroneous results, under BASIC-80, it was necessary to change the line to:

```
100 X%=RND(1)*N% + .5
```

Since the 0.5 addition is a floating-point number, it requires more memory space and takes longer than the addition of an integer. But this method does prevent BASIC-80 from returning a number outside the range of 1 to N%. In this case, the lowest value of the expression is 0.5, which rounds off to an integer 1, while the highest value, 10.4999 (9.9999+0.5), rounds off to an integer 10.

The situation could be further complicated if a BASIC were encountered that returned a full value of 1.0 from the random-number generator. In such a case, neither of the preceding methods would work to limit the range of the integer. In fact, if the random-number generator can return a 1.0 value, the IF...THEN... test of the final integer would be mandatory and would appear as:

```
100 X%=RND(1)*N%+1: IF X%>N% THEN 100
```

A simple way to determine how your random-number generator functions is to execute a small program of the form:

```
10 FOR X=1 TO 1000
20 Y%=RND(1)*5 + 1
30 IF Y%=>5 THEN PRINT Y%;"";
40 NEXT: PRINT
```

This displays integer values of either all fives or a combination of fives and sixes in lines across the terminal screen. If any output number is a six, the addition of the integer value in line 20 will not function to limit random selections properly. To verify it, substitute a +0.5 for the +1 in line 20 and reexecute the program. You should find that no integers other than five are displayed. In that case you always should use a limiting value for the added number that is 0.5 smaller than the actual limit you desire.

You also need to recognize that random numbers returned by simple RND() function calls are not evenly distributed across the range. BASICs are notorious for returning nonuniform distributions that don't approach either a "bell curve" or a "linear" frequency. Many articles on this subject have appeared in computer magazines during the past few years, including some very complex steps needed to obtain a uniform distribution. I'm not going to repeat that information or those procedures here; I will leave it to you to investigate the matter on your own. For my own purposes, I don't particularly care about numerical distributions—only about a randomized progression. Therefore, this quirk doesn't bother me at all, and I've never tried to program around it.

Random-Number "Seeding"

The technique for "seeding" the random-number generator differs from one BASIC to another. BASIC-80 (including MBASIC and GBASIC on the Apple II) provides a RANDOMIZE statement that causes the program to halt and request a seed number within a stated range that in turn "jumbles" the random-number generator. By entering a different seed number each time it is requested, you prevent the inadvertent duplication of a particular sequence. In BASIC-80 and the command programs compiled with BASCOM the random-number sequence is repetitive from one program run to another. Each time you start a program without seeding it, or if you enter the same seed number each time a program is started, the sequence of random numbers is the same. This can be useful in situations where you want to duplicate a previous run exactly—just use the same seed number or omit the RANDOMIZE call altogether.

BASICs such as Microsoft Revision 4.51 do not have the RANDOMIZE command, so any seeding or reseeding must be done by means of a keyboard input and a FOR...NEXT loop. For such BASICs, the appropriate substitution for the RANDOMIZE statement is a program line similar to:

```
20 INPUT"RDM NO.";X: FOR Y=1 TO X: Z=RND(1): NEXT
```

Entering different values for X from the keyboard executes the FOR...NEXT loop different numbers of times. This leaves the random-number generator at different positions in its sequence at the start of each run and before executing the remainder of the program.

Incidentally, some BASICs are nonrepetitive, so the generator is not returned to its starting point in the sequence at the beginning of a run. With this scheme it normally is not possible to duplicate a run because entering the same seed number just cycles the generator that much farther beyond the point where it left off. However, some interpreters use a negative argument such as RND(−1) to restart the random-number sequence, so debugging can be facilitated by using that call at the beginning of the program. All subsequent calls with a positive argument return the same sequence. Alternatively, a duplicate run may be obtainable through a power-down and power-up between each run with the subsequent use of the same seed value.

I've never decided whether I prefer a repetitive or a nonrepetitive random-number generator; each has its advantages. Where each run of a program can repeat the same sequence with the same seed number, testing and debugging the program is made easier by the ability to duplicate the same occurrences over and over again. A BASIC without the repetitive sequence is better for certain applications such as my word-puzzle enterprise because it helps prevent accidental duplication of a given puzzle manuscript and consequential copyright problems. As a result, I sometimes wind up doing my programming and testing with one version of the language and my actual production runs with another.

Defined User Functions

Microsoft and Applesoft BASICs (but not Apple Integer BASIC) offer you a means of defining your own functions within your programs. Once they are defined, you then can call those functions as needed, just as you would call intrinsic functions such as SQR(), SIN(), and so on. At first, this appears to be a very attractive feature, particularly when you have to perform some fairly complex operation over and over again at numerous places within the body of the program. However, the convenience of predefining functions is made available at a cost in execution time, and you must be careful not to overuse or misuse the defined-function capabilities.

When you determine that some operation lends itself to being predefined as a function because of its complexity, frequent repetition, or combination of both, you first have to devise and incorporate a statement DEF FN<name>[(<parameters>)]=<function definition> into the body of your program. The DEF FN... statement must be executed before the first function call to avoid an error message and program halt. Subsequently, whenever you need that function, you then can call it by using the program statement FN<name>[(<parameters>)].

The process of setting up the function is not very difficult as long as you remember five points. First, the <name> must be a variable name of the proper data type (integer, single- or real-precision, double-precision, or string) for the operation being defined. Second, the list of <parameters> in the DEF FN... statement is a "dummy list" but must correspond one to one with the number and data types of the values or variables passed by the FN call. Third, the <function definition> is limited to a single program line containing one continuous expression; you can't use loops, conditional tests, or other multi-statement definitions. Fourth, The DEF FN... statement must be executed *before* the first FN call to that function is encountered in the program. Fifth, the definition must be contained within a program—it may not be executed as an immediate command from the keyboard (an error results) and cannot be tested except as a numbered program line.

By predefining complex functions containing many characters, you can replace numerous occurrences of the same operations with a much shorter FN call, thus saving a lot of memory space when a given operation occurs very often. However, the memory savings and any convenience in programming often are offset by a serious loss in execution time. Remember that the defined function is stored in memory, so its use requires that the BASIC interpreter first locate it and then execute it. Time is required to locate the function, pass the parameters, execute the function, and pass the results back to the mainline program.

Personally, I find very few uses for the DEF FN... and FN statements unless I've reached a point where memory conservation is critical and saving a few bytes or a few hundred bytes at the cost of slowed execution means the difference between a successful run and an "out of memory" error. One exception is when I'm transferring programs back and forth between BASICs and anticipate problems with the random-number generator returning improper values. The need for the RND() function usually appears frequently throughout my own programs, and locating and then changing each occurrence can be a tedious task. Under that circumstance, I may set up a statement such as DEF FNA(B)=RND(1)*B+1 at the beginning of the program so I later can change a single line when it's necessary to use DEF FNA(B)= RND(1)*B+.5 to obtain properly "ranged" values.

This little programming convenience costs a lot of execution time. The following two routines show just how much time I can lose in 5,000 determinations of a random integer within a specified range. The routines are shown as run under Microsoft BASIC Revision 4.51. For BASIC-80 (Microsoft Revision 5.2), the integer addition of +1 for the computation was changed to a single-precision addition of +.5. For Applesoft, the integer addition was retained, but the integer variable X% in line 10 was changed to a real-precision X.

```
10 FOR X%=1 TO 5000
20 Y%=RND(1)*10+1
30 NEXT
```

[Microsoft Rev. 4.51: 54.4 seconds]
[Microsoft Rev. 5.2: 52.1 seconds]
[Applesoft: 55.4 seconds]

```
5 DEF FNA(B)=RND(1)*B+1
10 FOR X%=1 TO 5000
20 Y%=FNA(10)
30 NEXT
```

[Microsoft Rev. 4.51: 77.1 seconds]
[Microsoft Rev. 5.2: 74.5 seconds]
[Applesoft: 64.2 seconds]

Under Revision 4.51, the use of the defined function cost an extra 22.7 seconds, adding 41.7 percent to the execution time for the same operations without the function. For each of 5,000 computations, the call to the function and the passing of values added an average of 0.0045 second—a small cost by itself, but cumulative in a long run. Under BASIC-80, the function cost an additional 22.4 seconds, adding 43 percent to the time. Under Applesoft, it cost only 8.8 seconds and added only 15.9 percent. All three BASICs showed significant time losses. The smallest loss was suffered by Applesoft, making it the most likely candidate for using such functions. Nevertheless, the more times a random number is called using the defined function, the more memory is saved, but the more time is lost regardless of the interpreter being utilized.

I've also used the predefined-function capability when complex string operations are performed, but again with an overall loss of program efficiency. The two routines that follow take strings of English words stored as all uppercase letters in array elements S$(1) through S$(210) and convert them to words with initial caps and lowercase letters in array elements S1$(1) through S1$(210). The same word list is used in both cases, with variable I being the word count (210). Lines 1000 and 1010 form a 10-pass IF...THEN... repetition loop that extends the execution for more accurate timing. The CLEAR 20000 statement was deleted from line 10 for the Microsoft Revision 5.2 tests.

```
10 CLEAR 20000: DEFINT A-Z: DIM S$(210),S1$(210)
. . .
1000 W=1
1002 FOR X=1 TO I: S$=LEFT$(S$(X),1)
1004 FOR Y=2 TO LEN(S$(X))
1006 S$=S$+CHR$(ASC(MID$(S$(X),Y))+32)
1008 NEXT: S1$(X)=S$: NEXT
1010 IF W<10 THEN W=W+1: GOTO 1002
```

[Microsoft Rev. 4.51: 281.1 seconds]
[Microsoft Rev. 5.2: 224.1 seconds]

```
10 CLEAR 20000: DEFINT A-Z: DIM S$(210),S1$(210)
15 DEF FNS$(A,B)=CHR$(ASC(MID$(S$(A),B))+32)
. . .
1000 W=1
1002 FOR X=1 TO I: S$=LEFT$(S$(X),1)
1004 FOR Y=2 TO LEN(S$(X))
1006 S$=S$+FNS$(X,Y)
1008 NEXT: S1$(X)=S$: NEXT
1010 IF W<10 THEN W=W+1: GOTO 1002
```

[Microsoft Rev. 4.51: 391.5 seconds]
[Microsoft Rev. 5.2: 316.8 seconds]

For Revision 4.51, the defined function cost 110.4 seconds, adding 39 percent to the execution time required by the version without the function. For Revision 5.2, the cost was 92.7 seconds or 41 percent. With 2,100 strings being constructed in the 10 passes, this amounts to only 0.044 to 0.053 second per string, but, as you can see, the effects are cumulative and add up to a significant loss of efficiency. Again, the more times the function is used, the more memory space is saved, but the more time is wasted.

With the magnitude of the efficiency losses demonstrated, the use of a predefined BASIC function appears to offer no real advantage unless memory space is at a premium. Most programs should run considerably faster if each operation is written out in its entirety each time it's needed. If the DEF FN and FN statements must be used, at least avoid calling the functions from within long loops. Be especially careful with nested loops, where calling the function from one of the inner, more frequently used loops can cost a lot of time.

Constructing and Using Loops

The ability to construct and use program loops is one of the most powerful computing tools at your fingertips. With just a few keystrokes, you can devise powerful operations that can be performed hundreds, thousands, or tens of thousands of times. And they can be done far faster than you could ever hope to do them on a calculator or in your head.

Yet the construction of program loops tends to be a rather inexact science, with more variations and possible approaches than you might care to think about. In fact, at least one article has been published that talks about 24 fundamental ways to write a given loop, with minor variations providing more than 124 different ways—all accomplishing the same general purpose.[1]

[1]W. D. Maurer, "Twenty-four Ways to Write a Loop," *Byte*, volume 4, number 12 (December 1979), pp. 241-246.

I certainly don't intend to go through all those approaches in this book; I merely want to point out some of the possibilities. I also want to show that all of the numerous approaches are "correct" in that they yield the proper solutions but that the efficiency in terms of execution time differs from one method to another.

To set up a test case, consider the problem of having 10,000 numeric values stored in an integer array A(.) and having to move those values to corresponding elements of integer array B(.). One obvious way to accomplish the task would be to use a FOR. . . NEXT loop as illustrated by lines 100 through 104 of the following program for a Microsoft BASIC:

```
10 CLEAR: DEFINT A-Z: N=10000: DIM A(N),B(N)
20 FOR X=1 TO N: A(X)=X: NEXT
. . .
100 FOR X=1 TO N
102 B(X)=A(X)
104 NEXT
. . .
```

It should be obvious that there are at least four fundamental ways to write the FOR. . . NEXT loop using various combinations of variables, constants, positive stepping, and negative stepping. The question is, *are there differences in the amounts of time required to execute the loop?* By inserting a line between 20 and 100 that reads INPUT X$, the program can be halted until a Carriage Return is provided from the keyboard, making it possible to time only the loop of concern. The four variations and the times obtained with Microsoft BASIC Revision 4.51 are shown—Revision 5.2 (BASIC-80) runs out of memory with two 10,000-element arrays, and smaller arrays don't yield good timing intervals.

```
. . .
100 FOR X=1 TO N
102 B(X)=A(X)
104 NEXT
. . .
```

[59.3 seconds]

```
. . .
100 FOR X=1 TO 10000
102 B(X)=A(X)
104 NEXT
. . .
```

[59.3 seconds]

```
. . .
100 FOR X=N TO 1 STEP -1
102 B(X)=A(X)
104 NEXT
. . .
```

[59.5 seconds]

```
. . .
100 FOR X=10000 TO 1 STEP -1
102 B(X)=A(X)
104 NEXT
. . .
```

[59.5 seconds]

The timings remain the same whether the loop control is a variable or a constant, and there is an almost negligible difference of only 0.2 second (0.3 percent) for 10,000 operations between positive and negative stepping.

Meanwhile, the same loop can be written many different ways using an IF . . . THEN . . . statement instead of the FOR . . . NEXT loop. Once again, the question is what relative timings can be obtained and how they compare with the FOR . . . NEXT approach. As I said, I won't present all of the more than 124 possible ways to write the loop. I won't even attempt all 24 of the fundamental approaches. Instead, I'll provide a few examples and leave it to you, your imagination, and your computer to devise and test the others. For those I did choose to test, the routines, times obtained, and ending values of variable X with Microsoft BASIC Revision 4.51 were as follows:

```
. . .
1ØØ X=1
1Ø2 B(X)=A(X)
1Ø4 X=X+1
1Ø6 IF X< >N+1 THEN 1Ø2
. . .
```

[126.0 sec. X=10001]

```
. . .
1ØØ X=1
1Ø2 B(X)=A(X)
1Ø4 X=X+1
1Ø6 IF X< >N+1 GOTO 1Ø2
. . .
```

[124.8 sec. X=10001]

```
. . .
1ØØ X=N
1Ø2 B(X)=A(X)
1Ø4 X=X-1
1Ø6 IF X< >Ø THEN 1Ø2
. . .
```

[115.1 sec. X=0]

```
. . .
1ØØ X=N
1Ø2 B(X)=A(X)
1Ø4 X=X-1
1Ø6 IF X THEN 1Ø2
. . .
```

[103.0 sec. X=0]

```
. . .
1ØØ X=1
1Ø2 B(X)=A(X)
1Ø4 X=X+1
1Ø6 IF X=N+1 THEN 11Ø
1Ø8 GOTO 1Ø2
11Ø . . .
```

[132.5 sec. X=10001]

```
. . .
1ØØ X=1
1Ø2 B(X)=A(X)
1Ø4 IF X=N THEN 1Ø8
1Ø6 X=X+1: GOTO 1Ø2
1Ø8 . . .
```

[121.7 sec. X=10000]

```
. . .
100 X=N
102 B(X)=A(X)
104 X=X-1
106 IF X=>1 THEN 102
. . .
```

[115.1 sec.   X=0]

```
. . .
100 X=N
102 IF X<=0 THEN 110
104 B(X)=A(X)
106 X=X-1
108 GOTO 102
110 . . .
```

[122.3 sec.   X=0]

```
. . .
100 X=N+1
102 IF X=1 THEN 110
104 X=X-1
106 B(X)=A(X)
108 GOTO 102
110 . . .
```

[121.8 sec.   X=1]

```
. . .
100 X=0
102 B(X+1)=A(X+1)
104 X=X+1
106 IF X< >N THEN 102
. . .
```

[135.1 sec.   X=10000]

```
. . .
100 X=N+1
102 X=X-1
104 B(X)=A(X)
106 IF X>1 THEN 102
. . .
```

[114.4 sec.   X=1]

```
. . .
100 X=2
102 B(X-1)=A(X-1)
104 B(X)=A(X)
106 X=X+2
108 IF X<=N THEN 102
. . .
```

[94.0 sec.   X=10002]

Given just these few examples, you can see that there are quite a number of ways to accomplish the same thing but that there are some distinct differences in the speeds of execution and in the resulting values of variable X. In constructing any such loop, much depends upon the number of steps repeated, the positioning of the IF . . . THEN . . . test, and the internal efficiency of the BASIC interpreter. Note, for example, that the first two examples differ in that one has an IF . . . THEN . . . statement, while the second and 9.5 percent faster version uses the IF . . . GOTO . . . form. That particular comparison may not hold true for BASICs other than the one tested, and even in that version it doesn't always seem to be true for different applications.

Note also that an IF...THEN... comparison not involving an arithmetic step, such as that in the third example, gives a slight speed advantage over the first and second examples—in this case, it's up to 8.6 percent faster. Furthermore, a logical comparison with no explicit numeric value such as that in the fourth example further speeds the execution; the expression IF X THEN... is equivalent to but about 10.5 percent faster than IF X < > 0 THEN.... Finally, notice that the fastest of the IF...THEN... loops is the last one in which the loop is stepped by twos and has to execute only 5,000 times. Yet even this is not as fast as the FOR...NEXT loops cited earlier.

Whenever you construct loops, you have to be concerned about zero values, values exceeding the maximum limits, and the actual completion of the first and last (lowest and highest) iterations. It's quite possible that a loop you design may fail if the control variable is a zero. It may exceed the number of elements in a dimensioned array if the terminating conditions are not detected at the right time. It may fail to perform the first iteration or may not perform the last. In handling an array transfer such as the one used for these examples, check the B(0), B(1), and B(10000) elements to make sure they have the proper contents. For these examples, B(0) should be 0, B(1) should be 1, and B(10000) should be 10,000. With any other results, the loop is improperly constructed and is "wrong."

Therefore, you have to examine several facets of every loop. First, it must be "correct" and must yield the desired results under *all* conditions; you would be well advised to test the loop under "worst-case" conditions including control variables that are outside the expected range (zeros, negative numbers, and so on). Second, minimize the number of repeated statements within the body of the loop; repeating three statements usually is faster than repeating four, repeating four is faster than five, and so on. Third, minimize the number of arithmetic operations performed in the looping statements; a simple logical test such as IF X THEN... often runs faster than a numerical test such as IF X<>0 THEN... or IF X>0 THEN.... Fourth, if FOR...NEXT loops check out faster than IF...THEN... loops for your machine and typical applications, use them whenever and wherever possible. Fifth, check the comparative timing of IF...THEN... and IF...GOTO... statements for your own BASIC, and use the form that gives the best execution time; avoid the redundant form IF...THEN GOTO... that pops up frequently in published program listings.

Special FOR...NEXT Considerations

Believe it or not, BASICs differ in the way they execute the common FOR...NEXT loop. Not only do they differ, but the differences tend to be subtle ones, the explanations usually are buried in the instruction manuals where they're rarely noticed, and the failures are difficult both to recognize and to trace. Yet those differences can cause considerable problems in writing and adapting programs, particularly when attempting to transfer a program from one BASIC to another.

Control Variable Testing. The principal difference in FOR...NEXT loops relates to whether BASIC tests the controlling variable before or after execution of that loop. In the first case, a loop doesn't execute if the initial value of the controlling variable exceeds the final value specified. In the second case, the loop always executes once, regardless of the initial and final values of the controlling variable. It doesn't sound very important, but it can be a real problem in that it does not show up as an outright failure with a displayed error message but only as a discrepancy in the final results; even then, it may be intermittent.

For example, shortly after first acquiring my original Altair computer, I found that a number of my programs were failing to yield the correct results, not in every case or for every run, but intermittently. Typically, I might get an erroneous output in an average of one run out of eight. For quite a while, I couldn't trace the problem—every program step seemed perfect. Besides, if the program ran correctly once, why shouldn't it work right every time?

One day, I keyed in one of the many published versions of a *Startrek* game readily available to computer addicts. Behold! When I took a shot at a Klingon, he wasn't where he was supposed to be! Instead, the Klingon was located quite some distance away from where he was shown on the screen, sometimes in a completely different direction. It took many days to trace the problem to the FOR...NEXT loops that positioned the various elements of the game in numeric and string arrays. Through a long process of testing individual program segments individually and in various combinations, I eventually isolated the error and discovered that loops having an initial control value greater than the final value specified were executing one time and offsetting the data in the arrays by at least one extra and unexpected position. Where a flag or value was to be stored in a variable like X(10,15), it might actually be appearing in X(11,15), X(10,16), or X(11,16), depending upon which loops "malfunctioned." In other cases, I was getting nonzero values where I should have had zeros and vice versa.

In my previous experience with programming computers, all of the BASICs I had used were of the type that tested the control variable at the start of the loop. Therefore, they would skip any loop starting with something like FOR X=Y TO Z where Y was greater than Z. The program I had lifted from the publication also had been written for a BASIC that would skip a loop under that condition. But that wasn't the way the BASIC I was using had been designed. Buried in the instruction manual was the statement: "BASIC then executes the statements which follow the FOR statement in the usual manner. When a NEXT statement is encountered, the step . . . is added to the variable which is then tested against the final value." What I faced was a BASIC that always went through the entire loop one time before detecting the NEXT statement where it could test the control variable, and it would go through the loop whether or not I intended it to do so.

Going back through the *Startrek* game and all of my own programs, I added tests of the control variables' initial and final values before the FOR statements. If the loop began with the statement FOR X=Y TO Z, I preceded that statement with a test of the form IF X >Z THEN.... That test redirected program flow around the loop when the end value already was greater than the beginning value. Most of the questionable programs immediately became fully operational, and the intermittent errors disappeared from the outputs.

With BASIC-80 (Microsoft Revisions 5.1 and 5.2), the situation was reversed. According to the instruction manual, "The body of the loop is skipped if the initial value of the loop times the sign of the step exceeds the final value times the sign of the step." In other words, the loop would *not* be executed if the initial value already was beyond the range specified—the previous problem doesn't exist at all. Therefore, an IF . . . THEN . . . test of the control variable is unnecessary, redundant, and wasteful. Such statements expressly intended to prevent execution of a loop don't affect the actual program flow, but they do consume valuable time, especially when used in front of nested loops several levels deep. Therefore, improved program efficiency under BASIC-80 can be achieved by removing the IF...THEN... tests of loop variables from the program.

A quick and easy test of the way your BASIC handles the FOR . . . NEXT control variables is to run the following single-line program:

```
10 Y=0: FOR X=1 TO 0: Y=10: NEXT: PRINT X,Y
```

If your BASIC tests the control variables before executing the loop, the program displays the values 1 and 0 for X and Y respectively. This is typical of BASIC-80, including the MBASIC and GBASIC versions that run with the Microsoft SoftCard in the Apple II. If your BASIC doesn't test the control until the end of the loop, the program displays the values 2 and 10 for X and Y; note that the control variable X is incremented because of the implied positive step for the loop, so it will be "in error" as well. This operation is typical of Microsoft Revision 4.51, Applesoft, and Apple Integer BASIC.

Using results of the test, you should adapt one of the following approaches. The form for BASIC-80 is shown on the left, and the form for Applesoft and similar BASICs is shown on the right. When preliminary variable testing is needed, be sure to use it for each level of loop nesting. Of course, you need not incorporate the preliminary variable test if it is absolutely impossible for your program to have the initial control variable outside the desired range—but you had better be certain about the values, or you could wind up with some very odd results when your program prints or displays its outputs.

```
1000 FOR X=Y TO Z
. . .
1018 NEXT
1020 . . .
```

```
1000 IF Y>Z THEN 1020
1002 FOR X=Y TO Z
. . .
1018 NEXT
1020 . . .
```

Terminating FOR...NEXT Loops. There also are differences in the ways BASICs allow you to terminate a loop, either normally upon completion of all iterations or by force when a desired condition is satisfied before all iterations are completed. Having done a lot of my initial program development on the old versions of BASIC, which were quite flexible, I had developed some bad habits that created a number of problems when I converted my work to other BASICs.

First, you should have noticed that I've dropped the use of the variable name in the NEXT statement of most of the single loops presented as samples. That is perfectly acceptable for all of the interpreters I use except Apple Integer BASIC, which requires explicit closing of all loops with the variable name. However, some caution is necessary with nested loops, particularly when they terminate at the same point. A NEXT statement without a variable name closes only the most recently opened or innermost loop. For example, the following routine closes only the loop controlled by variable Z; the loops controlled by variables X and Y are still open, and subsequent use of a FOR X . . . or FOR Y . . . statement could result in an error message such as "FOR without NEXT."

```
1000 FOR X=1 TO 1000
. . .
1020 FOR Y=A TO B
. . .
1030 FOR Z=1 TO C
. . .
1035 NEXT
. . .
```

Suppose all three loops are to be terminated at line 1035. Since the preceding example would fail to close two of them, it would be necessary to use one of the following four methods:

Method 1

```
1035 NEXT Z
1036 NEXT Y
1037 NEXT X
```

Method 2

```
1035 NEXT
1036 NEXT
1037 NEXT
```

Method 3

```
1035 NEXT Z,Y,Z
```

Method 4

```
1035 NEXT:NEXT:NEXT
```

In an attempt to determine which of the four is the fastest, I set up the following little test routine, added each loop-termination method in turn, and executed the program under Microsoft BASIC Revision 5.2 (BASIC-80):

```
1000 FOR X=1 TO 200
1002 W=1
1020 FOR Y=1 TO 10
1022 S=10
1030 FOR Z=1 TO 5
1032 T=100
1035 . . .
```

Of the four loop-termination techniques, Method 4 ran in the smallest amount of time, with the NEXT:NEXT:NEXT statement allowing completion in 56.6 seconds. Method 2, with the three program lines but no variable names, was next in order at 57.1 seconds. Method 3 with a single-line NEXT Z,Y,X was next at 63.3 seconds, and Method 1 with three lines all containing the variable names was the slowest at 64.6 seconds.

The difference between the slowest and the fastest is 8.0 seconds. By using the slowest form, you would be adding 14 percent to the minimum execution time possible for these examples.

Some of my older BASICs also proved fairly liberal about the ways in which complex, conditional loop closures could be constructed. At one point, thinking I was being very clever, I started incorporating NEXT statements into conditional IF . . . THEN . . . ELSE . . . statements such as the following:

```
1000 FOR X=1 TO 5000
. . .
1020 IF FG>100 THEN BB=5: BC=1: NEXT ELSE NEXT
```

With those interpreters, this worked very nicely to detect the condition of a flag, use that condition to set two other flags, and reiterate the loop regardless of the detected condition. It did not work when the program was transferred to BASIC-80 for testing or compilation. Once out of the old BASIC, that type of statement caused a "NEXT without FOR" error message because the newer interpreters recognize the presence of two separate NEXT statements regardless of the conditional checks. Thus, they register the presence of two NEXTs for a single FOR. resulting in one NEXT being unmatched and in error. The BASCOM compiler is equally sensitive and proceeds to register NEXTs without FORs for all subsequent loops as well. To run correctly in all cases, the same routine had to be rewritten thus:

```
1000 FOR X=1 TO 5000
. . .
1020 IF FG>100 THEN BB=5: BC=1
1022 NEXT
```

I also encountered differences in the methods available for an early escape from a FOR. . . NEXT loop. With the older BASICs, it was fairly easy, requiring only a jump from anywhere inside the loop to the next statement to be executed after the loop. Apparently, those BASICs were structured so that encountering a FOR statement with a variable name used in an earlier, unclosed loop would simply close out that loop and open the next one automatically. Therefore, the simplest way to force an early exit was with something like this:

```
1000 FOR X=1 TO 5000
. . .
1020 IF FG>100 THEN 1024
1022 NEXT
1024 . . .
```

But this method turned out to be extremely unreliable with BASIC-80 and the BASCOM compiler. Although an error usually doesn't show up on a simple test with just a few FOR. . . NEXT loops, long programs are prone to develop an error condition somewhere through the remainder of the program when a NEXT statement is jumped. I sometimes found that the error messages "FOR without NEXT" and "NEXT without FOR" would be displayed with a line number when there was nothing wrong with the loop at that number. The actual cause of the error would be anything from 50 to 500 lines earlier in the program. I even had one program that wouldn't show the error until the second or third complete cycle of a multiple-cycle run when the unclosed loop had actually occurred during the first cycle.

Since the cause of the error condition and the error message could be so far apart in both the number of program lines and the elapsed time between them, this type of error was extraordinarily difficult to diagnose and eliminate once it appeared. Going back to the old adage about an ounce of prevention being worth a pound of cure, it was much easier to avoid the potential error condition than to correct it. As a result, I've totally abandoned the technique of jumping out of an incomplete loop and no longer will use it under any circumstances. Instead, I use techniques that trigger the termination of the loop by forcibly setting the control variables to values at or beyond the loop maximums. I then have a choice of either setting a new flag variable or using the control variable itself as a flag, depending upon how I choose to proceed after the loop termination.

There are several good, efficient, and error-free ways to shut down a loop prematurely. The one used at any given point in a program depends upon what has to be done once the loop has exited. In the simplest case, a condition is detected, the control variable is forced equal to the terminating condition, and execution continues normally at the next line, typified by the two routines:

```
1ØØØ FOR X=Y TO Z
. . .
1Ø2Ø IF FG THEN X=Z
1Ø22 NEXT
1Ø24 . . .
```

```
1ØØØ FOR X=Z TO Ø STEP -1
. . .
1Ø2Ø IF FG THEN X=Ø
1Ø22 NEXT
1Ø24 . . .
```

In the preceding examples, the detection of a desired condition for variable FG forces the control variable X to the value of Z in the right routine or zero in the left routine. It works just as well to set X equal to Z+1000 or −100 in the left and right routines respectively. In fact, any values work if they are outside the specified range for the control variable. In either example shown, the NEXT statement "thinks" the loop has been executed the desired number of times and exits immediately upon reaching the NEXT statement. It's important to remember that BASICs exit their FOR. . . NEXT loops with the control variable one increment step beyond the terminating value in the direction specified. Therefore, if forced only to the range limit, the left sample exits with X set to Z+1, while the right sample exits with X at −1. The same technique works for nested loops as long as each control variable is forced to its particular termination value. For example:

```
1ØØØ FOR X=1 TO A
1ØØ2 FOR Y=1 TO B
1ØØ4 FOR Z=1 TO C
. . .
1Ø2Ø IF FG THEN X=A: Y=B: Z=C
1Ø22 NEXT Z,Y,X
1Ø24 . . .
```

For multidirectional branching after exiting the loop, there are two fundamental approaches. In one, a separate flag variable is set to govern the branch, while the other makes use of the control variable itself. Consider these two examples:

```
1000 A=1: FOR X=Y TO Z           1000 FOR X=Y TO Z
. . .                            . . .
1020 IF FG THEN A=2: X=Z         1020 IF FG THEN X=Z+10
1022 NEXT                        1022 NEXT
1024 ON A GOTO 1026,9000         1024 IF X>Z+10 THEN 9000
1026 . . .                       1026 . . .
```

In the left routine, flag A is set to a value, the loop is forced to terminate, and the ON...GOTO... statement branches according to the value of A. The final control value is not used to govern subsequent operation. Of course, the loop may contain a number of different checks and forced terminations, each giving a unique value to variable A. The ON...GOTO... statement then may contain a great many more branches.

In the example on the right, control variable X is set to Z+10, the loop exits with X equal to Z+11, and the IF...THEN... branch is performed if and only if X is greater than Z+10. Since normal termination sets X equal to Z+1, that would allow execution to continue at line 1026. The abnormal, forced termination causes a branch to line 9000. Setting X equal to Z in line 1020 of this routine would not work, because the loop would exit with X equal to Z+1 whether the termination was normal or forced. However, setting X equal to Z+1 would force an exit with X equal to Z+2, and line 1024 then could test for X being greater than Z+1.

There are a great many variations on these approaches, with each being a function of exactly what needs to be done after loop termination, the depth of loop nesting, and so on. But they all serve to avoid potential problems of unmatched FOR and NEXT statements by making the program execute the NEXT statement with a terminating value in order to escape from the loop. As a result, they work reliably and without any chance for "sneaky" delayed error conditions in any of the different BASICs I normally use.

Reentering FOR...NEXT Loops. Sooner or later, you're apt to encounter a situation in which you want to reenter a FOR...NEXT loop and continue execution from the point of interruption without restarting the loop from the beginning. Your program can't jump right into the middle of the loop, or the first NEXT statement encountered will probably generate a "NEXT without FOR" error message. For the same reason, the jump can't be to the NEXT statement. Therefore, the only way to reenter is to jump to the FOR statement with the starting value for the loop control set to the desired value at which execution is to resume. In order to do that, the initial parameter to the right of the equals sign in the FOR... statement must be a variable and not a constant. Consider the following example:

```
1000 N=0
1002 FOR X=A TO 300
1004 INPUT "WORD "; S$
1006 IF S$="*END" THEN X=300: GOTO 1020
1008 S$(X)=S$: N=N+1
. . .
1020 NEXT
1024 IF X< 300 THEN 2000
1026 INPUT "MORE (Y/N) "; S$
1028 IF LEFT$(S$,1)="Y" THEN A=N+1: GOTO 1002
2000 . . .
```

In this routine, up to 300 strings may be entered into array S$(.) from the keyboard, with the routine keeping count of the number of strings actually entered with variable N. The entries may be terminated at any time by typing "*END" (line 1006), which forces the control variable X to the termination value and jumps to the NEXT statement. However, if fewer than 300 strings have been entered, the routine asks if more are to be entered (line 1026). If so, it resets the beginning value of the loop in variable A to a number that is one greater than the number of strings already entered (line 1028) and jumps back to the beginning of the loop. This type of structure can be used to terminate and reenter the loop as many times as necessary, without generating any error message or destroying any data already typed.

The same type of loop reentry can be adapted easily to almost any situation where there's a possibility of terminating the loop before all necessary operations have been completed.

Incidentally, jumping to a subroutine from a loop and returning via a GOSUB...RETURN sequence does not constitute an exit and reentry. Loops may contain GOSUB statements as needed. However, some BASICs such as Applesoft don't accept a transfer to an error-trapping routine with subsequent return to the middle of a loop. Under Applesoft, error trapping by means of the ONERR GOTO... statement disturbs the pointers and stack contents, so the return must be to the FOR... statement. This complicates the matter of writing loops subject to error trapping and makes it easy to end up in an infinite loop. Refer back to the section entitled "The LEN() Function" in Chapter 4 for additional details.

Timing of FOR...NEXT Loops. In Chapter 4, I established that controlling FOR. . . NEXT loops with integer variables and eliminating the variable name from the NEXT statement both served to decrease the overall execution time required by a loop. Those two techniques should be employed wherever they are allowed by the BASIC interpreter in use. Earlier in this chapter, I also presented some alternate approaches to terminating nested loops, along with some comparisons of the relative time saving that could be achieved with the various methods; essentially, I determined that closing nested loops with discrete NEXT statements not having variable names is the fastest method, thereby giving rise to multi-statement program lines appearing something like 1000 NEXT: NEXT:NEXT.

There remains one facet of FOR. . . NEXT loop timing that I have not yet examined in detail: the use of the STEP statement to govern the incrementing of the control variable. Many of the popular BASICs allow you to use an optional STEP that sets both the size and the direction of the iterations through the loop. For example, a STEP 2 statement causes the control variable to be increased in increments of two from the beginning value to the ending value. A STEP −1 statement causes the control variable to be decreased in increments of one. A FOR statement without a specified STEP is assumed to be a STEP +1 for positive increments of one.

At various times, articles have appeared advising against the use of the STEP statement, particularly for a negative step. These articles claim that a STEP statement increases the time required to complete the loop. That seems to be logical enough; after all, the STEP adds an extra program statement, and it seems plausible that going backward takes longer than going forward. The problem is that there often are occasions when it's desirable to use negative stepping to simplify a program operation, so it's necessary to know how much time, if any, may be lost to something like a STEP −1 statement. To find out, I tested the following routine under MBASIC (BASIC-80) running with 56K CP/M on an Apple II equipped with a SoftCard:

```
10 FOR X%=1 TO 15000
20 Y%=1500/100
30 NEXT
```

This routine is controlled by an integer variable with integer constants in the FOR statement and has an "implied" integer STEP +1. Using it as a baseline, I proceeded to modify line 10 systematically to check the comparative times using explicit positive and negative stepping under both integer and single-precision control. The modifications I used and the results I obtained were as follows:

1Ø FOR X%=1 TO 15ØØØ	125.3 seconds
1Ø FOR X%=1 TO 15ØØØ STEP 1	125.4 seconds
1Ø FOR X%=15ØØØ TO 1 STEP −1	125.5 seconds
1Ø FOR X!=1 TO 15ØØØ	136.9 seconds
1Ø FOR X!=1 TO 15ØØØ STEP 1	137.0 seconds
1Ø FOR X!=15ØØØ TO 1 STEP −1	137.3 seconds
1Ø FOR X!=1! TO 15ØØØ!	136.9 seconds
1Ø FOR X!=1! TO 15ØØØ! STEP 1!	137.Ø seconds
1Ø FOR X!=15ØØØ! TO 1! STEP −1!	137.3 seconds

Looking at these times in groups of three, it's obvious that the change from integer to single-precision control increased the execution time from just over 125 seconds to about 137 seconds. But it's also obvious that there's very little difference in each group among the timings without a STEP, with an explicit positive STEP 1, and with a negative STEP −1. For integer control, the difference between implied positive stepping and negative stepping for 15,000 loops is only 0.2 second for an increase of only 0.2 percent. For single-precision control, the difference is only 0.4 second for an increase of 0.3 percent.

All in all, that's not a very large difference. It's certainly not enough to worry about for most programming applications. If the loop were to execute continuously for 24 hours, the 0.3 percent increase would account for only 4.3 minutes, while the 0.2 percent increase would account for only 2.9 minutes. I'd say you're certainly not going to lose any noticeable amount of time by using negative stepping when and where you need it.

To illustrate how I often use negative stepping, consider a situation in which I have a list of N items in an array and want to perform some set of operations such as a search for particular values or string characters on each item. However, while I want the operations to be performed on the entire list, I don't want to start at the same point in the list each time I execute the loop. One way to approach the problem is to pick a random starting point, proceed upward from that point to the end of the list, and then return to a new starting point one item below the previous start and search downward to the beginning of the list. The controls to do exactly that would take the following form:

```
1ØØØ A=RND(1)*N+.5: B=1: IF A<2 OR A>N-2 THEN 1ØØØ
1ØØ2 FOR X=A TO N STEP B
. . .
1Ø2Ø NEXT
1Ø22 IF B=1 THEN A=A-1: N=1: B=-1: GOTO 1ØØ2
. . .
```

For this approach, the starting point is chosen at random but may not be less than 2 or greater than N-2. The step size is controlled by variable B, which is a +1 while searching upward from randomly selected point A through the end of the list at N. When the loop exits with a step of +1, the starting point is reduced by one to prevent duplication of the starting point, the ending point is set to the beginning of the list at item 1, the step size is switched to −1, and the loop is repeated. When the second pass is completed, the conditional test of line 1022 is false because B is set to −1, so the program continues from that point.

Special IF . . . THEN . . . Considerations

Whether you are using IF . . . THEN . . . statements to control loops or for simple program branching, there are a number of special considerations that affect the efficiency of a given program. Among these are the use of multiple conditions in the test, the use of the IF . . . GOTO . . . form, and the use of the IF . . . THEN . . . ELSE . . . form. As usual, the trick is to find the method that provides maximum execution speed in a particular system and under specific circumstances. It would be impossible to cover all of the variations and intricacies involved with using the IF . . . THEN . . . statement, but the examples I've chosen should be sufficient to indicate some general trends and lead you to devising and testing your own approaches.

Multiple-Condition Testing. As a matter of programming convenience, most BASICs allow you to test multiple conditions with a single IF . . . THEN . . . statement and logical or Boolean operators such as an AND or an OR. As a result, some very complex tests can be devised and used within a program, relying on the interrelationships of two or more otherwise independent variables. There are times when I've extended a single IF . . . THEN . . . statement to nearly the full 255-character line limit of my system, without spaces or other wasted characters.

However, complex testing statements aren't necessarily an advantage. Often they save some memory bytes but result in much longer execution times than might be achieved with several simpler tests. Take, for example, the three-condition test illustrated by the following "nonsense" routine executed by MBASIC (BASIC-80) under 56K CP/M with an Apple II and a SoftCard. For timing convenience, I've set up this routine for 10,000 iterations of a loop so that A always is a one, while B and C always are zeros.

```
10 A=1: B=Ø: C=Ø
2Ø FOR X=1 TO 1ØØØØ
3Ø IF A=1 OR B=2 OR C=3 THEN D=1ØØ
4Ø NEXT
```

[119.0 seconds   69 bytes]

The routine is simple, short, and straightforward. But there is a problem. I've kept the conditions on variables B and C from ever being true and made the condition on variable A true for every iteration. But line 30 has to test all three variables and all three conditions before it can perform the designated action of setting D equal to 100. In theory, this would be wasting a considerable amount of time. To check it, I modified the routine to test the condition of each variable separately, performing appropriate jumps as soon as the earliest desired condition is satisfied. Here is the revised routine:

```
10 A=1: B=0: C=0
20 FOR X=1 TO 10000
30 IF A=1 THEN 38
32 IF B=2 THEN 38
34 IF C=3 THEN 38
36 GOTO 40
38 D=100
40 NEXT
```

[67.0 seconds 107 bytes]

Despite taking 38 bytes more memory, this version requires 52 seconds less execution time than the multi-condition test of the first sample. This means a time saving of 43.7 percent by splitting the conditional tests. What's actually happening is that, because the condition of line 30 always is true, every iteration jumps directly to line 38. Lines 32, 34, and 36 never are executed in this case, and two conditional tests are eliminated.

But no real program is going to rely on satisfying the first condition every time. If it did, the other two tests would be redundant and could be eliminated completely. Therefore, it's also necessary to look at the timing when any one of the three conditions may be met. To do that, the two routines simply are changed as follows:

```
5 DEFINT A-Z
10 FOR X=1 TO 10000
20 A=RND(1)*3+.5: B=A: C=A
30 IF A=1 OR B=2 OR C=3 THEN D=100
40 NEXT
```

[224.6 seconds]

```
5 DEFINT A-Z
10 FOR X=1 TO 10000
20 A=RND(1)*3+.5: B=A: C=A
```

```
3Ø IF A=1 THEN 38
32 IF B=2 THEN 38
34 IF C=3 THEN 38
36 GOTO 4Ø
38 D=1ØØ
4Ø NEXT
```

[209.1 seconds]

These last two examples run more slowly than the first two, but that's of no importance for what I'm trying to demonstrate. What is of concern is the relationship between just these two, with the second, physically larger version running in 15.5 seconds less than the first and saving 6.9 percent of the execution time. Although the savings is not nearly as dramatic as the first pair of tests, it is large enough to be significant.

In the second routine, line 30 is executed for every pass. Line 32 is executed fewer times only when line 30 is false. Line 34 is executed the fewest times and only when lines 30 and 32 are both false. Therefore, the total number of tests is reduced in comparison with the "compressed" IF . . . THEN . . . test of the first example.

You might want to challenge the tests on the basis of the use of random numbers. After all, if the sequence of numbers is different between the two tests, the results should be different. And random-number generators are notorious for providing nonuniform distributions. Remember, however, that these tests were run under a version of BASIC-80 that provides exactly the same numerical sequence any time a program is run either without reseeding the random-number generator or with reseeding the same number. Under this particular BASIC, the same numerical sequence is provided for each test, so the results may be compared one to one.

This shows that you may find it advantageous to avoid long, complex IF . . . THEN . . . statements in favor of shorter ones organized in the order in which you expect the tests to be satisfied. This is an important point! For maximum efficiency, the individual tests must be organized so that the condition expected to be met most often always occurs first. Your goal is to minimize the number of tests that need to be performed to accomplish the desired program branches, and putting an infrequently satisfied condition before one met more often only serves to defeat the purpose of splitting the IF . . . THEN . . . statements in the first place.

Some other interesting things can happen in playing around with multiple-condition testing. Assume that you need to test three flags, each of which may have a value of zero or one. You want to perform a program branch if and only if all three flags have been set to ones. Once again, you have a number of ways of writing the IF . . . THEN . . . statement, although you almost are forced to use a single program line. The following example illustrates one way to accomplish the test and branch; it's incorporated inside a long loop strictly for timing purposes under MBASIC (BASIC-80) with the Apple II and the SoftCard.

```
5 DEFINT A-Z
10 A=1: B=1: C=1
20 FOR X=1 TO 10000
30 IF A=1 THEN IF B=1 THEN IF C=1 THEN D=100
40 NEXT
```

Systematically altering line 30 to use four different methods of testing and branching, the following times were achieved:

```
30 IF A=1 THEN IF B=1 THEN IF C=1 THEN D=100     [90.1 seconds]
30 IF A=1 AND B=1 AND C=1 THEN D=100             [92.2 seconds]
30 IF A+B+C=3 THEN D=100                         [72.8 seconds]
30 IF A AND B AND C THEN D=100                   [61.8 seconds]
```

You can see that the fourth version executes the fastest and uses only "logical" Boolean operators and comparisons with no numeric values. The second version, with a combination of logical operators and numerical comparisons, is the slowest, with a difference of 30.4 seconds between it and the fastest method. This is a slowdown of 49.2 percent when compared to the fastest version. For most of your programming, you should find that using logical operations and avoiding numerical comparisons provide a speed increase.

At the same time, you have to be careful in structuring your logical tests. For the above example, the statement IF A+B+C THEN... doesn't work without the numerical comparison. That logical condition is true if any one or any combination of the three variables has a nonzero value, so the statement does not test to make certain all three were nonzero simultaneously. That form is equivalent to the statement IF A OR B OR C THEN... or to an IF A=1 OR B=1 OR C=1 THEN....

Similarly, it is usually to your advantage to use an IF X THEN... rather than an IF X<>0 THEN... statement to test a single variable for nonzero status. But you have to be cautious about changing any IF X>0 THEN... statement to the same form because the IF X THEN... form is true if X is positive *or* negative, while you may wish to test only for the positive condition.

I suggest that you spend some time playing around with the logical or Boolean operators defined in your BASIC manual. Try to develop an intimate familiarity with AND, OR, NOT, XOR, IMP, and EQV operations that may be available with your system. Study the truth tables presented in the manual and construct some test routines using each operator. These items can be very valuable in reducing program run time, but they have to be understood and used properly. Be sure to test the effects of both positive and negative values, either separately or in appropriate combinations. Most manuals do not include negative values in the truth tables, and they can have some surprising results when encountered by a logical operator. To illustrate, consider the following routine:

```
1Ø FOR X=-5 TO 5: PRINT X;
2Ø IF NOT X-1 THEN PRINT "TRUE" ELSE PRINT "FALSE"
3Ø NEXT
```

You'll find that the word FALSE is printed only when X equals zero, and the word TRUE is printed for all other values. If you change line 20 to IF NOT X. . ., you'll find that FALSE is printed only when X is a positive one (+1). Testing IF NOT −X..., prints FALSE only when X is a negative one (−1). If the specific value is the one for which you intend to test, fine. Otherwise, you may be in trouble if you use the wrong test within your programs.

Using the IF...GOTO... Form. Many BASICs allow the use of an IF. . .GOTO. . . statement in place of the IF. . .THEN. . . when a branch to a program line number is desired. They also allow the use of an IF. . .GOSUB. . ., but that's a different situation. Normally, the IF. . .THEN. . . and IF. . .GOTO. . . are interchangeable for flow transfers to a new line, but the question of efficiency comes up again. I've had some programmers tell me that the GOTO form offers a distinct speed advantage because it uses memory addressing differently.

Personally, I never had noticed a difference, largely because I'd never paid much attention to it. So I decided to try it with one of the routines already tested in the previous section. I simply took a routine with several IF. . .THEN. . . statements and changed the appropriate lines to IF. . .GOTO. . . statements so the routine appeared as follows:

```
5 DEFINT A-Z
1Ø FOR X=1 TO 1ØØØØ
2Ø A=RND(1)*3+.5: B=A: C=A
3Ø IF A=1 GOTO 38
32 IF B=2 GOTO 38
34 IF C=3 GOTO 38
36 GOTO 4Ø
38 D=1ØØ
4Ø NEXT
```

[207.1 seconds]

In the earlier test of the same routine with THEN in place of GOTO in lines 30, 32, and 34, the execution time was 209.1 seconds. With this routine, the time was 207.1 seconds, saving a whole 2.0 seconds or 1.0 percent. Under continuous 24-hour loop operation, that would amount to a saving of 14.4 minutes per day. It's not much, but it might help a little when added to other time reductions.

Using the ELSE Statement. One other variation to the IF...THEN... conditional test involves the use of an IF . . . THEN . . . ELSE . . . form for multidirectional branching. Once again, it's necessary to take a look at the amount of time that may be gained or lost using that form in comparison with a default to a subsequent GOTO . . . statement. To check it out, I set up the following two routines under MBASIC (BASIC-80) on the Apple II with a SoftCard. As before, BASIC-80 provides the same sequence of numbers from the random-number generator for each run, so the tests are comparable.

```
5 DEFINT A-Z
10 FOR X=1 TO 1000
20 A=RND(1)*10+.5
30 IF A=5 THEN 40 ELSE 20
40 NEXT
```

[132.7 seconds]

```
5 DEFINT A-Z
10 FOR X=1 TO 1000
20 A=RND(1)*10+.5
30 IF A=5 THEN 40
35 GOTO 20
40 NEXT
```

[136.2 seconds]

Somewhat surprisingly, the ELSE statement saved 3.5 seconds or 2.6 percent of the execution time. I expected it to take a little longer or, at best, to break even. Note that the ELSE statement also eliminates the need for an extra line number, thus providing a potential means of reducing memory requirements. Most BASICs require as many as five bytes for the number and overhead associated with each added line, so the savings can mount up to several hundred bytes in a long program.

Neither Applesoft nor Apple Integer BASIC provides the ELSE statement. This makes it necessary to use explicit lines to construct multidirectional branches and complicates the procedure of writing some loops and other tests. Furthermore, Integer BASIC differs radically from Applesoft in handling the THEN condition. To elaborate: Applesoft ignores all statements following the THEN when the IF . . . THEN . . . expression evaluates as false. Integer BASIC ignores only the first statement following the THEN under the same condition, and subsequent statements on the same line are executed. Consider this example:

Special "BASIC" Tricks

A number of special tricks are available for reducing the memory consumption, execution time, or both, of BASIC programs you write. They may be used in addition to, not in place of, the techniques covered in previous chapters. Such things as reusing variable names, avoiding or minimizing the use of array variables in loops, forcing variable names to appear at the top of the "array table," eliminating unnecessary variables and constants from functions, and similar considerations all seem trivial and relatively unimportant. Yet these same items and many others all contribute to making a program more efficient and more effective than it might otherwise be. As with every trick I've demonstrated thus far, the impact of a single modification to a program or its use in a short program may be barely noticeable, but the cumulative effects of all tricks applied to long programs and lengthy processing runs become quite important.

It's my purpose in this chapter to define and quantify some, but by no means all, of the special tricks available to you. The material herein is far from an exhaustive study of the subject, but it should get you started in the right direction. As an example of just how important these things are, I've used them in my own applications and seen a program that took up to four hours suddenly finish its assigned tasks in about 30 minutes. Of course, there's no guarantee that the effects on your programming will be of the same magnitude; the impact is directly related to both the length and the complexity of the total program. Nevertheless, you should be able to achieve a significant and valuable increase in execution speed, particularly when you combine these approaches with the ones presented in the preceding chapters. As your programs grow longer and more complex, the impact will increase so that larger and larger amounts of time may be saved.

Manipulating the Variable Table

BASIC interpreters access the values for assigned variables by means of a "variable table." As each new variable name is used for the first time in a program, it is added to the end of that table. I'll avoid using the terms "top" and "bottom" in this context because not every computer supplier uses the same terminology. For my purposes, the "beginning" of the table is the first variable put into it, and the "end" is the last variable.

Every time the variable is used thereafter, BASIC must search the table until it finds that particular variable, with the search always proceeding from the beginning of the table to the entry being sought. As a result, variables entered toward the beginning of the table are encountered before those toward the end, and their values are available for use in the program much sooner. The more variable names are used in a program, the larger the table that has to be searched, and the longer it takes to locate a variable near the end of the table.

The implication is that a program can be made more efficient by controlling or manipulating the variable table to speed critical searches. Since the table is not directly accessible to the program or the programmer through BASIC, it's necessary to use a couple of special tricks that allow an element of indirect control. One involves the actual assignment of variable names, and the other involves using an extra program statement to force a critical variable to a position at or near the table's beginning.

Assigning Variable Names

The first step is to keep the table as short as possible. In order to accomplish that, it's necessary to use as few different variable names as is practical. That, in turn, leads to having to reuse as many names as possible and as often as possible throughout the program. This brings me back to the earlier subject of not structuring a program for readability of the listing. When readability is the primary concern, the tendency is to reassign new and "meaningful" variable names at various points throughout the program, which then increases the size of the variable table and extends the search time and overall execution time unnecessarily.

Long ago, I scrapped the idea of meaningful variable names and adopted a strict policy of using one- or two-character names and redefining them as often as I can. For example, I control all of my loops with the variables X, Y, and Z, which allows me up to three levels of nesting that use the same names over and over again. When I need more levels, I simply pick any one of the other, currently unused variables in the program and reassign it. Unless I can find no other way around the problem, I refuse to assign a new variable name for loop control. For single-level loops, where several FOR. . . NEXT statements are simply executed one after another, it's not uncommon for my listings to show five, ten, or more successive program loops all beginning with FOR X....

I do find, however, that I need to maintain a few "dedicated" variables to transmit a numeric value from one section of a program to another. One such might be the number of items or words contained in a string array, which then controls the ending point of loops, the number of iterations performed, the depth of a particular searching operation, and so on. In those cases, I always assign the same variable names from one program to another, so that I know which are the dedicated variables and which are the reassignable ones for any program listing I pick up. For example, I always maintain the number of words contained in the master string array with a variable named I. I always maintain the number of complete program repetitions performed in a variable named W. Then I know that in any program, the variables I and W are not available for reassignment until a new data base is read in or until the program recycles to its starting point for its next pass.

For complex programming, I've found it advantageous to set up a separate sheet of paper with an alphabetical list of variable names from A through Z, A1 through Z1, and so on arranged in vertical columns. As I write the program, each variable name is checked off as it's assigned. I use an "x" to mark those variables that are eligible for reuse and an "o" to mark those that are dedicated and not subject to reuse. Once I've finished writing and debugging the program, I then go back and "map" the appearance of every variable name according to its line number, make certain that the first occurrence of any variable name is absolutely and inescapably necessary, change any unnecessary variable names to reuse older names, and retest and "re-debug" the program.

While all those manipulations increase the program-development time and destroy the human readability of the listings, the speed advantages gained in long-term use of the program have proven well worthwhile. Incidentally, "mapping" software is available from various sources for many of the BASIC interpreters. Those specialized programs offer a real advantage in showing every programming element and the lines on which they occur, and they are well worth their prices. For my CP/M BASICs, I like a package called Prgm/Map from The Software Store (708 Chippewa Square, Marquette, MI 49855) because it maps variables, statements, commands, functions, referenced lines, and strings, all with a hard-copy printout. For Applesoft programs, I use the cross-reference feature of The Applesoft Programmer's Assistant in the Applesoft Tool Kit package, although it's not as thorough as I'd like and doesn't provide the hard copy I prefer.

Forcing a Variable Name into the Table

The second step is to examine the first occurrences of newly assigned variable names and force some of them to occur earlier so they are at the beginning of the variable table.

It's quite possible that you may be writing a long program and reach a point where there is no possibility of redefining an old variable name. Suppose this happens as you are writing a new loop that is going to involve hundreds, thousands, or tens of thousands of iterations, that the loop occurs far into the program, and that you have to assign one or more new variables. As I've pointed out, those new variables normally are added at the end of the variable table, which might already be quite large. At that point, the new variables are what I consider "critical names"—variables that have to be accessed a great many times by the interpreter and appear far down in the variable table.

Consider the following routine. I've used line 8 to simulate the variable assignments that might take place in a program before the desired loops are encountered. By line 10, the 23 variables from A through W have been defined and stored in the variable table, but X, Y, and Z have not. Therefore, X, Y, and Z would be added to the end of the table, and 10,000 computations of Z would involve the same number of X, Y, and Z searches through all the preceding variables already in that table.

```
5 DEFINT A-Z
8  A=1:B=A:C=A:D=A:E=A:F=A:G=A:H=A:I=A:J=A:K=A:L=A:M=A:N=A:O=A:
  P=A:Q=A:R=A:S=A:T=A:U=A:V=A:W=A
10 FOR X=1 TO 100: FOR Y=1 TO 100
20 Z=X+Y
30 NEXT:NEXT
```

[Microsoft Rev. 4.51: 119.4 seconds]
[Microsoft Rev. 5.2: 80.1 seconds]

Now I get a little sneaky and change line 8 so that variables X, Y, and Z are preassigned meaningless values before any other variables. Since they then are forced to appear at the beginning of the table, some reduction in execution time should be evident. The routine and timing then become:

```
5 DEFINT A-Z
8 X=1:Y=X:Z=X:A=X:B=A:C=A:D=A:E=A:F=A:G=A:H=A:I=A:J=A:K=A:L=A:
  M=A:N=A:O=A:P=A:Q=A:R=A:S=A:T=A:U=A:V=A:W=A
10 FOR X=1 TO 100: FOR Y=1 TO 100
```

```
20 Z=X+Y
30 NEXT:NEXT
```

[Microsoft Rev. 4.51: 43.6 seconds]
[Microsoft Rev. 5.2: 39.5 seconds]

Shocking, isn't it? By simply forcing the three variables to the beginning of the table rather than the end, the execution time is reduced by 75.6 seconds or 63.5 percent for Revision 4.51 and by 40.6 seconds or 50.7 percent for Revision 5.2. Now that's quite a reduction! In fact, I've found the deliberate manipulation of the variable table in this manner to be the single most important thing I can do to reduce the execution time of programs.

As a result, most of my own programs contain a definition line with seemingly unrelated numeric variables set equal to an integer and selected string variables set equal to null strings. That line always appears right at the beginning of the program to force the selected variables into the beginning of the table. The actual use of a given variable name may not appear again for several hundred lines, but the "critical" name has been positioned so that overall execution time for the program is optimized.

There are two points of importance in using this approach. First, it isn't necessary or even advisable to include every variable name in the "predefinition" line, only those involved in the critical loops. Second, the variables handled this way have to be determined experimentally. Since it's equally possible to impede execution by predefining the wrong variables, you have to try one set, test and time the operation, and then try and test another set, continuing until you find the set that works best. In general, the objective is to get the variables used most often in a program at the beginning of the table. Pay attention! I said the ones *used* most often, say in long loops, not necessarily the ones written in the most lines and expressions.

The same considerations affect the use of array variables. This time, the variable table has to be searched for the subscript; then the array table has to be searched for the variable affected by that subscript. The following three examples show the differences for three cases. In the first, the variables for loop control and subscripting default to the last entries in the variable table, and the desired array, Z(.), is the fifth of five arrays dimensioned. In the second example, the desired array is changed to the first one dimensioned (line 9), and a small reduction of time is achieved. In the third sample, the loop control and subscript variables are moved to the beginning of the tables, and a much greater time reduction is obtained.

```
5 DEFINT A-Z
8 A=1:B=A:C=A:D=A:E=A:F=A:G=A:H=A:I=A:J=A:K=A:L=A:M=A:N=A:O=A:
  P=A:Q=A:R=A:S=A:T=A:U=A:V=A:W=A
9 DIM A(100),B(100),C(100),D(100,Z(100)
10 FOR X=1 TO 100: FOR Y=1 TO 100
20 Z(Y)=50
30 NEXT:NEXT
```

[Microsoft Rev. 4.51: 69.9 seconds]
[Microsoft Rev. 5.2: 53.7 seconds]

```
5 DEFINT A-Z
8 A=1:B=A:C=A:D=A:E=A:F=A:G=A:H=A:I=A:J=A:K=A:L=A:M=A:N=A:O=A:
  P=A:Q=A:R=A:S=A:T=A:U=A:V=A:W=A
9 DIM Z(100),A(100),B(100),C(100),D(100)
10 FOR X=1 TO 100: FOR Y=1 TO 100
20 Z(Y)=50
30 NEXT:NEXT
```

[Microsoft Rev. 4.51: 65.9 seconds]
[Microsoft Rev. 5.2: 50.0 seconds]

```
5 DEFINT A-Z
8 X=1:Y=X:A=X:B=A:C=A:D=A:D=A:E=A:F=A:G=A:H=A:I=A:J=A:K=A:L=A:
  M=A:N=A:O=A:P=A:Q=A:R=A:S=A:T=A:U=A:V=A:W=A
9 DIM Z(100),A(100),B(100),C(100),D(100)
10 FOR X=1 TO 100: FOR Y=1 TO 100
20 Z(Y)=50
30 NEXT:NEXT
```

[Microsoft Rev. 4.51: 40.5 seconds]
[Microsoft Rev. 5.2: 36.3 seconds]

Most programming applications will be much more complex than these examples and will involve many more variables. As program complexity increases, the number of defined variables usually increases as well, so the relative positioning of the variables in the tables becomes more and more important.

Using Array Variables in Loops

The overuse or misuse of array variables can lead to a distinct loss of program efficiency, especially when loops that utilize a large number of iterations are involved. When a program calls an array variable, both the subscript and the variable have to be evaluated. In doing so, the BASIC interpreter has to search the variable table for each variable name occurring in the subscript before it can evaluate the subscript and begin its search of the array storage for the referenced value. Each subscript also requires additional memory each time it appears in the program, typically including six bytes for each set of parentheses, another five bytes for each integer variable in the subscript expression, and the bytes needed for the variable name itself. All in all, a costly situation at best.

I make it a habit to check all program loops for appearances of subscripted variables. When I find the same variable name and subscript appearing more than twice within any loop, I modify the program to set up a fixed, nonarray variable and then use that in subsequent computations. Often, that fixed variable name is one that has been forced toward the beginning of the variable table. The relative advantages do tend to fluctuate as a function of how many times the variable is used, the total number of variables in the program, the positioning in the variable table, the size of the dimensioned arrays, and numerous other factors. Yet the replacement of unnecessary array variables with fixed variables inevitably results in improved execution speed and usually reduces the overall memory consumption of the program.

The following two examples illustrate how this works. The routines are trivial numeric manipulations, but they show how the replacement can be accomplished to minimize array references in repetitive operations.

```
5 DEFINT A-Z
10 DIM A(100),B(100),C(100),D(100)
20 FOR X=1 TO 100: FOR Y=1 TO 100
30 D(Y)=X+Y
40 A(Y)=D(Y)+5
50 B(Y)=D(Y)+10
60 C(Y)=(D(Y)\B(Y))+B(Y)
70 NEXT:NEXT
```

[Microsoft Rev. 4.51: 321.0 seconds]
[Microsoft Rev. 5.2: 283.2 seconds]

```
5 DEFINT A-Z
10 DIM A(100),B(100),C(100),D(100)
20 FOR X=1 TO 100: FOR Y=1 TO 100
30 D=X+Y:D(Y)=D
40 A(Y)=D+5
50 B=D+10:B(Y)=B
```

```
60 C(Y)=(D\B)+B
70 NEXT:NEXT
```

[Microsoft Rev. 4.51: 293.0 seconds]
[Microsoft Rev. 5.2: 250.4 seconds]

For this particular set of examples involving 10,000 iterations of the Y loop, the elimination of several array references in lines 40 and 60 plus the setup of fixed variables in lines 30 and 50 resulted in a savings of 28.0 seconds or 8.7 percent for Revision 4.51 and 32.8 seconds or 11.6 percent for Revision 5.2. Variables B and D occur at the end of the variable table by default. I'll leave it to you to determine whether adding something like D=1 to line 5 will further improve the speed.

In many applications, I've seen even greater savings, sometimes amounting to 30 or 40 percent of the original execution time, depending upon all the other factors included in the particular program. As a general rule of thumb, the more array references eliminated from a given loop, the faster that loop will execute. For the two examples just presented, it's also interesting to note that the second version saved seven bytes, even though it actually contains a greater number of program statements.

Another factor often overlooked in the haste to get a program operational is the point at which a fixed or array variable is assigned a value in nested loops. In going through a large number of programs, both my own and those published by others, I frequently encounter a nesting that begins something like this:

```
1000 FOR X=A TO B
1002 FOR Y=C TO D
1004 Z=X/5
. . .
```

Notice line 1004. In this case, it's a simple, fixed variable, but it could just as easily be an array variable. It makes no use of the Y value yet is contained within the body of the Y loop where it has to be executed every time the inner loop is iterated. Since its value is strictly a function of variable X, it always evaluates the same for any single iteration of the X loop and wastes a lot of time in the position shown. It's far better to position that same computation thus:

```
1000 FOR X=A TO B: Z=X/5
1002 FOR Y=C TO D
. . .
```

Suppose the X loop ranges from 1 to 100 and the Y loop also ranges from 1 to 100. In the second form, Z would be evaluated 100 times. But in the first form, the value of Z would be computed 10,000 times, of which 9,900 computations are totally wasted. *Watch out for this one!* It's very easy to misplace a computation like this, and it most often happens in lengthy or deeply nested loops when the programmer suddenly realizes a value is needed and just drops the computation in at that point rather than backing off to an earlier loop where it would be more appropriate.

Zeroing Array Variables

It's common to reach a point in a program where it becomes necessary to "zero" an entire numeric array or set an entire string array to null strings. Nulling string arrays is particularly important in programs that use many of those variables because it releases unneeded string space for other uses, especially at the next occurrence of a string-space garbage collection. However, it doesn't free up the string-array pointers—only the actual number of bytes occupied by characters contained within the strings. Remember that dimensioning a string array only sets aside space for memory addresses at which the strings can be found. To clear the pointer space, it's necessary to "erase" the array, not merely to set the strings to nulls.

There are at least two ways an array can be zeroed. The first and most obvious is to execute a loop that sets each numeric element to zero or each string element to a null string. The following example illustrates the technique and shows the time required to zero three large numeric arrays and null a single large string array. Remember that the address pointers for the string array remain unchanged and that the CLEAR 10000 statement isn't used under Microsoft Revision 5.2.

```
10 CLEAR 10000: DIM A(100,10), B(100,10), C(100,10), S$(100,10)
. . .
1000 FOR X=1 TO 100: FOR Y=1 TO 10
1002 A(X,Y)=0: B(X,Y)=0: C(X,Y)=0: S$(X,Y)=""
1004 NEXT:NEXT
```

[Microsoft Rev. 4.51: 29.4 seconds]
[Microsoft Rev. 5.2: 31.5 seconds]

When the BASIC being used offers an ERASE statement, the same operation can be performed with the following approach:

```
10 CLEAR 10000: DIM A(100,10), B(100,10), C(100,10), S$(100,10)
. . .
1000 ERASE A,B,C,S$: DIM A(100,10), B(100,10), C(100,10), S$(100,10)
```

[Microsoft Rev. 4.51: 2.1 seconds]
[Microsoft Rev. 5.2: 2.1 seconds]

The second approach is simpler to write into the program and is much faster than the loop method. It also provides some additional benefits. For one, the redimensioning can be to any array size desired, so it would be possible to eliminate two-dimensional arrays and set up new arrays with only a single dimension, smaller arrays, and so on. For another, it allows arrays to be eliminated entirely by not redimensioning them, thus freeing up all of the previously reserved space. For yet another, it clears the string-array pointers, so string space may be made available to nonarray string variables under some BASICs or to any string or numeric uses under BASIC-80 where string space is not allocated separately.

The erase-and-redimension technique has one major drawback. It won't work for a program being processed by Microsoft's BASCOM compiler or certain other compilers. The compiler does not recognize or accept an ERASE statement, so an immediate "redimensioned array" error is detected. This is because compiled programs handle variables and arrays in a different manner than interpreted programs, and the memory utilization does not allow array space to be "disassigned." Typically, the BASCOM compiler includes the array space in the body of the compiled code, with every element having an assigned memory location (one reason why disk files output by the compiler are extremely large). At the same time, the compiler offers such tremendous speed advantages that zeroing or nulling arrays with a loop or series of loops is not a major factor in the overall run time.

A few BASICs offer yet another way to zero arrays. If the interpreter has a MAT statement or function, it also serves as a way of accomplishing the task. However, none of the BASICs I can run on my own systems have that statement, so I'm unable to provide a comparison with the preceding approaches. If you have such a BASIC, you might want to try the MAT statement and time it in comparison with the loop approach to determine whether or not it gives you an advantage.

I must introduce one other consideration here. Many programmers fall into the habit of starting their programs with a DIM statement for arrays and immediately progressing into a loop to set all numeric array values to zeros and all string values to nulls. With the exception of Apple Integer BASIC, every other version I use makes that an absolute waste of time. When first dimensioned (or redimensioned), all array variables are set to zeros or nulls automatically. There is absolutely no reason to repeat the operation with an explicit loop except with unusual interpreters such as Integer BASIC.

You also have to remember that using a subscripted variable without having first dimensioned it typically performs an automatic dimension operation for 10 elements. That is, executing a statement containing X(1) or X(A) without a prior DIM X(<n>) statement is equivalent to having executed a DIM X(10). Later in the program, a DIM X(<n>) statement not preceded by an ERASE X statement causes a "redimensioned array" error, and any subscript larger than the default 10 will cause a "subscript out of range" error. It's a good habit to dimension all subscripted variables and not rely on the default conditions in this case. Furthermore, you should try to do all initial dimensioning within the first two or three lines of the program rather than scattering DIM statements around.

Using Default Conditions

BASIC interpreters are jammed full of so-called default conditions. Forget to dimension an array but use a subscripted variable, and the system defaults to an array with 10 elements. Fail to allocate string space with a CLEAR statement under Microsoft BASIC Revision 4.51, and the system defaults to 100 bytes for strings. Leave out the memory size desired, and the system defaults to using the maximum amount of memory available. Omit a "range" expression from a function, and the system often defaults to a "1" for the beginning or "worst-case" condition. That last item can be especially important.

By specifying a value for an item that has a system-default value, you often end up inhibiting or limiting some system activity. Usually, the limits you program against something like an intrinsic function involve some internal computations or retrieval processes within the interpreter, processes that consume a finite amount of time. As long as you need the limit, specifying it explicitly is fine. But often the range you might choose to specify coincides exactly with the default parameters, at which time you waste a portion of the program's time in evaluating some expression unnecessarily.

To demonstrate how this works, consider a couple of the intrinsic string functions in Microsoft BASICs. First, there would be a case where it's necessary to determine the ASCII code of the third letter in each of 210 English words. By definition, the ASC( ) function returns the ASCII code of the *first* character in the string used as the argument, so either of the following two examples will work. They differ only in that the first routine returns a single character from the third position of the word, while the second example returns a string of all characters beginning at position three. The loop controlled by variable X merely repeats the entire operation a hundred times for convenience in timing it. The CLEAR 20000 statement is not used in the Microsoft Revision 5.2 tests.

```
5 CLEAR 2ØØØØ: DEFINT A-Z: DIM S$(21Ø)
. . .
1ØØ FOR X=1 TO 1ØØ: FOR Y=1 TO 21Ø
1Ø2 A=ASC(MID$(S$(Y),3,1))
1Ø4 NEXT:NEXT
```

[Microsoft Rev. 4.51: 173.2 seconds]
[Microsoft Rev. 5.2: 162.1 seconds]

```
5 CLEAR 2ØØØØ: DEFINT A-Z: DIM S$(21Ø)
. . .
1ØØ FOR X=1 TO 1ØØ: FOR Y=1 TO 21Ø
1Ø2 A=ASC(MID$(S$(Y),3))
1Ø4 NEXT: NEXT
```

[Microsoft Rev. 4.51: 157.5 seconds]
[Microsoft Rev. 5.2: 148.3 seconds]

By simply removing the specified length of the string from the MID$() function in line 102, some 15.7 seconds or 9.1 percent of the original time was shaved off the operations under Revision 4.51, and 13.8 seconds or 8.5 percent under Revision 5.2.

Now consider the case where it is desired to return a string S1$ that contains the rightmost characters of some other string S$ beginning at position N of the original. There are three rather obvious approaches using the function RIGHT$(S$,LEN(S$)–N+1), the function MID$(S$,N,LEN(S$)–N+1), and the function MID$(S$,N). In the first two, the length of the returned string is calculated explicitly from the length of the original and the first character position desired. In the last one, the length is allowed to default to all characters following the specified character position, giving a much simpler expression for evaluation and, one would expect, a much faster operation. The following three examples illustrate the timings obtained when the three methods were tested in 100 passes through a list of 210 strings.

```
5 CLEAR 2ØØØØ: DEFINT A-Z: DIM S$(21Ø)
. . .
1ØØ N=3:FOR X=1 TO 1ØØ: FOR Y=1 TO 21Ø
```

```
102 S1$=RIGHT$(S$(Y),LEN(S$(Y))-N+1)
104 NEXT: NEXT
```

[Microsoft Rev. 4.51: 287.6 seconds]
[Microsoft Rev. 5.2: 257.7 seconds]

```
5 CLEAR 20000: DEFINT A-Z:DIM S$(210)
. . .
100 N=3:FOR X=1 TO 100: FOR Y=1 TO 210
102 S1$=MID$(S$(Y),N,LEN(S$(Y))-N+1)
104 NEXT: NEXT
```

[Microsoft Rev. 4.51: 317.1 seconds]
[Microsoft Rev. 5.2: 284.0 seconds]

```
5 CLEAR 20000: DEFINT A-Z: DIM S$(210)
. . .
100 N=3:FOR X=1 TO 100: FOR Y=1 TO 210
102 S1$=MID$(S$(Y),N)
104 NEXT: NEXT
```

[Microsoft Rev. 4.51: 190.5 seconds]
[Microsoft Rev. 5.2: 168.8 seconds]

Indeed, the third and simplest form is fastest. With either BASIC interpreter tested, calculating the length of the returned string for the MID$() function in the second example takes about 1.7 times longer, and calculating the length for the RIGHT$() function in the first example takes about 1.5 times longer.

In a parallel situation, assume that it's necessary to locate the first position, if any, of the letter "A" within each of the same words. In this case, the two equivalent routines could appear as follows:

```
5 CLEAR 20000: DEFINT A-Z: DIM S$(210)
. . .
100 FOR X=1 TO 100: FOR Y=1 TO 210
102 A=INSTR(1,S$(Y),"A")
104 NEXT: NEXT
```

[Microsoft Rev. 4.51: 158.5 seconds]
[Microsoft Rev. 5.2: 147.3 seconds]

```
5 CLEAR 20000: DEFINT A-Z: DIM S$(210)
. . .
```

```
100 FOR X=1 TO 100: FOR Y=1 TO 210
102 A=INSTR(S$(Y),"A")
104 NEXT: NEXT
```

[Microsoft Rev. 4.51: 139.7 seconds]
[Microsoft Rev. 5.2: 130.5 seconds]

In this case, just removing the starting position for the string search from the INSTR() function in line 102 and allowing it to default to the first character position reduced the time required by 18.8 seconds or 11.8 percent for Revision 4.51 and by 16.8 seconds or 11.4 percent for Revision 5.2.

Going one step more, BASIC-80 (Microsoft Revision 5.1 or 5.2) allows the entire argument to be left off the RND() function so a simple RND function with no argument is exactly equivalent to an RND(1). This is not allowable on Microsoft Revision 4.51 or Applesoft BASICs, but it does have an effect on the speed of BASIC-80:

```
100 FOR X=1 TO 10000: Y=RND(1): NEXT   [70.3 seconds]
100 FOR X=1 TO 10000: Y=RND: NEXT      [59.3 seconds]
```

By eliminating the argument from the function, the returned random numbers remain the same (no seeding or reseeding), but the time is reduced by 11 seconds or 15.6 percent for the 10,000 loop iterations. The second version also saves the memory bytes otherwise needed for the parentheses and integer argument.

Eliminating a single variable or constant in this way may not make any real difference if the operation is performed only occasionally. But it can make a very distinct difference when the process is repeated again and again and again, say within a deeply nested FOR. . . NEXT loop. For maximum programming efficiency, strive to make use of the default conditions whenever and wherever you can get by with them.

Even variable arrays can be affected. Under most BASICs, a DIM X(10) actually assigns eleven subscripted variables ranging from X(0) through X(10). BASIC-80 is a possible exception since it contains an OPTION BASE statement that can declare a 1 as the minimum subscript value. Given the presence of the zero elements of arrays, many programmers, including me, prefer not to use them as parts of the sets of values. Simply stated, using the zero elements may save some memory bytes but can complicate programming later on when positions in the array have to be handled on the basis of some numeric sequence minus one. For example, 210 array elements would be stored as X(0) through X(209), and the eighth element would actually reside at X(7). In fact, the need to perform numerous subsequent subtractions can slow the entire program down.

Instead, I prefer to use each zero element as a separate storage location for temporary or semipermanent results obtained during execution. For example, when I want to know the first word in a list that begins with the letter "Q," I search the list from S$(1) through S$(n), locate that word, and store it temporarily in S$(0). By making this a uniform approach from one program to another, I know that the zero elements of arrays always are available to me as intermediate storage locations. I can treat each of these elements in much the same manner as a machine-language "accumulator," shifting data in and out or performing specific operations on a particular element—all without having to alter the contents of the other array elements.

I even apply the same technique to handling string data as numeric ASCII codes. It sometimes happens that I can perform complex word manipulations involving numerous arrays more easily, faster, and in less memory with individual ASCII codes than with intact strings. Take, for example, a situation where I have 200 English words stored in string array S$(.), with no word allowed to exceed 10 characters in length. A routine that I might use to set up the initial ASCII array would appear as follows:

```
10 CLEAR 20000: DEFINT A-R,T-Z: DEFSTR S: DIM S(210), L(210,10)
. . .
100 FOR X=1 TO 210: L(X,0)=LEN(S(X))
102 FOR Y=1 TO L(X,0): L(X,Y)=ASC(MID$(S(X),Y)):NEXT
104 NEXT
```

If I were to use the zero elements of the L(.) array to hold the ASCII codes for letters, I would have a minus one shift in both the word locations and the letter locations. As a result, the ASCII code for the fifth letter of the ninth word would actually be found in L(8,4). For my purposes, I prefer to have it in L(9,5) where I feel it belongs. So I use the zero element in the Y direction to hold the length (number of characters) of each word, which is a value I often need throughout the program. Therefore the array elements from L(1,0) through L(210,0) are numeric values representing individual word lengths. Meanwhile, I reserve the zero elements in the X direction from L(0,0) through L(0,10) to hold any 11 values I need to store, such as total words in the list, number of program repetitions needed, number of repetitions already performed, specific flags, and so on.

In short, I avoid using zero elements for regular array values, but I do make use of most of the zero locations for other purposes, thereby reducing the number of other variables and arrays that might otherwise be necessary. As usual, this is a technique that each programmer has to try and test individually. Furthermore, it may improve a program in one case or degrade performance in another.

Using Subroutines

Subroutines provide a handy way of minimizing the number of programming lines and statements as well as the memory space required for identical operations performed at various points in a program. Most BASICs provide a means by which the programmer can utilize subroutines written either in BASIC or in assembly language. Those written in BASIC are accessed by the GOSUB... RETURN or ON...GOSUB...RETURN statement, with the mainline program containing the GOSUB... and the subroutine containing the RETURN. Those written in assembly language are accessed by either the CALL... statement or the USR <n> function.

Since this book does not deal with assembly-language programming, I'm not going to go into detail on those subroutines. To use them properly, you have to know and feel comfortable with assembly-language programming. There also are a great many differences in the methods employed by different computer systems and BASICs to store the subroutines in memory, address them from the BASIC program, and pass the parameters back and forth between the subroutines and mainline programs. I will point out, however, that assembly-language subroutines offer a distinct speed advantage for complex operations, largely because they are closer to the computer's inherent binary language and don't require the continuous interpretation provided by BASIC.

What I am going to do is devote attention to subroutines written in BASIC and contained wholly within BASIC programs. There are several fundamental points that have to be made. First, any subroutine may be called from any place in the program, including other subroutines, and it may be called as often as necessary. This gives subroutines a considerable degree of "power" in that a routine can be written once, executed from many different calls through the program, and even moved intact from one program to another if it is stored on disk and "merged" into another program.

Subroutines also make life much easier for a programmer in that the algorithm and the program coding have to be written only once. For many of my own applications, particularly those involving a lot of string handling, I've developed a modular approach in which I store a library of "standard" subroutines as ASCII disk files and simply merge them from the disk files into each new mainline program as they are needed.

When one subroutine is called by another it is considered "nested," and the allowable depth of subroutine-to-subroutine transfers or the level of nesting is a function of the BASIC and the memory size in use. Microsoft BASICs do not impose a fixed limit on the number of nesting levels. However, in any one computer system there is a practical limit determined by the size of memory available. Each "active" GOSUB . . .

requires five or six bytes of memory (depending upon the BASIC) to store the address needed by the RETURN statement to transfer program control back to the mainline program or the preceding subroutine level. Applesoft, on the other hand, imposes a fixed limit of 25 levels, after which an "out of memory" error occurs regardless of the actual amount of memory remaining.

Nearly all modern BASIC interpreters use the RETURN statement in the subroutine to transfer control back to the *program statement* immediately following the GOSUB... most recently executed. This means that several GOSUB... statements may appear on the same program line, and each will be executed in the order of occurrence. This holds true for the Microsoft and Applesoft BASICs. For instance, the following program line would first transfer to the subroutine at line 1000. Upon return, it would then transfer to the subroutine at line 2000. The process would repeat for each subroutine call in sequence, with the mainline program proceeding to the next line following 100 only after the subroutine at line 400 has been executed.

```
100 GOSUB 1000: GOSUB 2000: GOSUB 3000: GOSUB 4000
```

However, there are a few BASICs still around that transfer control back to the *program line* following the GOSUB.... The distinction is important because those BASICs do not handle the preceding example properly. The return from the subroutine at line 1000 would be to the next line number, so the subroutines at 2000, 3000, and 4000 would *not* be executed. To accomplish the same progression of transfers under such an interpreter, it would be necessary to put each GOSUB... statement on its own line to form the following sequence:

```
100 GOSUB 1000
102 GOSUB 2000
103 GOSUB 3000
104 GOSUB 4000
```

Subroutine versus Mainline Programming

While subroutines are quite useful in simplifying a program and avoiding redundant coding that would otherwise occupy and possibly waste computer memory, they do have a cost. Each transfer to and from a subroutine takes time, so the advantages of convenience and memory savings have to be weighed against the disadvantage of slowed execution. As an illustration of how this works, consider the following examples. In the first, a simple random-number calculation is included within the body of the FOR...NEXT loop. In the second, the same routine is performed by a subroutine called from the loop. For the

Applesoft test, the DEFINT statement was removed from line 10, and variable name Y() was changed to Y%().

```
10 DEFINT A-Z: DIM Y(5000)
20 FOR X=1 TO 5000
30 Y(X)=RND(1)*X+.5
40 NEXT
```

[Microsoft Rev. 4.51: 64.1 seconds]
[Microsoft Rev. 5.2: 67.0 seconds]
[Applesoft: 70.5 seconds]

```
10 DEFINT A-Z: DIM Y(5000)
20 FOR X=1 TO 5000
30 GOSUB 9000
40 NEXT
50 STOP
9000 Y(X)=RND(1)*X+.5
9002 RETURN
```

[Microsoft Rev. 4.51: 71.0 seconds]
[Microsoft Rev. 5.2: 73.1 seconds]
[Applesoft: 77.6 seconds]

In each case, the subroutine caused an increase in execution time. For Revision 4.51, the increase was 6.9 seconds or 10.7 percent. For BASIC-80, it was 6.1 seconds or 9.1 percent. For Applesoft, it was 7.1 seconds or 10.1 percent. This indicates that every transfer of control performed to and from a first-level subroutine takes from 0.0013 to 0.0014 second, depending upon the BASIC being used. Since the transfer of control does take time, it's often advisable to avoid subroutines for simple one- to four-statement lines. Instead, the use of subroutines should be reserved for those computations involving a number of separate steps and usually requiring several lines of program code. When you have to repeat the same program coding, put the simple operations right into the mainline program, and put the complex ones into subroutines.

Transfers to and from subroutines from within FOR...NEXT loops are perfectly acceptable to any BASIC I've used. They pose a danger only if the subroutine alters the loop-control variables in any way. If you call a subroutine from within a loop that is under control of variable X, you cannot safely use another loop controlled by X within the subroutine. In some cases you might get a "FOR without NEXT" or "NEXT without FOR" error; in others, you will "butcher" the value of X and lose control of the mainline loop. You can, however, use a deliberate alteration of X in the subroutine to force early termination of the mainline loop, but you have to make certain that the program flow and results are what you really want to achieve. When subroutines are called from within nested loops, the same considerations affect the controlling variables for each loop.

Positioning a Subroutine

The Applesoft programming manual contains an interesting statement worthy of investigation. Specifically, it says, "when APPLESOFT encounters a new line reference... it scans the entire user program starting at the lowest line... frequently-referenced lines should be placed as early in the program as possible." This leads many programmers to use a GOTO... statement at the beginning of the program to transfer control to a mainline section appearing at the end. The space between the initial GOTO... and the mainline section then is filled with frequently called subroutines.

As usual, the question of whether or not there is a real gain in execution speed must be examined. It's also necessary to take a look at whether this is unique to Applesoft or extends to other BASIC interpreters. To check it out, I modified the little subroutine test conducted previously to add 101 program lines between the subroutine and mainline program. Line numbers 100 through 200, in increments of 1, all contained the statement X=1, were never executed, but forced the physical separation of program elements. In the first test series, I put the subroutine at the end of the program, while the second series had it positioned at the beginning. The Applesoft programs differ from the versions shown only in that the DEFINT statement is omitted from line 5 and variable Y() is named Y%().

```
10 DEFINT A-Z: DIM Y(5000)
20 FOR X=1 TO 5000
30 GOSUB 9000
40 NEXT
50 STOP
100 X=1
. . .
20 X=1
9000 Y(X)=RND(1)*X+.5
9002 RETURN
```

[Microsoft Rev. 4.51: 71.0 seconds]
[Microsoft Rev. 5.2: 73.1 seconds]
[Applesoft: 104.8 seconds]

```
10 DEFINT A-Z: DIM Y(5000)
20 GOTO 500
30 Y(X)=RND(1)*X+.5
40 RETURN
100 X=1
. . .
200 X=1
500 FOR X=1 TO 5000
502 GOSUB 30
504 NEXT
```

[Microsoft Rev. 4.51: 71.0 seconds]
[Microsoft Rev. 5.2: 73.1 seconds]
[Applesoft: 76.5 seconds]

Look at the time comparisons between these two programs, as well as the earlier version of the subroutine test without the intervening lines from 100 through 200. Neither of the Microsoft BASICs shows any effect as a result of repositioning the subroutine; the timing is exactly the same in all three tests under both of these interpreters. Frankly, I've never been able to detect any impact with any subroutine or any positioning variation under Microsoft BASICs.

But Applesoft is a completely different matter. As shown, positioning the subroutine at the start of the program gives a 28.3-second advantage. That's a speed increase of 27 percent over positioning the subroutine at the end. If you refer back to the version without the intervening lines, you'll find that moving the subroutine to the start of the program demonstrates a 1.1-second advantage over even the short version.

The implication is clear. First, subroutine positioning affects only Applesoft and similar BASICs, not Microsoft interpreters. Second, the subroutines referenced most often should be placed at or as near as possible to the beginning of the program and in the order of descending frequency. With Applesoft, the amount of time saved by placing subroutines properly is far too large to ignore, no matter how inconvenient the structure is. Other BASICs that may have the subroutines appearing anywhere without adverse effect allow the programs to be written in the form most convenient to the programmer.

I have a distinct preference for locating the subroutines at the end of a program; I find that placing them at the beginning is an outright nuisance. When I lift a program from another source or develop my own software, I like to debug individual sections or modules as I go along. When the subroutines are at the beginning of the program they're in the way, and I find it increasingly difficult to do the debugging because I have to key in many of the subroutine lines before I can test the mainline sections of concern. If I try to approach it from keying the mainline program and then keying only the subroutine affected, I have to jump back and forth between widely separated sections, often renumbering lines to make additional room for new routines. With nested subroutines, the situation deteriorates rapidly, and I may be forced to key most or all of a program before I can do any debugging at all. The time needed to isolate and correct problems then increases dramatically.

With most BASICs, I can simply "tack on" subroutines when and where they are needed, but Applesoft doesn't allow me that luxury without sacrificing program efficiency. So a tradeoff is necessary. I have to content myself with increased effort and time to key and test the program just to allow Applesoft to achieve its maximum speed of execution.

Recursive Subroutines

A "recursive" subroutine is one that loops back on itself, creating increasing levels of nesting without returns. Normally, this is a programming error; it is roughly equivalent to falling into an infinite loop. However, at least one such recursive subroutine is extremely useful under certain BASICs and demonstrates one way in which BASICs differ. The routine I'm speaking of is a single line:

```
1Ø IF FRE(X)<1ØØ THEN RUN ELSE PRINT FRE(X);:GOSUB 1Ø
```

This is a rather slick little memory test for Microsoft Revision 4.51 and similar BASICs. It simply progresses through memory, pushing return addresses into the stack until free memory decreases to less than 100 bytes. At that point, it "reruns" itself and starts all over. The screen display shows lines of decreasing numbers designating the unused memory. If the program hangs, there is a defective memory location, and it tests all memory locations "above" BASIC itself plus 100 bytes.

However, this little program does not function properly under BASIC-80 (Microsoft Revision 5.1 or 5.2). There the stack size is limited to that specified in a CLEAR... statement, so an "out of memory" error occurs when that space is consumed. However, it does demonstrate what happens when the CLEAR... statement is used to change the stack size. On my 64K machine, the default stack is 256 bytes, this routine will repeat itself 86 times before running out of stack space, and the free space for each iteration is reported as an unchanging 34,995 bytes. If I use the CLEAR... statement to increase the stack to 5,000 bytes, I get many more repetitions, each showing a lower but unchanging amount of free memory.

As written, the routine won't run under Applesoft; the normal negative numbers returned by the Apple II for free memory hang the routine. However, it can be modified:

```
10 PRINT FRE(X),:GOSUB 10
```

Under Applesoft, this routine executes exactly 25 times and prints a constant −18,450 free bytes (for a 48K system without DOS). It yields an "out of memory" error on the twenty-sixth try, confirming the Applesoft manual's statement that nested subroutines are limited to a maximum of 25 levels.

Using Disk Files

When running under a disk-operating system (DOS), BASICs generally offer the programmer a choice of two file-handling techniques—random access and sequential access. Each has its advantages and disadvantages for specific applications, and you'll find that you have to adopt the technique most suitable to your needs at any one point in time.

As the name implies, a random-access file allows you to read data from or write data to a file at random. You can record or retrieve from any numbered "record" you desire without having to read through all the data preceding that record. This provides a fast method of retrieving individual items from large accumulations of data. Additionally, when a random file is "opened," you can read from one record, write to another record, read from another, and so on. In short, you can mix storage and retrieval operations as you please.

A sequential-access file may be used to read or write data only in consecutive order from beginning to end. When it is opened as an "input" file, data may be read but not written. When it is opened as an "output" file, data may be written but not read. Incidentally, opening a file as an output file under most BASIC interpreters automatically "erases" the contents of a previous file having the same name. Therefore, it is usually not possible to store off data in a file and later reopen it for output to add or append more data to the same file (except under Applesoft, which does feature an append operation). Instead, it's usually necessary to open the old file for input, open a second file for output, read from one and write to the other, write the new data, close the files, kill or delete the original, and rename the new file.

Random-Access Disk Files

The manual for Microsoft BASIC-80 makes a clear statement concerning one advantage of using random files:

> Creating and accessing random files requires more program steps than sequential files, but there are advantages to using random files. One advantage is that random files require less room on the disk, because BASIC stores them in a packed binary format. (A sequential file is stored as a series of ASCII characters.)

I'll agree with the first part of the statement completely. Random-access files do require more program steps, both for storing data and for retrieving it later. There are advantages inherent in being able to access any record at random, as long as such access is needed. I'll disagree with the second part unless it is qualified to define the type of data, record size, and so on. As just one case in point, it is possible to waste a lot of disk space by using random-access files for string data to be stored and retrieved in purely sequential order.

Microsoft BASICs store all data in string form when using a random file. That means numeric data have to be converted to strings for storage and converted back from string to numeric form upon retrieval. The process of converting from numeric data to strings is performed by the MKI$(), MKS$(), and MKD$() functions for integer, single-precision, and double-precision values respectively. The process of converting the strings back to numeric values is performed by the CVI(), CVS(), and CVD() functions.

On disk, integers are stored as two "packed" bytes, single-precision numbers as four bytes, and double-precision numbers as eight bytes. That does provide a disk savings for numeric data—double-precision numbers having up to 17 significant digits require only eight bytes of disk space. However, the savings are realized only if all the bytes of a record, typically 128, are used.

In contrast, string data are not packed; the strings are stored in ASCII form, so there is no specific reduction in the number of bytes consumed. Because of the way random-file records are prepared, there may even be a significant waste of disk space with string data when all of the available bytes in a record cannot be used.

To oversimplify the matter, a single record for a random file is transferred as a unit of data to or from a random-file buffer maintained by the BASIC interpreter. In order for a record to be read onto the disk, that record first must be constructed in the buffer by the program, and the entire buffer then is transmitted to the disk. For the record to be read back, the entire record must be transmitted to the buffer, and the buffer then must be "decoded" by the program.

Take a case in which numeric data are stored with 100 integers in array A%(.), 100 single-precision numbers in array B!(.), and 100 double-precision numbers in array C#(.). For one reason or another it's necessary to store the data as 100 records, with each record containing one element of each array. When a specific record is retrieved, it then would return one value of A%(.), one of B!(.), and one of C#(.). The following routine could be used under a Microsoft BASIC to set up the buffer and store the data onto disk:

```
1000 OPEN "R", 1, "DATA"
1002 FIELD #1, 2 AS A$, 4 AS B$, 8 AS C$
```

```
1ØØ4 FOR X=1 TO 1ØØ
1ØØ6 LSET A$=MKI$(A%(X)): LSET B$=MKS$(B!(X)): LSET C$=MKD$(C#(X))
1ØØ8 PUT #1
1Ø1Ø NEXT: CLOSE
```

Line 1002 sets up or "fields" the random-file buffer, assigning three fields to the three values. Note that each field is assigned as a string variable and that the length of each field corresponds to the number of bytes for the numeric data type; the fields may be longer than required if wasted bytes can be tolerated, but they never can be any shorter.

Line 1006 packs the numeric data into strings and sets those strings into the variables named in the FIELD statement. The LSET statement forces the characters to the leftmost position of the field, filling any unused bytes to the right with spaces; an RSET statement also is available that forces the characters to the rightmost bytes, padding unused bytes to the left with spaces. Although there are no unused bytes for the fields set up, it's still necessary to use either an LSET or an RSET statement to set the values into the buffer. Finally, line 1008 contains the PUT #<file number >[,record] statement that writes the buffer to the disk.

To get a single specified record back from the disk file at a later time, it would be necessary either to have the buffer already fielded as necessary or to re-field it. The latter is preferred because the buffer may be "clobbered" during the interim. Knowing a specific record number, determined by variable N, the procedure would look like this:

```
1ØØØ OPEN "R", 1, "DATA"
1ØØ2 FIELD #1, 2 AS A$, 4 AS B$, 8 AS C$
1ØØ4 GET #1, N
1ØØ6 A%(N)=CVI(A$): B!(N)=CVS(B$): C#(N)=CVD(C$)
1Ø1Ø CLOSE
```

For a total retrieval of all three arrays, say in another program, the corresponding routine would be:

```
1ØØØ OPEN "R", 1, "DATA"
1ØØ2 FIELD #1, 2 AS A$, 4 AS B$, 8 AS C$
1ØØ4 FOR X=1 TO 1ØØ
1ØØ6 GET #1
1ØØ8 A%(N)=CVI(A$): B!(N)=CVS(B$): C#(N)=CVD(C$)
1Ø1Ø NEXT: CLOSE
```

In these examples, a total of 14 bytes per record actually are fielded and used for data storage. With a typical record length of 128 bytes, 114 of those bytes are wasted, making for very inefficient data storage.

BASIC-80 does allow you to correct the problem by specifying the overall record length in the OPEN statement; Microsoft Revision 4.51 and some other BASICs do not have any such provision. To make maximum use of the disk space under BASIC-80, line 1000 of each routine would have to be rewritten to define the record size, thus:

```
1000 OPEN "R", 1 "DATA", 14
```

Under versions other than BASIC-80, the record length is fixed, and even moderately efficient disk use could be achieved only by using several sets of fields for each record—which often involves some complex contortions in setting up the FIELD statement. That in turn would complicate the use of the file to retrieve a specific set of data because it would be necessary to locate the record number and then the position of the needed data set within that record.

Now consider the case where it's necessary to store string data, specifically a list of 200 words contained in array S$(.) and ranging in length from a minimum of 3 to a maximum of 15 letters. Also assume that the BASIC fixes the length of a random-file record at 128 bytes or characters. The length of any field must accommodate the longest possible word in the array, so every field must be at least 15 bytes. One possible routine would be:

```
1000 OPEN "R", 1, "DATA"
1002 FIELD #1, 15 AS P$(1), 15 AS P$(2), 15 AS P$(3), 15 AS P$(4),
     15 AS P$(5), 15 AS P$(6), 15 AS P$(7), 15 AS P$(8)
1004 FOR X=8 TO 200 STEP 8
1006 FOR Y=1 TO 8
1008 LSET P$(Y)=S$(X-8+Y)
1010 NEXT
1012 PUT #1
1014 NEXT: CLOSE
```

There are two problems here. First, only 120 of the 128 available bytes per record are fielded and used. For the 25 records required for the entire 200-word array, that wastes 200 bytes of disk space. The second and much more serious problem is that most of words stored are going to be considerably shorter than 15 letters or bytes. That means that a 3-letter word in a 15-byte field would waste 12 bytes of disk space.

In my own data-base structure, I maintain a statistical average length of six letters per word, so the average waste would be nine bytes per word. That factor alone would provide an average waste factor of 1,800 bytes per 200-word disk file. Adding the 200 bytes unused at the ends of the records means a waste of 2,000 bytes. Since the 200 words actually use only 1,200 bytes, the waste exceeds the used space and means that some 62 percent of the total disk area is "down the drain." With BASIC-80 and its provisions for altering record lengths, I can eliminate some of the waste and simplify the routine by writing it thus:

```
1000 OPEN "R", 1, "DATA", 15
1002 FIELD #1, 15 AS P$
1006 FOR X=1 TO 200
1008 LSET P$=S$(X)
1010 NEXT
1012 PUT #1
1014 NEXT: CLOSE
```

This eliminates the 200 wasted bytes on the tail ends of the records, but it does nothing to relieve me of the 1,800-byte overhead associated with short words. In fact, I've never found a satisfactory method of storing these types of data lists so that I don't have that overhead. Of course, limiting the maximum word length to something less than 15 letters would lower the numbers, but the overhead always exists. Essentially, the more words I store off, the more disk space I waste.

To further complicate matters, putting a word of less than maximum length into the random-file buffer pads the unoccupied letter positions with spaces. With an LSET statement putting a three-letter word in a 15-byte field, there are 12 trailing spaces added; an RSET statement would merely change it to 12 leading spaces. During the storage process, this isn't a problem beyond wasting space; it does, however, affect a program when the list is retrieved for later processing. At that time, the words are returned complete with the padding spaces, and applying a LEN() function to any word in the list would indicate a length of 15 characters, regardless of the number of actual letters.

It happens that my own applications depend upon an accurate determination of the length of each word to govern other operations, so it's impossible to allow a variable such as S$(12) to contain the word "TASK" plus 11 spaces and register as being 15 letters long. It also wastes that same average 1,800 bytes of string space in RAM for a 200-word list. Therefore, I have to use a time-consuming process of "stripping" each word before using it in other program steps. The whole process might look like this:

```
1000 OPEN "R", 1, "DATA"
1002 FIELD #1, 15 AS P$(1), 15 AS P$(2), 15 AS P$(3), 15 AS P$(4), 15 AS P$(5),
     15 AS P$(6), 15 AS P$(7), 15 AS P$(8)
1004 FOR X=8 TO 200 STEP 8: GET #1
1006 FOR Y=1 TO 8: S$(X-8+Y)=P$(Y): NEXT
1008 NEXT: CLOSE
1010 FOR X=1 TO 200: L=15: FOR Y=15 TO 1 STEP -1
```

```
1012 IF MID$(S$(X),Y,1)< >"^" THEN L=Y: Y=1
1014 NEXT: S$(X)=LEFT$(S(X),L):NEXT
```

Lines 1000 through 1008 get the words from the disk and put them into the string array, complete with the trailing spaces. Lines 1010 through 1014 then locate the rightmost nonspace character, set the length L to that position, and alter the array element to the leftmost characters up to and including that length. There are any number of alternative methods for stripping the trailing spaces, but all involve a character-by-character search of the string, all take time (as long as five to seven minutes for some of my lists), and all effectively negate any speed advantage random-access files might otherwise have. The only remaining point in favor of random access for word lists is the capability of retrieving or changing individual records. Yet my own applications turned out to need beginning-to-end reading anyway, so even that advantage was lost.

Sequential-Access Disk Files

As I've indicated, sequential-access files are handled so that data are written or read in order from beginning to end. Furthermore, an open file must be designated as either "output" or "input" for writing and reading operations respectively. Unless true random access is needed, as for alternate reading and writing to the same file, proper use of the sequential method can save both time and disk space, especially for string data.

Going back to the same example of a 200-word string array to be stored as a disk file, the routine for sequential handling is much simpler than that for random handling. For one thing, there is no need to field a buffer. For another, short strings are not padded with spaces, so disk space is more completely filled with letters. Here is the routine I normally use:

```
1000 OPEN "O", 1, "DATA"
1002 FOR X=1 TO 200
1004 PRINT #1, S$(X);",";
1006 NEXT: CLOSE
```

Notice line 1004, which is contained in the loop controlled by variable X. For each of the 200 words stored, it's necessary to "delimit" each word with a comma so the words can be separated upon being read back later. The sequence of semicolon, comma in quotes, and semicolon tells BASIC to write the word, put a comma in the next available byte, and hold that position while waiting for the next word. It does cause a final comma to be written in the file as though there would be another word to follow, but that extra comma never has done me any harm. If you happen to object to that final comma, the routine is easily modified:

```
1000 OPEN "O", 1, "DATA"
1002 FOR X=1 TO 199
1004 PRINT #1, S$(X);",";
1006 NEXT: PRINT S$(200): CLOSE
```

If you were to examine the disk contents directly, you would find a "continuous" string of characters with no intervening spaces from the beginning of the file to the end. The space "wasted" for the 200 commas would be offset by not wasting 200 spaces at the end of each 128-byte random-file record. Furthermore, the average 1,800-byte loss suffered by padding words with spaces in each random file is eliminated entirely.

Getting the data arrays back into memory from a sequential file is comparatively easy, requiring only a simple routine such as the following:

```
1000 OPEN "I", 1, "DATA"
1002 FOR X=1 TO 200: INPUT #1, S$(X): NEXT: CLOSE
```

There are no buffers to be fielded and no spaces to be stripped off. The delimiting commas are not included in the returned strings, and the S$(.) array now holds exactly the same words as when it was written to the file. No muss! No fuss! No bother!

For this particular type of application, I've found three advantages to sequential storage. First, the sequential file actually reads faster than a random file. Second, the delay of several minutes to strip down the retrieved data is eliminated entirely.

Third, I am able to compress my disk storage by nearly two-thirds. When I used random files, I could fit only 63 or fewer files of up to 220 words each per side of a single-density eight-inch diskette. With sequential access, I can fit about 180 files on the same magnetic surface. With several dozen diskettes previously devoted to storing word lists, the two-thirds reduction freed up a lot of useful storage space and saved a considerable amount of money because I didn't have to buy new diskettes. However, under the CP/M operating system, this led to a problem in that only 64 files are allowed per disk directory. But combining multiple files under one name (for "indexed" retrieval) or altering the directory parameters is a moderately painless way out of the problem.

I don't want you to get the wrong idea! Sequential files aren't always better than random files, nor are random files always better than sequential ones. The method you choose for any given program must be tempered by the application, the way you want to retrieve the data, and the way your own BASIC handles the files and any buffering they require.

Under Apple II DOS, the fielding of a random buffer is eliminated, but other complexities are introduced when random-access operation is selected. According to *The DOS Manual* published by Apple Computer, Inc.:

> Unlike the fields in sequential files, which may be of almost any length, the records in a random-access file are of specified *fixed length*. The first time you WRITE to any particular record in a [random-access] file, enough space is set aside on the diskette for a complete, standard-length record, whether or not the record is actually filled. So random-access files don't necessarily represent an efficient use of space.*

It's essential that you try the various file techniques for yourself. If you have a doubt as to which would be better or faster for a particular application, try it both ways. Don't rely on the information in the manual for all possible cases, because manuals are written in general terms and are designed to cover the broadest possible range of applications.

Closing Disk Files

You may have noticed the previous examples all closed the disk files with a simple CLOSE statement that did not specify the file number. The defined syntax for Microsoft BASICs is CLOSE [<f>], where f is the number under which the file was opened. The unnumbered form I've used closes *all* disk files, and it offers certain advantages.

First, closing all files provides an element of "safety." On many systems, files that are open for sequential output (writing) or random access could be "trashed" by an abnormal program termination such as a power interruption, a system reset, a drive malfunction, transient electrical surges, and so on. That could be costly in terms of lost data because the file then might not be usable when the system is reentered. By closing all files immediately after reading or writing data, the chances of having a vulnerable open file during an abnormal condition are minimized, and the integrity of the stored data is protected to a greater extent than if the files were left open throughout the run.

Second, file numbers can be reused as desired, provided an assigned number is freed up by being closed. Effective reuse of file numbers can contribute to a saving in required memory space. It's quite possible to have a single file number used for a sequential output file, a sequential

---

*Used with permission of Apple Computer, Inc.

input file, and a random-access file within the same program. It's even possible to flip back and forth between them as often as necessary. Most programming can be done without having more than one disk operation under way or more than one file open at one time. Therefore, most programs can be structured to use only one file number, reassigning that number over and over again in OPEN statements. If disk accesses are frequent, there may be a noticeable slowdown in the program's execution speed, but delays in programs with infrequent disk accesses aren't a major problem.

The advantage is that a typical BASIC allows the number of desired disk files to be specified when the interpreter is loaded. For example, BASIC-80 typically loads with three disk files allocated by default, but the load can be modified under user control to specify fewer or more files as necessary. Each file specified requires that a block of memory be set aside for manipulating it. As a result, several hundred bytes of memory can be freed for the program's other uses by reducing the file allocation. Maximum memory when disk accesses are required is freed when BASIC is loaded with only one file allocated and that file number is used over and over again. In any event, holding the allocation to the bare minimum required by the program and reassigning file numbers as often as possible can make the difference between a successful run and an "out of memory" error for a large program.

The third advantage of closing all files and reassigning numbers as needed is that there's no need to keep track of the open and closed files throughout the program. With many file numbers allocated and some being open while others are closed, the programmer is burdened by having to remember which files are open or closed at any time. A mistake in opening an already open file or one of the wrong type yields an error message during the run. Sometimes, that error occurs far into the run, necessitating a complete rerun of a long program.

Overall, it makes more sense to close all files instead of closing individual ones and worrying about things that could go wrong later. It also makes more sense to close them immediately upon completing the reading or writing operations instead of waiting until the end of the program run.

Choosing an Efficient Algorithm

All the individual techniques and tricks that help speed up a program's execution are useless if an inefficient algorithm or formula is selected to solve the computation problem at hand. Even while setting up the algorithm and before you start to code the first line of the program, you have to be aware of the BASIC features available on your system. Then you can pick and choose those that show the most promise of enhancing program performance.

Take the relatively simple task of determining whether a given integer is odd or even—that is, can the integer be divided evenly by two? Perhaps the single most often cited approach is to perform a test of two divisions, appearing as the program statement IF INT((X+.5)/2)= X/2.... For many BASICs, it's also one of the most inefficient ways because it involves a real-precision addition, two real-precision divisions, a call to the INT() function, and excess parentheses. To establish a baseline for comparison, consider the following routine in which this approach is used to set up two arrays; one array is used to store the even numbers from 1 to 5,000, and the other holds the odd numbers across the same range. As I will show, the execution time can be improved by subsequent and simple modifications to the algorithm.

```
10 DEFINT A-Z: DIM EV(2500), OD(2500)
. . .
100 EY=0: OY=0: FOR X=1 TO 5000
102 IF INT((X+.5)/2)=X/2 THEN EY=EY+1: EV (EY)=X ELSE OY=OY+1:
    OD(OY)=X
104 NEXT
```

[Microsoft Rev. 4.51: 135.9 seconds]
[Microsoft Rev. 5.2: 130.6 seconds]

A simpler and faster way of doing exactly the same thing is to change line 102 to eliminate the real-number addition:

```
10 DEFINT A-Z: DIM EV(2500), OD(2500)
. . .
100 EY=0: OY=0: FOR X=1 TO 5000
102 IF INT(X/2)=X/2 THEN EY=EY+1: EV(EY)=X ELSE OY=OY+1: OD(OY)=X
104 NEXT
```

[Microsoft Rev. 4.51: 124.5 seconds]
[Microsoft Rev. 5.2: 120.0 seconds]

Both routines accomplish exactly the same thing. The only difference between them is that the "mistake" of adding 0.5 as a real number delays completion; in these cases, the delay amounts to 8.8 to 9.1 percent of the faster execution times. Yet some BASICs allow an even faster approach using integer division. If you'll recall, I've already demonstrated that integer division, denoted by a backward slash under Microsoft BASICs, runs faster than regular division. Since these operations are limited to dealing only with integers, integer division is well suited to the application. The same routine then can be written thus:

```
10 DEFINT A-Z: DIM EV(2500), OD(2500)
```

```
100 EY=0: OY=0: FOR X=1 TO 5000
102 IF X/2=X\2 THEN EY=EY+1: EV(EY)=X ELSE OY=OY+1: OD(OY)=X
104 NEXT
```

[Microsoft Rev. 4.51: 103.2 seconds]
[Microsoft Rev. 5.2: 98.5 seconds]

When it's available, an integer division test IF X/N=X\N THEN... provides the fastest and easiest way to determine whether integer X is evenly divisible by integer N. By comparison, regular division with an INT function, in this application, is 21 to 22 percent slower than integer division. The preceding example works for all cases and for all values of N, as long as the variables are not real numbers (contain no decimals). Take the case where it's necessary to know how many and which integers between 1 and 5,000 are evenly divisible by six. Some simple modifications to the previous routines result in a new routine of the following form:

```
10 DEFINT A-Z: DIM D(2500): N=6
. . .
100 Y=0: FOR X=1 TO 5000
102 IF X/N=X\N THEN Y=Y+1: D(Y)=X
104 NEXT
```

[Microsoft Rev. 4.51: 76.2 seconds]
[Microsoft Rev. 5.2: 74.2 seconds]

Line 104 exits with Y set to 833, indicating the number of integers meeting the condition of line 102. The first 833 elements of array D(.) contain the actual integers evenly divisible by six, arranged in increasing numeric order.

As a practical application of this approach, I'm often faced with a situation in which I have a hundred or so strings to be printed out in four columns on a page. To avoid possible problems, I find it necessary to set up a range that is evenly divisible by four, zero or null any array elements between the last one used and the end of the range, and then print. The simplest way to accomplish this is to use the following routine:

```
1000 N1=N+1
1002 IF N/4< > N/4 THEN N=N+1: GOTO 1002
1004 FOR X=N1 TO N: S$(X)="": NEXT
1006 FOR X=4 TO N STEP 4
1008 LPRINT S$(X-3),S$(X-2),S$(X-1),S$(X)
1010 NEXT
```

Pay particular attention to line 1002. This tests the value of N to see if it's evenly divisible by four. If not, N is incremented by one and the test is repeated. This repeats until the test condition is satisfied, at which time N is evenly divisible and can be used as a control value for other operations. If you think about it, you'll see that the iteration can be performed only one to three times before the condition is satisfied. Line 1004 then nulls any strings between the original end of the array and the new end to prevent any strings from a previous pass being printed. Lines 1006 to 1010 then print the four columns.

You've probably noticed that the first three routines of this section set up EV(.) and OD(.) arrays for even and odd numbers respectively but were not the most efficient means of accomplishing that particular objective—not even the one demonstrating integer division. Those loops were set up strictly to perform repetitive operations. If you actually were to need arrays of even and odd numbers for some application, you could set them up much faster with this routine:

```
10 DEFINT A-Z: DIM EV(2500), OD(2500)
20 FOR X=2 TO 5000 STEP 2: Y=X\2
30 EV(Y)=X: OD(Y)=X-1
40 NEXT
```

[Microsoft Rev. 4.51: 34.1 seconds]
[Microsoft Rev. 5.2: 31.0 seconds]

To further amplify the importance of designing an efficient algorithm, consider a problem I encounter quite frequently. In this situation, I have to set up an array containing a random sequence of integers. At a later point in the program that array could be used to randomize the order of other operations by, for instance, printing the elements of such a string array, reordering the sequence in which elements of some other array are searched or tested, or performing any operation I don't want to do in strict ascending or descending numeric order.

I also impose certain restrictions on the random-number array. First, a definite range is specified for the random numbers, and the number of elements in the array exactly matches the number of integers in that range. Second, no array element may contain a value that is the same as the subscript of the element; that is, R(27) may not contain a value of 27. Third, every integer in the range must be used once and only once, so no two array elements may have the same value.

There are at least two ways I can approach the problem. The first involves setting up a loop that selects a random integer for each iteration. That integer is checked to make sure it is not the same as the iteration number. Then the selected integer is compared with each element already stored in the array to make sure it doesn't duplicate any other integer. Finally, having passed the tests, the counting variable for the array is incremented, and the selected integer is stored as an element with that subscript. The routine I use appears something like this:

```
1Ø DEFINT A-Z: A=63: DIM R(A)
. . .
1ØØØ B=Ø: F1=Ø: FOR X=1 TO A
1ØØ2 R=RND(1)*A+.5: IF R=A AND X=A THEN F1=1: GOTO 1Ø16
1ØØ4 IF R=X THEN 1ØØ2
1ØØ6 IF B<2 THEN 1Ø14
1ØØ8 F2=Ø: FOR Y=1 TO B
1Ø1Ø IF R=R(Y) THEN F2=1: Y=B
1Ø12 NEXT: IF F2 THEN 1ØØ2
1Ø14 B=B+1: R(B)=R
1Ø16 NEXT: IF F1 THEN 1ØØØ
```

[Microsoft Rev. 5.2: 85.1 seconds]

In this case, the range of random integers, specified by variable A, is from 1 to 63. The IF...THEN... test in line 1002 is necessary to prevent being caught in an "infinite loop" when the only unused integer remaining for the last iteration is the same as the number of the iteration; in this case it would be R equal to 63 when X equals 63.

The question, of course, is whether or not there's a faster way to do the same thing. It turns out there is a better way! Strangely enough, the faster method involves using string equivalents for checking whether or not an integer has been used before. A single INSTR() function then can check a single string instead of having to perform an element-by-element search and comparison pass through the R(.) array. The routine I prefer to use takes the following form:

```
1Ø DEFINT A-Z: A=63: DIM R(A)
. . .
1ØØØ S$=" ": F1=Ø: FOR X=1 TO A
1ØØ2 R=RND(1)*A+.5: IF R=A AND X=A THEN F1=1: GOTO 1ØØ8
1ØØ4 IF INSTR(S$,STR$(R)+" ") OR R=X THEN 1ØØ2
1ØØ6 R(X)=R: S$=S$+STR$(R)+" "
1ØØ8 NEXT: IF F1 THEN 1ØØØ
```

[Microsoft Rev. 5.2: 17.9 seconds]

The routine is physically much shorter; it executes in 67.2 seconds less time for a savings of 79 percent. Since this test and the preceding one with the array check are conducted under BASIC-80 without reseeding the random-number generator, both routines returned exactly the same contents for the R(.) array.

There are a couple of points of interest here that aren't immediately apparent. First, the single spaces used as quoted strings in lines 1000, 1004, and 1006 are necessary to prevent the routine from considering one number to have been duplicated just because its digits are contained in another number or the test string. Without the spaces, the integer 4 could be rejected when any number such as 48 already has been used; with the spaces that cannot happen. Second, the IF . . . THEN . . . test in line 1002 is still necessary to prevent being trapped in an infinite loop should R, X, and A all have the same value.

Because most BASICs limit the maximum length of a single string to 255 characters, this method works only as long as fewer than 65 random integers are involved and are included in the range from 1 to 64. When more numbers are needed, several parallel test strings must be set up, with one for values from 1 to 64, the next for 65 and up, and so on. Even with that, the routine always seems to maintain a significant speed advantage over constantly searching through the R(.) array.

Reiterating my earlier stand on programming techniques, I can't say that one approach is right and another is wrong. Every routine in this section accomplishes its intended purpose, so it is "correct" in the context of doing the job. The only differences are in the efficiency with which the tasks are accomplished, so there is a temptation to call an inefficient or less than efficient method "wrong." But many of the techniques are judgment calls on the programmer's part, and every programmer has individual preferences and styles. The thing to remember is that you have to develop your own style, and it's certainly not going to hurt you to develop one that provides maximum utilization of your computer's capabilities.

"Punch Up" BASIC

With this book, I've provided you with an introduction to a facet of programming you may not have recognized before. I've tried to demonstrate the importance of undertaking critical examinations of everything from individual program statements and functions to the overall design of an algorithm. But what I've given you is nothing more than a bare introduction to the subject, touching lightly and incompletely on many different facets. From this point, it's up to you to define and refine your own techniques and approaches.

Programming any computer, whether in BASIC or in some other language, is indeed a combination of art and science. To a large degree, the science is developing the method of solution for a problem. The art is applying the capabilities of the computer and its language to that solution. As you progress from simple to complex programs, your knowledge of the techniques available and the pros and cons of various approaches will grow. I believe I've given you a push in the right direction, guiding you into the considerations of speed and memory consumption that will either help or hinder your programming efforts.

I've also tried to demonstrate that BASIC isn't as bad a language as some people claim. It's not perfect, but you can push it, squeeze it, and punch it up to a point where it will do a respectable job—but only with a thorough analysis of the problem and solution and with a lot of thought about the language itself. BASIC won't ever match the efficiency and overall speed of some other languages (unless it is compiled), but it can be used effectively. Most of the gripes about how slow BASIC is are valid within a specified context, but all too often the same people who grumble and growl about the language are the ones who misuse or misunderstand it. If you don't set up your algorithms correctly or if you fail to use the most efficient statements and functions, it will be slow and cumbersome.

You can't just "whip off" a quick program and expect it to be perfect or even suitable. Instead, you have to write your program and then take it apart piece by piece, replacing each routine with a better routine if you can find one, replacing inefficient statements and functions with faster ones when they'll do the job, and removing all the "dead wood" such as spaces and remark statements. Yet no matter how far you go or how much time you spend modifying and improving, no program ever will be "perfect"; there's always room for improvement, always room for one more change, always a place to gain a few more seconds or fractions of a second.

ASCII Codes and Equivalents

Figure A-1 is the "standard" ASCII chart found in many computer and peripheral-device instruction manuals. It is reproduced here for your convenience. Figure A-2 is a similar chart showing the decimal values for the ASCII characters.

Table A-1 lists the ASCII characters and their decimal (base-10) and hexadecimal (base-16) equivalents. Note that the superscript "c" denotes

$b_4 b_3 b_2 b_1$	b_7 → b_6 → b_5 →	0 0 0	0 0 1	0 1 0	0 1 1	1 0 0	1 0 1	1 1 0	1 1 1
↓ ↓ ↓ ↓	COLUMN ▶ ROW ▼	0	1	2	3	4	5	6	7
0 0 0 0	0	NUL	DLE	SP	0	a	P	\`	p
0 0 0 1	1	SOH	DC1	!	1	A	Q	a	q
0 0 1 0	2	STX	DC2	"	2	B	R	b	r
0 0 1 1	3	ETX	DC3	#	3	C	S	c	s
0 1 0 0	4	EOT	DC4	$	4	D	T	d	t
0 1 0 1	5	ENQ	NAK	%	5	E	U	e	u
0 1 1 0	6	ACK	SYN	&	6	F	V	f	v
0 1 1 1	7	BEL	ETB	'	7	G	W	g	w
1 0 0 0	8	BS	CAN	(	8	H	X	h	x
1 0 0 1	9	HT	EM	)	9	I	Y	i	y
1 0 1 0	10	LF	SUB	*	:	J	Z	j	z
1 0 1 1	11	VT	ESC	+	;	K	[	k	{
1 1 0 0	12	FF	FS	,	<	L	\	l	¦
1 1 0 1	13	CR	GS	—	=	M	]	m	}
1 1 1 0	14	SO	RS	.	>	N	^	n	~
1 1 1 1	15	SI	US	/	?	O	—	o	DEL

NONPRINTING CHARACTERS (columns 0 and 1)

Fig. A-1. **"Standard" ASCII Character Conversion Chart.**

TENS \ UNITS	0	1	2	3	4	5	6	7	8	9
0	NUL	SOH	STX	ETX	EOT	ENQ	ACK	BEL	BS	HT
10	LF	VT	FF	CR	SO	SI	DLE	DC1	DC2	DC3
20	DC4	NAK	SYN	ETB	CAN	EM	SUB	ESC	FS	GS
30	RS	US	SP	!	"	#	$	%	&	'
40	(	)	*	+	,	-	.	/	0	1
50	2	3	4	5	6	7	8	9	:	;
60	<	=	>	?	@	A	B	C	D	E
70	F	G	H	I	J	K	L	M	N	O
80	P	Q	R	S	T	U	V	W	X	Y
90	Z	[	\	]	^	_	`	a	b	c
100	d	e	f	g	h	i	j	k	l	m
110	n	o	p	q	r	s	t	u	v	w
120	x	y	z	{	|	}	~			

Fig. A-2. **Decimal Values for ASCII Characters.**

Table A-1

ASCII Codes and Equivalents

Dec	Hex	ASCII	Dec	Hex	ASCII
Ø	ØØ	NUL (Ø^c)	22	16	SYN (V^c)
1	Ø1	SOH (A^c)	23	17	ETB (W^c)
2	Ø2	STX (B^c)	24	18	CAN (X^c)
3	Ø3	ETX (C^c)	25	19	EM (Y^c)
4	Ø4	EOT (D^c)	26	1A	SUB (Z^c)
5	Ø5	ENQ (E^c)	27	1B	ESC (escape)
6	Ø6	ACK (F^c)	28	1C	FS (L^{cs})
7	Ø7	BEL (G^c)	29	1D	GS (M^{cs})
8	Ø8	BS (backspace or H^c)	3Ø	1E	RS (N^{cs})
9	Ø9	HT (tab or I^c)	31	1F	US (O^{cs})
1Ø	ØA	LF (line feed or J^c)	32	2Ø	SP (space)
11	ØB	VT(K^c)	33	21	! (exclamation point)
12	ØC	FF (L^c)	34	22	" (double quote)
13	ØD	CR (return or M^c)	35	23	# (pound symbol)
14	ØE	SO (N^c)	36	24	$ (dollar sign)
15	ØF	SI (O^c)	37	25	% (percent sign)
16	1Ø	DLE (P^c)	38	26	& (ampersand)
17	11	DC1 [X-ON] (Q^c)	39	27	' (single quote)
18	12	DC2 [TAPE] (R^c)	4Ø	28	((open parenthesis)
19	13	DC3 [X-OFF] (S^c)	41	29	) (close parenthesis)
2Ø	14	DC4 (T^c)	42	2A	* (asterisk)
21	15	NAK (U^c)	43	2B	+ (plus sign)

Table A-1

ASCII Codes and Equivalents (continued)

Dec	Hex	ASCII	Dec	Hex	ASCII
44	2C	, (comma)	86	56	V (uppercase)
45	2D	- (hyphen)	87	57	W (uppercase)
46	2E	. (period)	88	58	X (uppercase)
47	2F	/ (forward slash)	89	59	Y (uppercase)
48	3Ø	Ø (numeric zero)	9Ø	5A	Z (uppercase)
49	31	1 (numeric one)	91	5B	[(open bracket)
5Ø	32	2 (numeric two)	92	5C	\ (backslash)
51	33	3 (numeric three)	93	5D	] (close bracket)
52	34	4 (numeric four)	94	5E	^ (caret)
53	35	5 (numeric five)	95	5F	_ (underline)
54	36	6 (numeric six)	96	6Ø	’ (accent mark)
55	37	7 (numeric seven)	97	61	a (lowercase)
56	38	8 (numeric eight)	98	62	b (lowercase)
57	39	9 (numeric nine)	99	63	c (lowercase)
58	3A	: (colon)	1ØØ	64	d (lowercase)
59	3B	; (semicolon)	1Ø1	65	e (lowercase)
6Ø	3C	< (less-than sign)	1Ø2	66	f (lowercase)
61	3D	= (equals sign)	1Ø3	67	g (lowercase)
62	3E	> (greater-than sign)	1Ø4	68	h (lowercase)
63	3F	? (question mark)	1Ø5	69	i (lowercase)
64	4Ø	@ ("at" symbol)	1Ø6	6A	j (lowercase)
65	41	A (uppercase)	1Ø7	6B	k (lowercase)
66	42	B (uppercase)	1Ø8	6C	l (lowercase)
67	43	C (uppercase)	1Ø9	6D	m (lowercase)
68	44	D (uppercase)	11Ø	6E	n (lowercase)
69	45	E (uppercase)	111	6F	o (lowercase)
7Ø	46	F (uppercase)	112	7Ø	p (lowercase)
71	47	G (uppercase)	113	71	q (lowercase)
72	48	H (uppercase)	114	72	r (lowercase)
73	49	I (uppercase)	115	73	s (lowercase)
74	4A	J (uppercase)	116	74	t (lowercase)
75	4B	K (uppercase)	117	75	u (lowercase)
76	4C	L (uppercase)	118	76	v (lowercase)
77	4D	M (uppercase)	119	77	w (lowercase)
78	4E	N (uppercase)	12Ø	78	x (lowercase)
79	4F	O (uppercase)	121	79	y (lowercase)
8Ø	5Ø	P (uppercase)	122	7A	z (lowercase)
81	51	Q (uppercase)	123	7B	{ (open brace)
82	52	R (uppercase)	124	7C	| (vertical bar)
83	53	S (uppercase)	125	7D	} (close brace)
84	54	T (uppercase)	126	7E	~ (tilde)
85	55	U (uppercase)	127	7F	DEL (delete or rubout)

a two-key command in which the Control key is pressed and held while the designated key is pressed. Similarly, the superscript "cs" denotes a three-key command in which both the Control and Shift keys are pressed and held while the designated key is pressed. Key conventions are those for the Hazeltine 1500 terminal and may differ for other keyboards, particularly for the three-key commands and the NUL character; consult your terminal documentation.

If you've only recently begun to use a computer system, you may not be aware that the abbreviations for the first 33 ASCII character codes (decimal values from 0 through 32) have specific meanings. Since some literature uses the full "name" of the code rather than just the abbreviation, these names are provided in Table A-2 for your information.

Table A-2

Full Names of Selected ASCII Characters

Abbr.	Full Name	Abbr.	Full Name
NUL	Null (or Null Character)	DLE	Data Link Escape
SOH	Start of Heading	DC1	Device Control 1
STX	Start of Text	DC2	Device Control 2
ETX	End of Text	DC3	Device Control 3
EOT	End of Transmission	DC4	Device Control 4
ENQ	Enquiry	NAK	Negative Acknowledge
ACK	Acknowledge	SYN	Synchronous Idle
BEL	Bell (or Sound Bell)	ETB	End of Transmission Block
BS	Backspace	CAN	Cancel (or Cancel Command)
HT	Horizontal Tab	EM	End of Medium
LF	Line Feed	SUB	Substitute
VT	Vertical Tab	ESC	Escape
FF	Form Feed	FS	File Separator
CR	Carriage Return	GS	Group Separator
SO	Shift Out	RS	Record Separator
SI	Shift In	US	Unit Separator
		SP	Space

Appendix B

Numerical Systems and Conversions

Numerical Systems—Methods of Counting

As you read through the instruction manuals and other literature pertaining to your computer system, you will encounter such terms as "decimal," "binary," "octal," "hexadecimal," "bit," "byte," and other strange words used in association with numerical values. Few of the documents devote much, if any, space to defining those terms, leaving you in the dark as to exactly what may be meant in a particular instance or how to use the different numbering systems indicated.

This appendix is devoted to those subjects, showing the relationships among various numerical systems and their applications to computers. Conversion procedures and binary manipulations are provided. Admittedly, numeric systems are of greatest concern in low-level programming such as assembly or machine language; their application to high-level languages such as BASIC is less immediate. In fact, many BASICs can be used quite well with no knowledge of different numbering systems, and the need for this information may never become apparent.

On the other hand, languages such as Applesoft and Apple Integer BASIC make extensive use of things like hexadecimal numbers, primarily to address specific memory locations for built-in machine-language routines and subroutines, within the system monitor, for manipulating graphics, and so on. In other BASICs, calls to assembly-language subroutines written and loaded by the user also must be in hexadecimal form. Often the address or data entered through a BASIC program for such applications or the results returned involve a hexadecimal number. Of course, it can be a tedious nuisance to convert numbers back and forth, so it should help you to know a little more about such numbers and a few shortcuts for calculating decimal equivalents. Oddly, some BASICs that function very well without using "strange" numbering systems are provided with conversion functions, while others such as Applesoft that rely heavily on those alternate forms do not have built-in conversions.

Although you may or may not need the information presented in this appendix, you would be well advised to acquire a working familiarity with it. Then, should you encounter a situation in which you need to do a conversion or calculate an equivalent value in another system, you won't be at a total loss and won't have to scramble around looking for the procedural guides. Of course, this appendix presents only a sketchy outline and is not intended to be a comprehensive study of the subject. Should you find yourself needing more details, you can find them in many of the books specifically devoted to assembly-language programming of individual microprocessors.

The Decimal System

To begin any discussion of numerical systems, it's necessary to examine our normal method of counting. If you'll think back to your early education in basic arithmetic, you'll probably recall that we use a counting system based on the number ten and that we refer to this as the "decimal" system. Since primitive man first learned to count with his set of ten fingers, the normal numerical system developed around a "base" of ten elements. Had human beings been equipped with six fingers on each hand, we would probably count on the basis of twelve elements at a time, and the duodecimal system would be common in our everyday lives.

As numbers began to be written, and methods of arithmetic and mathematics were developed, ten symbols were developed to represent the basic elements of the counting system—actually nine elements plus a null or zero character. Hence, we have the "digits" 0 through 9 that we all use on a daily basis.

However, the existence of only nine separate and distinct digits or numbers for counting individual items left no single number that could be used to designate the tenth finger or the tenth element of any set of items. Thus we arrive at the two-digit numbers ranging from 10 to 99. In looking at the number 10, the digit 1 has been shifted one place to the left, while the rightmost position is filled with a null or zero character. The number 10 is correctly interpreted as meaning one group of ten plus no other single item. If the zero is replaced with a one, we have the number 11, which is interpreted to be one group of ten plus one more item. In a similar fashion, we can build other two-digit numbers such as 49, which indicates four groups of ten plus nine more items.

Of course, development of a counting system could have proceeded along the line of having a new and unique symbol for each new number needed. Imagine how complex that would make mathematics. Instead, grouping the nine basic symbols and the null with an implied multiplication provides a convenient shortcut and enables different arithmetic operations to be performed according to specific and reliable rules.

The approach for two-digit numbers works very well until we again run out of available symbols, something that happens once we've reached the number 99 or nine groups of ten plus nine more items. However, the next number in the sequence is equal to ten groups of ten plus no additional items, so we can take the number 10 that was invented earlier, shift it one place to the left, and fill the empty space with a zero. Behold! We now have the number 100! This may be interpreted as meaning ten groups of ten plus no single items, or as one group of a hundred, plus no groups of ten, plus no single items. Again, we find that we can apply the construction procedures used with two-digit numbers to create three-digit numbers such as 108 or 167. Following the pattern already established, 108 is equal to one group of a hundred, plus no groups of 10, plus eight individual items. Similarly, 167 is one group of a hundred, six groups of ten, and seven more items.

Whenever the available combinations of symbols are exhausted at numbers such as 999, 9,999, and so on, the next number in sequence is easily constructed by putting a digit 1 in the next position to the left and filling the rightmost spaces with zeros. Each time, a new grouping of numbers is created that is exactly ten times larger than the preceding grouping. For example, the three-digit 100 is exactly ten times larger than the two-digit 10, the four-digit 1000 is ten times larger than the three-digit 100, and so on.

Similar considerations may be applied to decimal fractions, except that decreasing values shift the digit 1 to the right and indicate a division by ten instead of a multiplication. Using a decimal point as a position indicator to separate numbers larger than one from those smaller than one, any empty spaces to the left of the digit are filled with zeros until the decimal point is reached. For example, the number 1.012 would be interpreted as one whole item plus no tenths of an item, plus one hundredth of an item, plus two thousandths of an item. Note that each digit location to the right of the decimal point becomes ten times smaller (or one tenth as large) as the next position to the left. This maintains the previously established pattern that each position moved toward the left increases the value, while each position moved toward the right decreases the value, in each case by a factor of ten.

Another way of saying the same thing is that a decimal number is a sum of positional terms, wherein each term represents the product of some *power* or *exponent* of ten. Moving from right to left across a number, the exponent or power of ten increases by one for each digit position. Moving from left to right, the exponent decreases by one for each position. A number such as 43,798 is the sum of the series of multiplication products: $(4\times10^4) + (3\times10^3) + (7\times10^2) + (9\times10^1) + (8\times10^0)$. Similarly, a decimal fraction such as 1.234 is the sum of the multiplication products: $(1\times10^0) + (2\times10^{-1}) + (3\times10^{-2}) + (4\times10^{-3})$. Note that, by mathematical definition, any number raised to the zero power is equal to one and any number raised to the power one is equal to itself. Furthermore, negative exponents are equal to the reciprocal of the power of the base number so that 10^{-1} equals 1/10 or 0.1, 10^{-2} equals 1/100 or 0.01, and so on. A more graphic representation of the same numbers shows:

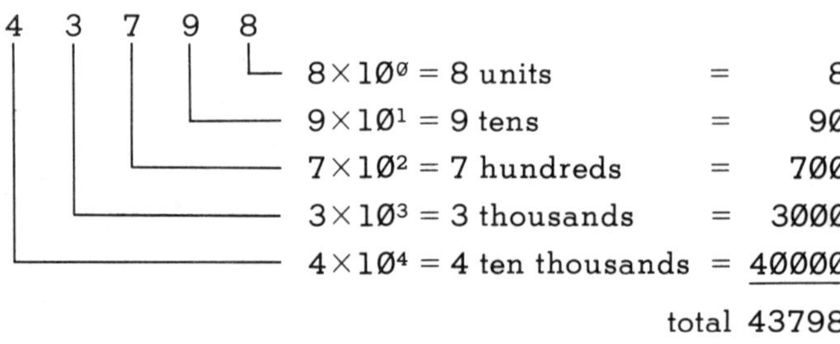

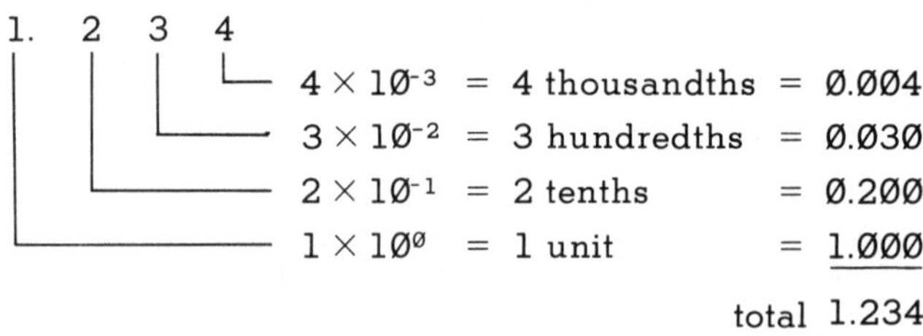

At this point, you're probably asking yourself, "So what?" After all, you don't normally think of everyday numbers in groupings like these, and you really don't have any reason to do so in daily usage. However, the ability to reason your way through such a procedure becomes critically important when you start to look at other possible numbering systems and the means by which to convert values from one system to another. As you'll see later in this chapter, the so-called binary system is limited to the two symbols 0 and 1, so the available representations of values with single symbols is exhausted by the time you count to the second item of a group. Similarly, "octal" numbering allows only eight symbols, and "hexadecimal" numbering allows 16 symbols. Therefore, each numerical system has specifically defined groupings of values, and an understanding of the methods used in making those groupings is vitally important to the understanding of each individual system.

The Binary System

All digital computer systems utilize the so-called binary system for their internal operations. Although few users see the binary numbers except under unusual circumstances or when they are called for by special applications, an understanding of the basic considerations that affect binary numbering is essential to an overall understanding of the computer. In addition, the binary system forms a basis on which to build the octal, hexadecimal, or other numbering system often used by a computer programmer for developing assembly-language programs and other applications not written in a high-level programming language such as BASIC.

Apple II users involved with graphics often have to deal with binary numbers because those numbers control the color of screen dots, whether a dot is on or off, and so on. Connecting peripherals such as printers often requires knowing whether parts of binary numbers are "set" or "cleared." There is a long list of such uses, so it certainly won't do you any harm to know something about the numbering system.

While the decimal system is based on a root number of ten, the binary system is based on a root of two. This is because electronic signals and relays have only two possible states—"on" (closed relay) and "off" (open relay). Therefore, only two values can be represented electronically—a zero for off or an open relay and a one for on or a closed relay. The numerical values 0 and 1 used to represent these two states are known as *bits* or *b*inary dig*its*.

Where the ten symbols of the digital system allowed up to nine separate items to be represented by one-digit numbers, the two bits of the binary system allow only a zero or a one to be represented by a single-bit number. By the second item, it's already necessary to start using a two-bit number, so two items are represented in binary as 10_2, three items are represented as 11_2, four items as 100_2, five items as 101_2, and so on. Note that the subscript 2 indicates the binary system; a decimal number could be written as 987_{10} but this is rarely done in practice except where there is a possibility of confusion between the numerical bases. Numbers written without a subscript or other explicit definition can be assumed to indicate a decimal value throughout this book and most other literature.

A decimal number already has been defined as a sum of positional terms, with each term representing the product of some power of ten. In the same manner, a binary number also is a sum of positional terms, but with each term representing the product of some power of two. Progressing from right to left across a binary number, the bit positions signify units (2^0), twos (2^1), fours (2^2), eights (2^3), sixteens (2^4), thirty-twos

(2^5), and so on. The sum of the individually calculated binary positions is identical to the decimal sum, so the decimal equivalent of a binary number may be determined by adding the values of the binary positions containing a one. As a graphic example, the following procedure may be used to determine the decimal value of the binary number 110011011:

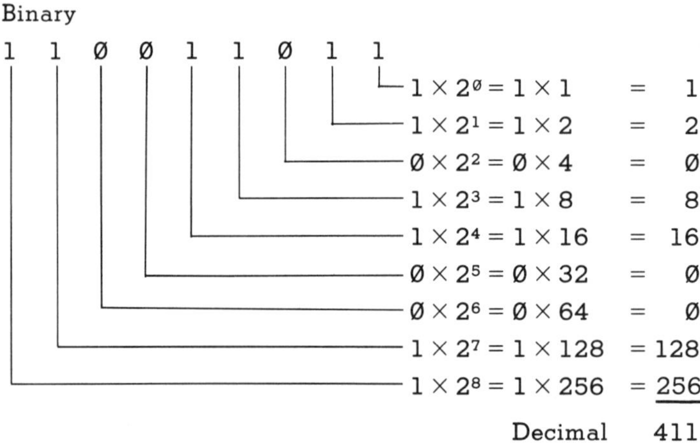

As you can see, the binary representation of a number can quickly become very cumbersome. For example, the decimal number 65,535 would be written in binary as 1111111111111111 (16 ones). Had humans evolved with single, digitless appendages, say tentacles, binary numbering probably would have evolved as a standard method of counting. As it happens, this system is completely foreign to our day-to-day existence and is very difficult to manipulate without a lot of practice.

Although binary numbering can be extremely difficult for the human mind to deal with, it nevertheless remains the only numbering system that a digital computer can manipulate directly. As a result, anything entered into a computer program eventually is converted to a binary representation, and this includes all numeric constants, addresses, instructions, and literal strings of letters. At the raw machine-language level, the entire universe exists only in binary codes.

To reach a compromise between this native machine language and something more easily handled by human minds, it's necessary to develop other intermediate numeric systems. Those systems in turn must provide a "shorthand" method for the human programmer yet allow quick and systematic conversion back to binary for the computer's use. Two of the possible solutions are the octal and hexadecimal systems described in the next two sections.

The Octal System

Since writing pure binary numbers is difficult, time-consuming, and prone to a great many human errors, modern digital computers provide the user with one or more alternate numerical systems that the machine can quickly convert into its binary codes. Such systems are developed by dividing the largest possible binary number the machine can use into groupings of bits known as *bytes* or *nybbles.* The number of bits available in a single byte or nybble of information determines the type of numbering system that can be used.

The octal system is one such numeric structure obtained when the bits are arranged in groups of three. Typically, the octal system is used with computers in which the maximum number of bits in a single binary number is evenly divisible by three, and it was particularly applicable to the 12-, 15-, and 18-bit minicomputers that were developed during the late 1960s and early 1970s. Many modern microcomputers that use 4-, 8-, or 16-bit binary numbers are better handled with other groupings, but they often retain some provision for the octal numbering system in order to provide a degree of system compatibility with other computers.

For the purpose of defining and illustrating the octal system, let's assume that we are dealing with an 18-bit computer. The largest binary number that can be represented in 18 bits is 111111111111111111 (18 ones), which is equivalent to a decimal value of 262,143. This binary number then can be divided evenly into six individual groups of three bits each and represented as 111,111,111,111,111,111 where each group could be considered either a byte or a nybble, depending upon the computer manufacturer's use or misuse of accepted terminology.

The most popular convention dictates that each three-bit grouping be termed a nybble. Some larger grouping of nybbles, say three 3-bit nybbles, then would constitute a byte. After all, a nibble of a sandwich is smaller than a bite. In that manner, six 3-bit nybbles or two 9-bit bytes would constitute an 18-bit *word.* For my purposes, I choose to refer to each 3-bit group as a nybble and reserve the term "byte" for a larger group of multiple nybbles.

Regardless of terminology selected, the maximum value of any one three-bit group or nybble is a binary 111 that evaluates to a decimal equivalent thus:

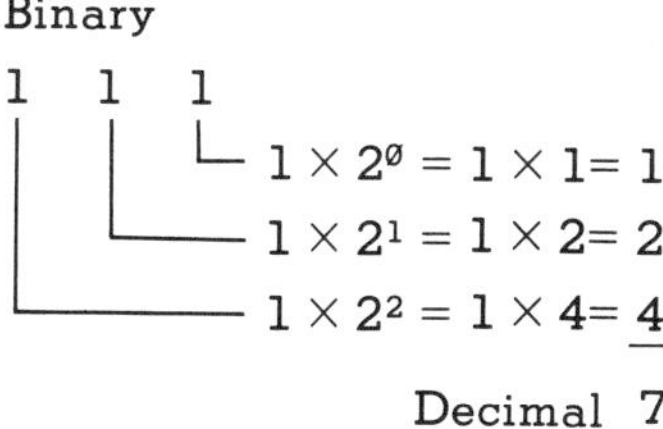

Therefore, a maximum of seven items may be represented by a single three-bit nybble, and any one nybble can be designated by a single numeric symbol or decimal equivalent from 0 to 7. This yields a system based on eight numbers, and it's called the octal system after the Latin *octo* for eight. It should be noted, however, that binary digits are referred to as bits, but octal digits are not called by any special name like "ocits"—they are called simply *octal digits.*

The obvious advantage in a numbering system such as this is that a long binary number can be represented as a much shorter octal number in which each octal digit directly represents a group of three binary digits. That's a two-thirds reduction in the number of characters that have to be handled. An 18-bit binary number now can be written as a six-digit octal number, making the task of writing such numbers considerably easier for the human mind and far less likely to suffer from errors of omitting, adding, or transposing individual digits. This becomes particularly evident with large numbers such as the previously cited binary value containing 18 ones—that same value can be written as 777777_8, where the subscript denotes the octal system. Incidentally, there are two different conventions in use for the subscript that denotes an octal value; one uses the numeric subscript 8 and the other uses the alphabetic subscript O or o. In either event, the meaning is the same.

Like the decimal and binary numbers already described, a given octal number denotes a sum of positional terms. In this case, however, each term represents the product of some power of eight. In reading across a binary number from right to left, the digit positions designate units (8^0), eights (8^1), sixty-fours (8^3), and so on. The decimal equivalent of an octal number can be calculated in a manner paralleling that used with binary numbers, determining the value of each position and adding those values to obtain a sum. To illustrate the procedure, the following example determines the decimal equivalent of 136542_8:

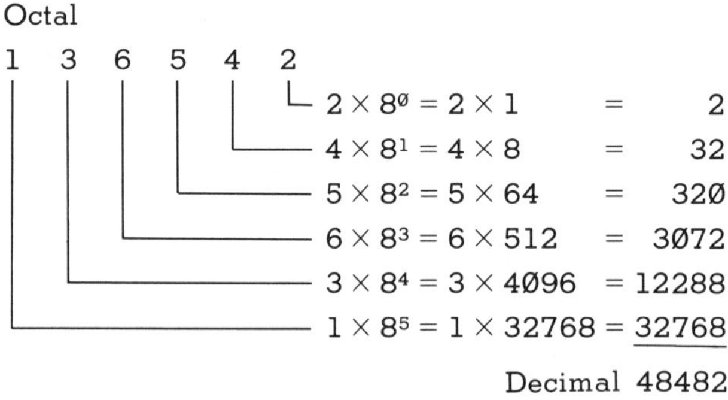

A similar procedure would be applicable to an octal fraction, so the evaluation of 2.6702_8 would proceed as follows:

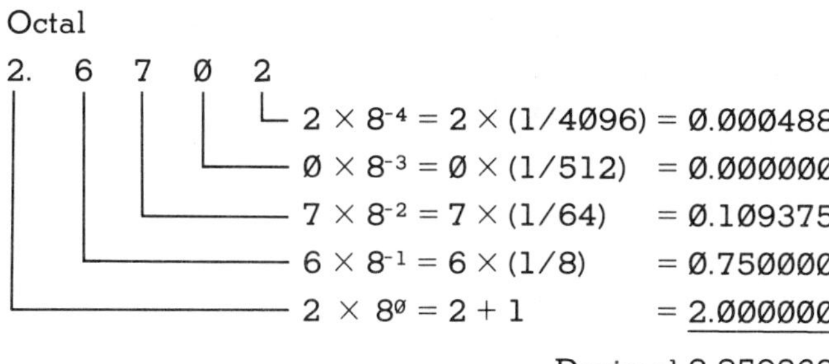

It's often useful to recognize the simple fact that an octal number never contains the numeric symbols 8 or 9. Any attempt to write an octal number containing either an 8 or a 9 is an error, and lists of octal numbers always should be checked for the presence of either of those two digits.

It's also important to point out that the actual maximum binary number that can be stored in a digital computer usually is one bit shorter than the total number of bits available might indicate. In an 18-bit computer, the actual maximum binary number would probably be limited to 17 bits in length rather than 18, and the leftmost bit position (known as the "high bit" or "most significant bit") would be reserved for a sign bit that would indicate whether the number is positive or negative. This would make the maximum integer value 131,071 rather than 262,143 as shown in the preceding example. However, the use of a sign bit does not affect the structure of a nybble other than to limit the value of the leftmost nybble to some value less than the maximum value that might otherwise be possible. To illustrate, the maximum octal value achievable from 18 bits has been shown to be 777777_8, but the maximum octal value from 17 bits would be 377777_8.

The Hexadecimal System

Another human-oriented shorthand alternative to the binary system is known as the hexadecimal system, more often called simply "hex." Where the octal system derived nybbles that consisted of three bits each, the hex system utilizes nybbles of four bits each. This approach most frequently is encountered in computers based on 8- or 16-bit binary numbers, but it also may be applied to 4-bit and 12-bit machines. Hex numbering is encountered frequently on personal computers since most are considered 8-bit machines and use 15 bits plus a sign bit (16 bits total) to represent the entire range of integer values they can handle, typically from −32,768 to +32,767. That 16-bit number or word then consists of four 4-bit nybbles or two 8-bit (2-nybble) bytes.

To illustrate, assume a computer utilizes 16 bits to hold a sign bit plus a 15-bit number. The largest integer this machine can represent in binary is 111111111111111 (15 ones), which can be grouped conveniently from right to left in fours as 111,1111,1111,1111. The maximum value of any one 4-bit group or nybble can be determined as:

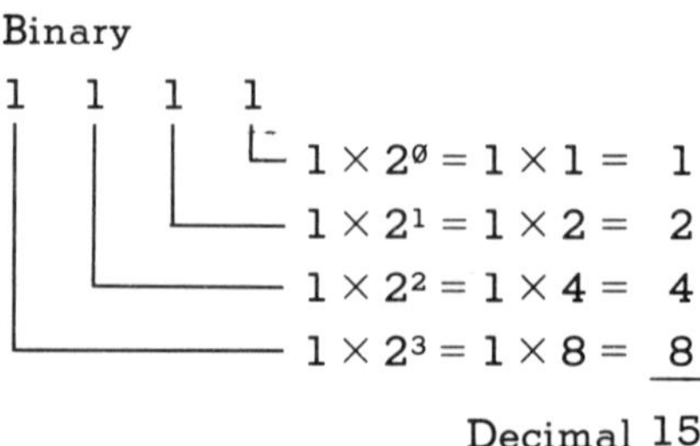

A maximum of 15 items can be represented with a single 4-bit nybble, and any possible nybble can be designated by a decimal equivalent ranging from 0 to 15. Obviously, this gives a numerical system based on 16 numbers—the system known as hexadecimal.

Now, however, there is a small problem. Our numerical symbology is limited to the characters we use as the numbers 0 through 9. It happened that both binary and octal systems could be accommodated with a smaller set of the same basic symbols since they did not require representing a value larger than decimal 9. With the hex system, we need 16 separate and distinct symbols, which is 6 more than we commonly recognize. Therefore, it becomes necessary to define some new symbols.

The definition of the new symbols is entirely arbitrary. Six characters such as #, $, %, &, *, and @ could easily have been selected. Alternatively, a whole new set of symbols could have been invented, but they probably wouldn't have been included on conventional typewriter keyboards. The most practical choice was to use some clearly logical progression with which everyone already was familiar. It happens that there is a set of symbols already arranged in a logical and meaningful order—the letters of the alphabet. So the standard convention has been to assign the first six letters of the alphabet (A through F) as the needed hex numbers extending beyond 9. Using this, the entire set of numbers in the hex system is defined as listed in Table B-1.

With an expanded set of symbols such as this, some very odd-looking numbers are possible, including strange combinations such as 10FB, CA25, BA, or FACB. Many first-time computer users panic when they initially encounter a number like this in their computer's output or in the instruction manuals. At first it's hard even to recognize such an item as a valid numerical value.

It's true that many computers do designate a hex number by either preceding it with an "H" or "&H" marker, following it with an "H", or using some other means of indicating that the value is in hexadecimal notation; however, a number that reads &HC85F can be even more shocking to the novice computer operator. In other machines such as

Table B-1

Hexadecimal Symbols and Decimal Equivalents

Hexadecimal Number	Decimal Value	Hexadecimal Number	Decimal Value
Ø	Ø	8	8
1	1	9	9
2	2	A	1Ø
3	3	B	11
4	4	C	12
5	5	D	13
6	6	E	14
7	7	F	15

the Apple II, extensive use is made of hex numbering in specifying memory addresses and other machine-specific items, but without any clear indication that the number is in hex notation. In such cases, only the instruction manual mentions the need for hex numbers, and the language itself expects any number encountered at that point to be hexadecimal.

There's really no need for concern. Hex numbers can be handled just as easily as octal numbers, and they are nothing more than a convenient shorthand for dealing with binary values. Hex numbers should, however, be identified as such whenever possible. The instruction manuals that come with a new computer or a new set of software should clearly indicate how to designate a hexadecimal or an octal number; a number written in text like this can be designated with a subscript such as $34A1_{16}$ or $34A1_H$. Either type of subscripting is correct, but the "H" subscript is commonly used simply because most computers use some variation of that letter to denote a hex value.

As with any other numbering system, the decimal value of a hex number can be determined by summing the values of the positional terms. However, each positional term now represents the product of some power of 16. From right to left, the positions designate the products of the hex digit times 16^0, 16^1, 16^2, 16^3, and so on. For example, the decimal value of $B5EF_H$ can be determined thus:

```
Hexadecimal
B  5  E  F
|  |  |  └─ 15 × 16^Ø = 15 × 1    =    15
|  |  └──── 14 × 16^1 = 14 × 16   =   224
|  └───────  5 × 16^2 =  5 × 256  =  128Ø
└────────── 11 × 16^3 = 11 × 4Ø96 = 45Ø56
                                   ------
                          Decimal   46575
```

Again, a similar procedure may be applied to hexadecimal fractions, so the evaluation of $1.2FA_H$ would proceed as follows:

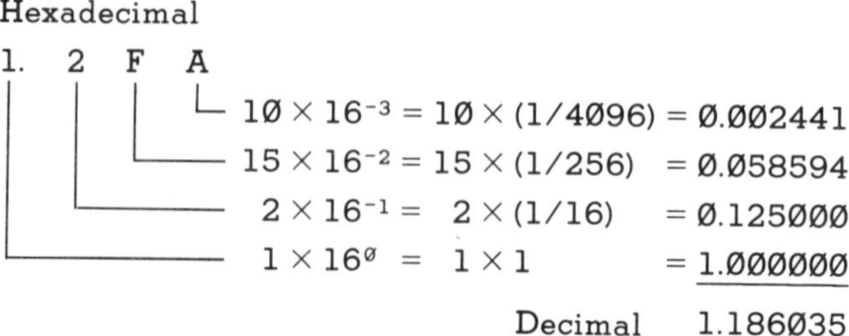

For many personal computers, the largest hex number without a sign bit that can be encountered is $FFFF_H$, which is equivalent to a decimal 65,535 or a binary number of sixteen ones. In many personal computers, two 8-bit bytes are combined to form 16-bit memory addresses and other values, hence $FFFF_H$ corresponds to the highest memory location that can be accessed directly with a single-number address. Therefore, this number defines the maximum number of bytes in such a computer's memory, resulting in what is called a 64-kilobyte or 64K system. The 64K designation is a misnomer; the computer actually has 65,535 bytes of memory. The 64K designation is a carry-over from the days when memory was provided on individual 4K circuit boards, each of which held 4,096 bytes. It was easy to denote the size of the system by simply multiplying the number of 4K boards by 4, so a 16-board system wound up being called 64K.

With one bit reserved for the sign designation, the maximum integer value that can be represented by 15 bits is $7FFF_H$ or a decimal 32,767. With the sign bit, integers therefore fall into the range of −32768 to +32767. In some systems like the Apple II, a sort of "wraparound" numbering is employed to represent values normally considered out of the acceptable range. For example, in determining free memory space, a negative integer might be returned. To get the correct positive value it then is necessary to add 65,536 to that negative number. For instance, adding 65,536 to a −20000 returned as free memory would indicate that 55,536 bytes remain free.

You should be aware that the word "byte" may be defined differently for various computer systems. In most popular personal computers, a byte indicates eight bits, and two such bytes are used together to make one 16-bit "word," memory address, or integer in the computer. In such a system, it takes two hex digits to define a single byte. However, the means of evaluating a hex number remains the same except that the rightmost hex digit gives the value of the rightmost or "least significant" four bits of the byte, while the leftmost hex digit gives the value of the leftmost or "most significant" four bits.

As a direct result, a 48K computer is defined to have 49,152 eight-bit bytes for a total of 393,216 bits of storage. With at least two bytes required for every word, the machine theoretically is capable of holding 24,576 words. However, some words such as those representing real numbers rather than integers usually require more than two bytes each, and multiple words may be needed to form a machine-language instruction, so the typical storage capability may be far less than 24,576 words.

Some Basic Number Comparisons

To further illustrate the differences between the various numbering systems, Table B-2 shows the relative values of some basic numbers:

Table B-2

Decimal, Octal, Hexadecimal, and Binary Comparisons

Decimal	Octal	Hexadecimal	Binary
1	1	1	1
2	2	2	10
3	3	3	11
4	4	4	100
5	5	5	101
6	6	6	110
7	7	7	111
8	10	8	1000
9	11	9	1001
10	12	A	1010
11	13	B	1011
12	14	C	1100
13	15	D	1101
14	16	E	1110
15	17	F	1111
16	20	10	10000
17	21	11	10001
18	22	12	10010
19	23	13	10011
20	24	14	10100
30	36	1E	11110
40	50	28	101000
50	62	32	110010
60	74	3C	111100

Table B-2

Decimal, Octal, Hexadecimal, and Binary Comparisons (continued)

Decimal	Octal	Hexadecimal	Binary
70	106	46	1000110
80	120	50	1010000
90	132	5A	1011010
100	144	64	1100100
1000	1750	3E8	1111101000
10000	23420	2710	10011100010000

Figures B-1 and B-2 are two "standard" hexadecimal conversion charts that should simplify working back and forth between hex and decimal numbering systems. Figure B-1 is best suited to converting values from hexadecimal to decimal notation, while Fig. B-2 is better for reverse conversions from decimal to hex.

Binary-Number Manipulations

I have shown how the various numerical systems are created and how they are related to one another. This appendix presents some of the ways in which binary numbers can be added, subtracted, multiplied, and divided. These are the four basic manipulations of concern in handling binary values, though most owners of personal and small-business computers rarely become involved in such procedures directly. Still, it's advisable to know the basic rules and to be able to apply them when the situation demands.

This appendix does not attempt a thorough description of all the aspects affecting binary manipulations as performed by a computer. Such topics as overflow, underflow, one's complement numbers, two's complement numbers, and the like are beyond the scope of this book. Besides, they really aren't necessary for the typical conversions and manipulations you'll be performing with a high-level language. However, they are critical considerations if you wish to program in assembly or machine language, including any effort you put into writing lower-level subroutines to be called from a high-level program. For those subjects and considerably more detail on the handling of binary and hexadecimal numbers, I'll refer you to virtually any one of the many books on programming individual microprocessors. A good description of the subject is contained in *Programming the 6502*, written by Rodnay Zaks and published by SYBEX, Inc.

HEX	0	1	2	3	4	5	6	7	8	9	A	B	C	D	E	F	00	000
0	0	1	2	3	4	5	6	7	8	9	10	11	12	13	14	15	0	0
1	16	17	18	19	20	21	22	23	24	25	26	27	28	29	30	31	256	4096
2	32	33	34	35	36	37	38	39	40	41	42	43	44	45	46	47	512	8192
3	48	49	50	51	52	53	54	55	56	57	58	59	60	61	62	63	768	12288
4	64	65	66	67	68	69	70	71	72	73	74	75	76	77	78	79	1024	16384
5	80	81	82	83	84	85	86	87	88	89	90	91	92	93	94	95	1280	20480
6	96	97	98	99	100	101	102	103	104	105	106	107	108	109	110	111	1536	24576
7	112	113	114	115	116	117	118	119	120	121	122	123	124	125	126	127	1792	28672
8	128	129	130	131	132	133	134	135	136	137	138	139	140	141	142	143	2048	32768
9	144	145	146	147	148	149	150	151	152	153	154	155	156	157	158	159	2304	36864
A	160	161	162	163	164	165	166	167	168	169	170	171	172	173	174	175	2560	40960
B	176	177	178	179	180	181	182	183	184	185	186	187	188	189	190	191	2816	45056
C	192	193	194	195	196	197	198	199	200	201	202	203	204	205	206	207	3072	49152
D	208	209	210	211	212	213	214	215	216	217	218	219	220	221	222	223	3328	53248
E	224	225	226	227	228	229	230	231	232	233	234	235	236	237	238	239	3584	57344
F	240	241	242	243	244	245	246	247	248	249	250	251	252	253	254	255	3840	61440

Fig. B-1. **"Standard" Hexadecimal-to-Decimal Conversion Chart**

Binary Addition

The first and most obvious way to manipulate binary numbers is to add them together to determine the sum of two or more values. There are three rules applicable to binary addition, namely:

1. $0 + 0 = 0$
2. $0 + 1 = 1 + 0 = 1$
3. $1 + 1 = 0$ with a 1 carried to the next position to the left.

5		4		3		2		1		0	
HEX	DEC	HEX	DEC	HEX	DEC	HEX	DEC	HEX	DEC	HEX	DEC
0	0	0	0	0	0	0	0	0	0	0	0
1	1,048,576	1	65,536	1	4,096	1	256	1	16	1	1
2	2,097,152	2	131,072	2	8,192	2	512	2	32	2	2
3	3,145,728	3	196,608	3	12,288	3	768	3	48	3	3
4	4,194,304	4	262,144	4	16,384	4	1,024	4	64	4	4
5	5,242,880	5	327,680	5	20,480	5	1,280	5	80	5	5
6	6.291,456	6	393.216	6	24,576	6	1,536	6	96	6	6
7	7,340,032	7	458,752	7	28,672	7	1.792	7	112	7	7
8	8,388,608	8	524,288	8	32,768	8	2,048	8	128	8	8
9	9,437,184	9	589,824	9	36,864	9	2,304	9	144	9	9
A	10,485,760	A	655,360	A	40,960	A	2,560	A	160	A	10
B	11,534,336	B	720,896	B	45,056	B	2,816	B	176	B	11
C	12,582,912	C	786,432	C	49,152	C	3,072	C	192	C	12
D	13,631,488	D	851,968	D	53,248	D	3,328	D	208	D	13
E	14,680,064	E	917,504	E	57,344	E	3,584	E	224	E	14
F	15,728,640	F	983,040	F	61,440	F	3,840	F	240	F	15

The following example applies these rules on a column-by-column basis in a graphic format to show how the binary numbers 11010 and 1011 are added together. For clarification, the decimal equivalents are shown, and the actual carries from one column to the next column left are included in the example. Like regular decimal addition, the process starts at the rightmost column and proceeds toward the left column.

	32s	16s	8s	4s	2s	1s	
Carries	1	1		1			
		1	1	Ø	1	Ø	= 26
+		Ø	1	Ø	1	1	= 11
Totals	1	Ø	Ø	1	Ø	1	= 37

Binary Subtraction

Another way to manipulate binary numbers is to subtract one from another to determine the difference. For this type of manipulation, there are four rules that must be applied:

1. $0 - 0 = 0$
2. $1 - 1 = 0$
3. $1 - 0 = 1$
4. $0 - 1 = 1$ with a 1 borrowed from next position to the left.

As an example, consider the subtraction of binary 10011 from 101101. Again, the problem illustrates the subtraction on a column-by-column basis from right to left, applying the preceding rules to each column in turn.

	32s	16s	8s	4s	2s	1s	
Borrows		1			1		
	(1)	Ø	1	(1)	Ø	1	= 45
−	Ø	1	Ø	Ø	1	1	= 19
Difference	Ø	1	1	Ø	1	Ø	= 26

As with decimal subtraction, the smaller number always should be subtracted from the larger number. If the desired difference is the smaller number less the larger number, the sign then can be changed from positive to negative. In the preceding example, 101101—10011=+11010 (45–19=+26), but 10011–101101=–11010 (19–45=–26).

Binary Multiplication

Multiplication is the third means by which binary numbers may be manipulated. There are three rules that apply to the multiplication of two binary numbers:

1. $0 \times 0 = 0$
2. $0 \times 1 = 1 \times 0 = 0$
3. $1 \times 1 = 1$

The multiplication process consists of a series of addition operations in which each digit of the multiplier is examined. If the multiplier digit is a 1, the multiplicand is offset or shifted the proper number of spaces to the left and added to the result. If the multiplier digit is a 0, a binary zero is added instead of the offset multiplicand. All of the rules of binary addition are in effect and must be observed at all times. The following example illustrates the multiplication of two binary numbers where 11010 is the multiplicand and 1011 is the multiplier. The "carries" for the addition process are not shown but do have to be included in the process.

```
                  1 1 Ø 1 Ø =   26
               ×    1 Ø 1 1 = × 11
                  ---------   -----
                  1 1 Ø 1 Ø
          +     1 1 Ø 1 Ø
          +   Ø Ø Ø Ø Ø
          + 1 1 Ø 1 Ø
          -----------------   -----
Product     1 Ø Ø Ø 1 1 1 1 Ø = 286
```

Binary Division

Division is the fourth and last of the basic binary manipulations with which you must be concerned. This process applies the rules of addition, subtraction, and multiplication in a method that involves successive subtractions. In approaching a binary division problem, the dividend is examined for the leftmost group of bits from which the divisor may be subtracted once, and a 1 is placed in the quotient over the last bit of the dividend group from which this subtraction can be performed. The next bit of the dividend is "brought down" to the right of the difference to form the least significant bit of a new dividend, and the procedure is repeated. Each time a subtraction is not possible, a 0 is placed in the quotient and the next bit of the dividend is brought down as shown in the following example.

```
          Ø Ø 1 1 Ø Ø 1
        -------------
1 Ø 1 ) 1 1 1 1 1 Ø 1
      - 1 Ø 1
        -----
          1 Ø 1
        - 1 Ø 1
          -----
              Ø 1
          -     Ø
              ---
                1 Ø
            -     Ø
                ---
                1 Ø 1
            -   1 Ø 1
                -----
                    Ø
```

The process is most easily followed in a graphic example, so the preceding procedure is provided to demonstrate the division of binary

1111101 (decimal 125) by 101 (decimal 5). Note that the leftmost bit group from which 101 can be subtracted is 111, so a 1 is placed in the quotient over the third dividend bit, the subtraction of 101 from 111 is performed, and the next bit of the dividend is brought down as the least significant bit of a new dividend. The process repeats until all bits of the dividend have been used and the quotient 11001 (decimal 25) has been calculated.

Numeric Conversions

A considerable amount of attention has been devoted to evaluating the decimal equivalents of binary, octal, and hexadecimal numbers, showing one way in which such numbers could be converted back to decimal values. However, little has been said about converting decimal numbers to one of the other systems, a procedure that is needed at least as often as the conversion back to decimal. Furthermore, there are other methods of determining decimal values that relieve you of calculating the individual powers of the base number, determining the product of the power times the digit, and then adding the individual products for each digit position. The remainder of this appendix is devoted to a description of these conversion procedures and is provided as a guide to effectively using numerical systems other than base 10.

If you're lucky enough to be using one of the high-level languages that has built-in routines for decimal-to-octal and decimal-to-hexadecimal conversions, your life is going to be a lot simpler. However, not all languages have those routines, so if yours doesn't you'll either have to program your own routines or rely on manual conversions when you need a value in a base other than ten.

In any of the numerical conversions, three separate cases must be considered: integers, proper fractions, and improper fractions. The procedures used for integers and proper fractions are similar but not identical, so improper fractions must be converted in separate stages for the integer and fractional portions, and the results of each stage must be combined to provide the final converted number.

Decimal-to-Binary Conversions

The conversion of a decimal integer to a binary integer is accomplished by a series of successive divisions by two (the binary base). After each division, the remainder is placed in the most significant bit (MSB) or leftmost position of the binary number being constructed. This applies whether the remainder is zero or one, and the procedure is repeated until a dividend of zero is obtained from the successive divisions. The following example illustrates the conversion of decimal 172 to a binary number:

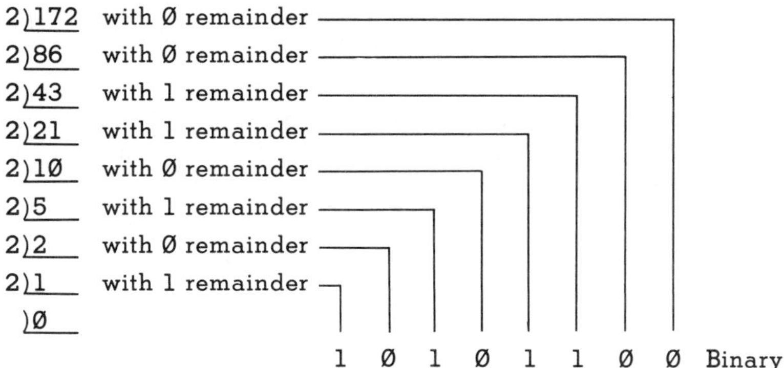

The conversion of a proper decimal fraction to a binary fraction is achieved with a series of multiplications by two—actually divisions by ½ or 2^{-1}. At each stage of multiplication, the integer portion of the product becomes the rightmost bit of the binary number, and the next multiplication is performed on only the fractional portion of the preceding product—the integer portion to the left of the decimal never is used in any multiplication step. The following example demonstrates the conversion of decimal 0.125 to a binary fraction:

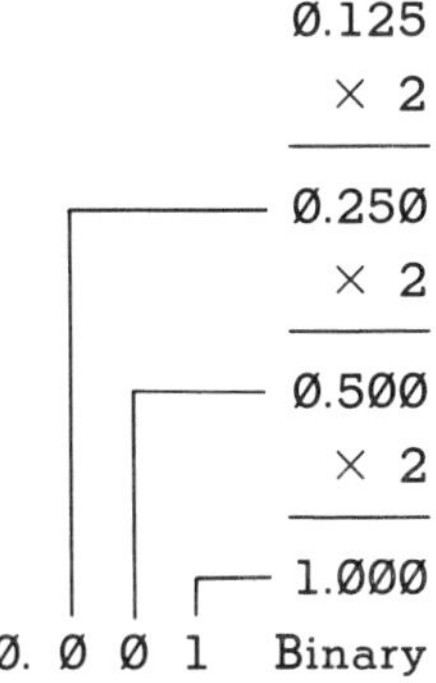

Had the decimal number been the improper fraction 172.125, each of the preceding two conversions would have been performed separately and the results combined to yield 10101100.001 as the improper binary fraction.

Binary-to-Decimal Conversions

The fastest and easiest way to convert a binary integer to a decimal number is through a series of successive multiplications and additions without calculating the powers of two at each bit position. This procedure starts with the most significant (leftmost) bit or MSB and multiplies it by two. The decimal value of the next bit is then added to the product, and the result is multiplied by two again. This procedure continues until the least significant (rightmost) bit or LSB has been added. Note that the rightmost bit signifies the number of units, so the procedure terminates with the addition and does not proceed to another multiplication. To illustrate, consider the conversion of binary 10011 to its decimal equivalent:

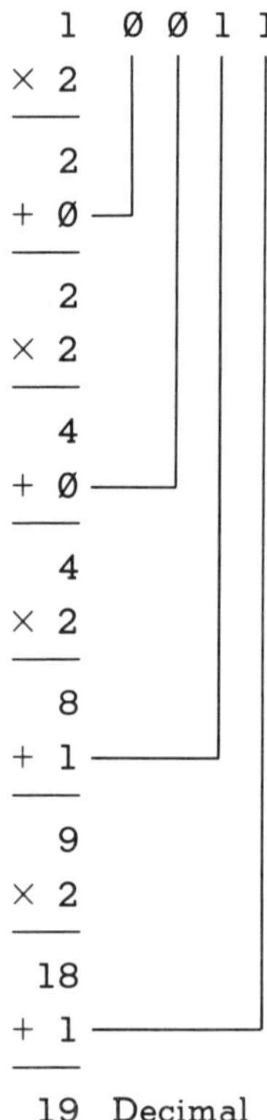

The conversion of a proper binary fraction is not readily handled in this fashion, so such a fraction should be converted by summing the products of the positional terms as described earlier in this appendix. Similarly, improper fractions should have the integer and fractional portions converted independently, with the separate results combined to yield the proper decimal fraction.

Decimal-to-Octal Conversions

The conversion of decimal integers to octal is essentially the same as converting them to binary, except that an eight for the octal base is used as the divisor instead of the two for the binary base. The mechanics of the procedure remain unchanged in that successive divisions are performed until a zero quotient is obtained, with the remainder at each step being placed at the most significant (leftmost) position of the octal number being constructed. The following example shows the conversion of decimal 2863 to its octal value:

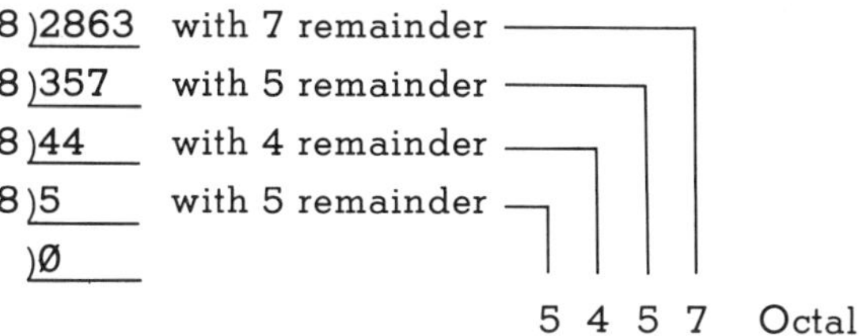

In a manner similar to the conversion to binary, the conversion of a proper decimal fraction to an octal fraction is achieved with a series of multiplications by eight—actually divisions by ⅛ or 8^{-1}. With each multiplication, the integer portion of the product is made the rightmost bit of the octal number, and the next multiplication is performed on only the fractional portion of the preceding product. The example shows the conversion of decimal 0.075 to octal.

In the preceding example, notice that octal 0.0463 is approximately 0.07495 rather than 0.075. Many decimal fractions cannot be converted to precise octal fractions within a reasonable number of digits, so you have to be content with approximations. The procedure illustrated can be carried to as many octal digits as desired, but exact conversions may not be found in all cases. Had I been converting the improper decimal fraction 2863.075, both of the above procedures would have been performed independently, and the results combined to obtain 5457.04631 as the improper octal fraction.

Octal-to-Decimal Conversions

An octal integer may be converted to a decimal number in exactly the same manner already demonstrated for binary integers. The only difference in the procedure is that the multiplier used at alternate steps is eight for the octal base instead of two for the binary base. This is illustrated by the following conversion of octal 472 to a decimal value.

```
  4  7  2
× 8  |  |
---  |  |
 32  |  |
+ 7 -┘  |
---     |
 39     |
× 8     |
---     |
312     |
+ 2 ----┘
---
314  Decimal
```

Like binary fractions, proper octal fractions are difficult to convert in this fashion. Such fractions should be converted by summing the products of the positional terms as described earlier.

Decimal-to-Hexadecimal Conversions

Converting a decimal integer to a hex number follows exactly the same successive-division procedure defined for binary and octal integers. However, the divisor in this case is 16 for the hexadecimal base. In these conversions, the remainders used to construct the hex number may be in the range of 0 through 15, and those from 10 through 15 must be written as the defined hex symbols A through F. The example provided illustrates the conversion of decimal 64932 to its hexadecimal equivalent; notice the treatment of the remainders in deriving the defined hex symbols.

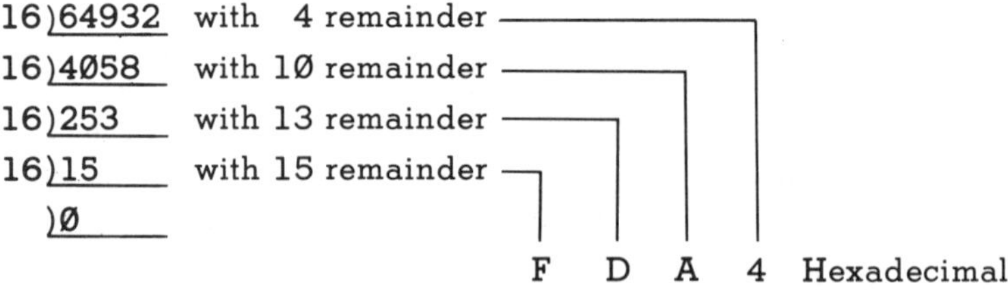

Converting a proper decimal fraction to a hex fraction also follows the procedure already detailed for binary and octal fractions. This time, the multiplier is 16 (or division by 1/16 or 16^{-1}). Again, it's necessary to convert the integer portion of each successive product to the appropriate hex digits, using A through F for the integers 10 through 15. The example illustrates the conversion of decimal 0.081 to a hex value:

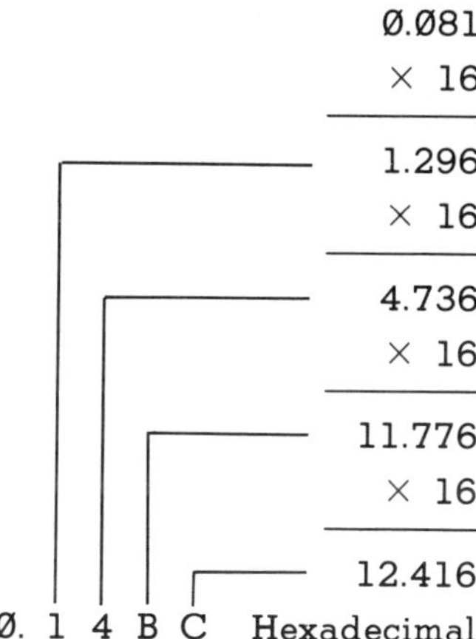

Hexadecimal-to-Decimal Conversions

The conversion of a hex integer to a decimal number follows the procedure described for binary and octal integers. This time, however, the multiplier used in alternate steps is 16, and some care must be used in making certain that the addition steps use the correct decimal equivalent of the hex digits A through F. The example illustrates the conversion of hex A6F1 to a decimal number:

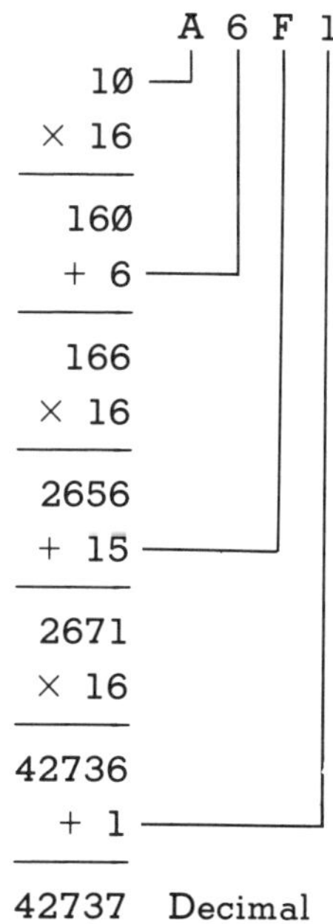

Binary-to-Octal and Octal-to-Binary Conversions

In converting back and forth between octal and binary numbers, consider each octal digit to be a group of three binary bits. Then evaluate each octal digit or group of three bits individually, applying the technique demonstrated earlier in this appendix under the description of the octal system for determining the maximum value of a three-bit nybble. The following examples are applicable:

Binary	1ØØ	Ø1Ø	111	
Octal	4	2	7	$= 427_8$
Octal	7	1	3	
Binary	111	ØØ1	Ø11	= 111ØØ1Ø11

Binary-to-Hex and Hex-to-Binary Conversions

Conversions back and forth between hexadecimal and binary numbers follow the same procedure as for octal and binary numbers. However, each hex digit is considered a group of four bits, and each group of four bits is evaluated as one hex digit.

Binary	Ø111	11ØØ	ØØ11	1Ø11	
Decimal	7	12	3	11	
Hex	7	C	3	B	$= 7C3B_H$
Hex	6	F	8	A	
Decimal	6	15	8	1Ø	
Binary	Ø11Ø	1111	1ØØØ	1Ø1Ø	= Ø11Ø11111ØØØ1Ø1Ø

Octal-to-Hex and Hex-to-Octal Conversions

The conversion between hexadecimal and octal numbers is best accomplished through an intermediate step utilizing either decimal or binary values. Perhaps the easiest way is to determine the binary equivalent of one number, regroup the bits, and then develop the other number from the regrouped binary. In regrouping the binary, be sure you proceed from right to left—regrouping from left to right will give an erroneous conversion.

Hexadecimal	D	Ø	9	B		
Binary Equivalent	111Ø	ØØØØ	1ØØ1	1Ø11		
Regrouped Binary	ØØ1	11Ø	ØØØ	Ø1Ø	Ø11	Ø11
Octal	1	6	Ø	2	3	3

Some "BASIC" Functions

For informational purposes, the first part of this appendix contains some BASIC subroutines for calculating square roots, natural logarithms, exponentials, sines, and cosines. Essentially, the subroutines perform the SQR(), LOG(), EXP(), SIN(), and COS() computations and may be used in place of those intrinsic functions (with a speed sacrifice) or on BASICs that allow real numbers but lack the built-in functions. All subroutines require the use of real numbers; they are not suitable for Apple Integer BASIC or other interpreters limited to integers only. All variables are considered to be real- or single-precision.

The second part of this appendix contains the computations of trigonometric functions that can be derived from other intrinsic functions or, with appropriate modifications, from the results calculated by the sine and cosine subroutines.

Subroutine for Square Roots

The following subroutine is equivalent to the SQR() function and may be used to compute square roots where X9 is returned as the square root of X1. The value of X1 must be established before the GOSUB 9000 to this routine. If X1 is less than zero, the square root is "imaginary" and cannot be computed by this routine—in that case, "SQUARE ROOT ERROR" and the value of X1 are displayed on the terminal, and the subroutine returns with X9 set equal to zero.

```
9000 IF X1 <0 THEN 9008 ELSE IF X1=0 THEN 9010
9002 X9=(1+X1)*.5
9004 X2=X9 : X9=(X2+X1/X2)*.5 : IF X9<X2 THEN 9004
9006 RETURN
9008 PRINT "SQUARE ROOT ERROR ";X1
9010 X9=0 : GOTO 9006
```

Subroutine for Natural Logarithms

The following subroutine is equivalent to LOG() and returns X9 as the natural logarithm of X1. The value of X1 must be set before the GOSUB 9300 to this subroutine. If X1 is equal to or less than zero, the natural logarithm cannot be computed, the subroutine displays "LOGARITHM ERROR", and the values of X1 and X9 are set equal to zero before returning.

```
9300 IF X1 >0 THEN 9304
9302 PRINT "LOGARITHM ERROR ";X1 : X9=0 : GOTO 9324
9304 X2=X1 : IF X1=>.75 THEN 9308
9306 X2=1/X1
9308 FOR X3=0 TO 200 : IF X2<=.15 THEN 9312
9310 X2=X2*.5 : NEXT
9312 X2=X2-1 : X4=X2 : X9=0
9314 FOR X5=1 TO 99 STEP 2 : X8=X9 : X9=X9+X4/X5-(X4*X2)/(X5+1)
9316 IF X9=X8 THEN X5=99 : GOTO 9320
9318 X4=X4*X2*X2
9320 NEXT
9322 X9=.69314718#*X3+X9 : IF X1<.75 THEN X9=-X9
9324 RETURN
```

Note that this subroutine and the LOG() function both return only the natural or Naperian logarithm. It may, however, be necessary to use logarithms based upon other systems such as decimal. In such cases, it's easy to compute the logarithm of any number X to any base N by simply dividing the natural log of X by the natural log of N—that is, solve the equation Y=LOG(X)/LOG(N) to have Y the desired log in the desired base.

Subroutine for Exponentials

This subroutine performs the EXP() function where X9 is returned as the value of e (the base of natural logarithms) raised to the power X1. The value of X1 must be set before executing the GOSUB 9400 to the subroutine. The "overflow" condition must be set to the maximum value of your system. For Microsoft Revision 4.51 BASIC, overflow occurs when X1 is greater than 87.3364. Similarly, the exponential is zero when X1 is less than −88.7227. In the event of an overflow, the message "EXPONENTIAL ERROR" and the value of X1 are displayed, and the subroutine returns with X9 set to zero (you can use machine infinity if you prefer).

```
9400 IF X1 >87.3364 THEN 9428
9402 IF X1<-88.7227 THEN 9430
9404 X2=X1/.69314718# : IF X1=>0 THEN 9408
9406 X2=-X2
9408 X9=1
9410 IF X2<1 THEN 9414
9412 X9=X9*2 : X2=X2-1 : GOTO 9410
9414 X2=.69314718#*X2 : X3=1 : X8=1
9416 FOR X4=1 TO 50
9418 X7=X8 : X3=X3*X2/X4 : X8=X8+X3
9420 IF X8=X7 THEN X4=50
9422 NEXT
9424 X9=X8*X9 : IF X1=>0 THEN 9432
9426 X9=1/X9 : GOTO 9432
9428 PRINT "EXPONENTIAL ERROR ";X1
9430 X9=0
9432 RETURN
```

Subroutine for Exponentiation

This subroutine accomplishes the task of exponentiation, effectively solving the equation X9=X1^ Y2 where X1 is the number to be raised to the power Y2. The result is returned in X9. Note that this subroutine relies upon calls to both the logarithm and the exponentiation subroutines already presented, so all three subroutines must be present.

```
9099 X0=1 : Y1=X1 : IF Y2=0 THEN RETURN
9100 IF Y1<0 THEN IF INT(Y2)=Y2 THEN X0=1-2*Y2+4*INT(Y2/2) : X1=-X1
9102 IF Y1<>0 THEN GOSUB 9300 : X1=Y2*X9 : GOSUB 9400
9104 X9=X0*X9 : X1=Y1 : RETURN
```

A special note on the use of exponentiation. Most BASICs support the SQR() function to solve for square roots, but they do not have features for solving other roots such as the cube root. Remember that the roots are the reciprocals of powers, so the exponentiation function can be used to duplicate those operations simply by making the exponent the reciprocal of the power. For example, the equation X=SQR(100) yields the same results as X=100^(1/2) or X=100^.5, any of which return X equal to 10. Note that the caret (^) is the BASIC symbol for exponentiation. Similarly the cube root can be computed with the statements X=27^(1/3) or X=27^.3333, each of which would return X equal to three. Any root of any positive number may be calculated in exactly the same way—merely enter the reciprocal as the power for exponentiation.

It's important, however, that you do not enter negative powers for exponentiation. In mathematical notation, it might be correct to write the cube root of X as either $X^{1/3}$ or X^{-3}, but the BASIC statements X=27^−3 or X=27^(−3) yield incorrect results. They do not cause an error message, but the computed response is far from the correct value.

Subroutine for Sines and Cosines

This subroutine calculates sines and cosines; it is equivalent to the SIN() and COS() functions. Variable X1 is the angle expressed in radians and must be set before the GOSUB . . . statement in the mainline program. The subroutine has two entry points so that a GOSUB 9000 returns the sine of the angle as X9, while a GOSUB 9002 returns the cosine as X9.

To calculate sines and cosines for angles expressed in degrees (and decimal fractions thereof) rather than radians, simply execute the statement X1=X1/57.295780# before performing the GOSUB . . . to the subroutine. This also works when using the SIN() and COS() functions for degree inputs.

```
9000 X2=X1 : GOTO 9004
9002 X2=X1+1.5707963#
9004 IF X2>-1.5707963# THEN 9008
9006 X2=-3.1415927#-X2
9008 IF X2<3.1415927# THEN 9012
9010 X2=X2-6.2831853# : GOTO 9008
9012 X4=X2 : X9=X2
9014 FOR X5=3 TO 99 STEP 4 : FOR X6=-1 TO 1 STEP 2
9016 X8=X9 : X4=X4*X2*X2/((X5+X6)*(X5+X6+1)) : X9=X9+X4*X6
9018 IF X9=X8 THEN X5=99: X6=1
9020 NEXT: NEXT
9022 RETURN
```

Subroutine for Tangents

In the absence of a TAN() function, determining the tangent of an angle is simply a matter of dividing the sine by the cosine; that is, the equation tan(x)=sin(x)/cos(x) is solved. To do this with the preceding routine calculating the sine and cosine, use the following subroutine that has X1 set to the angle and returns X9 set to the tangent.

```
9100 XA=0 : GOSUB 9000: XA=X9: GOSUB 9002: X9=XA/X9: RETURN
```

Subroutine for Arc Tangents

This subroutine computes the arc tangent of an angle specified in degrees as variable X1. The subroutine is equivalent to executing an X9=ATN(X1) statement. Upon return from the subroutine, X9 contains the desired arc tangent. Notice that this subroutine relies upon calls to an earlier subroutine to obtain the sine of the angle it needs.

```
9200 X0=X1 : GOSUB 9000 : X2=X9 : IF X1<0 THEN X1=-X1
9202 X3=0 : IF X1>1 THEN X3=1 : X1=1/X1
9204 X9=X1*X1 : X4=((2.86623E-03*X9-.0161657)*X9+
     .0429096)*X9
9206 X4=((((X4-.075289)*X9+.106563)*X9-.114209)*X9+.199936)*X9
9208 X9=((X4-.333332)*X9+1)*X1 : IF X3=1 THEN X9=1.5708-X9
9210 IF X0<0 THEN X9=-X9
9212 X1=X0 : RETURN
```

Miscellaneous Derived Functions

Many other functions can be derived from the few provided by the BASIC interpreter or obtained with one of the preceding subroutines. All require the ability to use real numbers, and all angles are expressed in radians. Often, these can be implemented with the DEF FN... statement when they have to be used more than once or twice in a program. Typically, this list is contained in the BASIC instruction manual furnished for the language, but they are included herein for your convenience.

Secant:	SEC(X)	= 1/COS(X)
Cosecant:	CSC(X)	= 1/SIN(X)
Cotangent:	COT(X)	= 1/TAN(X)
Inverse sine:	ARCSIN(X)	= ATN(X/SQR (X*-X+1))
Inverse cosine:	ARCCOS(X)	= -ATN(X/SQR (X*-X+1))+1.5708
Inverse secant:	ARCSEC(X)	= ATN(SQR(X*X-1))+ (SGN(X)-1) *1.5708

Inverse cosecant:	ARCCSC(X)	= ATN(X/SQR (X*X−1))+(SGN(X) −1)*1.5708
Inverse cotangent:	ARCCOT(X)	= −ATN(X)+1.5708
Hyperbolic sine:	SINH(X)	= (EXP(X)−EXP(−X))/2
Hyperbolic cosine:	COSH(X)	= (EXP(X)+EXP(−X))/2
Hyperbolic secant:	SECH(X)	= 2/(EXP(X)+EXP(−X))
Hyperbolic cosecant:	CSCH(X)	= 2/(EXP(X)−EXP(−X))
Hyperbolic tangent:	TANH(X)	= EXP(−X)/(EXP(X)+ EXP(−X))*2+1
Hyperbolic cotangent:	COTH(X)	= EXP(−X)/(EXP(X)− EXP(−X))*2+1
Inverse hyperbolic sine:	ARCSINH(X)	= LOG(X+SQR(X*X+1))
Inverse hyperbolic cosine:	ARCCOSH(X)	= LOG(X+SQR(X *X−1))
Inverse hyperbolic secant:	ARCSECH(X)	= LOG((SQR(X*−X+1) +1)/X)
Inverse hyperbolic cosecant:	ARCSCSH(X)	= LOG((SGN(X)*SQR (X*X+1)+1)/X)
Inverse hyperbolic tangent:	ARCTANH(X)	= LOG(((1+X)/(1−X)) /2)
Inverse hyperbolic cotangent:	ARCCOTH(X)	= LOG(((X+1)/(X−1))/2)

Rounding and Formatting

Frequently, it's necessary either to round off a real number, rather than truncate it, or to format a number to a fixed number of decimal places. Either operation can be accomplished quite easily in BASIC.

To round a number, simply add 0.5 to that number and perform an INT() function. For example, executing the statement X=INT(X+.5) rounds the value of X to the nearest whole number. Consider the case where X equals 9.49 so the statement would be equivalent to X=INT(9.99), which yields a truncated value of nine. On the other hand, if X equals 7.505, the statement is equivalent to X=INT(8.005), which yields an integer value of eight.

To force the number X to a given number of decimal places N, it's necessary to move the decimal point N places to the right, truncate the number with an INT() function, and move the decimal point back N places to the left. This is easily accomplished with either of the following two program statements, although the second form is preferred because it incorporates the rounding provision rather than just truncating:

```
X=INT((1Ø^N)*X)/(10^N)
X=INT((10^N)*X+.5)/(10^N)
```

As written, however, these two algorithms fail when applied to double-precision numbers under a Microsoft BASIC (Revision 4.51 or BASIC-80 Revisions 5.1 and 5.2). They work quite well for single-precision numbers, but applying them to double-precision numbers merely results in a slightly different number with as many (or more) decimal places as the original. In systematically trying to reduce these algorithms to something that would work correctly with double precision, I've traced the problem to the (10^N) expression used as the divisor. Whether that divisor is computed within the algorithm as shown or is calculated outside the algorithm and transferred in by means of a variable, the problem continues to exist. It also exists whether the divisor is computed as an integer, single-precision, or double-precision value.

In order to work with double-precision numbers under a Microsoft BASIC, I've found it necessary to alter the approach somewhat. In so doing, I recommend user-defined functions of the following forms:

```
DEF FNP#(N%,P#)=INT(N%*P#)/N%       [nonrounding]
DEF FNP#(N%,P#)=INT(N%*P#+.5)/N%    [rounding]
```

The program then calls these functions by setting P# to the double-precision value to be manipulated and N% to an integer *constant* that is an exponentiation of 10 dependent upon the number of decimal places desired. To illustrate how this works, consider the following sequence of calls to the rounding function to set the double-precision number 1.2345678 (in P#) to a desired number of places:

Function Call	# Places	Exponent	P1# Returned
P1#=FNP#(1,P#)	Ø	1Ø^Ø	1
P1#=FNP#(1Ø,P#)	1	1Ø^1	1.2
P1#=FNP#(1ØØ,P#)	2	1Ø^2	1.23
P1#=FNP#(1ØØØ,P#)	3	1Ø^3	1.235
P1#=FNP#(1ØØØØ,P#)	4	1Ø^4	1.2346
P1#=FNP#(1ØØØØØ,P#)	5	1Ø^5	1.23457
P1#=FNP#(1ØØØØØØ,P#)	6	1Ø^6	1.234568
P1#=FNP#(1ØØØØØØØ,P#)	7	1Ø^7	1.2345678

Obviously, the use of constants in this manner is cumbersome and consumes a lot of memory in a long program. Still, it's the only way I've found to make the algorithm work reliably for double-precision numbers. There is, however, a possible simplification if all conversions are to the same number of decimal places. As an example, take the case of an accounting program in which all values are to be reduced to two decimal places for dollars and cents. Since the number of decimal places is fixed, the defined functions can be rewritten as:

```
DEF FNP#(P#)=INT(100*P#)/100       [nonrounding]
DEF FNP#(P#)=INT(100*P#+.5)/100    [rounding]
```

Now the call to the function is simply P1#=FNP#(P#) without the need for the constant being repeated over and over again throughout the body of the program.

Commercial BASIC Enhancements

As I've indicated, some computers and some implementations of BASIC are limited by the lack of one or more built-in statements or functions. In many cases, however, you can find remedial routines in published sources such as magazines or books, or you can buy commercial software packages that will supplement your BASIC.

Using published sources, you do have the problem of transcribing the printed listings into your own computer—the price is right, but it can be a long and tedious procedure. Furthermore, there's no guarantee that what you copy will work the way you envision. There's also a copyright problem. You can use the materials in your own programming, but you legally cannot distribute what you've lifted, or anything derived from or depending on lifted material. If you write a program that depends on a published routine to provide a PRINT USING statement, you're not entitled to sell or even give the program to anyone else without first signing a license and paying what's usually a hefty copyright charge.

With commercial enhancement software, you eliminate the chore of keying the programs, but you still have the copyright problem. Many packages, such as those for the Apple II, are thoroughly locked up in copy-protection schemes so you can't even make a backup copy of what you've bought.

Yet, every once in a while, you could get lucky. You just might find a suitable package that is usable. That happened to me with the Apple II running Applesoft. I had to adapt a BASIC-80 program to Applesoft for possible resale, and I needed to emulate PRINT USING, INSTR(), and IF...THEN...ELSE... operations not available under Applesoft. While searching for something—anything—that would work, I finally stumbled across some suitable software in a package called *Apple Spice*

(Adventure International, Box 3435, Longwood, Florida 32750). I hesitate to cite a program like this by name, but I was so impressed by it that I thought it would be a worthwhile inclusion in this discussion. The software is inexpensive, does exactly what I expected, is provided on a copyable diskette, and can be used as part of other commercial packages without paying a royalty. The only restriction is that the supplier asks credit in the commercial works produced and that two copies of subsequent software be provided.

This particular package contains easily used routines to simulate the formatting capabilities of PRINT USING, search strings much like INSTR(), perform multidirectional branching like an IF...THEN... ELSE..., obtain an extended form of INPUT, and control screen-display formatting. Throughout, it's a utility that contributes nicely to getting the most use out of the Apple II.

The reason for mentioning this particular package is to point out that this type of software does exist. I know there are other packages like it for Applesoft; some may be better, others may be worse. Most likely, there are similar ones for other limited BASICs and other machines as well. All that's required is a bit of digging on your part to discover where and how to obtain them. The key consideration is that you can have access to missing functions and statements, can avoid convoluted programming to get around the missing items, and should be able to achieve high degrees of program efficiency and effectiveness. You're not limited to the computer supplier's concept of BASIC. I suggest that you be cautious in selecting and testing utility packages like this because they may not work as you would like them, but you should give them careful consideration as potential programming aids.

Sample Disk and Memory Tests

This appendix contains two sample programs. The first exercises the disk storage device and is a means of testing whether or not the drives are functioning properly. The second is a memory test routine that works on some systems to "peek and poke" patterns into memory locations, verifying that what the program gets back is the same as what it put into the location. Caution is advised in using these routines. They are designed to run on a 64K mainframe using Microsoft Revision 4.51 BASIC or an equivalent. Some modification may be necessary to run the programs on other systems, depending on the hardware and software characteristics of the particular machine, as well as the BASIC in use.

Disk Exerciser

This routine exercises the disk drives by writing 15 random files, each having 100 records. Either or both of the number of random files or the number of records per file may have to be changed to accommodate other systems; this program has been tested under Microsoft Revision 4.51 BASIC set up for 15 random files (its maximum) when loaded into the system. Essentially the program opens all files, writes the first record to each file, writes the second to each, and so on. Note that it doesn't just open a file and write all 100 records. The interleaving pattern being created is part of the disk exercise being performed.

Each record number written to the disk is unique and consists of a 128-character string, each character of which is the same. When read back from the disk, the character string is checked to make sure it has the proper contents. The readback proceeds on a random basis for 200 record numbers in each file. This is a "spot check" and is not intended to read every record of every file. If you want a sequential readback designed to check every record written, simply change line 110 to set RR equal to R1 instead of a random integer. A continuous error count is maintained by variable EC, but a properly functioning disk system with a good diskette should show zero errors.

The subroutine in line 9000 is used to position the printouts on an ADDS Regent 25® terminal so that each line overlays and replaces the prior one. You can change line 9000 for the addressable cursor operation of your own terminal or delete the addressing to allow continuous output down the screen.

```
10 PRINT CHR$(12) : CLEAR 2000 : DEFINT A-Z : DIM G$(15)
20 FOR I=1 TO 15
30 R=0 : C=0 : GOSUB 9000 : PRINT "OPENING FILE #";I
40 F$="B:TESTDA"+RIGHT$(STR$(I),LEN(STR$(I))-1)
50 OPEN"R",I,F$ : FIELD I,128 AS G$(I) : NEXT
60 FOR R1=1 TO 100
70 FOR F=1 TO 15
75 R=0 : C=0 : GOSUB 9000 : PRINT "WRITING RECORD #";R1; "FILE #";F
80 LSET G$(F)=STRING$(128,CHR$(R1+64)) : PUT F,R1
90 NEXT F,R1
100 FOR R1=1 TO 100
110 RR=RND(1)*200+1
120 FOR F=1 TO 15
130 R=0 : C=0 : GOSUB 9000 : PRINT "READING RECORD #";RR;"FILE
    #"F; "ERRORS =";EC
140 GET F,RR
150 IF G$(F)< >STRING$(128,CHR$(RR+64)) THEN EC=EC+1
160 NEXT:NEXT
170 R=0 : C=0 : GOSUB 9000 : PRINT "CLOSING ALL FILES";STRING$(65,32)
180 CLOSE
999 END
9000 PRINT CHR$(27)+"Y"+CHR$(R+32)+CHR$(C+32); : RETURN
```

Memory Exerciser

The following program exercises a portion of the computer's memory by poking locations with a given bit pattern, peeking those same locations to see what's there, and comparing the two. It makes four passes, with variable J set to 0, 85, 170, and 255. This pokes the four bit patterns 00000000, 01010101, 10101010, and 11111111, respectively. If any mismatch is found, the hexadecimal memory address, the number "poked," and the number "peeked" are displayed on the terminal. In a correctly functioning memory bank, there should be no displayed output other than the value of variable J printed when that value changes. However, the program ends normally with an error message attempting to poke the first location with J set to a value above 255.

This program is written for BASICs similar to Microsoft Revision 4.51 running on a 64K computer. To avoid destroying BASIC, it is necessary to limit the usable memory when loading the interpreter to 32,767 bytes or less, forcing BASIC into the lower 32K banks and allowing the test to be conducted on the upper two banks. Then, with power switched off, the bank select switches on the memory boards are used to interchange the upper and lower banks, power is applied, BASIC is loaded with a 32K maximum, and this program is run again to check the 32K not tested the first time around.

This program is not suitable for all systems, and I caution you against using it on any system that does not allow switch control of memory banks. Specifically, it's not suitable for the Apple II or similar machines in which reorganizing memory involves pulling and reinstalling chips.

```
1Ø J=Ø
2Ø FOR I=32768# TO 65535#
3Ø POKE I,J : IF PEEK(I)< >J THEN PRINT HEX$(I), PEEK(I), J
4Ø NEXT : PRINT J : J=J+85 : GOTO 2Ø
```

Some Useful Software

This appendix identifies some interesting and occasionally useful software for both CP/M and Apple II computers. The list does not include every possible package—not even every supplier of a particular program type. Instead, it lists representative products showing the range of assistance available for achieving improved efficiency and increased utilization of computer systems. The reader should carefully investigate and evaluate all available products of a given type before purchasing any. The software industry changes constantly, with old products discontinued and new products released weekly. Since it's impossible to provide a current and comprehensive list in a book of this scope, the list should be treated only as a starting point for surveying the field.

Owners of non-CP/M machines other than the Apple II should view this list as *typical* of products that may be available for any computer brand. Often, suppliers listed also provide versions for other machines such as the IBM PC, TRS-80, and so on. In addition, there are other suppliers not listed but unique to each computer brand. All products from all suppliers should be evaluated before deciding on one.

Inclusion in this appendix does not constitute endorsement of a product, nor is it a positive or negative recommendation. The list merely indicates a few selected packages felt to show promise in getting the most out of a computer, provided they are used correctly and in suitable applications.

Advanced Micro Techniques, 1291 East Hillside Blvd., Suite 209, Foster City, CA 94404.
DPatch™ is a disk-file recovery system for CP/M-based computers. It provides direct disk-file inspection (requiring user expertise in

disk formats and storage), easy recovery of accidentally erased or damaged files, and disk-surface certification to protect against using diskettes with damaged data blocks. Generally useful, but surface certification hasn't worked with some double-sided double-density disk drives.

Advanced Operating Systems, 4300 West 62nd St., Indianapolis, IN 46206.
The Programmer™ is a program writer for Apple II CP/M using either MBASIC or GBASIC (Microsoft BASIC-80 for the *SoftCard*). Unlike some other program-writing programs, it works without a data base management system. It can be used to generate an almost unlimited variety of programs coded in BASIC, but it doesn't always use the most efficient coding possible.

Adventure International, Box 3435, Longwood, FL 32750.
Apple Spice™ is an effective, easily used Applesoft enhancement that simulates PRINT USING, INSTR() (string search), IF... THEN...ELSE..., extended INPUT, and formatted screen output capabilities not otherwise available under the interpreter.

ALF Products, Inc., 1448 Estes, Denver, CO 80215.
Penulticopy™ is a high-speed, high-efficiency copy program for Apple II DOS. It is not a "nibble copier" and does not break copy-protection on commercial Apple diskettes. It provides simultaneous formatting, surface checking, and copying, thus eliminating some steps in making backups, second masters, and other copies of users' diskettes.

Blat Research & Development Corp., 8016 188th St. S.W., Edmonds, WA 98020.
Badlim™ is a diskette-certification program for CP/M-based systems. It locates bad areas on the media and "blocks" them from subsequent use by disk files. It has identified bad disks that were passed by the self-verification feature of this author's CP/M FORMAT.COM program. Thus, it has prevented data losses that otherwise would have cost many times the price of the program.

Borland International, 69 Upper Georges Street, Dun Laoghaire, Dublin, Republic of Ireland.
MenuMaster™ is a CP/M-based menu-creation utility with many applications. It generates the control menus for programs (BASIC) or CP/M system operations, providing information, programming steps, and functions necessary to create the program code easily. Being menu-driven itself, this program can simplify the writing of nontrivial application software in which the operations are easily understood and directed by even novice users.

Central Point Software, P.O. Box 19730-203, Portland, OR 97219.
The Filer™ is an Apple II disk utility with routines to copy individual files, change the DOS booting program, make fast diskette copies with read and write error checking (35, 40, and 70 track), adjust the drive speeds, and test the major disk-drive functions. It provides a degree of protection against common disk-caused data losses and system problems.

Creative Computing Software, 39 East Hanover Ave., Morris Plains, NJ 07950.
Disk Doctor™ is an Apple II disk utility for displaying and modifying diskette sectors, as well as formatting diskettes and verifying the media integrity. It does not include copying routines, drive tests, or similar functions.

Digital Marketing, 2670 Cherry Lane, Walnut Creek, CA 94596.
File Fix™ is a multi-purpose CP/M disk utility providing file recovery from accidental erasures plus other useful and practical functions. It includes verified file copying routines, "forged" linkages between user areas to save disk space, controllable "dumps" of disk files, and even a comparison routine to determine whether two files have the same contents.

Diversified Software Research, Inc., 5848 Crampton Ct., Rockford, IL 61111.
Diversi-DOS™ is a DOS speed-up modification for Apple II systems. It can provide significantly faster disk operations, although it's not usable with every commercial program or with software modified to change normal DOS functions.

Masterworks Software, Inc., 1823 W. Lomita Blvd., Lomita, CA 90717.
Masterdisk™ is an Apple II disk utility for searching and editing sectors, moving sectors between disks, undeleting erased files, determining sector usage, and performing high-speed single-drive disk copying. It's most useful for those having a working knowledge of Apple II disk-storage techniques.

MasterDOS™ allows customization of Apple II DOS with new commands, error messages, volume titles, and greeting-program names. It also can be used to free DOS sectors for other uses. Its primary purpose is to provide "file security" and prevent unauthorized tampering by using DOS terminology not easily recognized by unauthorized users.

Micro-Ware Distributors, Inc., P.O. Box 113, Pompton Plains, NJ 07444.

Nibbles Away II™ is an Apple II "nibble copier" for backing up "protected" and normally uncopyable commercial software packages. Making archival copies appears legal if the copies are for an authorized user's system backup only. It requires some knowledge of Apple II disk-storage techniques and parameters.

Omega Microware, Inc., 222 So. Riverside Plaza, Chicago, IL 60606.

The Inspector™ is a sophisticated Apple II disk utility for recovering data from damaged disks, finding and editing disk-stored information, searching and editing memory locations, and other applications. Users familiar with disk-storage techniques and memory utilization probably can use this program to good advantage.

Watson™ is an extension to *The Inspector* and adds features such as reconstructing the disk "volume table of contents," providing Hex and ASCII disassemblies, removing DOS from Apple II diskettes, checking whether disks are alike, and so on. Again, a working familiarity with disk and memory storage is essential to use this program effectively.

Locksmith™ is a "nibble copier" for backing up copy-protected Apple II diskettes. It includes a disk-surface verification to identify and prevent use of damaged or flawed disks, and it has a built-in drive-speed test with instructions for adjusting the drives. Because of its versatility, this nibble copier is most effective for knowledgeable users well versed in direct disk manipulations.

The Manager™ is an Apple II DOS-management system providing either of two functions. First, it can move DOS onto a 16K memory-expansion card, freeing about 10K of otherwise unusable RAM for programming use. Second, it can set up a 16K memory card as a fast but small disk-drive emulator for high-speed temporary data storage. It's applied easily and effectively, though it's not necessarily compatible with other commercial software.

P-80 Nut Software, P.O. Box 490, Lilburn, GA 30247.

Documenter™ is a novel, though somewhat limited, program to create flow charts from Applesoft programs. It can be useful if one likes the flowcharting technique and if the programs being charted are not overly complex. Intended as a final step in documenting a program, it's not a replacement for the normal flowcharting that should be part of the preliminary program development.

Pawluk Adv! (Nexus), 5455 Wilshire Blvd., Suite 802, Los Angeles, CA 90036.

Zip™ is a CP/M-based screen-formatting utility for CBASIC, Microsoft BASIC-80, and data base management systems. It can "draw" or "write" an input screen or output form under cursor control, automatically generating the program code for that screen or form. It stores a "program" on disk for merging into other programs. Properly applied, this can save time in programming input and output formats for different applications.

Quality Software, 6660 Reseda Blvd., Suite 105, Reseda, CA 91335.

Beneath Apple DOS (by Don Worth and Pieter Lechner) is a "must have" book for all Apple II users. It defines and describes the features of Apple DOS and Apple disk utilization not covered in standard system manuals, thus giving good insights into the use of magnetic media. It's particularly important to gain such an understanding to use nibble copiers and other disk utility programs effectively.

Bag of Tricks (Don Worth and Pieter Lechner) is a sequel to *Beneath Apple DOS* and provides useful and usable utility programs both in the book and on a prerecorded diskette. The emphasis is on protecting against and recovering from disk "crashes," but it also contains general utilities. One is a method for altering disk "skewing" or sector-access sequences to optimize storage and retrieval speeds—even for speeding up data-disk operations for certain commercial software such as word processors.

Sensible Software, 6619 Perham Drive, West Bloomfield, MI 48033.

Back It Up II™ is a nibble copier for backing up protected commercial software for the Apple II. Like others of this type, a thorough knowledge and understanding of disk-storage techniques is a definite advantage. On occasion, this program has been able to copy some software that other copiers couldn't seem to handle, but it's also failed to "grab" some with which others have succeeded.

Disk Recovery™ ***(The Scanner***™***)*** is an effective Apple II program for recovering erased disk files, scanning for and locking out bad sectors on a diskette, and so on. It does not provide direct disk editing facilities, but it works quickly, cleanly, and without extensive user knowledge of disk formats and storage techniques.

Super Disk Copy™ is a multi-function copying utility for the Apple II. It's not a nibble copier and isn't intended for copy-protected disks. It does provide several copying modes, diskette initialization, an ability to undelete erased files, a method to fix file sizes by eliminating unused sectors, and access to files stored with "illegal" characters in the directory to prevent access or tampering.

The Software House, 1542 W. Pepper, Mesa, AZ 85201.
EZ-Com™ is a CP/M-based programming aid facilitating the creation, use, and maintenance of modular software libraries. Menu-driven, it allows building program modules in virtually any language, storing them in an indexed library file, generating cross references and tables of contents, and then retrieving modules for inclusion in subsequent programming tasks. It can be used as a software data base to accumulate work on a daily basis and serves as a versatile tool.

The Software Store, 706 Chippewa Square, Marquette, MI 49855.
Disk Fix™ is a CP/M-based disk editor and file recovery utility. Its facilities move files from one user area to another, restore erased files, force a directory entry in one user area that accesses a file actually stored in another user area, restore a file containing a bad disk sector, and restore a file from a disk with a damaged directory. While the manual contains information on disk systems and storage, effective use does require some extra research into the ways CP/M uses the media.

Program Map™ is a CP/M-based cross-reference utility for Microsoft BASIC programs. It works with Revisions 4.51, 5.1, and 5.2 BASIC, and is applied to programs written thereunder. It outputs a map of the program elements complete with line numbers (in sequence) on which they occur. Output sections include variable names, BASIC statements and functions, numeric constants, referenced lines (called by GOSUBs, GOTOs, IF...THENs, and so on), and literal strings. This is useful in completing program documentation, editing programs for efficiency, debugging errors, and other steps that may be applied to make programs run better, faster, and more effectively.

SuperSoft, P.O. Box 1628, Champaign, IL 61820.
Diagnostics II™ is a general computer diagnostics package for CP/M-based systems. It runs extensive tests on the memory (four kinds of tests), CPU, disk drives, terminal display, and printer. It provides a good shakedown of the system and either ensures that major system components are functioning properly or helps isolate components that may be malfunctioning.

Disk Edit™ is a general disk-editing utility for CP/M systems. As usual for programs of this type, it assumes that the user is familiar with disk formats, file structures, storage techniques, and so on.

Disk Doctor™ is a CP/M-based program (Z-80 microprocessors only) that's supposed to undelete erased files, recover damaged files, and so on. This is a program I've been unable to test—it won't work with double-sided double-density disk drives present in my system, and I've not been successful in installing it on an Apple II.

Sympathetic Software, 9531 Telhan Drive, Huntington Beach, CA 92646.

Disk Prep™ exists for the sole purpose of testing Apple II diskettes for defective sectors and locking any of them out so they can't be used. The program is promoted as a means of testing or certifying the reverse side of diskettes, which it does, but there are many other reasons for not using the back sides. Even with this program, be prepared to lose files and data sometime later if you insist on using the back of the Apple diskettes. Be aware that similar disk-testing often is contained within other programs with additional editing and recovery facilities.

Taurus Software, 3685 Mt. Diablo Blvd., Suite 251, Lafayette, CA 94549.

CP+™ represents CP/M enhancements designed to make the system "user friendly." It accomplishes this through a series of selection menus on the screen instead of having to second-guess the normal CP/M commands. Whether this is an advantage is a matter of personal preference. Novice users are likely to appreciate the menu-driven selection; experienced users might feel they get in the way of quick, efficient system access.

XPS, Inc., 323 York Road, Carlisle, PA 17013.

Apple-Cillin II™ is a system diagnostic for the Apple II. It includes tests of motherboard and plug-in memory, the CPU, several peripheral cards, the keyboard, the video display, and the disk drives. The most used feature of the program is a disk-timing routine for adjusting the Apple drives. Not intended as a cure-all, it does provide a good indication that system hardware is or is not functioning normally.

Index

ABS, 96, 117, 120
Accounting, 61, 150
Accumulator, 27, 229
Adam Osborne & Associates, 43
Address, 1, 6-7, 23-24, 27ff., 40, 47, 62, 100-102, 116, 127
Adventure International, 287
Algebra, 44
Algebraic expression, 31
ALGOL, 30, 31
Algorithm, 34, 40, 64-76, 151, 244-250
Algorithmic language. *See* ALGOL
Altair, 7, 9, 88-90, 159-160, 163-164, 174, 197
American National Standards Institute. *See* ANSI
Ampersand, 164
AND, 207, 210
ANSI, 95, 130
Apostrophe, 151
Append operation, 236
Apple Computer, Inc., 5, 243
Apple II, 5, 7-9, 12-15, 21, 25-27, 42-44, 48, 65, 87, 259
Apple III, 12, 87
Applesoft Programmer's Assistant, 110, 217
Applesoft Tool Kit, 110, 217
Applesoft Tutorial, 5, 42
Apple Spice, 286
Applications software. See Software, applications
Arc tangent. *See* ATN
  subroutine, 283
Arithmetic, 131ff., 196
Array, 45, 101-103, 112, 121, 127, 137, 149, 153, 155, 157, 164, 178, 186, 191, 193, 196, 204, 206
  double precision, 137
  integer, 137
  random number, 247
  single precision, 137
  string, 77, 80, 104, 153-155, 157, 160-162, 180, 197, 217, 223, 229, 241, 247
  table, 32, 215, 219
  variable, 219, 223
  zeroing, 223
ASC, 96, 118, 167-168, 177, 225
ASCII, 12-13, 110, 116-118, 126, 167-168, 171, 175-176, 225, 229, 236-237, 251
  conversion chart, 251-253
Assembler, 29
Assembly language. *See* Language, assembly
Atari, 12, 44

ATN, 96, 118, 283
AUTO, 99
Automatic startup, 25

Backward slash, 143-144, 245
BASCOM, 33, 90, 100-103, 115, 140, 160, 163, 188, 201, 224
BASIC, 30, 31
  commercial enhancements, 286
  conversion, 85
  defined, 30
  enhancements, 36, 40
  implementation, 86
  learning, 42, 54
  portability, 41, 44, 85
  pros and cons, 39
  special tricks, 215
  techniques, 130
  understanding, 85
BASIC Computer Programs for Business, 43
BASIC Computer Programs for the Home, 43
BASIC for Home Computers, 42
BEEP, 92
Beginner's All-Purpose Symbolic Instruction Code. *See* BASIC
Binary, 259-260, 269-271
  addition, 269
  digits, 7, 29, 259
    See also Bits
  division, 271
  files, 109, 115-116
  format, 236
  manipulation, 268
  multiplication, 270
  numbering, 27, 66
    See also Numeric system, binary
  subtraction, 270
Bits, 7, 27-28, 255, 259
BLOAD, 109
Bookkeeping, 59, 64
Book-software packages, 43
Booting, 24-25, 155, 159
Bootstrap, 24
Branch, 44, 49, 106-107, 111, 117-119, 125, 165, 178, 198, 203, 207, 212, 230
BRUN, 115
BSAVE, 116
Bubble sort, 77-80
Buffer, 4, 101, 104-105, 110, 113, 123, 128, 237-238, 241-243
Bus
  address, 5
  data, 5
  S-100, 5, 7, 10, 48, 52, 56, 88-89, 140ff.
  status, 5
BUTTON, 96
Byte, 7, 53, 78ff., 100, 112ff., 127, 137, 255, 261ff.
  See also Bits

Calculating with BASIC, 43
CALL, 92, 100, 230
Cassette, 18, 20-21, 43-44, 55
  See also Tape
CATALOG, 99
Cathode-ray terminal. *See* CRT; Terminal
CDBL, 96, 118, 136
Central processing unit, 3-4.
  See also CPU
CHAIN, 92, 100-101, 115
Checkbook balancing, 44, 54, 58
CHR$, 80, 96, 118, 124-125, 160, 167-168, 171, 177
CINT, 97, 118
Circuit
  board, 5, 8, 24
  chip, 3, 52
  integrated, 3
CLEAR, 92, 100-103, 120, 152ff., 161ff., 174, 177, 225, 235
Clock, 18
CLOSE, 92, 101, 243
Closing files, 243
COBOL, 30-31
COLOR, 92
Commas, 241-242
Commodore, 44
COMMON, 92, 101, 115
Common Business-Oriented Language. *See* COBOL
Compiler, 32-33, 40, 48, 90, 100ff., 115, 140, 160, 163, 201, 224
Computer
  error. *See* Error, computer
  multiple-board, 5
  power, 7, 46, 54-55, 62, 230
  single-board, 5
  size, 7
  system, 3
Concatenation, 111, 164
CONSOLE, 92, 109-110
Constant, 45, 100-103, 117-119, 122ff., 131ff.

CONT, 99, 101, 103, 155
Control Program for Microprocessors. *See* CP/M
Control-C, 158
Control-D, 168
Control-G, 168
COS, 97, 119, 279, 282
Cosine. *See* COS
subroutine, 282
CP/M, 21, 33, 36, 88ff., 108-109, 115-116, 123, 140, 159, 161-163, 175, 207, 242
CPU, 4-6, 10, 27, 30
Create Word Puzzles with Your Microcomputer, 2, 152
Critical search, 216
CRT, 14, 80
See also Terminal
CSNG, 97, 118, 142
CVD, 97, 105, 119, 123, 237
CVI, 97, 105, 119, 123, 237
CVS, 97, 105, 119, 123, 237

Dartmouth College, 34-35, 86-87
DATA, 92, 101, 103, 114-115
Data types, 133
Debugging, 42, 54-56, 60, 69, 72ff., 101, 106, 234-235
Decimal fractions, 150, 257
Decimal point, 132
Decision, 1, 7, 88
Decision making, 49-50
DEF FN, 92, 102, 189, 190, 192, 283ff.
DEF USR, 92, 102, 127
Default conditions, 225
DEFDBL, 92, 102, 179-181
Defective diskettes, 53
Deferred commands, 91
See also Program statements
DEFINT, 92, 102, 161, 163, 179ff., 232-233
DEFSNG, 92, 102, 179-181
DEFSTR, 92, 102, 161, 163, 179-180
DELETE, 93, 99-100, 108
Depreciation, 57
Derived functions, 283
Device driver, 10, 14, 18
Digital Research, 21, 36
Digitizer, 18
Digits, defined, 256
DIM, 92, 102-103, 112, 122, 137, 149, 153, 155, 157, 162, 166, 224-225, 228
Dimensioning, 103, 149, 153, 186, 196, 219, 221, 223-225
Direct commands, 73, 91, 109, 111, 114, 155, 190
Disk, 9-11, 18-21, 23, 25, 36, 43-44, 52-55, 60, 69-70, 79, 82, 89-90, 100ff., 122, 123, 128, 168
file usage, 236
record, 236
test, 288
Disk operating system, 8, 21, 87, 128, 236
See also DOS
Division, 150
by zero, 134
integer, 143-146, 183, 245-246
real, 143, 146, 183, 245-246
two variables, 147
Documentation, 68-69, 76-79, 82-83
Dollar sign, 151, 179, 180
DOS, 21-22, 65, 87-89, 101ff., 236, 243
See also Disk operating system
DOS Manual, 243
Dot matrix, 15-16
DRAW, 92
Dummy list, 189
Dungeons and Dragons™, 65
Dynamic memory allocation, 160

EDIT, 99
Edit mode, 73
ELSE, 93, 106, 212, 286-287
END, 92, 101, 103, 116
EOF, 97, 119
EPROM, 8
EQV, 210
Erasable programmable read-only memory, 8
ERASE, 92, 103, 155, 223-225
ERL, 97, 104, 115
ERR, 97, 104, 115
ERROR, 92, 104
Errors
clerical, 51
computer, 46, 50-54
design, 52
FOR without NEXT, 199, 201, 232
formula too complex, 213
human, 51
illegal function call, 111, 165, 178
illegal quantity, 178
logic, 69, 73, 106
manufacturing, 52
NEXT without FOR, 74, 200-203, 232

Errors *(continued)*
out of date, 114
out of memory, 72, 82, 100, 152, 154-156, 190, 230-231, 235-236
out of string space, 152, 154-156, 162
overflow, 119, 135, 281
planning, 69
redimensioned array, 103, 224, 225
rounding, 150
subscript out of range, 74, 186, 225
syntax, 72, 74, 106, 151
trapping, 104, 111, 115, 178, 179, 204
type mismatch, 151
typographic, 73
Exclamation point, 133, 135, 151, 179
Execution speed, 138
EXP, 97, 119, 279-280
Exponent, 138, 258
Exponential
form, 135
subroutine, 280
Exponentiation, 67, 132
subroutine, 281
Exponent ranges, 135
Expression, 45, 100ff., 167

FIELD, 92, 104, 238-239
Fielding, 238ff.
File handling, 236
File numbers, 243
FILES, 99
Filing system, 55
Firmware, 24-26
FIX, 97, 120, 122
Fixed point, 45, 101, 132
Flag, 169-171, 197, 200, 202-203, 229
FLASH, 92
Floating point, 45, 87, 101, 132, 149
Floppy disk. *See* Disk
Flowchart, 60, 67ff.
Footnoting, 82
FOR...NEXT, 50, 72, 92, 104-106, 115, 117, 125, 139, 141, 160-161, 173-175, 178-179, 184-185, 188, 193ff., 201ff., 214, 217, 228, 231-232
Form Feed, 167
Formula Translation Language. *See* FORTRAN
FORTRAN, 30ff., 40
Forward slash, 143-144
FRE, 97, 120, 157ff.
Free memory, 9, 79, 154ff., 162-163
Fundamentals, 1, 3, 34, 42

Games, 54, 61-63
Garbage collect, 155ff., 171, 174, 184
GBASIC, 89ff.
GET, 92, 104-105, 121-122
GOSUB, 83, 92, 105-106, 111, 114, 279ff.
GOSUB...RETURN, 204, 230
GOTO, 44, 92, 106, 111, 114, 155, 233
GR, 92
Graphics, 10, 15, 18, 61, 89-90, 96, 112, 157-158, 259

Hardcopy, 14, 67, 109, 217
Hardware, 89, 91
defined, 22
failures, 53
HCOLOR, 92
HEX$, 97, 120, 123
Hexadecimal, 28-30, 112, 120, 127, 251, 263ff.
conversion chart, 269
symbols, 265
HGR, 93
High-level language. *See* Language, high-level; *individual languages*
HIMEM:, 93
HLIN, 93
Hobby, 61-62
HOME, 93
HPLOT, 93
HSCRN, 93
HTAB, 93

IBM Personal Computer, 21
IF...GOSUB, 211
IF...GOTO, 93, 106, 195-196, 207, 211
IF...THEN, 44, 49-50, 82, 93, 104, 106, 117, 124, 165-166, 170, 178, 185-187, 191, 194-196, 198, 200, 203, 207, 209, 211-214, 286-287
nesting, 106
IF...THEN GOTO, 106, 196
Imaginary roots, 125
Immediate commands, 91
See also Direct commands
IMP, 210
Implied LET, 93, 105, 108, 165
Income tax, 54, 57-59
Indexed retrieval, 242
INKEY$, 97, 120
INP, 97

INPUT, 44, 93, 105, 107-109, 193, 287
Input file, 236
INPUT#, 93, 107, 113
INPUT$, 97, 121
Input/Output Device, 10-11
  See also individual types;
  I/O device
INSTR, 97, 121, 168ff., 228, 248, 286-287
INT, 66, 74, 97, 120, 122, 148, 150, 245, 284-285
Integer, 45, 67, 87, 100ff., 131ff., 149, 186ff., 205-206, 212-213
Interactive, 33, 40, 73, 134
Interfacing, 11
Internal Revenue Service. *See* IRS
Interpreter, 32-33, 39-40, 48, 66, 78, 80-83, 134, 160, 175, 185, 188, 190-191, 195, 199, 201, 205, 216-217, 221, 224-227, 231, 234-236
Intrinsic functions, 36, 86-87, 91, 117, 225
Inventories, 55
INVERSE, 93
Invoice preparation, 61
I/O device, 11, 18
  See also individual types
I/O port, 116
IRS, 57-58, 64-65

Keyboard, 12ff., 44, 50ff., 59, 67-68, 70, 72-73, 75, 79, 89, 91, 101, 104ff., 120-121, 134
Keypunch, 19, 72
KILL, 93, 99, 108

Language
  assembly, 4-5, 26, 29-30, 34, 41, 68, 100-102, 112, 127, 230, 255
  high-level, 4-5, 23, 30-33, 255, 268
  machine, 4-5, 26-28, 31, 34, 39-40, 48, 101, 115-116, 157-158, 229, 255, 267
  standalone, 159
  universal, 42
LDOS, 22
Least significant bit, 266, 274
Least significant digit, 148
LEFT$ 97, 122-124, 152, 166-167, 172-173
LEN, 97, 122, 152, 177-179, 226, 240
LET, 44, 93, 108, 133, 165-166
Letter combination, 169
Lightning, 53
Limiting value, 187, 196
LINE INPUT, 93, 108-109
LINE INPUT#, 93
Line numbers, 78, 100, 104-106, 110-111, 114-115
LINK-80, 33, 140, 160, 163
LIST, 99, 109
LLIST, 99, 109-110
LOAD, 99, 109, 111, 114-115
LOC, 97, 122
LOF, 97, 122
LOG, 97, 123, 279-280
Logarithm. *See* EXP; LOG
  subroutine, 280
Logical comparison, 116, 196
LOMEM:, 93
Loop, 47-50, 67, 72, 74, 80, 84, 103ff., 115ff., 125, 128, 139, 146, 160-161, 173ff., 184, 196
  array variable in, 220
  construction, 192
  control, 139ff., 178, 194ff., 201ff., 214ff., 226, 232-233, 241
  critical, 219
  forced closure, 202-203
  incomplete, 202
  infinite, 204, 235, 248-249
  negative stepping, 205-206
  nesting, 48, 105, 117, 170, 192, 205, 216, 222, 233
  reentry, 203
  stepping, 193ff., 198, 205-207
  termination, 199ff., 204
  testing, 197
  timing, 205
  use, 192
  See also FOR...NEXT; IF...THEN; WHILE...WEND
Lower-case adapter, 13
LPOS, 97, 123
LPRINT, 93, 109-110, 112, 117-118, 125-126, 168, 173
LPRINT USING, 93, 110, 113
LSET, 110, 113, 123, 238, 240

Machine infinity, 119, 127
Machine language. *See* Language, machine
Magazine articles, 57
Magnetic media. *See* Mass storage; Disk; Tape

Mainframe, 11
Mainline program, 49
Mantissa, 138
Mass storage, 11, 18, 20, 36, 43, 55, 60, 75, 87
MAT, 104, 224
MBASIC, 89, 130ff.
Meaningful names, 76, 78, 216
Memory, 5
  allocation, 154, 171
  conservation, 138
  consumption, 137ff.
  management system, 8
  mapped video, 9, 14-15, 22, 87
  test, 235, 289
  See also RAM; ROM; PROM; EPROM
MERGE, 99-100, 110
Microprocessor, 3-4
  See also CPU
MID$, 93, 97, 110-111, 122-124, 126, 152, 165-167, 172-173, 175, 177, 226-227
Minicomputer, 19, 35
Misplaced computation, 223
MITS, 88-89
MKD$, 97, 119, 123, 237
MKI$, 97, 119, 123, 237
MKS$, 97, 119, 123, 237
Mnemonics, 29-31
Modem, 18
Morrow Designs, 7, 88
Most significant bit, 263, 266, 272-273
MPU, 4-5
  See also CPU
MSDOS, 21
Multiplication, 67, 140, 142-143, 150

NAME, 99
Negative argument, 188
NEW, 99, 101, 111
NEWDOS, 22
Nonprinting character, 118, 167
Nonvolatile memory, 8
  See also ROM
NORMAL, 93
NOT, 210
NULL, 99
Null string, 151, 153-154, 165, 181, 213, 219, 223
Number handling, 131
Numeric conversion
  binary to decimal, 273
  binary to hexadecimal, 278
  binary to octal, 278
  decimal to binary, 272
  decimal to hexadecimal, 276
  decimal to octal, 274-275
  hexadecimal to binary, 278
  hexadecimal to decimal, 277
  hexadecimal to octal, 278
  octal to binary, 278
  octal to decimal, 276
  octal to hexadecimal, 278
Numeric system, 255
  binary, 259-260, 269-271
  comparisons, 267
  decimal, 256
  hexadecimal, 263ff.
  manipulations, 268
  octal, 261-263
  See also Hexadecimal; Binary; Octal
Nybble, 261-263

OBASIC, 130ff.
Object program, 29
OCT$, 98, 123
Octal, 112, 123, 261-263
  digit, 262
ON ERR GOTO, 204
ON ERROR GOTO, 93, 111, 115
ON...GOSUB, 49-50, 93, 106, 111, 230
ON...GOTO, 49-50, 93, 111, 203
OPEN, 93, 104, 111-112, 239
Operator
  Boolean, 207, 210
  functional, 45
  logical, 45, 210
  relational, 45
OPTION BASE, 94, 102, 112, 228
OR, 207, 210
Osborne, 44
OUT, 94
Output file, 236

Packed bytes, 237
Parentheses, 221
Passing values, 191
PDL, 98
PEEK, 98, 104
Percent symbol, 133, 142, 151, 179
Peripheral, 11-12
  See also I/O device; *individual types*

Pigeonhole, 5
PLOT, 94
Plotter, 18
Pointer, 153-154, 157, 162, 204, 223-224
POKE, 94, 112, 178
POP, 94
POS, 98, 124, 128
Pound symbol, 133, 135, 151, 179
Power supply, 53
PR#, 109-110
Precision
  arithmetic effect, 138, 142
  comparisons, 131
  converting, 136
  double, 45, 102, 118-119, 123, 132-134, 137, 139, 150, 189, 285
  double arrays, 137
  loop effect, 139
  memory effect, 137
  mixed, 134
  real, 45, 133, 135, 137, 189
  single, 45, 102, 118-119, 123, 125, 132-134, 137, 139, 148, 189, 285
  single arrays, 137
  speed effect, 138
  See also Integer
Prgm/Map, 217
PRINT, 44, 80, 94, 110, 112-113, 117-118, 120, 125-126, 149, 160, 173
PRINT#, 94, 113, 117
PRINT USING, 94, 113, 150, 286-287
PRINT# USING, 94
Print zones, 112
Printer, 12ff., 87, 109-110, 116-118, 123, 126, 134
Problem evaluation, 60
Program
  accuracy, 131
  coding, 72
  command, 89
  compression, 78-79, 82, 86
  creation procedure, 60
  debugging, 73
  defined, 6
  efficiency, 131
  failures, 73
  flow, 44, 46, 49-50, 233
  line, 231
  mainline, 49, 103, 105, 110, 190, 231
  mapping, 217
  objectives, 63
  portability, 86
  protected file, 115
  running, 79
  statement, 36, 39, 72, 74, 76, 86, 91, 100, 231
  testing, 72, 73
  tight, 40
Programmable read-only memory, 7
Programming
  effective, 2, 85
  structured, 39-40, 79
Programming language. *See* Language
Programming the 6502, 69, 268
PROM, 7, 26
Punctuation mark, 74
PUT, 94, 104, 110, 113, 122, 238

Quotation marks, 151, 168

Radians, 118-119, 125-126
RAM, 7ff., 15, 18, 22, 25, 29, 33, 40, 152ff., 240
RAMCard, 8, 89
Random access, 21, 104-105, 112-113, 119, 122, 128, 236-237, 241, 243
Random access memory, 7
  See also RAM
Random file, 236
Random file buffer, 237-238, 240
Random number
  array, 247
  distribution, 187, 209
  generator, 72, 74, 113, 124, 149, 185ff., 209, 249
  seeding, 124, 188, 228, 248
RANDOMIZE, 94, 113, 124, 188
READ, 94, 101, 114
Readability, 41, 76-77, 79ff., 86, 114, 153, 216-217
Read-only memory, 7
  See also ROM
Real number, 119-120, 123, 125-126, 131-132
Record length, 239-240
Recordkeeping, 64
Redimensioning, 224
REM, 76, 79, 83, 94, 114, 153
Remark, 40, 41, 76ff., 82-83, 114, 153
RENAME, 99
RENUM, 99, 114
Repetitive operations, 46-48, 54, 57, 67, 82
Reserved words, 82
RESET, 99, 101

Reset key, 14
RESTORE, 94, 114-115
RESUME, 94, 115, 178
RETURN, 92, 105
RIGHTS$, 98, 122-124, 152, 166-167, 226-227
RND, 74, 98, 124, 149, 186-188, 190, 228
ROM, 7-9, 25, 33, 40
ROT, 94
Rounding, 91, 124, 134-135, 148ff., 184, 186-187, 284-285
RSET, 110, 113, 123, 238, 240
RUN, 94, 99, 103, 109, 111, 114-115, 160
Runtime efficiency, 41

SAVE, 94, 99, 115
Save time, 58
SCALE, 94
Scientific notation, 132
SCRN, 98
Separate program lines, 76
Sequential access, 104-105, 122, 236, 241
Sequential file, 107, 109, 111, 113, 117, 119, 121-122, 128
SGN, 98, 120, 124
Shift key, 13
SHLOAD, 94
Sign bit, 263
Significant digits, 138
SIN, 98, 125, 189, 279, 282
Sine. *See* SIN
  subroutine, 282
SoftCard, 89-90, 100, 105, 123, 130, 141, 144, 198, 205, 207, 210, 212
Software
  applications, 23, 290ff.
  defined, 22
  mapping, 217
  off-the-shelf, 42, 290ff.
  system, 23
  useful programs (list), 290ff.
  user, 23
Some Common BASIC Programs, 43
Source of income, 62
Source program, 29
SPACE$, 98, 125, 129, 173-176
Spaces, 76, 79, 108, 113-114, 122, 124-126, 240-241
SPC, 98, 125, 173
Special tricks, 215
Speech synthesizer, 18
SPEED, 94
SQR, 66, 98, 125, 135, 189, 279, 281
Square root. *See* SQR
  subroutine, 279
Stack, 32, 100, 105, 204, 235
Standardization, 87
Startrek, 197-198
Static, 53
Statistical analysis, 55
STEP, 94, 104, 146-147, 205-206
STOP, 80, 94, 101, 116
STR$, 98, 126-127, 160, 176-177
String
  array, 77, 80, 104, 153ff., 157, 160-162, 180, 197, 217, 223, 229, 241, 247
  data, 36, 45, 72, 96, 101, 105, 229, 237ff.
  handling, 151ff., 161ff., 184
  literal, 151ff., 189, 213
  space, 100, 120, 152ff., 171, 174, 223-224, 240
STRING$, 98, 126, 129, 175-176
Subroutine, 76, 86, 100ff., 127, 157-158, 168, 213, 230ff., 268, 279ff.
  nesting, 100, 105, 230, 236
  positioning, 233-235
  recursive, 235
Subscript, 102-103, 112, 149, 153, 157, 166, 180, 219, 221, 225, 228, 247-248
Subscript error. *See* Error, subscript
Substring, 165ff.
SWAP, 94, 116
Syntax error. *See* Error, syntax
SYSTEM, 99
System overhead, 10, 142, 150
System software. *See* Software, system

TAB, 98, 126, 149-150
Tabulation, 76, 126
TAN, 98, 126, 282
Tangent. *See* TAN
  subroutine, 282
Tape, 11, 18ff., 60
  See also Cassette
Terminal, 12-14, 87-89, 107, 112ff., 134
TEXT, 94
Text
  editor, 83
  window, 117
The Software Store, 217
Throughput, 15, 90
TRACE/NOTRACE, 95

TRON/TROFF, 95
TRS-80, 7, 22, 44
TRSDOS, 22
Truncating, 91, 124, 135, 148-150, 184-186, 284-285
Truth tables, 210
Turnkey machine, 25

Unattended operation, 59
Uploading, 159
Upper-case keyboard, 13
User software. *See* Software, user
User-defined function. *See* DEF FN; DEF USR
USR, 98, 100, 102, 127, 230
Utility programs, 23

VAL, 98, 126-127, 176-177
Variable, 45, 100ff., 131, 147, 216
  array, 220ff.
  control, 139
  critical, 216ff.
  dedicated, 217
  defined types, 179
  fixed, 221-222
  map, 217
  name, 216
  preassignment, 219
  table, 32, 216ff.
  types, 134
VARPTR, 98, 127-128
Vector Graphics, 14
Video display, 14
VLIN, 95
Volatile memory, 8
  See also RAM
VPOS, 98, 128
VTAB, 95

WAIT, 95, 116
Waste, 39-40, 54, 57, 78-79, 82
WHILE...WEND, 95, 117
WIDTH, 95, 117
WIDTH LPRINT, 95, 110, 117
Word processing, 2, 13, 17, 23, 26, 42, 55, 59, 61, 63, 79
WordStar, 79
WRITE, 95, 117
WRITE#, 95, 117

XDRAW, 95
XOR, 210
XPLOT, 95

Zero
  -character string, 151
    See also null string
  element, 102, 112, 127, 228-229
  values, 196